COGNITION IN ACTION

Cognition in Action

Mary M. Smyth
Peter E. Morris
Philip Levy
Andrew W. Ellis

Department of Psychology
University of Lancaster
Bailrigg
Lancaster LA1 4YF
U.K.

LEA LAWRENCE ERLBAUM ASSOCIATES, PUBLISHERS LEA
London   Hillsdale, New Jersey

Lawrence Erlbaum Associates Ltd., Publishers
Chancery House
319 City Road
London EC1V 1LJ

British Library Cataloguing in Publication Data

Cognition in action.
   1. Cognition
   I. Smyth, Mary M.
   153.4   BF311
   ISBN 0-86377-039-8
   ISBN 0-86377-040-1 Pbk

Typeset by Spire Print Services Ltd., Salisbury
Printed and bound by A. Wheaton & Co. Ltd., Exeter

Contents

ACKNOWLEDGEMENTS

We would like to thank Sheila Whalley, Sylvia Sumner, and Pat Keynes for typing parts of the manuscript.

Introduction

In this book we approach cognitive psychology from the standpoint of someone who is interested in what it has to tell us about how people carry out everday activities. That is, how people organise and use their knowledge in order to behave appropriately in the world in which they live. Each chapter in the book starts with an example (which makes up the first part of the chapter title), and then uses the example to introduce some aspects of the overall cognitive system. In this way the more general psychological functions described in the second part of each chapter title are introduced and explained.

Some of the examples we use are serious ones, like making a medical decision, and others are fairly trivial, like tapping your head and rubbing your stomach at the same time. In addition, some of the examples are simply used to introduce problems and questions about an aspect of cognitive functioning, and are not the topic of the chapter itself, whereas other examples, like reading a word or a book, do provide the topic for the whole chapter. This is partly because language processing is something we do every day, as well as a central research area for many psychologists. Other everyday activities may not themselves be studied directly by psychologists, or may only be studied as part of a wider enquiry.

So, for example, we use eyewitnessing in Chapter 10 to introduce many of the important issues in the study of memory, particularly memory for events which have happened to us. However, the chapter is not intended to be a comprehensive review of research on eyewitnessing. Again, in Chapter 2 we use face recognition to introduce questions about the recognition of faces, objects and words, and the chapter is not a review of all the face-recognition research. In most cases, the second part of the chapter title gives a wider view of what is to be covered within the chapter than does the example.

Cognition is concerned with knowledge, and cognitive psychology is concerned with the acquisition and use of knowledge, and with the structures and processes which serve this. The cognitive system, although it is complex, normally operates as a whole, and it can be misleading to separate out parts of the system for special attention without emphasising that each part can only be understood properly in its place in the functioning of the whole. Traditionally, textbooks on cognitive psychology have taken topics such as perception, memory and language as major themes, and in doing so have sometimes emphasised the component parts of the system while obscuring its purposes and functions.

Of course, to study any complex system it is necessary to introduce some sub-divisions, and the problem is to present these without leading readers to believe that a topic such as memory can be completely understood in isolation. Our solution has been to identify important components in the cognitive system, and to illustrate them through examples of cognition in action. So, for example, all cognition depends on our initial perceptions of the world, and perceptual processing is referred to over and over again throughout the book. However, perception plays an especially important part in reading and in recognising faces and by starting with these examples in the first two chapters we are able to highlight the major aspects of the initial perceptual components of the system.

Unlike other texts, we do not make a rigorous division into "stages" of cognitive processing, rather we emphasise different aspects of the system in different ways. For example, new information entering the system must be appropriately organised and classified, relevant old information must be retrieved to aid construction and interpretation, the elements of the old and new must be held in a temporary form while the new construction is assembled and decisions made, and a record of what has occurred becomes part of the store of information that is held for future use. Each of these aspects, and many others, can be emphasised in the context of a particular task, so we do not have chapters which treat cognitive processes or stages in isolation from tasks. Thus, while the book moves from what are traditionally "lower" aspects of cognition, such as perceiving faces and producing actions, to "higher" aspects such as comprehension and problem-solving, these are not seen as stages but as important parts of normal human functioning which cognitive psychology has approached in different ways.

Cognitive psychologists have in the past concentrated on experimental laboratory studies. Their research has sometimes moved a long way from the original questions they asked, and a very long way from cognition in action. This can make the topics seem both difficult and irrelevant to the student. Nevertheless, in many cases we do need to move into the laboratory to control some aspects of normal functioning in order to get a better understanding of how cognitive processes operate. What is important is that such research should give results which can be used to help us answer the original questions, or even to show us that they are not the best questions to ask. We have tried to select such research for this book.

In writing this book we have taken the view that the fact that research has been done does not necessarily make it relevant or important. This means that some topics which are found in other cognition texts do not appear here. We also feel that the fact that research was done some time ago does not make it irrelevant or unimportant. So, in some chapters, where there is a long tradition of research that seems to us to have approached problems in intuitively sensible ways, we have reported the work, even if it does not provide complete answers to our questions. Experiments and research programmes have little value by themselves, they only matter when they help us to understand something of how the cognitive system does, or doesn't, work.

We can all read words, recognise people we know, make decisions, read books, and tell tables from chairs. We normally take these abilities for granted. In this book we do *not* take such activities for granted: rather we start to ask the question "How *do* I do that?" We hope that students who are new to cognitive psychology will also start to ask themselves the same question so that they can begin to see what it is that cognitive psychologists study. We also hope that students who start to question their everyday abilities will come to understand why it is sometimes necessary to remove people from the everyday world into a laboratory in order to understand the processes involved in cognition.

This book does not present the argument that everyday cognition can only be studied in the everyday world, but rather that everyday cognition gives us our problems and our questions. Our answers, however we obtain them, must always relate back to cognition in action.

1 Reading Words: Sight and Sound in Recognising Patterns

Each of the chapters in this book will start with some familiar, everyday ability or task, and will go on to explore the cognitive capacities and processes that make that performance possible. Sometimes a chapter will stick closely to its opening scenario; sometimes it will use it as a springboard for a discussion of other, related aspects of cognition. The ability with which we open this chapter and the book is reading.

Reading is a skill that can very easily be taken for granted. We usually learn to read early in life, and by adulthood few of us can remember much about how that learning occurred. Reading is accepted as a simple, commonplace activity. If you go into the kitchen and find a note which says *Please wash the potatoes and put the casserole in the oven*, you may object to having to wait for your dinner, but you won't find it difficult to decide what *potatoes* means. A seven-year-old child, on the other hand, might have considerable difficulty in deciding what to wash and what to put in the oven.

Reading has been extensively studied by psychologists, partly because it is a skill that requires some effort to acquire (even if the effort is then soon forgotten), and partly because it is a specifically human, culturally transmitted cognitive activity. When Huey (1908) reviewed the first 10 or 15 years of experimental research on reading, he remarked that: "to completely analyse what we do when we read would almost be the acme of a psychologist's achievement, for it would be to describe very many of the most intricate workings of the human mind, as well as to unravel the tangled story of the most remarkable specific performance that civilisation has learned in all its history."

Psychologists have not yet finished unravelling the complexities of that remarkable performance, but they have made a start. We shall use the reading skill more than once in the book as a peg upon which to hang our discussion of cognitive processes. One reason for this is that reading *is* a real-world activity, not one invented for laboratory experimentation; another is that skilled reading requires and depends on a rich variety of cognitive abilities.

Where should the study of reading start? One obvious place might be the recognition of letter shapes, since letters are the building blocks of written words. But there is an even earlier stage in reading. Before you can begin to recognise a letter or the word in which it belongs, your eyes must first alight on the word. The eye movements made during reading are quite subtle and we begin with a discussion of them. Later in the chapter we consider the processes by which a written word evokes its meaning and sound in the reader's mind, and the role of context in helping or hindering word recognition. Chapter 9 examines the higher-level processes involved in comprehending and remembering lengthy passages of text, and reading in one form or another will be mentioned in several other chapters. We begin with the patterns of eye movements of skilled readers.

EYE MOVEMENTS AND INFORMATION UPTAKE IN READING

Normally when you read text you are concentrating on what it means and are quite unaware of your eye movements. Even if you attend to them you may not get an accurate feeling for what is happening. Next time you get the chance, observe someone intent on reading a book. You will see that their eyes do not move smoothly along a line of print, but progress by a succession of quick flicks interspersed by moments when the eyes are quite still. The stationary moments are called *fixations* and the flicks are referred to as *saccades* (the term used by the French ophthalmologist Javal who first reported them in 1887). Saccades and fixations are not unique to reading; they happen whenever we inspect a static scene. In fact, the only time we can move our eyes smoothly is when we are tracking a moving target. You can easily verify this by asking a friend first to fixate the tip of a pencil while you move it in a straight line, and then to move their eyes in a straight line without a target to follow. In the first condition you will observe smooth, continuous eye movements; in the second you will see saccades and fixations.

Figure 1.1 shows a passage of text and superimposed upon it a somewhat idealised representation of the eye movements that a normal reader would be expected to make. The circles above the words represent fixations, with the diameter of the circle indicating their likely durations (larger circles for longer fixations). The arrows show the saccades. Note that most saccades are forwards, but in reality some 10 or 20 per cent of eye movements (excluding those from the end of one line to the beginning of the next) go backwards to re-fixate words which have been fixated once already. These are called *regressions*.

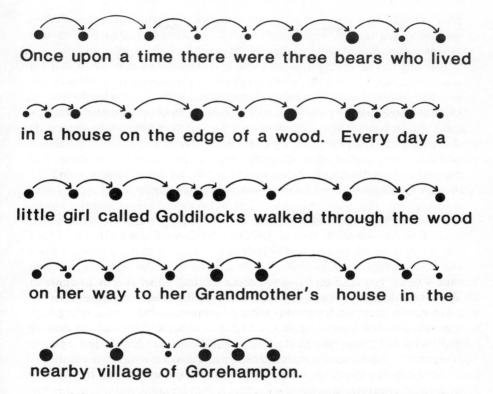

FIG. 1.1 The pattern of eye movements that a skilled reader might make in reading a passage of text. Circles represent fixations, with larger circles indicating longer fixations, and arrows represent saccades. (For simplification we have omitted the 10 per cent or so of backward, "regressive" eye movements that occur in natural reading.)

The average fixation of a skilled reader lasts 200–250 msec (i.e. between one-fifth and one-quarter of a second). The average saccade takes only 25–30 msec (a mere one-fortieth of a second). Compare these two figures and you will realise that a reader's eyes are in fact still—fixating—for about 90 per cent of the time in reading. It may *feel* as if your eyes are constantly moving when you read, but they are stationary for most of the time.

All of the uptake of useful information in reading occurs during fixations. We have known since the work of Dodge (1900) and Holt (1903) that little or nothing is perceived during a saccade (a phenomenon known as 'saccadic suppression'). Even a strong flash of light is unlikely to be perceived if it occurs entirely within a saccade (Latour, 1962). Suppression also extends into the first 60 to 80 msec of a fixation: Both in reading and viewing a scene it takes that long after a saccade before information begins to be utilised (McConkie, 1983).

But why is it necessary to make these eye movements at all? Why is it not possible to read a whole page of a book by giving it one long fixation in the middle? There are two reasons (at least). First, although it is likely that we can simultaneously extract meaning from more than one written word at a time (e.g. Allport, 1977), words in books cannot be understood separately and in isolation. Words in books come in sentences and must be processed one at a time, so that a picture of the grammatical sentence structure and the underlying message it conveys can be built up (see Chapters 8 and 9).

Second, the *quality* of visual information picked up declines rapidly with distance from the point of fixation. The reason for this is straightforwardly anatomical: Detailed vision is made possible by light-sensitive cells called *cones* in the retina at the back of the eye. The cones are densest, and afford the greatest acuity, in a central region of the retina called the *fovea*. That is the region upon which is focused light coming from the point on the page that is being fixated. Moving away from the fovea the density of cones in the retina decreases, bringing with it a corresponding decrease in visual acuity away from the fixation point. Reading requires reasonably high visual acuity. If letters or words are briefly displayed at various positions in the visual field, then the likelihood of being able to identify the stimulus correctly declines rapidly with distance away from the fixation point.

Although acuity declines more or less symmetrically around the fixation point, information uptake in reading is not symmetrical. For a start, attention is focused on the line you are presently reading—you do not normally process the lines above or below. Also experiments have shown greater uptake of letter and word information to the right of the fixation point than to the left. Rayner, Well, and Pollatsek (1980) showed that the "perceptual span" within which usable information is taken in extends some fifteen or so characters to the right of the fixation point but not more than three or four characters to the left (see Fig. 1.2). That this is a learned adaptation on the part of English readers to the left–right direction of English script is shown by Pollatsek, Bolozky, Well, and Rayner's (1981) demonstration that for readers of Hebrew (which runs from right to left), the perceptual span is assymmetrically biased to the *left* of the fixation point.

If the English reader's attention span takes in roughly twice as many letters to the right as to the left of the fixation point, then the optimum place to fixate a longish word would be about one-third of the way into it. And that, unsurprisingly perhaps, is where English readers do fixate. Rayner (1978) and O'Regan (1980) found that there is a preferred viewing location for words between the beginning and middle letter. This is

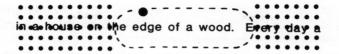

FIG. 1.2   The "perceptual span" in reading typically extends further to the right of the fixation point than to the left.

illustrated in Fig. 1.1 by the locations of the fixation dots in words like *house, through*, and *village*.

But fixating a word is only the first step in recognising and understanding it. Fixate a word in a foreign language, particularly one in an unfamiliar alphabet like Russian or Arabic, and you will be able to make very little of it. Fixate a familiar word in your own language and your own alphabet, however, and the word will activate in your mind its meaning and its sound with no apparent effort. How is this achieved? What happens inside your head when you fixate a familiar word that fails to happen inside the head of someone who cannot read your language? If we could answer that question completely we would have reached Huey's "acme." We haven't yet succeeded in doing so, but we can at least sketch the outlines of a plausible answer.

A PRELIMINARY ACCOUNT OF THE RECOGNITION OF FAMILIAR WRITTEN WORDS

Recognising Letters

The thousands of written words in the English language are assembled from a set of 26 letters. For reasons we shall review shortly, many theories of visual word recognition assume that at least some of the component letters of a written word must be identified before the word itself can be recognised.

We must be careful with terminology here. By "identify a letter" we do not mean name it. Identification involves the visual categorisation of a stimulus pattern such as a letter as an exemplar of a known type, in this case as a particular letter of the alphabet. Coltheart (1981) reported the case of a man who, following brain injury, could understand most written words, but could pronounce very few, and was rarely able to read aloud invented nonwords like ANER. His letter naming was also poor, yet he could reliably respond "same" to pairs of nonwords like ANER/aner and "different" to pairs like ANER/aneg. These decisions were possible because the man could still identify and compare the component letters of words or nonwords visually though he could no longer pronounce or name them.

Letter recognition is commonly assumed to be a necessary part of word recognition, but we have as yet only an ill-defined notion of how exactly it might be achieved. An early theory proposed that we might possess internal letter *templates* against which stimuli could be compared. You can think of these templates as stencils, which you could place over a letter to check for a match. The problem with this theory is evident from the limitations of machine systems that employ this mode of letter recognition. An example is the computer reading of the lettering on cheques. Those rather odd letter shapes are designed to be minimally confusable, and the systems that recognise them are very intolerant of even slight changes in letter shape. Yet as Fig. 1.3 illustrates, even within upper or lower case, the same letter can take a variety of different, if related, forms. It has not yet proved possible to design a template system which would correctly identify all the shapes in Fig. 1.3 as versions of the letter G while at the same time not being misled by a C, O or Q.

The problems with template accounts led some theorists to propose that letters are recognised in terms of sets of *distinctive features*. A distinctive feature is a property or aspect of an object that helps to distinguish it from other objects. The distinctive features of letters might include lines and curves in varying orientations. Thus, the features for the letter A might be [right-sloping oblique], [left-sloping oblique], [horizontal line]. That would not be enough, however, since there are many ways you could combine two sloping and one horizontal line without forming a letter A (see Fig. 1.4). The "features" therefore would need to include specifications of the *configuration* that the elements must adopt in order to be an acceptable letter.

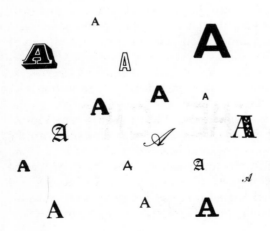

FIG. 1.3 Any template-based model of letter recognition would have great difficulty coping with natural variations in letter shape and size.

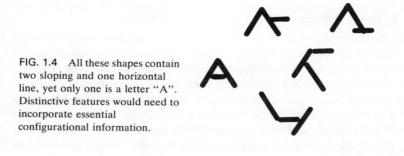

FIG. 1.4   All these shapes contain two sloping and one horizontal line, yet only one is a letter "A". Distinctive features would need to incorporate essential configurational information.

   As with templates, computer systems have been created which recognise letters using distinctive features (the system of McClelland and Rumelhart which we discuss later in this chapter is an example). But again as with templates, feature systems have their problems, as illustrated in Fig. 1.5. Particularly when one moves from print to handwriting, the variability of letter shapes becomes enormous, and it has yet to be proven that feature-based systems can cope with that variability any better than template systems. Additionally, as Fig. 1.6 shows, the same physical shape can be classified differently depending on the word-context in which it occurs. Such demonstrations undermine the assumption that letter recognition normally occurs prior to, and independently of, word recognition. As we shall see shortly, there is other evidence pointing to the conclusion that letter and word recognition are interacting rather than independent operations.

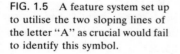

FIG. 1.5   A feature system set up to utilise the two sloping lines of the letter "A" as crucial would fail to identify this symbol.

FIG. 1.6   The same physical shape can be identified as two different letters depending on the context in which it occurs. In 1.6(a) the same shape is identified as an "H" in the first word and an "A" in the second; 1.6(b) will be read as either "went" or "event" depending on the surrounding context.

THE CAT

Recognising Words

When psychologists have turned their attention from letters to words they have tended to adopt the same sort of approach and to utilise the same sorts of explanatory concepts. It has often been proposed that there exists a separate "word recognition unit" for each familiar written word (e.g., Morton, 1979; McClelland & Rumelhart, 1981). The idea is that each word that a reader is familiar with and has encountered in print several times before is represented by a separate recognition unit. The word *farm*, for example, would be represented by a single unit that would be activated when the letters *f, a, r*, and *m* are recognised.

The alert reader may already have spotted one or two problems with this account. For a start, words, like letters, come in various forms. It would be inefficient to have separate word recognition units for FARM, *FARM*, farm, and *farm*, so we should perhaps prefer there to be just one unit capable of identifying these different instantiations of the same word. There are a number of ways this goal could be achieved. One possibility, shown in Fig. 1.7(a), would be to have the recognisers for each letter form feed directly into the word-recognition unit. Another possibility, favoured by Coltheart (1981) and illustrated in Fig. 1.7(b), has the recognisers for each common form of a letter feed first into an "abstract letter identity unit" for that letter. The abstract letter identity units would then pass activation up to the word level.

Evidence for a stage of abstract letter identities has been claimed by Evett and Humphreys (1981). Their experiments involved the rapid presentation of a sequence of four stimuli. The first was always a random jumble of letter fragments known as a "pattern mask." The second stimulus was a letter string called the "prime." The prime could be a real word or an invented nonword (like *crove* or *smife*), but was always displayed so briefly that subjects were never aware that it had been presented at all. The third stimulus in the sequence was the "target" word, which it was the subject's job to report. This again was brief, but long enough to ensure somewhere between 40 and 80 per cent correct identification depending on the condition under investigation. The fourth and last stimulus was always a repetition of the pattern mask. The four stimuli, MASK–PRIME–TARGET–MASK, followed each other in rapid succession without any gaps.

The key feature of the design was the relationship between the prime and the target. The prime was always presented in lower-case print and the target in capitals. If the prime and target were the same word (e.g. *point–POINT*) then identification of the target was significantly better than if the prime was a visually different word (e.g. *gravy–POINT*), despite the fact that the prime was never consciously perceived. A real-word prime

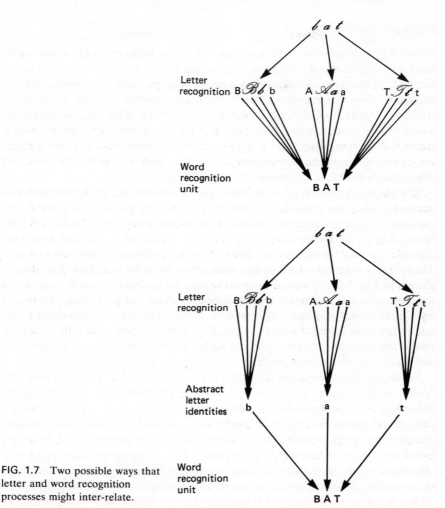

FIG. 1.7   Two possible ways that letter and word recognition processes might inter-relate.

which shared letters in common with the target (e.g. *paint–POINT*) also improved target identification as, importantly, did visually similar nonword primes (e.g. *pairt–POINT*). The magnitude of this effect was independent of the degree of physical resemblance between lower- and upper-case versions of a letter (that is, *a* would prime *A* as much as *p* primed *P*).

Evett and Humphreys take this result as supporting the concept of abstract letter identity (ALI) units. Take the case of the target *POINT* being primed by *pairt*. The prime is presented so quickly that subjects are not aware that anything has happened, and yet, according to Evett and Humphreys, in the few milliseconds that *pairt* is displayed, the letter units have been activated and, more importantly, they have transmitted information up to the ALI units. When *pairt* is replaced by *POINT*, three of the five appropriate ALI units are already active, and that degree of priming is sufficient to facilitate the perception of the target.

This sort of visual priming as a result of shared letters is much stronger when the letters in question occupy the same *positions*. We have talked so far as if there were only one abstract letter identity unit for each letter, which recognised its letter wherever it occurred. The problem here is that the words *was* and *saw*, *lose* and *sole*, *orchestra* and *carthorse* contain the same letters in different positions. Word recognition units must be informed not only of the occurrence of particular letters, but also of the positions those letters occupy (*Boston Philharmonic Carthorse* really doesn't look right, does it?).

One solution to this problem might be to propose a separate letter unit for each position that a letter can occupy. That way the component letters of *orchestra* and *carthorse* would activate completely different sets of letter units. Position-specific letter recognisers were favoured by McClelland and Rumelhart (1981) in an influential computer simulation of visual word recognition that we shall discuss shortly. Their system was, however, limited to a vocabulary of exclusively four-letter words, so that there were just four position-specific units for each letter. No one has yet shown that a system working on this principle could cope successfully with natural variations in word length from *hip* to *hippopotamus*.

Word Shape

One of the properties of the model shown in Fig. 1.3(b) is that information about word shape is lost very early on. Word recognition units are activated only by abstract letter identities and have no access to information about the shape of a word that is being fixated. There is a popular belief, however, particularly in the educational sphere, that word shape is an important clue to word identity. Thus readers might use the different outlines of the words *yacht* and *boat* (Fig. 1.8) to help discriminate between them and to help identify each word. Our model, however, denies any importance to word shape. How justifiable is this

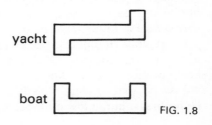

yacht

boat

FIG. 1.8

rejection? We should begin by noting that, at best, word shape could only play a relatively minor, supplementary role in reading. Groff (1975) showed that less than one-quarter of the commonest words found in children's readers had unique outlines. Word shape is also only a consideration with lower-case print—words in CAPITALS do not have such distinctive word shapes. Yet despite this fact, and despite the further fact that we surely encounter words far more often in lower-case print than in capitals, McClelland (1976) was unable to find any difference between lower-case and capitals in the accuracy with which words could be identified from a brief presentation.

A manipulation which grossly disrupts word shape is to present words in aLtErNaTiNg CaSe. This manipulation radically disrupts word shape but turns out to have only a small effect on word recognition (e.g., Besner, 1980). Cohen and Freeman (1978) measured the time taken to read aloud short passages printed either normally or in alternating case. Reading speed was reduced by 11 per cent for slower adult readers, but by a mere 2 per cent for faster readers. Importantly, these studies also found that the small disruptive effects of case alternation are no greater for familiar words than for unfamiliar words or invented nonwords, implying that the effect occurs at an early stage (e.g. letter recognition) rather than at access to word recognition units.

Finally, work on the effective span in reading has shown that when you are fixating a word, you are also picking up useful visual information from the next one or two words on the line. McConkie and Zola (1979) had subjects read text displayed on a computer screen in alternating case. They were able to change the display when the subject made a saccade, reversing the case of all the letters so that, for example, *cHaIr* would become *ChAiR*. If the subject was reading the phrase *On ThE cHaIr* and had been fixating the word *On*, then McConkie and Zola showed that a change from *cHaIr* to *ChAiR* as the eyes moved to fixate *ChAiR* did not increase the length of the fixation on *ChAiR* when compared with a condition in which the case was not changed during saccades. Thus the useful information picked up from upcoming peripheral words does not appear to include word shape.

INTERACTIONS BETWEEN THE WORD LEVEL AND THE LETTER LEVEL

Our preliminary account of word recognition had two stages; first the identification of letters, and second the identification of words. Many traditional cognitive theories might have assumed that the first stage must be *completed* before the second could begin; that is, that the identification of lines and curves as letters must be finished before the letter information could start to trigger word recognition units. However, McClelland and Rumelhart (1981) deliberately violate this assumption in their computer simulation of word recognition. In that simulation, as soon as a letter unit begins to be activated by featural information it starts to transmit activation up to the word units to which it is connected. What is more, the word units feed activation back down to the letter units which supply them.

What is the purpose of having letter units activated both from above (the word units) and below (the external stimulus)? The purpose in one sense is to explain a phenomenon known as the "word superiority effect." This effect was discovered by Reicher (1969) and Wheeler (1970), and has been the subject of much experimentation since (Henderson, 1982). In a typical experiment a subject is shown very briefly a letter string which could be a word (e.g. *MADE*) or a pronounceable nonword (e.g. *MIDE*) or a string of consonants (e.g. *MTDG*). The brief string is followed by a pattern mask of jumbled letter fragments which cuts out any short-term visual image of the stimulus (the so-called "iconic image"). The subject is then quizzed on what the letter in a particular position was (for example, following *MADE* the subject might be asked whether the third letter was *D* or *L*). In such circumstances, accuracy is greater for letters in words than for letters in nonwords or consonant strings. That is, although the subject is only ever being asked which of two letters occurred at a particular position, performance is enhanced if the target letter happens to be contained within a familiar word.

McClelland and Rumelhart (1981) successfully mimicked this effect in their computer simulation of word recognition, a simplified diagrammatic representation of which is shown in Fig. 1.9. The model has recognition units at three levels—a feature level, a letter level, and a word level. Because the model only recognises words written in capital (upper-case) letters in a particular typeface, the problems mentioned earlier about multiple and variable forms of letters are avoided. As was also mentioned earlier, the model only deals with four-letter words, making it feasible to have a unit for each letter at each of the four positions.

Units at each level send two sorts of connection to units at levels further down the line. The first are activating connections which seek to increase the level of activity in relevant higher-level units, and the second are inhibitory and seek to suppress activity in inappropriate higher-level units. Thus there will be at the feature level a unit activated by a vertical line at the left-hand side of a letter. It will send activation up to appropriate letter units (*B*, *D*, *E*, *F*, *H*, *K*, *L*, *M*, *N*, *P*, and *R*) and inhibition up to all other letter units. Suppose the word being recognised begins with an *M*. The letter unit for *M* will be achieved by the left-vertical feature detector, and also by feature units responding to the central oblique lines and the vertical line on the right. Letter units for letters sharing the left-vertical feature

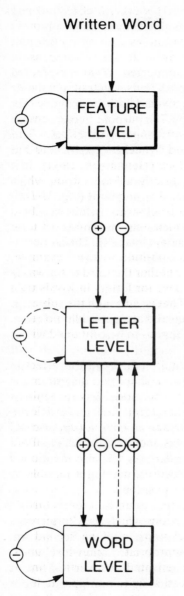

Written Word

Features identified in individual letters. Feature detectors inhibit one another.

Feature detectors activate position-specific letter detectors containing their feature and inhibit all other letter detectors.

Individual letters identified. Letter detectors receive activatory and inhibitory inputs from feature detectors, and activatory inputs from word level units. Inhibition between letter detectors is permitted in the R & M model but not used in the simulations.

Letter detectors activate word recognition units containing their letter and inhibit all other units. Letter detectors are, in turn, activated by feedback from the word level. Word-to-letter level inhibition is permitted in the model but not always used in the simulations.

Word recognition units respond to activatory and inhibitory inputs from the letter level and also mutually inhibit each other. The word recognized is the one whose activation level remains high while the others are suppressed.

FIG. 1.9   A simplified representation of the McClelland and Rumelhart (1981) computer model of visual word recognition (from Ellis, A. W. (1984) *Reading, Writing and Dyslexia: A Cognitive Analysis*. London: Lawrence Erlbaum Associates. Reproduced with permission).

will, in contrast, be inhibited by these other features, so the M detector at the letter level will emerge as the one most highly activated.

The initial detector will send activation in turn to word-level units for all words beginning with M ($MORE, MILL, MOAT, MADE, MALE$, etc.), and inhibit units for words not beginning with that letter. If the target word to be recognised happened to be $MADE$ it would be activated by the four appropriate letter detectors. $MILL$ would be activated by the initial M but would be inhibited by the A, D, and E. $MALE$ would receive three activatory inputs (M, A and E) and only one inhibitory input (D) so would take longer to be rejected. That rejection would, however, be hastened in McClelland and Rumelhart's model by the fact that there are additional inhibitory connections *within* the word level. As a word unit gains activation it seeks to suppress other units, and the strength of its inhibitory influence increases as its own level of activation goes up. This within-level inhibition, which also occurs at the feature and letter levels, causes the total system to settle down more rapidly, and speeds the identification of the letter string which has been presented to the computer.

We have now accounted for all the connections in Fig. 1.9 except those introduced to permit the model to simulate the findings on word superiority effects with which we began this section. Letters presented in familiar words, it will be remembered, seem to be identified more accurately at brief, masked exposures than letters in nonwords. McClelland and Rumelhart simulate this finding in the model by allowing activated word units to contribute to the current level of activity in letter-level units for the word's component letters. Consider the D in $MADE$. The first step towards its eventual identification as a D will begin with the activation of appropriate feature detectors. They will begin to feed activation into the letter unit for a D in a third position. At the same time, the letter units for an initial M, second A and final E will be warming up. While still less than fully activated, they will be passing activation up to the word unit for $MADE$. And as it begins to warm up it will feed activation back down to those letter units, thus hastening the moment at which they achieve maximal activation.

Now suppose the D had formed part of the nonword $MIDE$. Letter units would begin to be activated by the feature detectors and would, in turn, send activation up to the word level. But there is no word unit which would receive wholly activatory inputs—even units for similar-looking real words like $MILE$, $SIDE$, or $MADE$ will all receive at least one inhibitory input from $MIDE$. The word level will accordingly warm up much less than it did with $MADE$. The important consequence of this is that the top-down contribution of the word level to the activation of the letter units, and hence to the perception of component letters, will be less for nonwords than words. So when the presentation of a letter string is brief and curtailed by a pattern mask, the letter level will have made less progress in resolving the identity of the letters if they had formed a nonword than if they formed a familiar word. Consonant strings like *MTDG* will cause even less activity at the word level, so their perception will be even more heavily data-driven and slower as a consequence. In McClelland and Rumelhart's simulation such strings are the slowest to be identified, and in experiments on letter identification using human subjects they fare worst of all.

It is not only the word superiority effect that can be explained by allowing the word level to influence the letter level. Under certain conditions the effect of word-context may be so strong that it induces the illusory perception of a letter that is not in fact there. The classic demonstration of this phenomenon we owe to Pillsbury (1897). He deliberately smudged some letters in words or replaced them with others, then displayed the words briefly (though no briefer than an average fixation duration) to skilled readers. The readers were asked to indicate, with some estimate of their degree of confidence, *exactly* what they had seen. Pillsbury discovered that people would report with confidence having seen letters which had, in fact, been replaced by a smudge or by another letter.

Figure 1.10 (from Frisby, 1979) illustrates the power of context to induce letter restoration. Have a look at it. Now have another look—there is no *P* in *SPRING*!

In terms of the interactive activation model, what appears to be happening is this: You often do not need all of the letters in a word to activate its word recognition unit (e.g., *elxphxnt*; *gxrxffe*). If a letter has

FIG. 1.10 A dramatic illustration of the capacity of context to induce illusory letter perception (from Frisby, J. P. (1979) *Seeing: Illusion, Brain & Mind*. Oxford: Oxford University Press. Reproduced with permission).

been omitted from a word, either through a printer's error or an experimenter's deviousness, the remaining letters may be sufficient to activate the word unit. It will then feed activation back down to the letter units for all its component letters, *including the missing one*. It will be "seen" because it has been activated from within, not from without. The broader context in which a misprinted word appears is also known to affect the probability of illusory letter restoration, a fact we shall discuss later. Interactions between letter and word levels also help account for the effects of context on letter identification illustrated in Fig. 1.6(b).

A further important aspect of interactive models should be noted. Although the three stages of the McClelland and Rumelhart model are distinct and occur in sequence, processing of information at one level does not have to be completed before processing at the next level begins. Instead, as soon as activation starts to build up at one level it is transmitted to the next. Because of the additional feature of reverse, "top-down" flow of activation, higher levels can interact with and influence lower levels. The simulation thus avoids many of the unwanted features of earlier linear-stage models in cognitive psychology, at the same time providing a model of the way in which stored knowledge of the world (in this case, knowlege of the spellings of familiar words) can interact with incoming stimulus information to determine what is actually perceived.

We have dwelt at some length upon one particular model of word recognition. One reason for this is that the McClelland and Rumelhart model represents a use of computer simulation that is of most value and most interest to cognitive psychologists. The aim of its creators was more than just to get a computer to recognise words. They wanted their computer system to recognise words in the same way that human readers do. And when there was a mismatch between human and computer performance, the simulation was modified until a better match resulted. The simulation thus embodied a theory of how *we* do what we do.

Also, there often comes a point in the development of our understanding of a particular skill where our theories reach such a degree of complexity that it is useful to try and implement them on a computer to see if they are workable. In attempting to program a computer to simulate human performance, the psychologist may also come to appreciate previously unrealised problems and may indeed discover ways of solving them. Finally, when the program is run it may be found to have unanticipated properties which can then be compared against data from humans. An example of this is Rumelhart and McClelland's (1982) discovery that the perceptibility of a nonword is determined by how many real words it resembles rather than, for example, whether or not it is pronounceable.

Cognitive psychologists do not, by and large, believe that humans are "just computers"—a computer doesn't get depressed when its team loses;

it doesn't aspire to a lifestyle beyond its means; and its work doesn't suffer because it is lovesick. But there are *aspects* of what we can do that computers can also do quite well, and trying to persuade a computer to do something that most of us can do effortlessly can be an instructive exercise for the psychologist.

ROUTES FROM PRINT TO MEANING AND SOUND

The word-recognition processes we have outlined so far apply to the case of a reader fixating a familiar written word. In this instance word identification is followed by accessing the word's meaning (its "semantic representation"), which may be followed by activating the word's spoken form. This last stage would account for the "voice in the head" that many people report as normally accompanying their reading. There are good reasons for arguing that where familiar words are concerned, this voice is activated last, after meaning has been processed. First, the voice in the head gives words and phrases appropriate emphasis, colouring and intonation, which cannot be done unless the meaning is grasped. Second, the inner voice assigns the appropriate sound-form to words whose pronunciation varies according to their meaning (e.g. "Goldilocks caught her dress on a thorn. There was a large *tear* in it. She began to cry. In her eye a *tear* formed and trickled down her cheek.") Here, then, is one route through the word-recognition apparatus:

Written   IDENTIFY   IDENTIFY   ACCESS   ACCESS
word → LETTERS →   WORD → MEANING → PRONUNCIATION

We shall see later in the chapter that this scheme is probably too simple. It seems likely that in addition to a route from "identify word" to "access pronunciation" via "access meaning", there is also a route which allows familiar words to access their pronunciations directly from word recognition, without going through their semantic representations. Thus our scheme should possibly look more like:

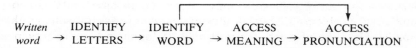

Written   IDENTIFY   IDENTIFY   ACCESS   ACCESS
word → LETTERS → WORD → MEANING → PRONUNCIATION

Not all letter strings encountered in reading form familiar words. Young or unskilled readers frequently come across unfamiliar words on the printed page, and skilled readers occasionally do: the place-name Gorehampton at the end of our Goldilocks passage (Fig. 1.1) being an example. In Fig. 1.1, Gorehampton was shown as receiving multiple, prolonged fixations, the typical pattern for unfamiliar words (Buswell, 1937).

Normal readers are not helpless in the face of unfamiliar written words. During the prolonged fixations they first identify the component letters (as with familiar words), then slowly "sound out" the word in their heads. This involves breaking the word down into its component letters or letter groups, then translating each into the appropriate sounds, thereby assembling a pronunciation for the word. Quite often a word whose written form is unfamiliar will be one that the reader has heard before and knows the meaning of. There is a chance, then, that once the sound-form of an unfamiliar word has been assembled it will be recognised and understood. This mode of word recognition is sometimes referred to as "phonic mediation" because the sound of the word mediates the access to its meaning (Ellis, 1984). The mode can be induced in skilled readers by re-spelling familiar words in unfamiliar ways (e.g. *Wunss uppon a tyme thear wur thrie beirs hoo livd inn a hows onn the ej ov a phorrest*). We may represent the phonic mediation routine as follows:

| *Written word* | $\rightarrow$ | IDENTIFY LETTERS | $\rightarrow$ | APPLY LETTER–SOUND CORRES-PONDENCES | $\rightarrow$ | IDENTIFY SPOKEN WORD-FORM | $\rightarrow$ | ACCESS MEANING |

One line of evidence pointing to the independence of the visual, whole-word recognition routine and the phonic mediation routine comes from the effects of brain injury on the reading performance of previously skilled readers. Reading disorders caused by brain injury in adulthood are known as *acquired dyslexias*, and several different patterns of reading impairment have been identified (Ellis, 1984). Of interest to us here are reports of patients who have lost the use of one of the two proposed routines for visual word recognition but retained the other. Least disabling for the already fluent reader is impairment to the phonic mediation routine, a condition sometimes referred to as "phonological dyslexia." Such patients can still recognise all (or most) of the words that they had learned to recognise visually before their brain injury: all they cannot do is "sound out" unfamiliar words or invented nonwords (Patterson, 1982, and Funnell, 1983, provide detailed case reports).

The contrasting pattern of loss of the visual, whole-word routine with preservation of phonic mediation is conventionally referred to as "surface dyslexia." Case reports can be found in Patterson, Marshall, and Coltheart (1985). Although such patients often retain a limited "sight vocabulary," many words that were formerly recognised visually as wholes now appear unfamiliar, with the result that the patient must attempt to read them by phonic mediation. This can be successful if the word they are attempting to read has a "regular" spelling–sound correspondence (e.g. *pistol* or *boat*), but words with irregular correspondences (e.g., *sword*; *yacht*) are apt to be mispronounced and hence not comprehended.

Dyslexia can also occur in developmental forms that can bear a resemblance to the acquired forms, but there are reasons to be cautious in attempting to draw parallels (Ellis, 1985a). Reading is a skill we learn, not one we are born with, and it is too late and restricted an arrival on the evolutionary scene for us to have evolved any inbuilt mechanisms specific to dealing with the written word. It follows, then, that developmental reading problems are likely to arise because a child suffers from a disorder, possibly a slight and subtle one, to some cognitive process which is necessary for the full and complete acquisition of literacy but which is not only involved in reading or writing.

A good illustration of this point is provided by Campbell and Butterworth's (1985) analysis of the reading problems of a 20-year-old student. This bright student, RE, had experienced considerable difficulty learning to read at school and, as often happens, became a "behaviour problem." Her mother eventually taught her to read by abandoning the "phonic" methods that had been tried with RE and concentrating instead on whole-word "look-and-say" methods. By dint of great application RE acquired a sight vocabulary sufficient to allow her to make progress at school and gain entrance to university.

RE's problem came to the attention of Campbell and Butterworth when she admitted in a psychology seminar that she could only read a new word aloud once she had heard someone else say it. More formal testing revealed that although she could read "by sight" uncommon or difficult words like *phlegm*, *catacomb*, and *subtle*, she had great difficulty reading aloud even the simplest invented nonwords like *hoz* or *bant*. When she succeeded it seemed to be through a strategy of basing her response on a similar-looking real word. Thus she pronounced *bant* correctly, but only after a 15-second pause, and only after admitting that she "thought of Bantu and knocked off the 'u'."

So far RE's profile resembles that of an acquired "phonological dyslexic" (good visual, whole-word recognition with poor phonic mediation), but Campbell and Butterworth were able to tie her problems to a developmental difficulty that was not restricted to reading. RE was found to have great difficulty in consciously comparing or manipulating the sound patterns of words in general. She would read two words aloud correctly but then be unable to say whether or not they sounded the same (*reign/rain*) or rhymed (*rough/fluff*). She was poor at indicating the number of sounds in a word (*theach* = 3; *stint* = 5) and was equally poor at a language game which required her to reverse ("spoonerise") the initial sounds of the names of pop starts (*John Lennon*–"Lon Jennon"; *Bob Dylan*–"Dob Bylan").

In all of these tasks RE tried to work with the visual appearance of words rather than their sounds. Thus she could judge rhyme correctly when two words looked alike (*match/catch*) but falsely asserted that pairs like *post/lost* rhymed, and failed to spot the rhyme in visually dissimilar pairs like *true/shoe*. Her estimates of numbers of sounds in words tended to be based instead on numbers of letters, and she made errors in the spoonerising task through her stragey of reversing letters rather than sounds (*Phil Collins*–"Chil Pollins," not "Kil Follins").

These deficits appeared even when the tasks were presented entirely auditorily, with spoken stimuli requiring spoken responses. Campbell and Butterworth (1985) conclude that RE lacks conscious access to the sound-forms of words. She cannot inspect or analyse the sound patterns of words internally, a skill that appears to be necessary for the development of the phonic mediation route but which is not essential for developing a visual sight vocabulary. A remark RE once made is revealing in this regard; she said, "I could never understand when teachers said 'listen to the word in your head'. I don't hear words in my head."

HIGHER-LEVEL CONTEXT EFFECTS IN READING

Earlier we saw how the context in which a letter appears (whether in a word, a pronounceable nonword, or an unpronounceable letter string) can affect its perceptibility. Here we shall ask whether the same applies at the word level. Does the context in which a written word appears affect the ease with which it can be recognised or understood?

The first modern experiment on this issue was reported by Tulving and Gold (1963). They assembled a set of sentences in which the final word was highly appropriate to the preceding sentence context (e.g. *The skiers were buried alive by the sudden AVALANCHE*). In their experiments subjects would be shown some or all of the sentence context and would then be shown the final word very briefly. At first the exposure time for the last word would be so short that the subjects would be unable to report it. The context would then be shown again and the target word displayed for a slightly longer time, and so on until the subject correctly reported what the final word was. Tulving and Gold found that having the context available reduced the exposure duration at which the final word could be accurately identified, and that the effect increased as more context was supplied.

Similar results were obtained by Tulving, Mandler, and Baumal (1964) and, independently, by Morton (1964), and led researchers to conclude that readers utilise the context of what they have just read to assist ongoing word recognition. That assertion is still presented as received wisdom in many textbooks, but it is the fate of all received wisdom to be challenged and qualified, and this one has proved no exception.

We remarked at the outset of this chapter that work on reading has been less dogged than many areas of cognitive psychology by the problem of "ecological validity" (i.e. the artificiality of some laboratory tasks designed to study cognition). However, it could be argued that the Tulving and Gold experiment might induce in subjects different strategies from those employed in normal reading. Put yourself in the shoes of a subject in this experiment and ask yourself how *you* would have approached it. You see an incomplete fragment of a sentence—*The skiers were buried alive by the sudden.* . . . Then, after a short delay, you see a very quick flash. All you pick up is the fact that it's a longish target word. That excludes some possibilities already (e.g. *flood, fall*) but leaves several open (*snowball, rockfall, avalanche,.* . .). You are then shown the context again, followed by a longer, though still brief, look at the target. This time you see that it's a longish word *and* that it begins with *a* and ends with *e*. You're home and dry—it's got to be *avalanche*. Naturally, if you're one of those subjects receiving shorter context fragments (e.g.—*alive by the sudden.* . .), then the number of possible completions will tend to be higher and you are likely to need a rather longer look at the target word and pick up rather more letters before you guess it correctly.

When the procedure and the likely resulting strategy for a subject in this sort of experiment are spelled out in this way, there are several reasons why one might query any simple generalisation from it to normal reading. First, in normal reading, words are not presented at brief exposures determined by the experimenter. Fixations on words typically *are* brief (200–250 msec), but in normal circumstances the reader is free to prolong a fixation for as long as is necessary to identify the word. This suggests that fixations should be shorter on predictable words than on unpredictable ones, a sugestion that was confirmed by Ehrlich and Rayner (1981). In their study, fixation durations on words predictable from the preceding context were not only shorter than on unpredictable ones (221 msec vs. 254 msec), but the probability of skipping a word (failing to fixate it at all) was also higher for predictable than unpredictable targets.

So highly predictable words in natural texts tend to be skipped over and, when fixated, to receive a briefer glance. But how predictable is "highly predictable"? In the Ehrlich and Rayner study it was very high indeed. Their predictable targets were words which, if deleted from the text, had a 90 per cent or higher probability of being correctly restored by subjects asked to supply the missing words. It is possible that, for skilled readers of the sort used in these studies, this level of predictability is necessary before contextual facilitation can be observed.

Fischler and Bloom (1979) presented incomplete context sentences followed by either a word or a nonword. The subject's task was to press one button if the target was a word, and another if it was a nonword (a "lexical decision task"). Fischler and Bloom found that the time to judge a letter string to be a word was reduced if the word was a very highly probable completion of the incomplete sentence (e.g. *She cleaned the dirt from her . . . SHOES*), but less probable, though still sensible completions (*. . . from her . . . HANDS*) were not facilitated. Gough, Alford and Holley-Wilcox (1983) presented the first eight words of sentences selected at random from the *Reader's Digest* to subjects who were asked to guess the ninth word. If the ninth word happened to be a so-called "function word" like *the, at, him* or *from*, predictability was around 40 per cent, but for "content words" of the sort used in typical experiments (*hands, shoes, avalanche*, etc.), predictability was a mere 10 per cent (i.e. guessed correctly by only 1 in 10 subjects). Yet Fischler and Bloom failed to find any contextual facilitation in their lexical decision task when the predictability of word targets fell below 90 per cent, and the Ehrlich and Rayner study of fixation duration only looked at very high levels of predictability.

So do readers utilise context to assist in the recognition of words at normal levels of predictability? The answer to that question would appear to be "Yes, but only sometimes," and the key to understanding when and where is to ask the related and important question, "Why *should* anyone utilise context to assist ongoing word recognition?" As Forster (1981) noted, using context to predict likely upcoming words cannot be a simple and straightforward matter, but probably requires extensive cognitive resources. For the skilled reader in normal circumstances, is it worth bringing those extensive resources to bear for the sake of a few milliseconds' saving in recognition time per predictable word?

Stanovich and West (1979) found no contextual facilitation from incomplete sentences to target words presented in clear, sharp print, but when the contrast on the target words was reduced, making them harder to read, a facilitation effect emerged. On reflection this makes sense. Theories of *how* context exerts an influence on word recognition commonly propose that high-level semantic processes dealing with the meanings of words or sentences are able to affect the activation levels in word recognition units (e.g. Morton, 1969). That is, recognition units can be "primed" by contexts so that less stimulus information (e.g. a briefer exposure or shorter fixation) is necessary for likely words to be identified than unlikely ones. Such priming will be particularly useful (and detectable) when stimulus-driven recognition is slow because reading conditions are difficult—hence the interaction between stimulus quality and context observed by Stanovich and West (1979) and others. The notion that context may be exploited most when recognition based solely on print information is slow may also explain the finding that younger and/or less skilled readers appear to make more use of context than do older and/or more skilled readers (Stanovich, West, & Freeman, 1981).

Stanovich (1980) reviewed the literature on the use of context in skilled and unskilled reading and argued for an "interactive-compensatory model" of individual differences. He suggested that although utilising context predictively might be cognitively demanding, it will aid reading fluency when "bottom-up" recognition of words from print is slow and possibly error-prone. This will tend to be the case for children and older but relatively unpractised readers. As reading skill increases, visual processes become faster and more efficient, and consequently the need to use context to compensate for slow stimulus analysis decreases. Under normal reading conditions, Stanovich argues, skilled readers make little predictive use of context (a claim echoed by Mitchell, 1982). The capability remains however, and can be brought into play under the conditions discussed earlier where stimulus quality is poor.

SUMMARY

Reading is an acquired skill which requires the involvement of perceptual, linguistic, and general cognitive processes for its successful execution. As such it is a natural object for psychological investigation. The reading of text requires a well co-ordinated pattern of eye movements involving fixations (moments when the eyes are stationary, and during which visual information is taken in) and saccades (rapid eye movements between fixations). At each fixation, visual information is registered from within an area around the fixation point known as the "perceptual span." In English readers this is biased to the right of the fixation point.

Letter recognition has been much studied as an example of skilled pattern recognition. "Template" and "feature"-based models have been proposed, but it has not yet been established that either of these can cope adequately with the naturally occurring variability of letter shapes or with the influence of context on letter identification.

There is evidence that the different forms a letter may take converge upon a level of "abstract letter identities" prior to actual word recognition. Word shape seems to play only a minimal role in skilled word recognition. Letter and word recognition processes appear to interact in subtle ways rather than occurring as sequential stages. The McClelland and Rumelhart (1981) computer simulation of word recognition embodies one possible account of the form that interaction might take, and at the same time provides an explanation of various phenomena concerning letter, word, and nonword recognition.

Cognitive psychologists have identified several routines for accessing meaning and pronunciation from print. Familiar written words are probably identified from their visual forms without the mediation of the word's sound-form. It seems likely that the pronunciation of a familiar word can be accessed either via the word's meaning or more directly from the stage of visual word recognition. Unfamiliar written words can be read aloud using a knowledge of letter–sound correspondences in English, and may then be identified if the visually unfamiliar word is familiar in its spoken form. Different patterns of reading disorder in both acquired and developmental dyslexics can be analysed in terms of impairment to one or other of the different reading routines.

Finally, readers appear to be able to utilise the context in which a word occurs to aid ongoing word recognition, though it seems that context is utilised more by poor and beginning readers than by skilled readers who may only use context extensively when stimulus quality is poor.

In Chapter 2 we consider other forms of pattern recognition, notably the recognition of familiar faces and objects, and discuss similarities, differences, and interrelationships between object, face, and word recognition. We have focused in this chapter largely on word recognition because other aspects of language processing are dealt with elsewhere in the book, notably in Chapters 8 (sentence processing) and 9 (comprehending and remembering text).

A broader introduction to reading and its disorders can be found in A. W. Ellis (1984), *Reading, Writing and Dyslexia*; more advanced treatments are given in D. C. Mitchell (1982), *The Process of Reading*, and L. Henderson (1982), *Orthography and Word Recognition in Reading*.

2 Recognising Faces: Perceiving and Identifying Objects

It is a busy Saturday afternoon in your town. The streets are swarming with shoppers pushing and shoving. You are trying to find a pair of shoes you like and wondering why on earth you didn't do your shopping mid-week when things were quieter. In the distance you notice two people walking towards you. The one on the left you recognise immediately as your grandmother; the one on the right you do not recognise.

What could be a more commonplace and everyday occurrence than recognising the face of someone you know? We do it all the time—at home, at work, watching television, in town . . . "But," asks the cognitive psychologist, "*how* do we do it? *How* do we recognise the lady approaching us as granny? What processes go on in our minds that allow us to identify the lady on the left as familiar while rejecting the person on the right as unfamiliar?" Like word recognition, face recognition must be a matter of achieving a match between a perceived stimulus pattern and a stored representation. When you get to know someone, you must establish in memory some form of representation or description of their appearance. Recognising the person on subsequent occasions requires the perceived face to make contact with the stored description, otherwise the face will seem unfamiliar and you will fail to recognise him or her.

Few cognitive psychologists would depart from our account so far. The problems arise when one tries to be more specific. What form does the internal representation of a familiar face take? How are seen faces matched against stored representations? In what sort of memory store is the representation held? How does seeing a familiar face trigger the wider knowledge you have about that person, including their name? When you see a familiar person, he or she is often moving against a complex visual background: How does your visual system isolate elements of the whole visual scene as constituting one object (a person) moving in a particular way at a particular speed? These are some of the questions a complete theory of visual processing should be able to answer, and some of the questions that are addressed in this chapter. In the previous chapter reading was both the real-world example and the main topic in the chapter. We use face recognition in this chapter to introduce some of the important questions about how we perceive and recognise objects in general, not just faces.

RECOGNISING FAMILIAR PATTERNS

There are lots of faces visible in the shopping crowd, but you recognise only one of them. How? A ploy commonly adopted by cognitive psychologists when trying to understand how the mind performs a particular task is to ask how we could create an artificial device capable of performing the same task. How could we, for example, program a computer to recognise a set of faces and reject others?

First of all the computer would need to memorise somehow the set it had to recognise. It would then need to compare each face it saw (through a camera input, for example) with the set stored in memory to see if there was a match. If a satisfactory match was achieved the face would be "recognised"; if not, it would be rejected as unfamiliar.

Now within those broad outlines there are a number of options available regarding the possible nature of the representation of each face to be stored in memory and the manner in which the perceived face could be compared against the stored set. We could, for example, store the description of a person's face in terms of a list of *features* (a feature being a property of an object that helps discriminate it from other objects). Granny's face might then be held in memory as a feature list something like:

+ white hair
+ curly hair
+ round face
+ hooked nose
+ thin lips
+ blue eyes
+ round gold-rimmed spectacles
+ wrinkles

and so on. The features of each face to appear before the camera could then be compared against the stored list. If all features agreed then the face would be recognised as Granny's, but if the person before the camera had, say, a long, thin face rather than a round one it would be rejected as unfamiliar. This would be a *feature-based* model of recognition.

There is no denying that features play a role in face recognition, or that some features are more important than others. In free descriptions of unfamiliar faces subjects utilise features, mentioning the hair most often,

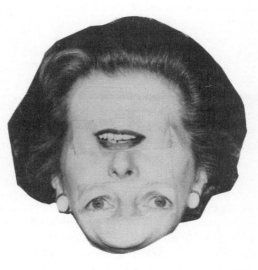

FIG. 2.1   The scrambled face of a well-known person illustrates the importance of configuration in pattern recognition (from Bruce, V. & Valentine, T. (1985) 'What's up? The Margaret Thatcher illusion revisited *Perception* **14**, 515–516. Reproduced with permission.

followed by eyes, nose, mouth, eyebrows, chin, and forehead in that order (Shepherd, Davies, & Ellis, 1981). As faces become familiar there is evidence of a decreasing reliance on external features such as hairstyle, colour, and face shape towards a reliance on the internal features of eyes, nose, and mouth (Ellis, Shepherd, & Davies, 1979). This may be because hairstyle in particular can change, and so is a relatively unreliable cue to recognition, whereas internal features are comparatively stable and reliable.

The problem with any simple feature-based model is illustrated by Fig. 2.1. A "scrambled" face contains the same features as a normal face, but their *configuration* has been altered. Although it may be possible to recognise the scrambled face of a well-known person, it is much harder than recognising a normal face. Also, as Fig. 2.2 shows, varying the configuration of a fixed set of features can substantially alter the appearance of the face.

Because of the significance of configuration in face recognition, theorists have often favoured some form of template account (Ellis, 1975). As we saw in Chapter 1, templates have difficulty if the stimulus pattern is not in exactly the same orientation as the original pattern from which the representation was formed. This could be overcome for faces if several templates were stored for different views of familiar people (full face, profile, three-quarter view, rear view, etc.). Although the extrapolation should only be made with extreme caution, there is evidence from work with monkeys to suggest that those animals do indeed store a fixed set of views of faces they have learned to recognise (Perrett et al., 1984).

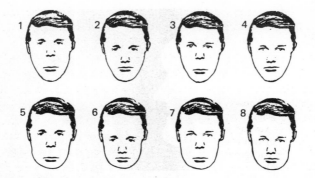

FIG. 2.2   Each pair of faces (1 and 2; 3 and 4; 5 and 6; 7 and 8) differ only on the configuration of their internal features. (Adapted with permission from Sergent, J. (1984). An investigation into component and configurational processes underlying face perception. *British Journal of Psychology*, **75**, 221–242).

SEEING OBJECTS

Your grandmother is moving through a crowd of shoppers carrying a couple of bags. Parts of her periodically disappear from view when she passes behind a bench seat, or when another shopper passes in front of her. Your visual system is confronted with a kaleidoscope of patches of light of different colours, reflecting off surfaces of objects at varying distances, moving in varying directions at varying speeds. What you *perceive*, however, is a coherent scene composed of distinct objects set against a stable background. This unified impression is the *end product* of processes of visual perception which psychologists have sought to understand.

Some of the first psychologists to be interested in how we perceive one part of a visual display as belonging with another were the German Gestalt psychologists. From just before the First World War, Gestalt psychologists, led by Wertheimer and his students Kohler and Koffka, concentrated upon the way in which the world we perceive is almost always organised as whole objects set against a fixed background. Even three dots on a page (see Fig. 2.3) will cohere as a triangle. Our perceptual systems are organised to

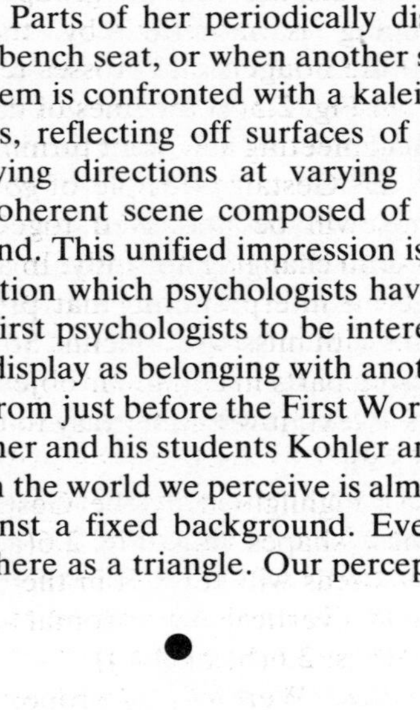

FIG. 2.3   Three simple dots on a page cannot but be seen as a triangle.

FIG. 2.4 Rubin's well known ambiguous figure which can be seen as either a black vase against a white background or two white faces against a black background (but not both at once).

derive forms and relationships from even the simplest of inputs. Sometimes the input can be interpreted in more than one way and the result is a dramatic alternating in our perception. The face–vase illusion (Fig. 2.4) devised by the Gestalt psychologist Rubin is a well-known example. The information in the picture allows it to be interpreted either as a vase or as two faces. When the interpretation shifts, the part that had been the figure becomes the background, and vice versa.

The Gestalt psychologists formulated several principles to describe the way in which parts of a given display will be grouped together (see Fig. 2.5(a)). However, grouping is modified by the similarity of components. So, in Fig. 2.5(b) the noughts and crosses tend to be seen in lines because they are similar. In Fig. 2.5(c) the lines of dashes are seen as crossing one another, rather than meeting at a point turning at an angle and moving away. This illustrates the Gestalt principle of *good continuation*, which maintains that elements will be perceived together where they maintain a smooth flow rather than changing abruptly. In a similar way, the perceptual system will opt for an interpretation that produces a closed, complete figure rather than one with missing elements. Sometimes this can lead to the overlooking of missing parts in a familiar object. If you had not been primed to look for it by the text, it would be easy to overlook the gap in one of the letters in Fig. 2.5(d).

Other perceptual preferences highlighted by the Gestalt psychologists were for bilaterally symmetrical shapes (e.g. Fig. 2.6(a)). Other things being equal, the smaller of two areas will be seen in the background, and this is enhanced by them being in a vertical or horizontal arrangement (see the black and white crosses in Figs. 2.6(b) and (c)).

To summarise their principles, Wertheimer proposed the Law of Pragnanz. This states that, of the many geometrically possible organisations that might be perceived from a given pattern of optic stimulation, the one that will be perceived is that possessing the best, simplest, and most stable shape.

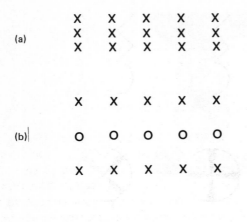

(a)

(b)

(c)

(d) **HELLO**

FIG. 2.5 Examples of Gestalt principles in action. a) *Proximity*: The arrangement of the crosses causes them to be perceived as being in columns rather than rows. b) *Similarity*: The similarity of the elements causes them to be perceived as being in rows rather than columns. c) *Good continuity*: causes you to interpret this as two continuous intersecting lines. d) *Closure*: The gap in the O is perceptually completed.

Although we have illustrated the Gestalt principles using very simple examples and illustrations, their application to normal, intricate visual processing is in the way they assist the visual system to unite those components of the visual array that constitute single objects. There are other cues that assist in this unification.

All the cues discussed so far apply to stationary objects, but additional cues arise when an object moves. If an object is moving it will cover progressively more of the visual field if it is approaching, less if it is going away, and will successively obscure and reveal the background over which it passes. This movement is a major source of object perception. Elements that move together are usually perceived as being part of the same object, a principle known to the Gestalt psychologists as *common fate*.

Research in visual perception continues to identify further visual cues to object recognition (Bruce & Green, 1985). An example would be *granularity*. If two regions in the perceptual field have the same overall brightness but differ in the spatial distribution of their elements, then regions of uniform granularity are perceived as separate. This is more easily demonstrated (Fig. 2.7) than explained.

FIG. 2.6   a) Organisation by lateral symmetry. The symmetrical form on the right is much more easily perceived as a coherent whole than the assymetrical form on the left. b) The preference here is to perceive the smaller area as the figure and the larger as the ground—i.e. as a black cross on a white background. c) If the larger area is to be perceived as the figure—a white cross on a black background—then orienting the white area around horizontal and vertical axes makes this easier.

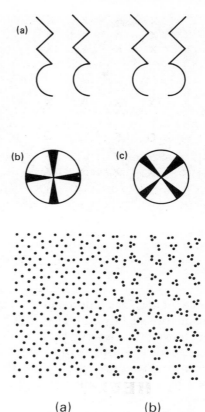

FIG. 2.7   With the spatial density of the dots held constant, an area with altered granularity is perceived as separate (from Bruce, V. & Green, P. R. (1985) *Visual Perception: Physiology, Psychology and Ecology*. London: Lawrence Erlbaum Associates Ltd.)

(a)   (b)

Granny's granularity, her good continuation, the common fate of her parts, and so on, will all help you unify those components of a 'buzzing, blooming visual array which belong together as the parts of a single object. It is convenient for the purpose of illustration to isolate each cue and demonstrate it in simplified form, but in the real world these cues are all operating together, and their function is to assist the visual system in identifying objects in the visual scene with a view to recognising them for what they are. Camouflage in the natural world can, incidentally, be analysed as a variety of attempts to disrupt and confound those visual cues, making an object hard to distinguish from the background scene.

DISTANCE AND MOVEMENT

As soon as you become aware of Granny's presence in the crowd, you also have an impression of how far away she is. Judgement of the relative distances of visible objects is an important aspect of perception.

FIG. 2.8   Julesz dot patterns (see text for explanation (from Julesz, B. (1964) Binocular depth perception without familiarity cues. *Science*, **15**, 356–62. Copyright 1964 by the American Association for the Advancement of Science, and reproduced with permission.

One source of distance information is the stereoscopic information provided by the two slightly different views of the same scene obtained by our two eyes. Given the disparity between the images to the two eyes it is possible to calculate the distance of an object, because the closer an object is, the greater is the disparity between the two different views of it. Stereoscopes, in which two different pictures are presented to each eye, each picture representing what would be seen if the actual objects were presented in a three-dimensional world, were invented in the 1830s by Wheatstone and have been popular at various times since for the vivid three-dimensional experience they produce.

There is still considerable dispute about how exactly the discrepant information from the two eyes is combined to allow depth to be computed. The traditional view was that the images from each eye were separately processed and then fused together (e.g. Sherrington, 1906). However, the work of Julesz (1971) has suggested that this is not so. Julesz developed the *random dot stereogram* (see Fig. 2.8). This consists of patterns of black and white dots. Viewed without a stereoscope the two patterns shown in Fig. 2.8 look similar. If, however, the patterns are projected one to each eye, a central square of dots will be seen floating closer to the observer. The reason is that the two random-dot stereograms are not identical. The right-hand one has a square part of the left-hand pattern shifted to the right and the space remaining filled with random dots. To the retina of each eye this provides the same information that would be seen if that square was actually in front of the rest of the main square, and it is seen in that way when the stereoscopic information is combined. What Julesz random-dot stereograms demonstrate is that one can see stereoptically without having to first recognise and fuse an object separately for each eye. When seen separately we cannot see the object, the square, which only appears when the images are combined.

Monocular Depth Cues

We have discussed depth perception using two eyes, but even with one eye closed we can normally judge how far away an object is. With one eye closed we could still shake hands with our grandmother's friend! There are many cues to distance in most static visual scenes. First there is the relative size of known objects—the farther away your grandmother is, the smaller the area of the retina upon which her image is projected. Second, things that are closer will often be superimposed upon and obscure parts of the view of things farther away. Shadows give impressions of solidity and depth to individual objects. The texture of the things we perceive becomes less obvious and finer at greater distances. Especially in a man-made world of straight lines, right angles, and flat planes, perspective is a strong depth cue. As they recede into the distance, parallel lines converge, and line drawings that incorporate such features give a strong impression of depth (see Fig. 2.9).

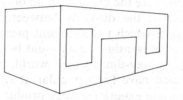

FIG. 2.9   Converging lines give a strong impression of depth.

By careful building it is possible to construct visual displays that set monocular cues against one another. A famous one is Ames' room. In Fig. 2.10, photographed inside the room, it appears as if the person on the right is very much bigger than the one on the left, yet both are normal-sized adults. In Ames' room the normal depth cue of our knowledge of relative sizes is overwhelmed by the manipulation of the perspective provided by the decorations on the walls. To the viewer the room looks rectangular because the decorations which look like doors and windows appear as they would do in a normal rectangular room. In fact, the room increases in distance and height away to the left and the decorations are trapezoidal, not rectangular. The person who appears smaller is much farther away than the other one.

A moving person or object supplies additional information to help in the judgement of distance. The farther away a moving object is, the slower it

FIG. 2.10   Ames' room (see text for explanation). Used by permission of
Eastern Counties Newspapers Ltd.

will move through the visual field. When we are ourselves moving, then the
world that we see seems to flow past us. The speed and direction of the
optic flow provide excellent information about the direction and speed of
our travel. Gibson (1966, 1979) has argued strongly that too much
emphasis in psychology has, in the past, been placed on the perception of
static, very simple displays by static observers in a highly uniform, often
visually degraded environment. Our perceptual systems have actually
evolved to cope with a visually extremely rich world in which we are
constantly moving and experiencing changes in the visual array, and the
cues afforded by movement and change are important in determining the
interpretation we place upon a visual scene.

When it comes to grouping elements of an array together as components
of a single object, or judging how far away that object is, then the processes
involved are likely to be the same whether or not you recognise the
individual object concerned (they will treat Granny and the unfamiliar lady
walking alongside her alike). For the remainder of this chapter we return to
the processing of familiar objects, concerning ourselves with such things as
how, having recognised an object, you retrieve the relevant information
about it that you have stored in memory (including its name), and what
role context plays in the recognition of familiar objects.

OBJECT MEANINGS AND OBJECT NAMES

When you espy Granny walking towards you, the act of recognition is typically accompanied by more than just a feeling of familiarity. Something of what you know about her also springs to mind. You may remember that she is a little hard-of-hearing and resolve to speak clearly; you may remember that she is critical of what she considers untidy appearance and surreptitiously try to spruce yourself up; you may remember that she holds strong political opinions somewhat different from your own and make a mental note to steer clear of contentious topics. You will also usually be able to remember her name.

That is what *normally* happens, and what *should* happen, but we all know that our cognitive processes sometimes let us down. Young, Hay, and Ellis (1985) persuaded 22 volunteers to keep diaries of their everyday errors and problems in person recognition. A total of 1008 incidents were recorded. They fell into several different categories, of which we shall consider four. The first type of error was the simple failure to recognise a familiar person: 114 such incidents were recorded. The explanation for such errors is presumably the failure of the perceived face to access the internal stored representation of the familiar person's appearance. A common cause of such an error is that the person's appearance has changed, and so no longer provides a good match to the stored representation. Someone you know but fail to recognise may, for example, have cut their hair and shaved off a beard, or lost weight dramatically, or may have aged 15 years since you last saw them.

The second type of error reported was the misidentification of one person as another (314 incidents). Such errors tended to be short-lived and to occur under poor viewing conditions (e.g. a brief glimpse of someone). Usually the misidentification took the form of mistaking an unfamiliar person for a familiar one (thinking the person walking towards you is your granny then realising she is a stranger). Usually there is a degree of visual similarity between the two people. The explanation here would be that the similarity is sufficient to momentarily activate the stored representation of the familiar face, though a second and better look reveals the discrepancies and hence makes the perceiver aware that an error has been made.

Young et al. (1985) collected 233 reports of a third type of error. This involved seeing a person, knowing they are familiar (i.e., that you have seen them somewhere before), but being quite unable to think who they are, where you know them from, or what their name is. Typically this happened with slight acquaintances (rather than close friends or relatives) encountered out of their usual context; for example, seeing a clerk from your bank out shopping in the street.

The fourth and final type of error is the inability to remember someone's name (190 incidents). In over 90 per cent of these instances the diarists reported being fully aware of who the person was in the sense of what their occupation was (99 per cent) and where they were usually seen (92 per cent), but the name remained elusive. There seems to be something different, and something difficult, about names.

Young et al. (1985) interpret the fact that you may be able to recall all you know about someone except their name as suggesting that names may somehow be stored apart from the other information you possess about familiar people. They argue that satisfactory face recognition requires the involvement of at least three separate mental systems. The first is the *face recognition system* in which the stored representations of familiar faces are held. The second is a *semantic system* in which is located all the general knowledge you possess about people you know. Third and last is a system from which the spoken forms of words, including names, are retrieved. The term "lexicon" is commonly used to refer to an internal word-store of this sort, and we shall dub this system the *speech output lexicon* (see Chapter 7) for a further examination of this mental component).

There are various ways that these three systems could be arranged in the mind. Figure 2.11 shows the arrangement that is suggested by the pattern of errors discussed previously, and also by the sorts of logically possible recognition errors that seem *not* to occur. It is an arrangement in which the three systems exist in a linear sequence, and in which access to the information held in each system is triggered by activity in the preceding one.

Failure can occur at any point in the sequence. If a familiar face fails to activate its representation in the face recognition system, then you fail to recognise someone you know. If a face incorrectly activates a representation because of resemblance between two people, then you misidentify one person as another. If a facial representation is correctly accessed, but the appropriate semantic knowledge is not retrieved, then the face "rings a bell"; that is, it feels familiar without any more detailed information about the person becoming available to you. Finally, if both the face recognition system and the semantic system perform their designated functions properly, but the speech output lexicon refuses to yield up the name that goes with the face, then you recognise the person but cannot recall their name.

We mentioned that the non-occurrence of certain logically possible types of error can be an important constraint on a theory. To take one example, there is no reason in principle why you should not see a face and think "That face looks familiar, and I know his name is Joe Bloggs, but I can't think what he does or where I know him from." This failure (absence of semantic information in the presence of familiarity and name) seems, however, never to occur in normal conditions. In terms of Fig. 2.11 this is because semantic information is needed in order to retrieve the name, and the name cannot be retrieved without it.

Face
recognition
system

↓

Semantic
system

↓

Speech
output
lexicon

↓

Speech

FIG. 2.11 A possible
arrangement of three functional
cognitive sub-systems involved in
the recognition and naming of
familiar faces.

THE ROLE OF CONTEXT IN OBJECT RECOGNITION

In Chapter 1 we argued that the context in which a word is encountered may affect its ease of recognition. Object recognition is clearly determined in large measure by the visual description of an object, but objects are also normally perceived in contexts. Does the context in which an object appears affect the speed or accuracy with which it can be recognised for what it is?

Subjects in Palmer's (1975) experiment were asked to identify briefly presented line drawings of objects. On some trials they were first given a picture of a scene (e.g., a kitchen scene) to inspect. The briefly presented object drawing which followed could then be either appropriate to the preceding scene (e.g., a loaf of bread) or inappropriate (e.g., a drum). Accuracy of object identification was highest when the object picture followed an appropriate scene, and lowest when it followed an inappropriate one. With no preceding scene, accuracy was intermediate. We may say, then, that the context provided by an appropriate scene *facilitates* the subsequent recognition of a briefly seen object whereas that provided by an inappropriate scene *inhibits* subsequent recognition.

The equivalent experiment with faces (e.g., presenting President Reagan's face against a background of the White House or the Taj Mahal) has not, to our knowledge, been conducted. Experimenters have, however, asked whether one person's face is more easily recognised if it is seen immediately after the face of a second person with whom the first is associated than if it is seen after the face of an unassociated person. "Association" here means pairs of people who share a common occupation and/or tend to be seen together (e.g., Starsky and Hutch, Ronald and Nancy Reagan, Prince Charles and Princess Diana).

Bruce and Valentine (1986) presented a mixed sequence of famous and unknown faces to subjects. Their task on being shown each face was to press one button as quickly as possible if the face was familiar (a famous face) and press another button as quickly as possible if the face was unfamiliar (an unknown face). Bruce and Valentine showed that where two famous faces occurred together in the sequence, the time taken to respond to the second face by pressing the "familiar" button was less if the first face was associated (e.g., Starsky preceded by Hutch) than if the first face was unrelated (e.g., Starsky preceded by Princess Diana). The mean reaction times were 731 msec in the first condition, compared with 857 msec in the second. By extrapolation, the time needed to recognise your granny should be less if you have just seen your grandfather than if granny is encountered unexpectedly.

It would appear, then, that the recognition of an object can be facilitated by the context in which it is seen—either the general background context as in Palmer's (1975) object-recognition experiment, or the other objects recently recognised as in Bruce and Valentine's (1986) face-priming experiment. But *how* can context influence recognition? We have already argued that recognition occurs when an analysed pattern accesses and activates a stored representation. One possibility proposed by Seymour (1973) and Warren and Morton (1982) for objects, and by Hay and Young (1982) and Bruce (1983) for faces, is that context works by contributing some activation to the representations for patterns that the context suggests are likely to be perceived. Representations that are already partially activated from within by the context will then require less input from the stimulus pattern to be fully activated and to trigger recognition.

Inspecting a kitchen scene will, on this account, cause partial activation of the stored representations of the appearance of objects likely to be encountered in a kitchen (loaves of bread, forks, casseroles, cookers, etc.). Each of these visual patterns will be recognised more easily as a result of this priming than if it suddenly intruded into, say, a jungle scene. Similarly, if Nancy Reagan's face appears on the television you will recognise her more easily if you have recently recognised Ronald.

Why Use Context, and When?

The classic demonstration of contextual influences on recognition comes from work on "ambiguous figures" such as the one shown in Fig. 2.12. This can be seen as either a rat or a man. Bugelsky and Alampay (1962) showed that subjects who saw the figure after recognising a drawing of a çat tended to perceive it as a rat, whereas subjects who had just recognised a drawing of a woman tended to perceive it as a man.

It can be argued, though, that ambiguous figures are unnatural and unlike anything normally encountered. Normal rats and men differ in size, colour, shape, texture, and so on, and you would never experience any difficulty deciding which you were looking at. The same objection could be levelled against the use of line drawings of objects in Palmer's (1975) experiment, or flat, black-and-white photographs of faces in the experiments of Bruce and Valentine (1986). Is context only used to aid in

FIG. 2.12 Bugelsky and Alampay's (1962) ambiguous rat–man figure.

the recognition of such impoverished stimuli? Is the recognition of normal, solid, coloured objects subject to any contextual facilitation?

Work on word recognition in reading has repeatedly shown that as stimulus quality becomes poorer, so readers make more use of context to assist ongoing word recognition (see Chapter 1). Bruce and Valentine (1986) found that priming played a greater part in face recognition when the faces were blurred than when they were clear, and Sperber, McCauley, Ragain, and Weil (1979) found the same result for object (line drawing) recognition.

So the influence of context does seem to diminish as viewing conditions improve. The question then becomes, "Are natural viewing conditions always good?" We would suggest not. Consider an ancestor of ours out hunting for food. The quarry might itself be dangerous—a sabre-toothed tiger, say, or a mammoth—so it may be vitally important to recognise the prey for what it is as quickly as possible. Viewing conditions will *not* always be ideal: The animal may be some distance away, partly obscured by vegetation; the hunt may be progressing in a blizzard or twilight gloom. A glimpsed form *may* be ambiguous—is it a mammoth or just a large rock? Under such conditions the ability to prime representations and so reduce the amount of stimulus input required to effect recognition could literally make the difference between life and death and the occasional false recognition of a rock as a mammoth would be of little importance.

Natural selection may have operated in the past to favour organisms whose visual systems can be biased from within to assist pattern recognition under difficult viewing conditions. In our modern cossetted world with its artificial lighting where we hunt only in supermarkets, such contextual facilitation may be little needed. We come to think of natural viewing conditions as optimal viewing conditions, whereas in many natural cases they are far from optimal. To the modern recogniser, contextual facilitation may be of only occasional value, as when driving in a blizzard or trying to spot granny in the fog, but when our pattern recognition systems were originally evolving it may have been crucial.

WORDS AND THINGS

In this chapter we have discussed the processes involved in recognising objects, and took recognising a familiar face as a commonplace example. In Chapter 1 we explored the processes involved in recognising written words. How similar are these two forms of recognition? Do they share any cognitive operations in common? We consider these and related questions briefly in this section.

First think about looking at the face of an unfamiliar person, then looking at an unfamiliar word. Because the face is new to you there will be no recognition as such, but that does not mean you can do nothing with the face. There are many judgements you can make about an unfamiliar face—you can form an opinion about the person's sex, their approximate age, whether they look happy, sad, worried, and so on. You may be wrong in some of your judgements, but that does not prevent you from making them.

In these respects unfamiliar words seem different. Words don't look old or young, happy or sad. On the other hand, whereas there is no way of deriving an unfamiliar person's name from their face, you can attempt to name (pronouce) an unfamiliar word with some hope of success.

There thus seems little to be gained from comparing the processing of unfamiliar words and faces. The situation is more promising, however, when we switch our attention to familiar words and familiar faces. We have argued that in order to recognise a face you know or a word you know, the face or word must access and activate a stored representation that was established when the pattern was learned. Thus the word *politician* is only recognised when the letter string on the page activates the appropriate word recognition unit, and Ronald Reagan's face is only recognised when the stimulus pattern in the photograph activates the appropriate internal representation in the face recognition system.

The two processes look formally similar, but can we extend the comparison further than that? For example, do face and word representations intermingle in one larger visual pattern recognition system? The answer to this question appears to be, probably not. In Chapter 1 we discussed patients with "surface dyslexia" whose brain injury leaves them unable to recognise many written words as familiar letter strings, though they can still sound them out using low-level spelling–sound correspondences and can attempt to recognise the word from the assembled sound form. The brain injury these patients have sustained appears to have impaired the set of visual word recognition units that have been amassed in the process of learning to read yet there is no necessary corresponding impairment of face recognition (Patterson, Marshall, & Coltheart, 1985). Conversely, patients suffering from "prospopagnosia" may lose the capacity to recognise familiar faces without any corresponding impairment of word recognition (Hécaen, 1981). Such a dissociation between face and word recognition suggests that although the systems responsible for the two modes of recognition may operate along similar lines, they are nevertheless distinct systems, not two aspects of the functioning of one broader system. Similarly, the recognition of objects can be impaired independently of impairment to face or word recognition, suggesting the involvement of a third recognition system for objects (Ellis & Young, in press).

Even if the processes that mediate the recognition of, say, a telephone are different from those which recognise the written word *telephone*, it would be very odd if the *semantic* knowledge accessed from the two inputs—what telephones are, how you get them to work for you, etc.—were different in the two cases. Semantic knowledge influences recognition processes through the phenomenon of "semantic priming," a type of context effect. Recognising a word like *knife* is made faster and more accurate if you have just recognised a related word like *fork* or *spoon* (Meyer & Schvaneveldt, 1971). The same holds for object (or picture) recognition: A picture of a knife will be recognised more quickly and more accurately if you have just seen a picture of a fork or a spoon (Guenther, Klatsky, & Putnam, 1980). Importantly, semantic priming also occurs between words and objects: Recognising the word *knife* is primed by preceding it with a picture of a fork, and vice versa (Guenther et al., 1980).

This implies that objects and words contact the same body of stored knowledge, which then feeds activation back to all recognition systems, preparing them for items that are likely to be perceived in the near future (for semantic priming must surely be a mode of perceptual anticipation or preparation).

We have argued that the names of objects (including faces) are accessed via and after the activation of their semantic representations (what or who they are). Potter and Faulconer (1975) found that subjects can make semantic decisions about objects (e.g., "Is it living or nonliving?") faster than they can name them. This is clearly compatible with the proposed sequence of activation of semantic and name information. Potter and Faulconer found the reverse pattern for words, however: Semantic decisions on words were slower than naming responses. The conclusion that word meanings are therefore accessed via their sound-forms cannot hold for familiar words of the sort used in this study, for reasons discussed in Chapter 1. Warren and Morton (1982) argued that the Potter and Faulconer pattern of results could be explained if objects access their semantic representations first and their names second, whereas words access the two simultaneously but with the route to word pronunciations (names) being faster than the route to meanings (semantic representations). Young, McWeeny, Ellis, and Hay (1986) found a comparable result for naming and classifying the faces and written names of famous personalities: Subjects could classify a face as belonging to a politician faster than they could name it, but could pronounce a politician's written name faster than they could classify it.

These experiments provide the evidence alluded to earlier that written words can access their pronunciations directly following recognition as well as accessing them via semantic representations. Objects and faces, on the other hand, may only be able to access their spoken names via semantic representations.

A Combined Model

The simple model of the recognition of familiar faces presented in Fig. 2.11 contained three components: the face recognition system, semantic system, and speech output lexicon. We have just argued that familiar objects and familiar words have their own separate recognition systems, but that they

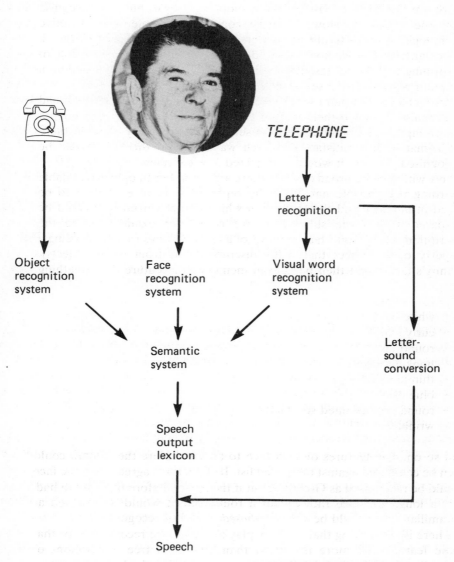

FIG. 2.13   A simple functional model combining face, object and word recognition.

converge upon the same knowledge store (the semantic system). There is similarly no reason to argue that object names and the pronunciations of familiar words are retrieved from anywhere other than the same speech output lexicon from which people's names are retrieved.

We thus have three recognition systems converging upon one semantic system and one speech output lexicon. There are, however, additional processes associated with visual word recognition. First, word recognition is probably preceded by a stage of letter recognition. Second, there appears to exist a separate process of letter–sound conversion available for assembling pronunciations for unfamiliar written words. Finally, there is arguably a direct connection from the visual word recognition system to the speech output lexicon which allows the pronunciations of familiar words to be retrieved in parallel with their meanings rather than sequentially (as seems to be the case for faces and objects).

This sort of theorising in terms of separate cognitive systems and their interconnections lends itself to diagrammatic expression. Figure 2.13 presents the model just outlined. Readers may care to test their understanding of the model by predicting the effects of loss through brain injury of particular components or particular connections, either singly or in combination. What symptom-patterns are permitted by the model? What are prohibited (and hence would falsify the model if discovered)? Alternatively, what experiments might you carry out on normal subjects to test the predictions of the model?

SUMMARY

Word recognition in reading, the topic of Chapter 1, involves pattern recognition of a sort, but face and object recognition are arguably more natural forms of pattern recognition. Recognising a familiar face must involve comparing a perceived stimulus pattern against a set of stored representations. Once again, simple template and feature models have problems coping with the variability of natural patterns (e.g., familiar faces in different orientations, with changing hairstyles, etc.). Where faces are concerned, the visual system appears to try to counteract the variability of external features like hairstyle by an increasing reliance on internal features as the basis of the recognition of familiar faces.

Faces and objects are normally encountered against a complex, changing visual background. Psychologists have made some progress in identifying the cues that enable elements of a visual array to be grouped together as parts of the same object. Such grouping is a necessary preliminary to recognition. The cues underlying distance and movement perception have also been analysed in some detail.

It is commonly assumed that word, face, and object recognition converge on a common "semantic" stage at which is held knowledge of the meanings and uses of words, the uses and properties of objects, and the characteristics and personalities of people. A model was presented to account for the interconnection between the cognitive processors responsible for different types of recognition, for comprehension, and for naming, using as sources of relevant evidence the recognition problems experienced by both normal and brain-injured individuals. The possible role of context in face and object recognition is discussed and compared with its role in word recognition (cf. Chapter 1).

This chapter and the preceding one have concentrated on the more peripheral aspects of recognition. We turn in Chapter 3 to an examination of that central stage where word, face, and object concepts intermingle and to the study of the form such conceptual representations might take.

A deeper, more thorough account of visual perception which covers both information-processing and "Gibsonian" perspectives is provided in V. Bruce and P. Green (1985), *Visual Perception: Physiology, Psychology and Ecology*. Aspects of the more particular topic of face recognition can be found in G. Davies, H. Ellis, and J. Shepherd (1981), *Perceiving and Remembering Faces* and H. Ellis, M. Jeeves, F. Newcombe and A. Young (1986), *Aspects of Face Processing*.

3 Telling Sheep from Goats: Categorising Objects

Has the origin of the phrase 'telling the sheep from the goats" ever puzzled you? It has a biblical flavour and it means something like "telling the believers from the unbelievers," but why sheep and goats? After all, believers and unbelievers may not look very different but sheep and goats definitely do. A sheep is covered with curly fleece, has a weak-looking face, skinny ankles, is rather plump, and may or may not have horns. A goat is thin, with straight hair, a strong face, long legs, and may or may not have horns. Both kinds of animals have legs, heads, eyes, and so on, but they share these with a great many other animals so they are not very useful in discriminating one animal from another. The description given above relates to sheep and goats in England and in other parts of northern Europe. Yet in countries around the Mediterranean, animals grazing on a hillside cannot be classified so easily by a northern visitor. They have not got a lot of fleece but they are not as thin as goats. Their faces don't fit either the strong goat or the weak sheep. There are flocks of them, which seems more sheep-like than goat-like. Altogether, it is not very easy to tell sheep from goats.

The tourist's classification of sheep and goats breaks down in the Mediterranean, but for the local farmer the distinction will be an important one. It may not be an easy distinction to make at a distance, so it becomes important to bring the flock together in order to distinguish sheep from goats. The example is important because it shows us that we take our systems of categorisation very much for granted; and that they depend on the situations in which they were learned, and the purposes which make them necessary. After all, if no one made a distinction between sheep's milk and goat's milk, or sheep's meat and goat's meat, there might not be much need to tell sheep from goats. It is also important because it directs us to ways in which we might extend our classification in order to apply it to things we have not met before. Telling sheep from goats is an example of categorisation. However, the chapter is more generally about how we organise our knowledge.

Putting things into groups is one of the most basic ways to organise what you know. If you cannot categorise you have to meet each object or event in the environment as a new thing, so you would have to keep on learning how to deal with it. If you learn that a berry of one particular shade of red makes you sick when you eat it, you could subsequently avoid all berries, but that means that you can generalise to small round things regardless of their colour. To avoid all red berries means that you have to lump together the many hundreds of shades of red which the human eye is capable of discriminating. So either you create a category of small round things, or you create a category of small, round red things, or you go further and add other features of the bush, the situation, and so on. Our experience of relevant instances is necessarily limited and so, usually, is our ability to analyse all the factors involved. When we categorise we are making up our minds about the meaning of things or how to behave towards them. In general, "categorising serves to cut down the diversity of objects and events that must be dealt with uniquely by an organism of limited capacities [Bruner, Goodnow, & Austin, 1956, p. 235]."

The range of things that we can classify is not limited to physical objects with some similar perceptual characteristics. When we try to identify a famous face we often attach a label like "politician" or "TV actor" to it before we can retrieve the name; these are groups of people whose *behaviour* provides the basis for the classification, although their appearance may help a little. We can also make more abstract classifications like "believer" and "unbeliever," which make appearance a poor indicator, and even cast doubts on behaviour as the basis for identification. We classify and categorise everything, from animals to emotions and from the concrete to the abstract. Indeed, we have to think of our knowledge of the world and our abilities to form categories as being tightly bound together.

The process of abstraction is, however, the key activity underlying a concept. "Abstraction" can imply many things. The isolation of a subset of features most relevant to the concept is one aspect of abstraction, as in our attempts to say in what ways sheep and goats are alike and different. The tolerance of a certain amount of variability in the way features are expressed is another aspect. In Chapters 1 and 2 we saw examples of our ability to tolerate variability in stimuli in the recognition of objects and words. In general, the process of abstraction identifies something beyond the immediate and the particular, allowing us to match up things and to retrieve things previously experienced that may bear upon the current experience. So the study of concepts is but one way of probing into the structure of our knowledge. In this chapter we look at categorising and concepts as one way of studying the question "How are all the things we know organised in our heads?" Later chapters will develop further answers to the same question.

CONCEPT IDENTIFICATION

Categorising results in concepts, that is, in abstract knowledge that is not linked to individual instances. To know about "chair" or "fear" does not necessarily mean remembering a particular chair or a particular fear. Try thinking of "chair." It means something to sit on, a piece of furniture, it has four legs (but some chairs do not), it has a back, it might have arms, it might be hard or soft, low or high. It is not a simple idea and defining a chair is much more difficult than pointing to one or finding one to sit on. How do we get such a concept?

To investigate the origins of concept formation the Russian psychologist Vygotsky (1934/1962) used a set of 22 blocks that differed in colour, shape, height, and area. They were divided into four groups and given nonsense names so that *lag* meant tall and large, *bik* meant tall and small, *mur* meant short and large, and *cev* meant short and small. The shapes and colours were irrelevant to these groupings; only the height and area were important. These Vygotsky blocks were presented to both children and adults in a similar way. The blocks were mixed up and the subject was shown one of them and given its name, then asked to pick out all the others which might be of the same group. After this had been done, the experimenter picked up one of the wrongly selected blocks, gave its name, and then asked the subject to continue finding the first group. As this process continued adult subjects came to create concepts which related characteristics of the blocks and the nonsense words.

Young children do this task quite differently from adults. At first children put the blocks into unorganised heaps, or they simply select the items which are nearest to the one they are shown. Then they move to what Vygotsky called "complexes"; they put all the red things together, or they chain items so that when given a big red circle they next choose several red items but a red triangle is followed by a blue triangle, some more blue items follow, then a particular blue item precipitates another switch. The "complex" is not a concept because it does not rise above the elements but is tied to them.

Rising above the elements requires subjects to identify blocks having the same name, attending to values of just two particular features of the blocks in combination and ignoring other features. This is a reasonable first approximation to what concept formation means. Vygotsky's general aim was to gain an understanding of the relation between thought and language, and early American studies of concept formation had a different theoretical perspective, but, as we shall see, their laboratory tasks implied definitions of a concept which were similar in several respects to Vygotsky's.

Associationism

The early American research on concept formation grew out of association models for stimulus–response learning. These models suggested that each time an example of a category was encountered, the link between the concept and all of the features of the example of the concept were strengthened. So, for example, a child learning the concept of *flower* could be told that a daisy is a flower. This leads the child to link the features of daisies (such as many petals, size, different-coloured centre) with the term "flower." Subsequent examples of flowers, such as a rose and a tulip, would strengthen certain features, like petals and stalks, but not others, like specific colour and size. Eventually, therefore, the child will selectively learn the importance of each of the features involved in the concept of a flower.

The first experimental study of this process was carried out by Hull (1920). He required his subjects to learn to say distinct sounds, such as "li"

Word	Concept	Pack I	Pack II	Pack III	Pack IV	Pack V	Pack VI
oo							
yer							
li							
ta							
deg							
ling							

FIG. 3.1   Stimuli used by Hull (1920). Six of the Chinese radicals that Hull used are shown here. First, the subject was shown a Chinese character and guessed its "name" (e.g., oo); then the experimenter gave the correct name and so on. Characters with the same radicals always were given the same name so that after going through several packs of characters, the subjects improved their performances and were eventually able to correctly name characters they had never seen before.

and "ta", to each of a set of 12 Chinese characters (see Fig. 3.1). He then switched to a second set of Chinese characters and taught the same sounds to them. Within all the Chinese characters were features, known as radicals, common to both of the characters that were taught to go with the same sound. Hull continued by teaching new characters, again containing the same radicals. He found that the subjects became quicker at learning which sound went with which character, and they could often guess the correct response prior to it being taught. Hull interpreted this as the steady strengthening of the associations between the names (sounds) and the features (radicals) common to each new Chinese character, so subjects began to detect the features which were determining whether a character was a "li" or a "ta."

One important observation made by Hull was that many of his subjects could respond consistently correctly but were not able to describe what it was about the Chinese character that made them classify it in that way. Hull introduced the term "functional concept" for the situation in which a person can respond correctly but is unable to say why. One consequence of this was that in much of the subsequent research the concepts that the subjects had and the methods by which they went about developing their concepts were inferred from the subjects' responses. Subjects were rarely asked what they were doing.

Hypothesis Testing

The view that concepts are learned slowly through the selective association of features without people ever really knowing what is going on, was opposed by psychologists who realised that people often made an effort to look for patterns in their experiences. The difference appears when subjects are asked to carry out tasks in which the features can readily be detected and can be combined in various ways to make up hypotheses about concepts. So, if shown a sheep/goat animal you might say that it has no curly fleece so it cannot be a sheep. When told that there are some sheep without curly fleeces you change to looking for something else which determines whether an animal is a sheep or not.

The most widely quoted research on hypothesis testing in concept formation was carried out by Bruner, Goodnow, and Austin (1956). They used 81 cards, on each of which there was a pattern made up of four dimensions (shape, colour, number of borders, number of objects), and each dimension could have one of three values. The patterns were therefore made up of combinations of the following: object shapes (circle, square, cross); colour of objects (red, green, black); number of objects (1, 2, 3); and number of borders (1, 2, 3). The experimenters defined a particular concept and the subject had to guess what it was. The three main

CA-C

types of concepts studied were: (1) concepts with single values on one dimension (e.g., *red*); (2) conjunctive concepts requiring particular values on two dimensions (e.g., *circles and two borders*); (3) disjunctive concepts, where the concept had one value on one dimension *or* one value on another dimension, (e.g., *blue* or *cross*).

In one procedure, subjects were shown the cards one by one and they guessed whether or not the pattern was an instance of the concept. The experimenter told them each time if their guess was correct. Bruner et al. identified two distinct strategies at this task. In what they called the *wholist* strategy, the subject tried to remember all the attributes of instances identified as members of the category. In the *partist* strategy, subjects focused on one hypothesis at a time (e.g., that the concept was *red*), retained it if successful in predicting the next card and formed a new hypothesis if it failed. Some subjects get thoroughly exasperated with the task, as you might expect.

A second procedure was to show all the cards at once and let the subjects ask questions about them. This is similar in some ways to the situation that Vygotsky used, except that no name was provided for the concept. In this form of the task more strategies for solving the task were revealed. In *successive scanning*, subjects began with one hypothesis and changed if it failed. *Conservative focusing* was the technique of picking a positive instance and selecting subsequent cards so that one attribute changed at a time. In *focus gambling*, several attributes were changed each time. In principle, subjects might attempt to use *simultaneous scanning* in which they begin with all possible hypotheses and proceed to eliminate them, but as you can imagine this is difficult to sustain. Indeed, all the strategies make a considerable demand on memory if previously discarded hypotheses are not to be tried again and the new hypotheses are to be based upon instances that are plausible in the light of earlier cards. It was found that subjects were more efficient when they used the wholist and focusing strategies.

In Hull's task, the Chinese characters were highly unfamiliar to the subjects and the features relevant to the concept must initially have appeared to be well-integrated with other features. Recall also that most of Hull's subjects could not give an account of how they achieved success. In the study by Bruner et al., the stimuli consisted of familiar, nameable and spatially separated features and the features were elements of well-defined sets like shapes and colours. More immediately than in Hull's task, the subjects were faced with the question of what makes the stimulus array a positive instance. The "strategies" and "hypotheses" referred to by Bruner et al. are likely to be ones of which the subjects may have been partially aware. The existence of hypothesis-testing strategies was, however, inferred from the series of choices that the subjects made, not by asking them how they did the task. Unfortunately, there are limitations to what can be inferred about the strategies of subjects from their choices. In these early experiments the stimuli had so many attributes and so many possible rules relating them that it was very difficult to show that people did use strategies and hypotheses.

A much simpler task was used by Levine (1966) in order to show that hypothesis testing was occurring, and that there was some memory of old hypotheses which had been thrown out. Levine showed his subjects pairs of letters on a card. The letters differed in four ways; the letter itself (T or X), its colour (black or white), its size (large or small), and its position (left or right). The experimenter picked one of these eight possible characteristics to be the concept on a particular trial. The subjects were shown four cards, one after the other. For each card they indicated which of the two items—the one on the left or the one on the right—was the member of the target class and they were told whether they were correct or not. The order of one possible set of four cards is shown in Fig. 3.2. As you can see from the figure, the first card allows the subject to cut the number of hypotheses from 8 to 4. If "right–large–black–T" includes the relevant characteristic, then "left," "small," "white," and "X" are no longer possible hypotheses. After a second trial the number of possible hypotheses is cut to two and after the third trial it drops to one. If subjects could remember all the things they had rejected on each trial then they should be able to make the correct judgement by the fourth trial. Levine then allowed subjects to continue with four more trials in which they were shown the same sort of cards and asked to pick the items which had the relevant attribute, but this time they were not told whether they were correct or not. If subjects do have only one hypothesis left then they should go for one attribute, say

Trial	Stimulus	Correct	Possible hypotheses
1	X **T**	right	right, large, black, T
2	T **X**	right	right, black
3	**T** X	left	black
4	**X** T	left	black

FIG. 3.2 A sequence of trials using Levine's task, showing how the subject could in principle select the correct hypothesis after three trials with feedback of the correct response. (Taken from Levine, M. (1966). Hypothesis behaviour by humans during discrimination learning. *Journal of Experimental Psychology*, *71*, 331–338. Copyright 1966 by the American Psychological Association and reprinted by permission.)

black, regardless of the shape, size, or position of the letter. If they have more than one hypothesis then they will not be consistent during these four trials without feedback. Levine found that subjects had not managed to develop a commitment to only one hypothesis at this stage, but that they tended to have about three. As there were eight possible hypotheses at the beginning this is reasonably good performance.

Levine's subjects must have been remembering something about the hypotheses they had rejected, because they tested fewer than the maximum number of hypotheses, even though they had not got the correct one. So suggestions that there was no memory of earlier stages, based on work by Restle (1962) and Bower and Trabasso (1964), could not be correct. It is however, possible that hypotheses are forgotten gradually over several trials rather than on any one trial, particularly as the hypotheses are quite difficult to distinguish from one another. Hypotheses may be forgotten in some situations but not in others.

Some Limitations of the Laboratory Studies

Levine's (1966) experiment is commonly and correctly taken to demonstrate that people do indeed form hypotheses which they test and reject. If you look at the task again you will probably find it hard to think of anything else that subjects could do. They are being asked to use "black" as a relevant attribute when only one attribute *is* relevant, but they are not being asked to learn what "black" means, or to use the term correctly. In the experimental tasks subjects are typically asked to guess what the experimenter is thinking. However, in real life as in our "flower" example, concepts normally require both the selection of certain features, such as stalks and petals, in spite of their variability in shape, size, and colour, and the correct use of a name in application to somewhat novel instances, to new variations of these features. Hypothesis testing does occur in experiments and may occur in concept formation, but this is unlikely to tell the whole story.

When people form hypotheses in concept identification experiments they do not choose the rules at random, but rather they bring in their previous knowledge of the ways in which things are likely to go together. Heidbreder (1946) illustrated this by showing pictures to which names had to be learned. On each trial the picture was changed but it retained one characteristic, e.g., being a face, being circular, having a particular number of items. Heidbreder showed that people were quickest at learning the concrete classes like "faces" and "buildings," were poorer at learning more abstract concepts (e.g., shapes) and worst of all when "number of things" was the feature to be abstracted. It is not easy to identify that what pictures have in common is "threeness," but it is easy to say that they are all pictures of faces, which is a much more natural way to judge pictures.

Nor do subjects choose attributes at random. Among the flower designs used by Trabasso (1963), features like the colours, shapes, leaves, and stem branchings could all be distinguished but they were not all treated equally. He found that on average only about 4 errors occurred when subjects learned a classification based on colour, while 19.5 errors were made when the rule was based on the angle of the leaves. This does not mean that colour is always the most relevant attribute in deciding whether something is in a class or not. The attribute "white" is an important characteristic of milk, chalk, and snow, but it occurs less readily to people as a characterstic of sugar or baseballs (Underwood & Richardson, 1956). For some categories colour is a dominant attribute and so acts as a major cue in a sorting task; but not so for other categories.

The line of research outlined in the preceding paragraphs concentrates on the features of objects that go together. The view implied by the studies is that all the instances of a concept share common properties and that these properties are necessary for something to belong to the category as well as sufficient to guarantee category membership. However, there is a difficulty with the idea that features are necessary and sufficient for defining a concept. If this were the case, then looking up a word in a dictionary would be a very straightforward way of understanding its meaning. The dictionary would list all the features of a sheep that make it a sheep. The *Concise Oxford Dictionary* defines sheep as "kinds of wild or domesticated, timid, gregarious, woolly, occasionally horned, ruminant mammal." Unfortunately "gregarious" means "living in flocks," and "flock" is "a number of domestic animals, usually sheep, goats or geese." So, a sheep is a mammal which lives in groups like sheep do. Not surprisingly, we learn few words by looking them up in a dictionary; rather we meet them in a context that enables us to give some sense to the dictionary definition.

There are further problems with the view that features are necessary and sufficient for making decisions about category membership. One is that decades of effort by philosophers and linguists have failed to discover the defining properties that such a view would imply. The philosopher Wittgenstein (1958) identified the problem as follows:

> Consider for example the proceedings we call "games." I mean board-games, card-games, ball-games, Olympic games, and so on. What is common to them all?—Don't say "There must be something common or they would not be called games," but *look* and *see* whether there is anything common to *all*.—For if you look at them you will not see something that is common to

all, but similarities, relationships, and a whole series of them at that . . . I can think of no better expression to characterise these similarities than "family resemblances" [pp. 31–32].

This idea has been taken up by many researchers. When the features of members of a category are spelled out, they do not wholly overlap, and they are rarely necessary or sufficient to determine category membership (Hampton, 1979).

Real-world objects do not fit into just one category. A sheep is a ruminant, a mammal, and an animal. In the category "animal" it is joined by many creatures that share few attributes, although it is more similar to other ruminants. The tomato is not even easily classified as a fruit or a vegetable, because it is often used as a vegetable, but when the definition is made in terms of the relationship of the tomato to the tomato plant, then it is a fruit. This problem leads us into another one, which is that some members of a category are "better" examples than others. A sheep is a representative animal, a snake is not. So, while hypothesis testing and association of features are useful in some situations, they are not readily applied to how we develop real concepts. We need to explain how we come to use shared meanings yet can not explain how we reliably label objects in terms of rules about features.

NATURAL CONCEPTS

Natural categories like "chair" do not contain perceptually identical instances. Chairs vary considerably in their appearance and, somewhat relatedly, in their functions. Studies by Eleanor Rosch and her co-workers in the 1970s were especially responsible for shifting focus away from artificial stimuli and the view that categories could readily be defined in terms of common elements. Rosch (1978) has emphasised that natural or cultural categorisation is not arbitrary but is structured according to two principles. The first concerns the *perceived structure* in the world. If the objects in the world were made up, like many laboratory stimuli, from arbitrary combinations of attributes such as colour, size, and shape, then we might end up with no basis for classification. We do not, for example, have an obvious name for "red, small, square objects," nor for many other combinations of attributes. The wide variety of things called "chairs" has a strong commonality of *function*. Some pairs of chairs share many perceptual features, but others very few, rather in the way that pairs of members of the same family often vary in the kind and degree of resemblances that they show. It is naturally occurring assemblies of attributes and their relationship to function which is important and which makes it impossible to view categorisation as like the logical task of taking all attributes, putting them in combinations, and giving names to the combinations. Feathers, wings, and beaks are frequently observed to go together, but not petals, wheels, and fur. We experience the world as structured by the frequency with which some perceptual and functional attributes occur together.

The second principle emphasised by Rosch is that of *cognitive economy* in categorisation. What of all the things in the world do we give a name to and what names do we most frequently use? We could develop a classification system with as many layers of categories as we choose, but the principle of cognitive economy suggests that in cultural practices a compromise is achieved between specificity and generality of reference and between richness and sparsity of implication. We require cues to similarities for some purposes and we need cues to make some distinctions. Not all levels of categorisation are equally useful. When the principles of cognitive economy and the perceived structure of the world are put together, they suggest that there is one level of categorisation which is the mose useful. Rosch called this the *basic level*.

At the basic level of categorisation are the concepts which are most commonly used and among the first to be learned. Rosch, Mervis, Gray, Johnson, and Boyes-Braem (1976) asked subjects to list all the attributes they could think of for items that seemed to be at this basic level, such as chair, car, and pants. They also argued for a higher or *superordinate level*, which is less specific than the basic level, and for a *subordinate level*, which is more specific. So they also asked subjects to list attributes of furniture, vehicles, and clothes (superordinate) and kitchen chair, sports car, and Levi's (subordinate). Each person wrote attributes for only one of the levels. If you try the task yourself you will probably find that there are not many attributes of "furniture," that "chair" has a large number, and that "kitchen chair" has most of the attributes of chair with a few extra ones.

Subjects found it hard to produce attributes for superordinate categories. For "clothing" there were two—you wear it and it keeps you warm. For "pants" (American for the British basic category of "trousers") there were six characteristics or attributes, including being made of cloth and having two legs. The subordinate category of "Levi's" added only one more attribute to those at the basic level—they are blue. Because most of the attributes are produced for the basic level and also show up differences between categories, this is the level that is most useful, reflects the structure of the world, and allows for cognitive economy.

There is more evidence that one level of categorisation is the most useful. When asked to name objects or to classify assemblies of objects, people most often adopt the basic-level terms. When you use items that are classified in the same way at the basic level you make similar movements.

So sitting on different chairs involves actions that are more similar than walking on rugs or taking books out of bookcases, although both rugs and bookcases are furniture. Putting on any pair of trousers involves actions that are similar, and quite different from putting on a jacket or a hat. Finally, items from a basic-level class are often so similar in shape they may sensibly be "averaged"; for example, two cars (basic level, "cars") are more alike in this respect than a car and a bicycle (superordinate level, "vehicles"). Overall, the notion that there is one level of category which make most sense in ordinary life can be argued for with some conviction.

Basic-level categorisation has also been found by Berlin (1978) in studies of the folk-biological classifications of plants and animals in non-Western cultures. He concluded that at one level of categorisation of a diversity of plants or animals, the perceptual and behavioural similarities seem to "cry out" to be labelled; at a lower level of categorisation, the culture requires some further distinctions to be made for certain purposes among things having high similarity. Similarly, Newport and Bellugi (1978) confirmed the psychological salience of Rosch's three category levels in the operation of American Sign Language used by the deaf. The English language itself gives some evidence about the existence of these levels. Subordinate category names like "kitchen chair" and "sports car" are compounds that include the basic-level concept.

It could be argued that basic-level concepts have developed in one of two ways. The common words that we learn early help to organise our experience and become more central than other category names that we learn later. The alternative is that basic perceptual and cognitive organisation of the world is primary and names follow that. Mervis and Crisafi (1982) investigated this using artificial categories. Subjects had to sort items into groups but were not given names for them. The responses tended to use the middle level of the possible categorisations, even though there were no names to support the distinction.

There are, of course, some words whose meanings have not developed exclusively from everyday interaction with the world, and these have definitions that do largely constrain or even determine their meaning. For example, we have the "triangles" and "squares" of geometry, "water" and "copper sulphate" of chemistry, and "velocity" and "inertia" of physics. The meanings of these terms in science are restricted, just like the strongly conventional definitions of some terms used in specialist domains such as ballet, the skilled trades, various professions, and in religions. The main impact of Rosch's work is not to say that a culture can not give rise to terms which are satisfactorily defined in terms of attributes, but that many of our natural categories can not readily be explained in this way.

Prototypes

The work on basic-level categories is a description of what our categories are, not of how we acquire them or of how we actually use them. However, the finding that some category members are more typical than others has pointed to a way in which classification might be carried out. Oranges and apples are good examples of fruit, tomato and olive are not, yet they are all in the same family. Rosch and Mervis (1975) found that members of a class regarded as "typical" shared more features with other members of the class than non-typical members did. Some members of the category "vehicle" share wheels and windscreens with many other members, but a few vehicles, like wheelbarrows and elevators, share only the attributes of carrying things and moving. Indeed, it is arguable whether wheelbarrows and elevators are vehicles at all. They could also be garden implements and parts of buildings. This means that "car" is typical whereas "wheelbarrow" is untypical and gives rise to boundary disputes.

The clearest cases of category membership are referred to as *prototypical* cases (Rosch, 1978). Prototypicality has a number of effects on the way in which people make judgements about whether items belong in a class or not. Adults are faster to respond "true" to statements like "A robin is a bird" than to statements like "A penguin is a bird." Children show even greater reaction-time discrepancies between judgements of good and poor representatives of a category, a fact which supports the earlier observations that children do not learn about fruit from pomegranates and olives.

These observations help to describe the structure of what we know, but they do not as yet tell us how we know it. Could we use some kind of holistic organisation of the most "central" features to give us a way of making judgements about whether items belong to a class or not? Is this what a prototype is? In order to answer this question we have to start to control the stimuli again, even if this produces "unnatural" categories. Look at the faces in Fig. 3.3. The upper five faces represent category 1, the lower five faces represent category 2. If you study those faces can you decide what it is that makes a face fit into category 1 rather than category 2? Could you place new faces into the categories? If you were doing the task, would you match all the features of a new face to those already in the category, or would you try to create a pattern that was the most "central" face possible in the category and then match new faces to it? The second strategy involves the use of a prototype face, one which is not present in the display but which is a good average of all the relevant features.

This was the task that Reed (1972) presented to his subjects. The faces differed on four dimensions, namely, eye separation, height of mouth, height of forehead, and nose length. Subjects classified new faces and were

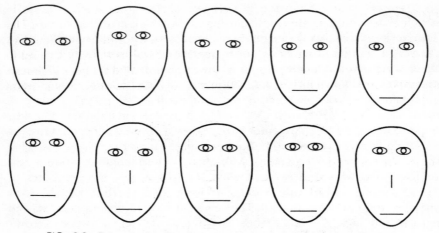

FIG. 3.3 Faces used in Reed's categorisation task. (Taken from Reed, S. K. & Friedman, M. P. (1973). Perceptual vs. conceptual categorisation. *Memory and Cognition*, *1*, 157–163. Copyright 1973 by the Psychonomic Society, Inc., and reprinted by permission.)

asked how they had done it. The majority of the subjects (58 per cent) said that they formed an abstract "image" of what a category 1 face should look like and what a category 2 face should look like and then matched each new face to the abstractions. A good number of subjects (28 per cent) used a feature frequency strategy in which they took each feature in the new face and looked at how many times it matched a feature in the category sets and then chose the category with the highest number of matches. Two other strategies were found, both using the whole face. In the nearest-neighbour strategy, some subjects (10 per cent) compared all the faces with the new face, picked the one which looked most similar and put the new face in the same category. In the average-distance strategy, subjects (4 per cent) tried to compare the new face with each of the 10 given faces and to come up with an overall judgement. These decisions that subjects made about the faces reflected the predominance of a prototype strategy.

Most of the subjects in Reed's experiments claimed to use either features, whole-pattern judgements, or prototypes. They could also have used a mixed strategy, such as using a prototype plus instances of the category. There is evidence that subjects who look at a large number of cases do actually remember some of the particular instances, and not just an abstraction as some theorising about prototypes theory would suggest (Hayes-Roth & Hayes-Roth, 1977). Another possibility is that with a large number of instances several prototypes are developed. The overall category of "games" could be regarded as several sub-categories each with its "typical" game. Neumann (1977) investigated the different ways in which a task could be approached using two kinds of artificial stimuli. The stimuli were faces that varied on three dimensions (overall length, length of nose, and number of wrinkles), or rectangular patterns that also varied in three ways (overall length, length of lower section, and number of lines). Examples are shown in Fig. 3.4. There were five levels of each dimension

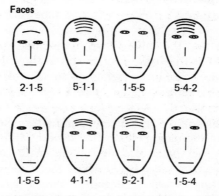

Note: Numbers indicate age, face length and nose length

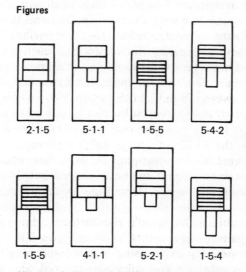

Note: Numbers indicate height of overall rectangle, layers in upper rectangle, and height of bar in lower rectangle

FIG. 3.4 Neumann's faces and rectangular patterns. (Re-drawn from Mayer, R. E. (1983) *Thinking, Problem Solving and Cognition*. New York: W. H. Freeman & Co. Copyright 1983 by W. H. Freeman & Co. and reprinted by permission.)

ranging from 1 (small or few) to 5 (large or many), and subjects were shown stimuli made up of combinations of the three dimensions. They were never shown any stimuli on which the dimensions were rated at 3 (middle sized), but they saw several stimuli with the extreme values 1 and 5, and a few with the values 2 and 4. So, the figure or face could have the three dimensions at 1–5–2 on one trial and 4–1–5 on another.

Two kinds of prediction can be made from Neumann's study. One is that subjects will tend to take an average of each dimension they see on the repeated faces or patterns, so they will build a prototype which is roughly 3–3–3. The other is that the subjects will remember the features which they actually saw, and as they saw more 1s and 5s they will remember the extremes. Subjects were tested by being asked to look at new faces or patterns and to say whether they had ever seen them before. For the faces, they tended to recognise the 3–3–3 version, that is, the prototype or average on each dimension. For the rectangular patterns subjects tended to recognise the extremes, so they said they had seen the 1–1–1 version or the 5–5–5 version when they had not done so. The material being classified had an important effect on the ways in which the objects were classified, with the faces resulting in one prototype whereas the rectangles were divided into two classes on the basis of the most common features.

In general, the laboratory studies of classification have indicated that people can use many ways to classify new items. Both analytic and non-analytic strategies can have advantages for particular types of task. Some studies suggest that analytic knowledge of rules is available (Reber & Allen, 1978), and analytic strategies are cued by very salient attributes (Reber, Kassin, Lewis, & Cantor, 1980). But if the relevant attributes are not obvious then an overall match is likely to be attempted.

Problems with Prototypes

Rosch (1978) was careful to point out that the notion of a prototype does not define the processes of learning about categories, nor those involved in making category judgements; nor does it define the manner of representing prototypes. Prototypes "exist" in the sense that there are a number of phenomena to do with variation in typicality that we hope to account for by using the concept. Clearly, the concept of a "prototype" itself is still in a somewhat exploratory state of definition!

The subjects in Reed's study reported a variety of methods for classifying faces, and Neumann's subjects used different methods for different kinds of stimuli. We can see that "prototype" can be thought of in several different ways. One kind of prototype might be constructed and operate as an average of the examples we have available. This is an especially plausible method when many or most of the important features can be averaged one by one and perhaps the average may generate some kind of abstraction, a kind of template. A second kind of prototype can be thought of as an unevenly dispersed "crowd" of examples in our head, the more commonly experienced ones—and probably, therefore, the ones thought to be more typical—being more frequently represented, more closely packed together in the "crowd," and these more easily come to mind when we use the category. Thus, a subject in Reed's experiment need not average but could report that a new face has more "nearest neighbours" in one category than another. Another way of operating would be to use an abstracted form of prototype for the most typical examples of a category, but to decompose the prototype and examine particular instances from experience when problematic objects arise.

Several views of what a prototype is can be sustained, as can some variants of feature analysis and of template matching, processes referred to in Chapters 1 and 2. Speculatively, it may be that our active representations and hence our processing methods can vary with the questions put to us and the kinds of instances we are asked to deal with. We are quick, for example, to confirm that a robin is a bird; indeed, we will be aware that it is a very typical bird and be satisfied to describe it as close to being a prototypical bird. In many features it is close to average, but it is certainly not close to "average bird-coloured," whatever that might be. However, asked whether a penguin is a bird, we will probably pause to examine features of both a penguin and prototypical cases, unless of course we have been alerted by previous questions to the full range of the category "bird." Overall, we are probably capable of using a variety of methods in assigning things to categories. Specific definitions of "prototype" may be too rigid on present evidence, and the notion of schemas may have a contribution to make. Schemas are discussed more fully in Chapter 9, but the relevant point to note here is that they can ignore dimensions which are not necessary and use those which are (Anderson, 1980).

Concepts can also be learned in many different ways, and some of the learning has to override more natural groupings. We said earlier that a sheep was a ruminant (we can see it chew), and that it was an animal (we can see it move), and also a mammal. But we have to learn that being a mammal (warm-blooded, suckling young, and so on) is a sub-category of animal. Some categorisations based on biological taxonomies override our informal decisions. A whale is more like a fish on most of the dimensions on which it could be measured, yet we can learn to override that similarity. It is even possible to hold two different categories at the same time. For many people, mammal is what they mean by animal. Dogs are animals, so are cows and sheep, but snakes and birds are snakes and birds. Even when we know from our education that "animal" covers sheep, snakes, and birds, we can continue to use the informal meaning for most purposes.

The core definitions that lie at the centre of our concepts may be different from the attributes we use naturally to decide whether an object belongs to one category or another. Acts of close discrimination between categories may call upon processes that do not wholly overlap with those involved when we identify an object in which its primary functions are evident from the context. Concepts have many tasks to perform for us and their response to particular contexts and their relation to other concepts leads us to consider their place in the wider structure of our knowledge.

CONCEPTS IN THE STRUCTURE OF KNOWLEDGE

All the knowledge of meanings that we have can be thought of as making up our semantic memory. We use this memory in many situations, noticeably when we understand what someone is saying to us, or when we read a story. We cannot do much without it, and we can study its operations in many different tasks. Simple activities, like telling sheep from goats or deciding whether pomegranates are fruit, use comparatively small units of knowledge, while comprehending stories uses large frameworks or schemas, yet each can tell us something about the way in which our general knowledge of the world is organised.

If you show people a list of words taken from categories such as flowers, animals, furniture, and months of the year, with the categories jumbled together, and then ask them to recall as many as they can, they will tend to recall them in clumps, category by category (Bousfield, 1953). If the words are presented in the first place according to categories, they are remembered far more easily (Bower, Clark, Lesgold, & Winzenz, 1969). Clearly, prior knowledge about kinds of knowledge makes it easier to learn structured lists, and one way to explain this is to say that our knowledge about the world is stored in memory in an organised way. Information about several different types of flower may be stored in such a way that accessing information about one flower may activate information about other flowers, as though we have a major entry for "flowers" in our heads and related information is held close by. This would mean that concepts and categories could play an important role in the way in which information is stored in memory.

How could information in memory be structured? If we think about many of the natural concepts we have discussed so far, the idea of hierarchies—of classes and sub-classes—is a plausible one. One account of a hierarchical structure was put forward by Collins and Quillian (1969). They suggested that semantic memory was made up of a set of concepts represented by nodes in a network and that all the properties of things are stored at the nodes in the most economic way possible. Consider the

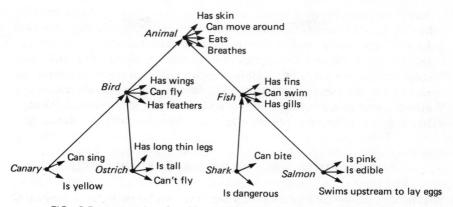

FIG. 3.5 A sample of a hierarchial network as a hypothesis about the organisation of semantic knowledge. Based upon Collins and Quillian (1969).

hierarchy of nodes shown in Fig. 3.5, which shows a familiar relationship among animals, birds, fish, and some exemplars. Features are shown at each node so that, for example, the things that birds have, but most animals don't have (e.g. feathers) are "stored" at the "bird" level. Features shared by all animals (e.g. has skin) are stored at the "animal" level, and the lowest level allows distinctions to be made between particular birds (e.g. is yellow). This model makes a lot of intuitive sense, and Collins and Quillian devised an experimental procedure that allowed them to test whether the diagram successfully represents a semantic structure, the way in which meanings are connected.

If you ask "Is a canary yellow?" and time how long it takes people to say "yes" and then compare that time with the time it takes to decide whether a canary can fly, or whether a canary has skin, you will find that some answers are made more quickly than others. In fact, answers to questions which relate items at the same level in the hierarchy are answered most quickly, those which are one level apart are reasonably quick and those which are two levels apart are slowest of all.

Unfortunately, while everything works neatly for canaries being birds, the model does not hold up to other kinds of test. If you ask "Is a bat a precious stone?" you should have to search all over the network to find out that "bat" and "precious stone" are not related. However, that question is actually answered very quickly, whereas "Is a bat a bird?" takes a much longer time. The degree of similarity or relationship between the concepts determines the speed of the reply, not the structure of the network (Smith, Shoben, & Rips, 1974). Worse still for the simpler models, the degree of typicality affects the time it takes to make a decision about category membership. It takes longer to answer "Is a chicken a bird?" than it does to answer "Is a sparrow a bird?" This is just what we would expect from study of natural concepts, but it shouldn't happen if "chicken" and "sparrow" are both at the same level in a hierarchy.

Collins and Loftus (1975) produced a refined and elaborated version of the Collins and Quillian model which was no longer structured hierarchically but instead used the principle of semantic relatedness or distance. Concepts are interconnected and the links can be strong or weak, depending on how often they have been activated. Search for an answer proceeds by *spreading activation* so that when one concept is processed, activation spreads to neighbouring ones. The more often activation spreads between two concepts, the more they are linked, so "sparrow" and "bird" are linked more strongly than "chicken" and "bird". The model allows comparison of the features shared by the concepts, but, in addition, hierarchical relationships are also represented. This is necessary because if you are asked "Is a sparrow a wren?" the activation from the two concepts would spread through the same features, so a link would soon be made. To prevent an erroneous "yes" answer, there has to be some way of recognising very quickly that "wren" and "sparrow" are both instances of the same higher category of birds. The hierarchical aspects become just further features in the network rather than the main basis for its structure.

This brief sketch of just two ideas about how relationships between concepts are represented indicates something of the challenge to our understanding of concepts. The theories work for some questions but not for others. Whatever we propose must ultimately answer a lot of questions about how we acquire concepts, how we see similarities and differences, how we assimilate later knowledge, how we use knowledge from different perspectives and how we restructure it. The story is necessarily incomplete, but Chapters 9 and 10 especially take up some issues about the way in which our knowledge is structured. Meanwhile we turn briefly to point to the way we use concepts to evaluate new experiences.

Concepts and Induction

When we meet examples of a new class of objects, we use our old knowledge to help us get to know the new. For example, the old knowledge can be represented by well-practised analysers like those we come to have in reading, or our old knowledge can be a source of hypotheses or guesses about why a new word has been assigned to a novel collection of objects. Indeed, it is hard to imagine what wholly "new" information would be like, so commonly do we discover something of apparent relevance in our previous knowledge. Now, the acquisition of natural concepts probably occurs most often by the non-analytic route, as functional concepts in Hull's terminology. With no laboratory simplification of the stimulus array and with "trials" haphazardly spread over days and months, young children rapidly acquire high reliability in naming common objects. They even on occasion overextend category names to similar but different objects, showing that something—perhaps a shape or an action—is perceived as having something in common with something previously experienced and labelled. Real-world objects, such as dogs and tables, exist in such detailed variety. Children, and people generally, show remarkable ability in abstracting what might be the esssential features and in making up for the gaps in their experience. Experience of a small number of tables or dogs is sufficient. The fact that a child may sometimes confuse one kind of object with another, say mistake a goat for a sheep, is perhaps the more remarkable for the child's near-recognition than for the error. After all the error implies that a flexibly intelligent knowledge structure is being brought to bear upon current experiences.

Not only is a process of analysis and abstraction in evidence in such cases, but the process which allows us to generalise, to make up for the gaps in our knowledge, deserves attention. This process is sometimes termed *induction*, in which instances of something induce us to offer a generalisation that we cannot wholly justify because the evidence is incomplete. To understand how concepts and beliefs from current knowledge help us to make sense of new information, try the thought experiment which Thagard and Nisbett (1982, pp. 380–381) suggested:

> Imagine you are exploring a newly discovered island. You encounter three instances of a new species of bird, called the shreeble, and all three observed shreebles are blue. What is your degree of confidence that *all* shreebles are blue? Compare this with your reaction to the discovery of three instances of a new metal floridium, all of which when heated burn with a blue flame. Are you more or less confident of the generalization "All floridium burns with a blue flame" than you were of the generalization "All shreebles are blue"? Now consider a third case. All three observed shreebles use baobab leaves as nesting material, but how confident do you feel about the generalization "All shreebles use baobab leaves as nesting material"?

You will probably share the intuitions of undergraduate subjects who felt that the generalisation about the metal floridium is more certain than the assumption of uniform coloration of shreebles and that the generalisation about their nesting materials is least secure. Professional philosophers and psychologists also agreed with this ranking of the generalisations. We can readily justify these intuitions in terms of our partial knowledge of metals and of birds and their nesting materials. What does this tell us about the nature of the concepts of "metal" and "bird"? Thagard and Nisbett point to our background knowledge of the variability of kinds of things as a major determinant of our confidence about generalisation from a given number of instances. We have to have a notion that something is a *kind of thing* and we have to appreciate that instances are liable to show *variability* to some extent. Clearly we tend to operate with a belief that the individual instances of any metal do not vary very much with respect to the properties under consideration, and therefore we believe that a very small number of instances give us sufficient information to allow a judgement. This might mean that even for non-experts "metal" is a concept having some very clear and defining attributes. Similarly, experts and novices bring to bear some formal or informal knowledge of the variability in colour of birds of the same type, and the even greater variability in nesting materials. It does not take an expert to suggest that if baobab leaves are not available for nesting materials in an otherwise suitable environment, the shreebles will probably find something else that will serve. We can do this even if we can not quite put our finger on how we come to think this.

Most studies of concepts, especially those using artificial stimuli, have focused on the categorisation of concrete objects using perceptual features. The processes involved in such tasks must have much in common with those for word, object, and face recognition discussed in Chapters 1 and 2. Yet the study of concepts has always promised to take us closer to an understanding of higher processes such as judgement, language use, and thinking. Recall, for example, that Vygotsky's aim was an understanding of the relation between language and thought. The thought experiment offered by Thagard and Nisbett reminds us that concepts can carry higher-order kinds of "features," that is, features of features and rules about features, beyond those that we immediately experience. In particular, they remind us that our concepts act as firmly held hypotheses and beliefs when we receive new information. The observations that we were invited to adopt as "givens" provoke certain ready-made assumptions in us. Floridium *is* a metal, we were told, and it is a feature of metals that samples of a metal do not vary much with respect to some of its properties. Features (e.g. properties of a metal and of metals) can have higher-order features (e.g. degree of variability). Hardness, melting temperature, and colour of flame are among those features which are likely to be marked as "constants," whereas the size and shape of pieces of metal are variable and even irrelevant immediate perceptual features.

In general, the study of concepts has given us some clues about how our knowledge is organised, but the traditional studies, often focusing on physical things and stimuli constructed from perceptual features, leave much to be understood about particular areas of our knowledge. The development of the more automated recognition processes discussed in Chapters 1 and 2 impinges on the phenomena of categories and concepts, and these in turn form the basis for higher processes in learning, understanding, and thinking, topics that are taken up in many different ways in later chapters.

SUMMARY

The task of "telling the sheep from the goats" illustrates many of the issues to do with acts of categorisation and their relation to concepts. This chapter first reviewed some of the many laboratory studies that have used constructed stimuli to demonstrate the manner in which concepts may come to be identified. When the concepts are defined by rules applied to salient perceptual attributes of the stimuli, many subjects engage in something akin to hypothesis-testing behaviour. When the concepts are based on more complex perceptual arrays, a less analytic process of abstraction is in evidence. This process probably applies most commonly to naturally occurring concepts which are often hard to define by rules. Typically, both perceptual and functional features are involved, at least for those concepts signified by concrete nouns.

Natural concepts also display properties beyond those observed in the early laboratory studies. The co-occurrence of features in the environment, both physical and cultural, leads to structure and non-arbitrariness in the things we come to name. The most commonly used levels of categorisation accord with the principle of cognitive economy, the basic level signifying a sufficient amount of similarity among members and a sufficient differentiation between categories. Members of a category often show variation in "typicality." The notion of a prototype, an abstract representation of the most typical members of a category, is beginning to account for a number of phenomena, both naturally occurring ones and some found in the laboratory.

Hopes that the study of concepts would lead to an understanding of the relation between language and thought and of the structures underlying learning and thinking have not yet been fulfilled. Rather, these topics are approached from several other directions in many of the chapters that follow. The many chapters gathered in E. Rosch and B. B. Lloyd (Eds.) (1978), *Cognition and Categorization*, give a wide variety of perspectives on structure, process, and representation of concepts; and the review by D. L. Medin and E. E. Smith (1984) in the *Annual Review of Psychology* should prove accessible to a beginning student.

4 Reaching for a Glass of Beer: Planning and Controlling Movements

Reaching out to pick up a glass of beer may not seem like a very difficult activity, at least in the early evening. The glass is on the table, you reach, pick it up, carry it to your mouth and drink. No one stops to ask "How did you do that?" and you would be very surprised if they did. The ease with which we do this makes us think that there is nothing to explain and we may want to move on to more difficult, and therefore more interesting, activities. However, it is just these very simple activities that can often be the most difficult to explain. In other chapters of this book we discuss how you might read a word, like *beer*, or how you would recognise the face of an acquaintance in the bar. These are also easy to do, and they don't need much explanation in ordinary life, but when we think about how we do them we realise that reading words and recognising faces are complex activities.

The study of how we make movements is important to cognition because our thought processes only have an effect on the world if they result in movement, including the movements that produce speech. However, it is not always recognised that the questions we can ask about our knowledge of movements are similar to those we can ask about other kinds of knowledge. We can ask about the nature of the movement knowledge, about how it is stored in memory, and about how we use it to plan and prepare the actions we actually produce. Questions about how we represent the meanings of words, or how we store and use visual patterns like faces have already been raised in earlier chapters and we address this kind of question in all the chapters of this book.

In this chapter we concentrate on movement itself, and we start with the simple example of reaching out to pick up a glass. This is a simple everyday example that we take for granted and we will use it here as the first of several activities that give us insight into our movement plans. Later we consider other activities such as catching a ball, long-jumping, throwing a parcel, typing, and playing the piano. Picking up a glass involves getting the hand from one place to another, and this change in position of a part of the body is central to making any kind of movement at all. If drinking beer isn't something which you do then you could replace the work "beer" in what follows with "tea", "lemonade", "pina colada" or whatever feels appropriate to you.

REACHING AND GRASPING

When you reach for a glass your movements seem smooth and well organised; you don't knock the glass over, and you don't take an inordinately long time to make the movement. These are aspects of your performance that we want to try to explain. Reaching is something that happens very early in life, but we are not going to consider how the baby's primitive reaching becomes the adult's skilled movement. Reaching is such a well-learned activity that you probably do not know how you reach for a glass, never mind how you plan and control the reach. How do you score on these three questions: Can you make the reach as well with your eyes closed as with them open? When you reach, do you keep your hand flat until you contact the glass and then curl your fingers? Would you reach in the same way for a wide glass and a narrow glass?

In order to obtain some basic information on how people reach out and pick things up, Jeannerod (1984) filmed subjects reaching for objects of different sizes and analysed the pattern of their movements and how long it took for each part of the pattern to be produced. He found that the movement could be broken down into two main phases, the reach phase and the grasp phase. The reach phase basically involves aiming the hand in the direction of the target and moving it the correct distance. The second phase of the movement, the grasp, begins during the reach, and reflects judgements about the size and shape of the object to be picked up. When subjects began to reach, their fingers were partly bent and the tips were close to the thumbs. During the first part of the movement the fingers began to stretch and the gap between finger and thumb grew larger. After about three-quarters of the movement duration the finger gap was reduced in order to fit the size of the target object. This grip size changed with object size so that the fingers were quite far apart for a large object and close together for a small one, but the size of the grip had no effect on the time it took for the overall reach phase. Figure 4.1 shows a record of reach and grasp for one subject on one trial. The fastest part of the reach (the steepest slope) occurs at the same time as the extension of the fingers. The slowest part, where the slope is flattened at the end of the movement, corresponds with closing the fingers to make the grip the right size. That is, the timing for the reach and the grasp show considerable correspondence. There appears to be one overall timing pattern for the two components of the action, and they are fitted together quite neatly.

Jeannerod asked subjects to reach when they could see their hands and when their hands were out of sight. He found that being able to see the

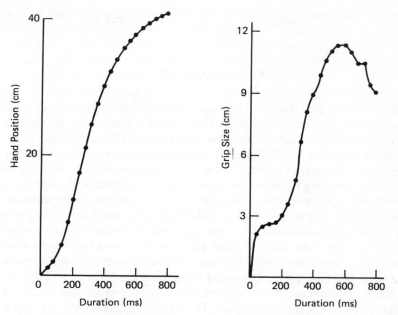

Fig. 4.1 Position profiles of the two components of a reaching movement as a function of time. Left: arm trajectory. The beginning of the low-velocity phase occurs at 560 msec, that is, in this case within 70 per cent of completion of the movement. Right: finger grip. The greatest grip opening also occurs at 560 msec. From Jeannerod, M. (1984) The timing of natural prehension movements. *Journal of Motor Behavior*, *16*, 235–254. Copyright 1984 Heldref Publications and reprinted with permission.

hand meant that the reach was more accurate, but this did not lead to a change in the relative timing of the two components. So, of the three questions we asked earlier, the answers are: yes, reaching with vision is more accurate than reaching without vision; yes, you do start to curl your fingers before you reach the glass; and yes, the amount you open or close your fingers does relate to the size of the glass. Most importantly, observing what happens during reaching allows us to see that parts of the pattern produced are co-ordinated in time, and so must be planned together rather than one after the other.

MOVING TO A TARGET

The first phase in reaching is aiming to a target, and aiming occurs in many other situations. If you want to type a letter you need to know how to aim a finger onto a typewriter key, but you also need to aim if you want to punch someone on the chin, or turn the knob on the cooker before the milk boils over. Aiming is even simpler than reaching and it allows us insight into one of the most basic questions about how we make movements. That is, what do we plan, and what do we change while the movement is going on? One of the earliest studies of movement produced some answers to this question. It was carried out by Woodworth (1899). His subjects drew with a pencil backwards and forwards between lines on a piece or paper attached to a rotating drum. The movements were made to the beat of a metronome so that Woodworth could investigate how hand movements were made at different speeds, and the rotation of the drum meant that any changes in the speed of the movements could be seen as changes in the slope of the pencil marks that were produced. At slower speeds Woodworth found that there were two phases to movement with eyes open: an initial one which was fast and came close to the target, and a second phase which guided the pencil more accurately to the target (see Fig. 4.2).

Woodworth's "two-phase motor unit" can be observed if you hold your arm straight out to one side and then move it fairly quickly so that you touch the tip of your nose with your index finger. Unless you are quite happy to run the risk of sticking your finger in your eye you should notice

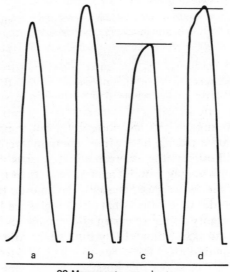

20 Movements per minute

FIG. 4.2 Tracings of different sorts of movements: (a) eyes shut, left hand; (b) eyes shut, right hand; (c) eyes open, left hand; (d) eyes open, right hand. Rate, 20 movements per minute. The movements with eyes shut were supposed to be equal to each other. Those with eyes open were required to terminate on a line ruled on the paper. These are selected records, not continuous ones. (From Woodworth, 1899).

that there is a fast phase followed by a homing phase just before you touch your nose. However, if the movement is very fast, this two-part movement is not observed. When Woodworth's subjects moved back and forward between their target lines 140 times per minute they were much less accurate overall, and they did not show the slower second phase. The accuracy of their fast movements seemed to reflect only the accuracy of the first part of the two phases, the initial impulse to move. A great deal of subsequent research has confirmed that fast movements are generally less accurate than slow ones and that slow ones tend to have two main phases.

In order to start a movement, and to complete it quickly (or without being able to see what you are doing), you have to control two things. One is the amount of force you use to get the movement going, and the other is the amount of time for which the force is applied (Schmidt, Zelaznik, Hawkins, Frank, & Quinn, 1979). If you want to make a long movement quickly then you need to exert more force in the first place. If you miscalculate the amount of force then you make a mistake. It is likely that the more force you should have exerted, the more errors occur, so fast movements (when a lot of force is required) will lead to more mistakes than slow movements. This account has been refined by Meyer, Smith, and Wright (1982), who suggest that there may be a sequence of force impulses applied during the movement, but both accounts relate to situations in which you move very quickly to a target, and the speed is more important than the accuracy when you arrive. However, when you want to reach for a glass accuracy is important, otherwise some of the beer could be wasted. How can you reduce error in reaching for the glass?

Correcting an Aimed Movement

Jeannerod's filmed observations and Woodworth's early study give us one obvious answer to the problem of making movements more accurate. You can watch them and decide whether they are going to get to the right place and make some alterations if they do not. This means that it will take longer to make the movement because one or more corrections will have to be planned and organised, and this takes time. Keele and Posner (1968) estimated how long it took for subjects to correct the accuracy of their aiming movement using vision. They did this by asking subjects to make a 6-inch movement at several different speeds. In one condition subjects could see the target and their hand during the movement; in a second condition the lights in the room were turned off as soon as the movement was started. Keele and Posner found that movements that took 190 msec to complete were made with the same accuracy whether the lights were on or not, but that movements that took 260 msec or longer were more accurate when the light was on. They concluded that it took between 190 and 260 msec to make a correction to a movement based on visual information.

A much shorter time for altering movement on the basis of visual feedback has been estimated by Carlton (1981). He had subjects make a movement of a set size to a set target 50 times but prevented them from seeing their hand and the stylus for most of the movement. Analysis of films of some of the movements showed that when subjects could not see their hands until 93 per cent of the movement had been made, they were able to change the rate at which they were accelerating within about 135 msec from the moment at which the hand became visible. The task was well learned and performed accurately, and very small adjustments were in fact made, so it seems likely that the time it takes to use visual information will depend on the accuracy of the initial impulse. This may not seem like a very relevant finding, as even the most dedicated beer drinker is unlikely to reach for a glass in the same place 50 times within a few minutes, but it does alert us to the possibility that the planning of a simple movement and the detection of error are not entirely independent.

We have already said that very fast movements tend to be less accurate than slower ones, even when there is no time for a correction, because of the variability in the initial force impulse. However, movement accuracy and movement time will not always be related in the same way, especially if it is necessary to use vision to achieve a high level of accuracy. To show that there is a relationship between the size of the target (the accuracy of the movement), the initial impulse, and the possibility of correction, Wallace and Newell (1983) asked subjects to make movements over a range of movement distances to targets of different sizes, and to make some of the movements in the dark. Short movements to wide targets, which are easy and take a comparatively short time (Fitts, 1954), were not affected by the presence or absence of visual information, but vision was needed for some other combinations of movement distance and target size. When vision *was* needed it took 200–250 msec to use it. Movements to very small targets needed vision to be performed accurately, although they took the same overall time as longer movements to larger targets. This rather complicated relationship suggests that visually based corrections are more important when high accuracy is required.

The task being carried out affects the time it takes to make a visually based correction, and the possibility of visual correction can affect the way the movement is planned. We cannot say that a fixed length of time must elapse before a visual correction can be made (Elliott & Allard, 1985). So, how long will it take you to correct your reach for a glass of beer? Different experiments give different estimates of the time taken to use visual feedback depending on the combinations of movement distance, speed, and practice that are used, and whether subjects know that vision will be available or not. In Carlton's task, as in many of those we have discussed, the target actually stopped the movement, so terminal velocity does not need to be controlled too finely. Instead, it is important not to make an error to the side of the target, or to move too far or not far enough. Practice reduces the amount of sideways error so all that is needed is minor adjustment. If you reach for a glass, however, the target does not stop the movement; in fact the glass will be knocked over unless the movement is properly controlled. The time to correct error is therefore likely to be in the range suggested by Keele and Posner (1968) and Wallace and Newell (1983), if not more.

Correcting Using Proprioception

Many studies of movement have shown that there are occasions when being able to watch the movements we make does not seem to change their accuracy. That is, we are able to control some movements, or parts of movements, in another way. One contender for this role is a different kind of perceptual processing, one which involves information about the position of the body itself. *Proprioceptive feedback* which is derived from receptors in muscles, joints, and skin, could be used to make sure that a movement was proceeding as planned (Crossman & Goodeve, 1963). The time it takes for a person to react to proprioceptive input can vary, depending on the nature of the task, but it is less than that for visual input. Chernikoff and Taylor (1952) found the average proprioceptive reaction time to be 120 msec in a task that did not involve well-learned movement, so control could be exerted more quickly than vision would allow. Annett, Annett, Hudson, and Turner (1979) analysed errors in putting pegs into holes, and found that the time from hitting the edges of the hole by mistake to getting the peg securely in place was 118 msec, which again is shorter than a visual reaction time for the same correction.

Although proprioceptive information is of great importance in many aspects of movement, we cannot use it to obtain information about the position of a limb in relation to a position in the environment. Imagine trying to find a light switch in the dark. If you reach out and miss you do not know the size of your error, or what direction to move in next. If you can see your hand the relationship between the position of the hand and the position of the light switch is direct. If you cannot see you have to hunt around. So, if you control a movement by feel you can only do so if you know what the movement should feel like. You can not detect that you have picked the wrong movement in the first place and that you are going to miss the target.

THE CONSTRUCTION AND ORGANISATION OF MOVEMENT PROGRAMS[1]

When you decide to reach for something you have to turn that decision into instructions which will move the appropriate limb to the correct place. There are of course several ways in which you could move your right hand from one place to another. You could move from the elbow only, or from the shoulder, or you could combine the two. You could even hold all your arm joints fixed and move your whole upper body instead. Some of the possible combinations will never appear, because co-ordination between parts of your body is already structured and organised into groups (Turvey, 1977), and some of the calculations about the best combinations of movements to use will be constrained by the situation you are in so that, for example, you might hit someone with your elbow if you moved in a particular way. The kinds of advance calculations that might determine the combination of limbs you use to reach are extremely complicated (Hinton, 1984), and we are going to consider some much simpler questions about simple reaching.

Simple Movements

If you reach for a glass you will use one hand and arm, you will reach in one direction, and for a specific distance. Do you plan, or program, the reach for one arm, then program the direction, then the extent, or is there a different order, or does all the planning happen at the same time? It is not easy to see this kind of planning happening in everyday life, unlike planning what we are going to say (see Chapter 7), so we need to look at experiments that allow us to measure the time it takes to start movements, and then use that as an indicator of what is happening in programming the movement. Using the time it takes to react is a very common technique in all of cognitive psychology. The basic argument is that if more processing is required then the reaction time (RT) will be longer. If movements are programmed in advance, then more programming should require more time, so more complex movements could take longer to prepare than simple ones. More specifically, if programs are built up in steps which become more and more detailed, then any changes to the program at a high level should take longer than changes at a low level, because everything has to be re-organised if a high-level component is changed.

---

[1]In British English "programme" is the more common spelling, but "program" has come to be acceptable in relation to computers. As we are using "movement program" by analogy to "computer program" and the term "motor program" is a technical term in the literature on movement control, we have decided to use the computer, or American, spelling.

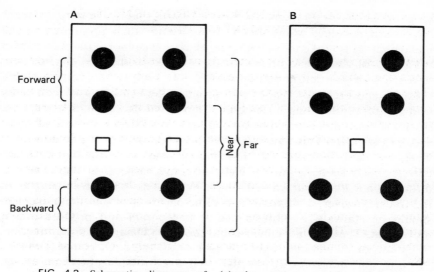

FIG. 4.3 Schematic diagrams of: (a) the response panel used by Rosenbaum (1980), and (b) the corresponding stimulus panel used by Larish and Frekany (1984). In (a) the square buttons are the starting position and the round buttons are the targets. In (b) the large round shapes are target lights which indicate exactly which button on (a) is to be pressed.

It is worth pointing out here that there is a difference between the *decision* about the choice of the movement (where do I want to move to?) and the choice of the movement itself (how do I make the move?). We are dealing with the second part of the process here, but the link between the two is an important part of movement planning and it can be difficult to separate them. Rosenbaum (1980) used a "precuing" technique to investigate how programs are organised. Subjects started with their index fingers on two buttons and moved as quickly as possible to one of eight other buttons (see Fig. 4.3). They moved either the right hand or the left hand, the movements were either towards the body or away from the body, and the movements were either long or short. Subjects were warned (or precued) about one element of the movement—hand, direction, or extent—and later they saw a coloured light which told them exactly which movement to make. The results of the experiment showed that any kind of advance planning made reaction time faster, but there was no indication that it took longer to replan one aspect of the movement than another. Unfortunately, it is not entirely clear that the subjects knew exactly where they were moving *to*. Because the experiment used different coloured lights to specify responses, the subject had to recognise the colour and remember which position it stood for before starting to program. This means that other decision processes could have been going on after the stimulus, as well as the programming itself (Goodman & Kelso, 1980). That is, the subjects might have been deciding where to move to, rather than programming the movement. This is like the situation in which you cannot work out which of the glasses on a table is yours, so you don't know whether it would be easier to reach with your left or right hand.

Larish and Frekany (1985) tried to isolate the two kinds of decision by using a reprogramming technique. They used Rosenbaum's response system so movements could be for the right or left hand, forward or back, and long or short. This time, however, all three aspects of the movement were cued in advance by illuminating one of eight lights which corresponded spatially to the eight response targets, so there was no difficulty in working out where to move to (see Fig. 4.3). On 25 per cent of the trials, however, a different light came on to signal that the movement should be started, so subjects had to reprogram and produce a new movement. The new movement could require a change of arm, direction, or extent, or a combination of any two, or all three. Of course, the time taken to start a movement was increased when it had to be changed, but what is important is that some of the changes took longer than others. The reaction times showed that it took longer to reprogram when direction was changed than it did when arm or extent were changed, and that changing an arm took longer than changing extent. In addition, if direction was changed it did not matter if something else was changed as well and if arm was changed it did not matter if extent was changed as well. So, the order of programming seems to be direction, arm, extent. If you have to change the direction of the movement then you reprogram the whole thing, but if you have to change extent that is all you change.

This result supports the view that there is an order in which we program movements, with direction first and extent last. Why should this be? When you program forward movement you organise a particular pattern of activity in groups of muscles. This pattern would be quite different if the movement were backward, whichever hand and arm was used, so the pattern is not specific to one particular set of muscles—right or left hand, for example. Given the pattern of activity, the specification of particular muscle groups comes next (e.g. right hand), and to program extent or distance, you change the force that has to be applied. This account makes considerable sense, but it probably isn't the whole story. The experiments are conducted on quite a limited set of movements and we can not generalise too far from them.

Sequences of Movement

When you reach for a glass you have to organise some of the reach in advance because you have to co-ordinate groups of muscles. You may use feedback near the end of the reach to check on accuracy as you get close to the glass itself, but the reach is a reasonably discrete event and is over quite quickly. Imagine that instead of reaching for your glass you turn to ask your friend to name the tune that is running through your head, because you cannot decided what it is. You refuse to sing it but you are prepared to tap out the rhythm on the table top. You know the rhythm before you start, but how many taps would you prepare before beginning? How does the tune get turned into a sequence of movements? You might just set up a long string of taps, or you might use the structure of the tune to organise taps into groups which then get expanded into movements. We can use reaction time to investigate how much of a sequence is programmed in advance, and how the structure of the sequence affects the way the program is organised.

Henry and Rogers (1960) asked subjects to respond to a tone in one of three different ways. One involved lifting a finger from a reaction key, and this took less time to initiate than reaching up to grasp a tennis ball on a string, which in turn took less time to initiate than a movement sequence which included hitting a ball, pressing a key, and grasping a ball. This was interpreted as showing that advance planning took longer with more alternatives, but as the movements began differently it may be that it was the start which was planned, not the whole sequence. Inhoff, Rosenbaum, Gordon, and Campbell (1984) used a much simpler task and asked subjects to respond as quickly as possible to a signal by pressing once with the index finger, or with the index finger followed by the middle finger, or by the index, middle, and ring fingers. They found that the time to react increased each time another finger press was added, even though the sequences began in the same way, so more advance programming occurred each time another movement was added to the sequence.

So, as one might expect, adding more bits to a sequence does lead to more advance programming, but it does not tell us about the structure of a program, so the next point to consider is how the different components of a sequence are represented before they are produced. Again we use a very simple task, that of making short (*dit*) and long (*dah*) presses on a Morse code key. Klapp and Wyatt (1976) asked subjects to make one of four movement combinations of key presses (*dit-dit*, *dit-dah*, *dah-dah*, and *dah-dit*) in response to one of four signal lights, and they measured the time it took to start the first key press. They found the longest reaction times when the first part of the combination was *dah* rather than *dit*, but the reaction time was shortened if the second item was the same as the first. So *dah-dah* was produced more quickly than *dah-dit*, and *dit-dit* was faster than *dit-dah*. These two findings suggest that there are two components in the pre-programming of these simple activities. To produce *dah* first takes longer because it requires a slower movement which is more complicated to program into the force impulse discussed earlier. The effect of repetitions indicates that there is another level of programming that relates to the elements in the action. If two elements are the same it takes less time to organise them, so repetition is specified at a level above force.

More evidence that sequences of movements are structured in levels comes from a study by Rosenbaum, Kenny, and Derr (1983), who asked subjects to make repeated tapping patterns with different fingers. These went: right middle, left middle, right middle, left middle, right index, left index, right index, left index, and instead of looking at how long it took to start a sequence, Rosenbaum et al. looked at the times that elapsed between each tap. They found the longest gap in the centre of the sequence when the pattern changed from middle to index finger, with slightly shorter gaps between the first and second pairs in each half. They argued that the sequence was broken into two between the middle and index fingers, and then into two again between the pairs of right and left taps, and that this structure was reflected when the sequences was translated into the individual finger movements that produced the taps.

When we produce a series of movements, like tapping out a rhythm, we start with the intention to produce something which sounds like the rhythm, and we turn that overall intention into a set of units which reflect the structure of the rhythm itself. Depending on the complexity of the output there may be several levels in this structure. A structure in which there are higher levels that can be said to control lower ones is often called a *hierarchy*, which basically means that the details of organisation at one level do not need to be known at a higher level. When we come to turn the structural representation into movements we may use the hierarchical structure to guide the translation of specific responses (e.g. move right middle finger) into the force impulses that will produce the movement. We return to the idea of levels of planning of output later in this chapter, and in Chapter 7 on the production of speech, but first we consider the nature of the memory representations for the actions we use to produce particular movements.

DEVELOPING MOVEMENT SCHEMAS

When I reach for a glass of beer, pick it up, carry it to my mouth and drink, an observer will not notice details of the movement. I will simply have lifted the glass. Yet if the glass is completely full I will have to exert more force to lift it than if it is half empty, so the instructions to move will be different although both the intention and the description will remain the same. The ability to cope with variation within the same action has to develop with time and experience. We probably do not think of reaching for a glass as requiring a great deal of acquired skill, and perhaps an example used by Pew (1974) is more compelling. Pew observed post-office workers sorting packages. The sorter stood near the source of the packages, between 5 and 10 feet away from a set of 25 mailbags. As each package appeared it was examined and then thrown into the correct mailbag. The packages were of many different shapes and sizes, the sorter was different distances away from each of the mailbags and could be standing in slightly different positions on different occasions, yet accuracy in getting the package into the mailbag was extremely high. What interested Pew was the nature of the learned knowledge for throwing parcels, which the sorters had developed over time. It seemed implausible that they would have stored in memory instructions for every distance they had seen in the past, or every packet weight which they had felt. Pew's view, and that adopted by many others since, was that a generalised schema for movements of a particular class is developed with experience.

Before we consider the nature of these schemas for movement in more detail we need to consider the word "schema," which is used in many contexts in psychology. In general, it refers to a knowledge structure that does not contain specific information about a particular movement or event. When Bartlett (1932) adopted the concept of schema from its use by Head, he stated that: " 'Schema' refers to an active organisation of past reactions or past experiences, which must always be supposed to be operating in any well-adapted organic response [p. 201]." We discuss in Chapter 9 how schemas can be used to explain the way in which past experience can be used to make sense of similar situations when they recur, but in the present context another quotation from Bartlett is more appropriate, because it is specifically directed at movement control. He wrote about making a stroke in tennis or cricket and commented that: "When I make a stroke I do not, as a matter of fact, produce something absolutely new, and I never merely repeat something old. The stroke is literally manufactured out of the living visual and postural 'schemata' of the moment and their interrelationships [p. 202]."

A more detailed account of these generalised schemas[2] for movement has been put forward by Schmidt (1975). In Schmidt's account there are several stages involved in making simple movements. First the overall situation has to be sized up and the appropriate type of action selected, and this means using the appropriate schema. Then the initial conditions such as how heavy the parcel is and how far away the mailbag is have to be assessed and translated into decisions about how to make the schema specific for that particular movement. This means calculating the specific values for parameters in the general program for these movements. "Parameters" in computer programs take particular values when a program is run, but can be different on every occasion, depending on the

---

[2]The Latin plural of "schema" is "schemata," the term Bartlett used. We prefer to use the plural form "schemas."

requirements of the situation. Parameters for movement programs would include force and time, which we have already discussed in our consideration of simple movements.

The memory representation or schema is a set of rules or procedures developed from past movements, which acts as a plan for future ones. However, Schmidt's account also allows us to deal with the problem of how we know what movements feel like without doing them, or how we know what to expect when we make a movement, by suggesting that there are stored schemas for the sensory consequences of movements as well as procedures for how to produce them. These perceptual schemas allow us to think about movement without doing it, as well as allowing us to judge the correctness of a movement without any information about it from the environment. This is a situation with which many of us are familiar. We throw a piece of paper at the wastebasket and feel that we know whether or not it is going to go in. More skill may be shown by the basketball player or the golfer: They may also feel that an effort will be successful before the outcome is known. This information could be extracted from the trajectory of the paper, the basketball, or the golf ball, rather than from knowledge related to body movement, but an experiment by Henderson (1975) does suggest that we can judge success even when we cannot see the trajectory.

Henderson asked novice and expert dart throwers to throw at the centre of a target. As the dart left the subject's hand it crossed a beam so that the lights were turned out. The throwers had to judge the accuracy of the throw before they saw what they had done. They were also asked to estimate the size of their error if they felt one had occurred. The experts made more accurate throws than the novices and they did know when they were accurate, so they were able to judge without information from the environment. However, experts didn't seem to be as good as novices at judging how big their errors were, possibly because they have developed the ability to tell good throws from bad without having to identify the bad ones.

Schemas for Writing and Catching

What kind of schema might we have for a well-learned skill like writing a particular letter? When we write we make finger movements that move the pen up and down, finger movements that move the pen from side to side, and movements at the shoulder joint that move the hand across the page. Vredenbregt and Koster (1971) have shown that a mechanical model with two electric motors that drive a pen horizontally and vertically can simulate many aspects of handwriting. The diagonals and curves are the result of interactions between the forces produced by the two motors. We can think of the two sets of muscles that move the fingers as operating in a very similar way. Basically they make vertical movements or sideways movements and the force used has to be carefully timed. Changes in the amount of force exerted vertically can lead to an increased stroke in order to produce an *l* rather than an *e* and allowing all impulses to last longer makes the writing larger (Wing, 1980). Individual handwriting styles will depend on the stored procedures that each person has learned for producing these forces in the sets of muscles. However, these procedures are not specific to the muscles that move the fingers. If you write on a blackboard you will use your whole arm, yet your handwriting style will be recognisable. You would probably produce the same style if you could write with the pen between your toes. What is important is that the sequences of timed impulses used to produce letters can be translated into action for any pair of muscle groups that operate at right angles to each other. The stored schema for writing a letter is a generalised program concerned with relative forces and their duration.

Many of our movements, such as reaching and catching, have not been learned in the same way as we learned to write letters, but we can also consider the nature of the schemas that have developed for them. Both reaching and catching are carefully organised in terms of the timing of the components and, in addition, the timing of a catch must be related to external events. If you try to catch a ball you must get your hand to the right place at the right time or you will miss. You also have to start to close your fingers before the ball arrives or it will bounce off your palm. Alderson, Sully, and Sully (1974) analysed film of one-handed catching in two situations, one in which the hand was held down next to the thigh before the catch began and one in which the arm was held straight out from the shoulder so that the hand was already close to the path of the ball. The initial part of the movement was quite different in the two movements, but in the last fifth of a second before contact with the ball, changes occurred in the orientation of the hand which rotated it into the correct position, and started the grasp. These changes were the same for the two movements. As in reaching there are two major components in the catching performance, one of which (moving the hand into the path of the ball) is different for each catch, while the other (the sequencing of the grasp) is the same for all balls of the same size. The schema for catching has to contain both the overall structure of the action and the structure of the grasp component, and either of these may be varied for different catches.

MAKING SEQUENCES FLEXIBLE

We have been trying to understand some of the programming and use of memory representations that take place when we make comparatively simple movements. Although we have emphasised advance programming, other factors are important in controlling our actions. If, like some

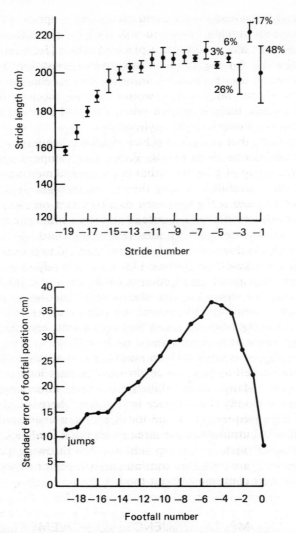

FIG. 4.4   (a): Means and standard deviations of stride lengths over six run-ups for an Olympic long jumper. Run was over 4 m with 21 strides (first two not shown). Stride −1 is the stride onto the take-off board, stride −2 is the preceding one, etc. Numbers printed over the last strides are statistical estimates of the percentage adjustment made on the stride. (b): Standard errors of the distances of the athlete's footfalls from the take-off board. Footfall 0 is the one aimed at the board, footfall −1 the penultimate one, etc. From Lee, D. N., Lishman, J. R., & Thomson, J. A. (1982) Regulation of gait in long jumping. *Journal of Experimental Psychology: Human Perception and Performance. 8*, 448–459. Copyright 1982 by the American Psychological Association and adapted by permission.

neurologically impaired patients, you cannot use proprioceptive input from your joints and muscles, then you will find it very difficult to perform simple sequences like crumpling a piece of paper (Jeannerod, Michel, & Prablanc, 1984). An emphasis on advance organisation does not mean that we cannot use perceptual information to change sequences of movements. If we did not, we would be like mechanical toys which continue to move their legs even when they fall over, instead of being skilled, adaptive movers in the environment.

You may think that you *can* produce inflexible sequences of movement, and you would not be alone in this. Skilled long-jumpers, for example, try to develop a run-up of a fixed number of paces, and measure distance from the board quite carefully, making the run-up as regular as they can. Yet they do not produce a fixed pattern of movement on each run-up (Lee, Lishman, & Thomson, 1982). Instead, they maintain a consistent stride pattern until they are a few strides from the board. At that point the consistency breaks down and stride length is altered to produce an accurate position on the take-off board (see Fig. 4.4). This adjustment is based on visual information about the position of the board and involves a change in one aspect of the stride pattern, the vertical impulse of the step. The vertical impulse determines how long the flight time for the stride will be. Thus, programming does not mean that movements are run off regardless of what comes out or how relevant it is.

The long-jumper is trying to run quickly to a particular position in the environment as well as to produce thrust from that location to carry the body forward. Many other skilled acts use information from the environment to modify performance in advance. There are also many cases in which the consequences of one movement are evaluated and used to alter subsequent output (we have already seen that feedback is used in this way when postal sorters develop schemas for throwing parcels.) Some kinds of feedback are crucial to continuing good performance even though performance may continue without them.

COMPLEX SEQUENCES OF MOVEMENT

We started this chapter by looking at reaching and aiming to a target, because many of the more complicated activities we engage in involve reaching to targets. Piano playing and typing are good examples of such complex tasks, as we have to put a finger on a key in a particular position in space, in order to produce a note or a letter. The overall intention may be a very high-level one indeed (like playing a Bach fugue or writing a novel) but it has to end up as a long sequence of aiming movements. Extended sequences of movements are not run off like the music on a record, rather they are organised according to the structure of a piece of music, or the material that is to be typed. We have suggested that structured sequences are translated into elements which will in turn be used to produce the motor output with appropriate parameters such as force and time. We will now examine this approach using typing and piano playing in turn.

Typing: Some Data and a Model

When we think of typing we know that the typist does actually produce a series of key presses which occur one after the other and that a good typist can do this at the rate of 500 key strokes a minute (about 100 wpm). Typists can tell us a certain amount about what they do, but their perceptions of their performance are sometimes not borne out when tested. For example, some typists feel that they can scan quite a long way ahead on a page, and that this helps them to maintain a smooth output. However, Shaffer (1973) found that good, fast typing (100 wpm) was achieved when typists could see 8–9 letters in advance and did not improve if more letters were shown. For slower typists, preview led to good results with fewer letters and overall it seems that typists look ahead for just as much as it takes one second to type: any further look ahead adds nothing more to the skill. Shaffer also looked at the role of the material being typed and found that there was little difference between the typing speed for ordinary connected text and for nonsensical passages which contained real words in random sequences. However, presenting letters in random order led to a drop of about 50 per cent in overall speed. These results suggest that organising continuous typing requires knowledge of letter combinations in the language being typed. The responses have to be organised first at the level of letters before being turned into movements that will press the keys.

Does this mean that we know that the movements are organised in the order in which the keystrokes make the letters appear on the page? Gentner, Grudin, and Conway (1980) filmed a 90 wpm typist and looked at the order in which the movements were begun. The movements are described as being like "the movement of sea grass weaving in the waves . . . all in motion at the same time [Norman & Rumelhart, 1983, p. 47]" and they did not support the view that each finger made a stroke in turn. For 21 per cent of the keystrokes analysed, the movements did not begin in the order in which the keys were eventually struck. In these cases the finger movements that resulted in the second of two keystrokes started before the finger movements that produced the first one. This means that the commands for future keystrokes influence the current position of the hand and finger.

On the basis of these observations, and data taken from the kinds of errors that typists make, Rumelhart and Norman (1982) produced a model for typing which they tested by running it as a computer simulation. A simulation is not intended to mean that typists are computers, but rather the degree to which the simulation behaves like a real typist is used to evaluate how similar the processes built into the model can be to the processes in the human typist. The model is called an "activation triggered schema system" and a schema is defined as an organised unit of knowledge which can have other schemas nested within it. That is, schemas are hierarchically organised, with high-level ones being "parent" schemas to others which are "child" schemas, but these in turn can act as "parents" for other still lower levels. The idea of activation used here is similar to that used in the McClelland and Rumelhart (1981) model of word recognition discussed in Chapter 1, although in this case output units are activated.

The schema for a word to be typed activates child schemas for the keypresses that correspond to the letters in the word. These in turn act as parent schemas to excite arm, finger, and hand movements. An actual movement of a particular finger in a particular direction will only occur if the schemas or knowledge units are activated sufficiently. Activation can be damped down by inhibitory links between schemas. Once a keypress has been produced, that unit is de-activated. Norman and Rumelhart argue that an orderly sequence of output is not planned in advance. Instead, several keystrokes are in competition to occur as early as possible and it is the amount of activation that leads to one appearing in the correct serial order. Advance preparation is explained by the activation of commands for future keystrokes which influence the current position of the hand and finger, but there is no organised string of letters planned before they are produced.

The kinds of mistakes people make when they type can provide evidence for models of typing. Basically, a typing error means selecting the wrong letter, the wrong hand, the wrong finger, or the wrong position for a finger. Grudin (1983) has found many substitutions between hands ($n \rightarrow v$), between fingers ($a \rightarrow s$), and within fingers ($n \rightarrow b$). These errors could occur because the keystrokes are in competition with each other and this sometimes leads to the wrong movement appearing before the correct one has received enough activation. This would mean that substitution errors should be made more quickly than normal keystrokes. Omission errors are likely to occur when the same letter has recently been typed and so been de-activated. When Grudin considered the timing of substitution errors he found that the interval before an error was not shorter than normal, as the model predicted. Instead of keystrokes being produced on a first-come, first-output basis, Grudin suggested that the overall timing of responses is regulated by a central timekeeping system using an internal clock. This means that some overall control of the output is necessary.

The model of typewriting that we have been considering makes many predictions about typing performance, some of which are supported by the error data, while others are not. Data from the timing of patterns of responses are also a little ambiguous. Shaffer (1978) found that the first three letter of *whig* are typed differently from the first three letters of *whim*, as the model would predict, but that the differences were not exactly those proposed by Rumelhart and Norman. It may be that the observations that movements are started in a different order from the order in which the keys are pressed does not mean that responses are in conflict. Shaffer (1982) has argued that the results are due to a process of grouping keypresses which allows whole sections to be considered before the first response starts. This means that variations in the timing of responses which result from the wish to put expression into them could be dealt with. It is difficult to add expression when all the responses are fired off as quickly as possible. These two approaches to typing are in opposition, and we consider piano playing in the next section in order to try to resolve the dispute. However, there is general agreement that the knowledge used to produce response output is hierarchically structured and that high-level units are broken down into lower-level ones as output is produced.

Timing and Expression: Playing the Piano

In earlier sections we discussed timing without considering how it was done. Is there an internal clock that we can use to make sure that we time movements correctly? In the study of typing some theorists have suggested that there is no need for an internal clock, whereas others consider that this is the only way to explain the findings. Perhaps typing and the other tasks we have been looking at are not the most suitable activities for investigating the full exent of our timing abilities. After all, the typist is not required to do anything more than produce accurate keystrokes as quickly as possible.

When we consider a musician the picture is a very different one. A good pianist sight-reading a piece of music reads notes on a page and produces finger movements on a keyboard in response. However, there is more to playing than this. A competent player can play all the notes in the correct order, but an excellent player also adds expression to that order, and has to use knowledge of the type of music being played and its conventions in doing so (Sloboda, 1983). The difference is a bit like that found between a drum machine which produces exact intervals between sounds, and a real drummer, whose intervals will be less exact, but for most of us, more interesting to listen to.

When we consider piano playing we have to stop thinking of sequencing as being the production of one movement at a time, because the piano player is producing different notes, often in different rhythms, with the right and left hands (see Chapter 5). Shaffer (1981) has shown that an expert pianist playing two successive performances of a Bach fugue which he had not played for many years, structured the timing of the two performances in a very similar way. The analysis broke the music down into units with the four-bar phrase at the highest level, and the quarter bar at the lowest. The timing relations were closest at the highest level of the analysis and least similar at the lowest level, which suggests that overall there was hierarchical planning of timing for the piece of music. One very interesting finding concerned a set of errors that the pianist made in one performance. Unlike a typist's errors, these did not produce nonsense. The harmonic structure of the music was maintained and the rhythm was not disrupted.

To produce an underlying beat the timing in music has to be controlled by a mechanism that uses an internal clock, but if we can only produce the correct beat there is no expression. Playing expressively includes playing away from the beat and then returning to it. The mechanism that does this has to be responsive to timing, which is a property of the representation of the structure of the movement. So timing has to have two levels, one for a clock which produces regular intervals and one which actually produces movements to produce notes at different points in time relative to the beat. These two levels of timing control do not seem to be totally independent (Clarke, 1982). If the overall speed or tempo is changed, this affects the relative timings within sections of the music and is not independent of them, because expression of interpretation of the music involves both.

The pianist's knowledge of the type of music he was playing in Shaffer's study meant that he had procedures stored in memory for producing certain types of rhythmic patterns, arranging the fingering of notes and chords and planning the phasing of a sequence. These procedures allowed a representation of the structure of the music to be built up a section at a time when he was sight-reading correctly, and they also affected the section built up when a sight-reading error occurred. The abstract structural representation of a piece of music in the mind of the player is the first of two major stages of output organisation. The second stage, which represents the commands that will specify movements and involves memory units like those discussed earlier, is derived from the first.

Although the details will be very different, we should be able to use such a framework to account for simple movements with one force impulse and little accuracy, like banging your fist on the table to attract attention, or those as complex as producing different sequences of force impulses, of different intensity and at different times, simultaneously with the right and left hands as a concert pianist will do. It is because there *is* more to moving than simply giving commands to muscles that we have included this chapter in a book on cognition, and have treated movement planning as a structured hierarchical process.

SLIPS OF ACTION

Errors in what we do can give us insight into how what we do is planned and controlled. When a typist types the wrong letter, or a pianist makes a sight-reading error, we can ask what it is about the way they carry out the task which allows these errors to be produced. However, for most of us, typing errors, or hitting a golf ball too hard, or missing the double twenty on the dart board, may not be the most noticeable mistakes in the long sequences of movements that we produce throughout an average day. We make mistakes that are not described at the level of the accuracy of our movements, but at the level of the overall actions we intend to carry out. That is, we intend to play darts but get distracted by seeing a friend, or we intend to make a pot of tea but forget to add the hot water after the kettle has boiled. Such errors are not movement errors, but we can take some of the explanations we have used in discussing sequences of movement and apply them to these more general situations.

It isn't very easy to study the errors people make in normal life, and it certainly cannot be done in a laboratory. One way round this is to ask people to keep diaries in which they record deviations from their intentions. Reason and Mycielska (1982) did this in two studies in which they collected a total of 625 errors from 98 people. This pool of 625 slips was analysed into four categories. In the first, an intended action was repeated unnecessarily (e.g. sugaring coffee twice). In the second, the intended actions were made, but in relation to the wrong object (e.g. throwing a dirty shirt into the toilet instead of the laundry basket). In the third, unintended actions became incorporated into the sequence (e.g. taking out own front-door key when approaching a friend's house). In the final group, actions were left out of the sequence (e.g. going to bed fully clothed). All these examples are real ones and you can probably think of similar errors that you have made. Reason and Mycielska (1982) noted that many of these errors occurred in familiar and mostly constant environments and were associated with distraction and preoccupation.

Table 4.1 shows a somewhat different classification of slips carried out by Norman (1981). There are three overall categories, some of which have several sub-categories, and they include speech errors as well as other action slips. Norman has produced a model of everyday action in which the emphasis is very similar to that in the typewriting model of Rumelhart and Norman (1982) discussed earlier. The basic assumption is that we have large numbers of schemas, which are organised units of knowledge and are

TABLE 4.1
Norman's (1981) Classification of Action Slips Based on the
Presumed Source of the Errors

Slips that result from errors in the formation of the intention
  Errors that are not classified as slips: errors in the determination of goals, in decision
    making and problem solving, and other related aspects of the determination of an
    intention
  Mode errors: erroneous classification of the situation
  Description errors: ambiguous or incomplete specification of the intention
Slips that result from faulty activation of schemas
  Unintentional activation: when schemas not part of a current action sequence become
    activated for extraneous reasons, then become triggered and lead to slips
    Capture errors: when a sequence being performed is similar to another more frequent
      or better learned sequence, the latter may capture control
    Data-driven activation: external events cause activation of schemas
    Associative activation: currently active schemas activate others with which they are
      associated
  Loss of activation: when schemas that have been activated lose activation, thereby losing
    effectiveness to control behaviour
    Forgetting an intention (but continuing with the action sequence)
    Misordering the components of an action sequence
    Skipping steps in an action sequence
    Repeating steps in an action sequence
Slips that result from faulty triggering of active schemas
  False triggering: a properly activated shema is triggered at an inappropriate time
    Spoonerisms: reversal of event components
    Blends: combinations of components from two competing schemas
    Thoughts leading to actions: triggering of schemas meant only to be thought, not to
      govern action
    Premature triggering
  Failure to trigger: when an active schema never gets invoked because the action was
    preempted by competing schemas
    There was insufficient activation, either as a result of forgetting or because the initial
      level was too low
    There was a failure of the trigger condition to match, either because the triggering
      conditions were badly specified or the match between occurring conditions and the
      required conditions was never sufficiently close

---

related to each other in a hierarchical way. A high-level schema is a
"parent" schema, which has low-level "child" schemas controlled by it.
The child schemas can act as parent for the next level, and so on. Overall
intentions are related to the highest-order parent schemas. Because most
action sequences take time to be completed, several intentions may be
active at any one time. So, you could be intending to walk to the pub to
meet a friend, and also to post a letter on the way.

The schemas are hierachically organised, so once high-level schemas
have become activated the lower levels carry out their components without

referring back very much. The lower levels can be activated from higher levels, or they could be activated by events from the environment. Before a schema is used it has to be activated, and once activated it has to be triggered before the action will appear. So, as you set out to walk to the pub to meet a friend, the intention activates a host of schemas necessary for walking safely through the town and for following a well-known route. At appropriate points, say when you are at the kerb before crossing a road, the situation triggers the road-crossing schema and you will carefully survey the traffic and decide when to cross. In most cases, the rules for making decisions will be part of a practised schema and you will not have to think about what you are choosing to do.

In Norman's system, action errors can occur because of faults in activation or faults in triggering. So, you could activate the wrong schema (take out your key at a friend's door), or activation could be lost (you forget why you went into the kitchen). Your activated schemas could be triggered at the wrong time or they might not be triggered appropriately. These triggering failures often occur when there are several competing actions, so you might put the lid on the teapot and then pour the hot water.

Many of the errors described by Reason and Mycielska (1982) and Norman (1981) are very similar. Norman's theoretical model is, as we have seen, a competing schema one, in which there is lots of activation and errors creep in because of this. The account that Reason (1979) has put forward, and which Reason and Mycielska have expanded, is rather different. The basic hierarchical structure of action schemas still exists, but there is an overall intention system that organises plans for future actions, monitors and guides activity, reviews earlier actions, and if possible, corrects the consequences of errors. This system is limited in that it can only deal with one plan at a time, so when a plan has been organised it is passed to the action system to be implemented.

Reason's view of the organisation of a sequence of actions is that a hierarchical plan is built up in advance. So, to make a pot of tea, you boil the kettle, warm the pot, add the tea and hot water. Of course, boiling the kettle requires you to check there is enough water, and fill it up if there isn't, and boiling the kettle might be part of a number of other action plans as well as making tea. When the hierarchical action plan is implemented all the little movements involved in making tea will be produced as each sub-unit of the plan is carried out. In Reason's account the position in the plan sequence has to be maintained by some kind of internal counting system and errors like repeating an action occur because when the plan is implemented, the counting system "looses its place." This would also result in an action being dropped from the sequence entirely, so that no tea gets put into the pot. The errors result from the ways we have of keeping the place in a sequence of output. We said earlier that most errors occur when we are preoccupied and doing something which is quite familiar. This is because sub-schemas are run off without any checking on whether they are correct or not, and checking only occurs at critical decision points. If checking is not carried out, because we are busy planning something else, for example, then errors are not detected.

Norman and Reason have presented different models, which are similar in many respects to those put forward earlier for typing and playing the piano. They both agree that the organisation of action output is hierarchical, even at the level of the action, rather than the movements. One argues for competing activated schemas, whereas the other prefers a pre-organised sequence, but the data (the errors people make) do not as yet enable us to decide which is the best way to understand the high-level planning of action. In typing, we found that different theories made different predictions about the times between keystrokes, which could be evaluated by looking at performance. It is much more difficult to study high-level action plans in this way. This does not mean that we should not study such plans. What is likely to happen is that experimental analyses of activities like typing and the study of errors in action will converge, so that we will eventually be able to place the control of movement, the choice of individual movements and groups of movements, and the structure of our actions, into a single explanatory framework.

SUMMARY

In this chapter we have looked at the hierarchical nature of the construction and organisation of movement programs, at the general schematic form of the representation of movement, and the parameters, such as force and time, that are used to make a schema specific for a particular situation. Although movement is pre-programmed it is important to realise that what we actually produce can be affected by perceptual information received during the movement or the sequence of movements.

Typing and piano-playing are real-life tasks in which complex sequences of aiming movements are produced. These could be produced by hierarchically organised schemas competing to be produced or by building up sequences of responses in advance which reflect the structure of the task. When intricate rhythmic patterns are involved the knowledge of the structure of the music becomes so important that it suggests that we do build up a structured representation of the music, which is then translated into finger movements. These two ways of explaining the control of sequences of movements have also been used to account for everyday action plans and the errors we make in carrying them out. It is hoped that the control of movement and the study of everyday action will converge on a common solution to the problems of how we plan what we do.

Several of the issues raised in this chapter will be found in later ones. In the next chapter we return to movements in considering how we do two things at once, although we move beyond movement itself to consider many other types of activity. Planning output is an important topic in Chapter 7 on the production of speech, and the issue of memory schemas is central to the discussion of memory for events and stories in Chapters 9 and 10.

The treatment of the topics in this chapter is necessarily brief. Further reading can be found in M. M. Smyth and A. M. Wing (Eds.), (1984) *The Psychology of Human Movement*, and a somewhat different point of view, which we have not addressed here, can be found in J. A. S. Kelso (Ed.) (1982), *Human Motor Behavior*.

5 Tapping Your Head and Rubbing Your Stomach: Doing Two Things at Once

At a party, or sitting around with a group of friends, you might be asked to tap your head with one hand and rub your stomach with a circular motion with the other. You would probably find this quite difficult to do: People tend to tap and tap or rub and rub. It is this difficulty which makes the situation amusing. When you tap and tap instead of tapping and rubbing at the same time, one activity has captured some of the control of the other. There are many other situations in which we try to do two things at once, but we do not always find that one task captures the other. Children have been listening to pop music while writing essays for quite some time, and they tend to claim that no interference occurs, whatever their parents may say. You may find that you can talk easily to passengers while driving your car, but that you stop talking when approaching a hazard in the road. In this case there is no capture; rather one task is stopped entirely. If we are asked why these changes occur, most of us have answers that include paying attention, doing things automatically, or having some things in the background while others are more central. Psychologists interested in how people do things at the same time have put forward similar explanations, though usually in more complicated language.

In this chapter we consider what the relationships between two tasks tell us about how our cognitive abilities are organised. We will not be spending the whole chapter dealing with how you tap your head and rub your stomach. Instead, we use that example to discuss some of the properties of the way in which we control our limbs which might prevent us from doing two things at once. We then consider other constraints on what we can do, such as whether we can only make one decision at a time, or whether we have only a limited amount of attention which we can give to any tasks. Of course, the amount of practice and experience you have with an activity can alter your ability to do something else at the same time, and we will be discussing the effects of practice. The other tasks that we consider include typing and talking at the same time, and reading and writing at the same time, so we do move quite a long way from tapping your head and rubbing your stomach. However, the emphasis throughout the chapter will be on doing, and we are not primarily concerned with how much you can think about at one time. That topic will be dealt with in the next chapter.

SIMULTANEOUS ACTIONS WITH TWO HANDS

Can you tap your head and rub your stomach at the same time? Does it make a difference if you use your right hand to tap and the left to circle or the other way round? Why should this difficulty occur? Is there a link between the control of the two hands which puts a basic limitation on our ability to do two things at once? A simpler situation, and one that has been studied in laboratories rather than at parties, is one in which people are asked to move their right and left hands rapidly to different targets. These movements are aiming movements similar to those described in Chapter 4. When a "go" signal was given to subjects in an experiment run by Kelso, Southard, and Goodman (1979), they had to move both hands quickly from a position in front of the body to two targets placed to the sides. One target was further away and smaller than the other so that it was more difficult to hit it accurately. If the movements are made one at a time, it normally takes people longer to move to a small, distant target than to move to one which is close and large (see Chapter 4). However, Kelso et al. found that the two simultaneous movements reached the targets at the same time. The subjects seemed unable to make the movements independently of each other but slowed down easy movements so that they finished at the same time as difficult ones.

When we considered how movements are made (Chapter 4), we suggested that a motor program could have parameters that allowed it to be used for different movements of the same type. Schmidt, Zelaznik, Hawkins, Frank, and Quinn (1979) have suggested that when people make rapid simultaneous movements with two hands, some of the parameters applied to both hands have the same value (the movement time is the same), but other parameters are different (different forces have to be exerted to produce movements of different extent in the same time). So there is a sense in which we can make these two movements at the same time, provided we do not want the movements to be completely different. In these very simple situations people can not time movements of the two hands separately, and this may limit the ability to do two things at a time. However, if we think of co-ordinating two hands then the use of the same timing parameters for each of them would make the co-ordination easier.

Simultaneous Rhythms

If you have ever tried to become a drummer or a pianist, you will have experienced situations in which you have to try to make the two hands move at different times in order to produce interesting rhythms. Making sequences of timed rhythmical movements is very similar to tapping the head and rubbing the stomach and can be studied using very simple tapping tasks. Klapp (1979) asked people to press a key with one hand in synchrony with a light that came on at set intervals. He found that performance deteriorated if subjects also had to tap as quickly as possible with the other hand. However, if the two hands were co-ordinated so that one was tapping twice as fast as the other, there was no deficit. Again, the timing of movements seems to constrain what one can do with two hands at the same time. Yet it is possible for a drummer to produce movements of the two hands that are not synchronised at regular intervals. How does this happen?

Imagine trying to tap consistently (produce a beat) with one hand and then tapping a rhythm (like a repeated melody phase) with the other. Or try to do it using the example in Fig. 5.1. You should set up the beat with one hand (try the left) and then phase in the rhythm with the other. Switch hands and try again. Try tapping the beat with the right hand and the rhythm with the left foot. Did you find some of these combinations more difficult than others?

The rhythm in Fig. 5.1 is one of three that Ibbotson and Morton (1981) asked subjects to tap. They used university students, half of whom were musicians who had been playing an instrument for at least 6 years. They asked each subject to tap the three rhythms in twelve combinations of limbs (all possible pairings of two feet and two hands), so each person had 36 attempts. Ibbotson and Morton found that the musicians did much better overall than the non-musicians, some of whom were unable to tap at all with their feet. In addition, the non-musicians did best when the right hand had to tap the rhythm against a beat from one of the feet or from the left hand, and combinations in which one of the feet took the rhythm and one of the hands took the beat were very difficult.

Three observations can be made from this experiment. The first point concerns the relationship between the control of the right and left hands and of the hands and feet. Differences here were only found for non-musicians and so are related to the second point, which is that musicians found the tasks easier than non-musicians did. The third point concerns a detail about how the experiment was run: Subjects were not

FIG. 5.1   Rhythm and beat to be tapped simultaneously.

allowed many attempts at each condition, so they could not improve with practice.

As the two hands or feet need to be closely co-ordinated for many activities it does make sense for them to be dependent on each other. If we had to time each foot separately when we walk, the activity would be unnecessarily complicated. Co-ordination means the ability to regulate movement activity over many sets of muscles and different limbs. There is other evidence that such co-ordination involves dominance relationships in which one hand is more important than the other, and both hands are more important than the feet. Gunkel (1962) found that when subjects had to move one limb back and forward slowly and move another limb back and forward quickly at the same time the rhythms were not independent. Sometimes the movements were alternated so that when one hand was moving, the other was stationary, and vice versa. In addition, the feet were more likely to act together than the hands, and the right hand was relatively independent of the other limbs when it was used to make fast movements. Ibbotson and Morton's data agree with this. Instead of having independent control of the hands and feet we have different degrees of linkage, or coupling, between the limbs. This makes co-ordination easier in ordinary tasks because normally we are trying to use the limbs together, as we do in walking, and this requires us to move the hands and feet within a common temporal framework. We can do this by specifying timing parameters which are used for more than one limb. In order to do two separate things with two limbs we have to break some of these natural linkages.

Practice and Simultaneous Movements

Ibbotson and Morton (1981) did not allow their subjects to repeat combinations of limbs and rhythms. They argued that with practice subjects might be able to do the task but that it would not be possible to tell how they did it. One problem with practising doing two tasks at once is that it is possible to create a third task which is a combination of the first two, and then to do that one task using two limbs. The rhythm and beat patterns in Fig. 5.1 can be thought of as 6 events which involve tapping with one limb or tapping with two. Did you try to tap the rhythm with your foot and the beat with your right hand and find it totally impossible? Try the same combination again, but instead of trying to do both kinds of tapping separately try this:

Count:	One	Two-and	Three-and	Four
Tap:	Both	Both Foot	Both Foot	Both

("both" means tap with both limbs, and "foot" is foot only.)

If you count the rhythm only and unite the two tasks in one, it should become much easier. You have created a new task that does not require you to control each limb separately.

Doing two things at once is easier if those two things can be combined into a new activity, but does this mean that musicians are better at tapping rhythms because they can produce a new "third" task more easily than non-musicians? To answer this we have to look at complex rhythmic performance in which it is much less likely that the performer can be producing movements with one limb which are temporally linked to those produced with the other. When we look at the performance of good pianists we discover that there are few similarities between movements made with the right hand and movements made with the left.

Piano playing has been extensively investigated by Shaffer (1981), who attached a computer to a grand piano so that the time between the keystrokes and the intensity of every keystroke could be recorded during a performance. We have already mentioned this work in Chapter 4. In one performance a pianist played a study by Chopin in which one hand had to play a group of three notes in the time that the other hand played four. This 3 : 4 pattern occurred twice in each bar for about 60 bars in the music. The two hands had to produce differently timed finger presses and also to move up and down the keyboard at different times. The pianist had no difficulty in moving her hands across the keyboard at different times and she could produce more force in one hand independently of the other. In addition, she played three against four very fluently and allowed tempo variation, or rubato, in each hand separately. That is, she played different rhythms at the same time and allowed variation on the rhythm to occur in one hand which was not occurring in the other.

The pianist in Shaffer's study was able to move her hands in a way in which non-pianists in laboratory experiments cannot do. She appears to have independent control over both hands. However, this independence is produced within a framework for doing one task, playing one piece of music. To produce more force in one hand independently of the other, force has to be controlled separately for the two hands, but the relative force between the hands is part of an overall framework for what the music should sound like. The three-against-four rhythm produced by the two hands requires differently timed movements, yet they have to take their timing from one internal timekeeper, or clock, otherwise the correct overall rhythm would not appear. We can think of the central timekeeper being used to produce equal beats for each bar but these bar intervals have to be divided into three for one hand and four for the other. This creates a hierarchical structure in which timing the intervals and producing the movement control parameters are separate stages.

The skilled pianist can de-couple or unlink the more natural timing patterns used to produce co-ordinated movements in everyday life and this is an important part of the development of fine control of the hands. Marcel Marceau, the great mime, has extremely expressive hands. They can create walls, or butterflies, or convey emotion. One component of their expressiveness is Marceau's ability to move any finger forwards and backwards independently of all the others. Most of us find that if we try to move one finger the others move too—we cannot isolate our fingers.

There are many ways in which practice affects the organisation of our activities and we will deal with more of them in the later sections of this chapter. However, we can now think of the creation of new structures that give a tighter coupling of limbs than is normal and we can also think of breaking down the normal links and creating smaller and more specialised units. Both of these developments will have considerable effects on our ability to do two things at once.

PERCEPTION, DECISION, AND ACTION

In the previous section we considered some of the motor linkages that might make it difficult to do two things at the same time. However, tapping your head and rubbing your stomach, or even playing the piano or the drums, may not be the examples that come to mind when you think about doing two things at once. Most of us aren't too worried about chewing gum and walking at the same time, and we do consider, perfectly sensibly, that we can have a conversation about politics while driving home in the car. The latter activities are going on over the same section of the day; one of them seems to have a larger motor, or perceptual-motor, component than the other which is concerned with the organisation of an argument and the production of speech. There are many things we "do" which have a considerable component that is not directly apparent in our actions. You say "Shut up, I'm thinking" to a chattering friend because you are "doing" something that does not have a very large action component. We will return to the issue of what "doing" means in a later section, but first we will consider the meaning of "at once." What are you doing when you drive and talk at the same time?

Driving and talking may go on over the same extended period but it is possible that while you are thinking about what to say next you are not doing much driving. After all, there are many occasions when driving consists of little more than making occasional adjustments to a steering-wheel and occasional movements of one foot. If you see an obstruction ahead in the road you will have to do more driving-related actions and it is likely that your contribution to the conversation would stop. Is this because you don't actually drive and talk at the same time but alternate the two? Or is it because you have a certain amount of capacity for doing things, which gets filled up if one of them is difficult?

Probing Cognitive Tasks

One way to look at this problem is to ask someone to carry out one task and then to "probe" them by asking them to respond to something else while carrying on the first task. The diagram in Fig. 5.2 shows the structure of an experiment designed by Posner and Boies (1971) to investigate this issue. The subjects had to watch a screen on which two letters were presented, with a one-second delay between the two. They had to press one of two keys with the index finger of the right hand if the letters were the same and the other key with the middle finger of the right hand if the letters were different, and they had to respond as quickly as possible. This first or primary task required the subjects to recognise a letter, hold it in memory, recognise another, compare them, decide if they were the same or different and then decide which button to push and to move the correct finger. The most difficult part of the task is in the decision-making stage, although to an outsider none of the task looks very difficult. The secondary task was to press another key with the index finger of the left hand in response to a brief auditory tone which could occur at any time. Posner and Boies found that the time it took subjects to respond to the auditory probe varied depending on what they were doing in the other task. If the tone was presented just before, or at the same time as, the second letter, there was an increase in the time it took the subjects to respond to the tone. This suggested that there were times when it was difficult to do two things at once and times when it was easy. If the tone appeared during an easy part

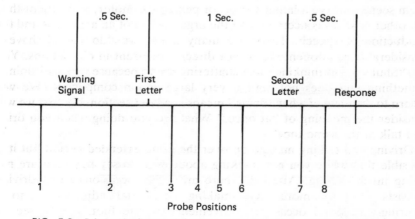

FIG. 5.2 Schematic diagram of a sequence of events in a letter-matching task used by Posner and Boies (1971), in which a series of auditory probes are placed at each of the indicated probe positions. From Posner, M. 1. (1973). *Cognition: An Introduction*. Glenview 111.: Scott Foresman and Co. Copyright 1973 Scott Foresman and Company and reprinted with permission.

of the first task there was no increase in the time to respond to it, but if it appeared when the first task was difficult then it was not possible to start responding to the tone until the difficulty had been dealt with, so the reaction time was longer. The Posner and Boies study has been covered here at some length because it introduced an important method for attempting to find out what was going on and when. However, later studies have altered the method slightly and produced different results. These changes in method result from changes in the theory of how we do two things at once, so we will deal with them later in the chapter. First we consider the general principles involved in the conclusion drawn by Posner and Boies.

The Psychological Refractory Period

Posner and Boies' result suggested that people could only cope with a certain amount of decision making or complexity at one time, and if something else came along to be dealt with it had to wait. Such a proposal had been put forward by Craik (1948), who thought that there might be a limit on what people could do because there was a single "computing" process that dealt with incoming information one step at a time. If a second input arrived while the first was being processed it would have to wait, so there would be an increased reaction due to the "psychological refractory period." There have been many experiments on the refractory period. In most of them the task is to respond to one signal as quickly as possible and then to respond to a second signal. The typical finding is that if the second

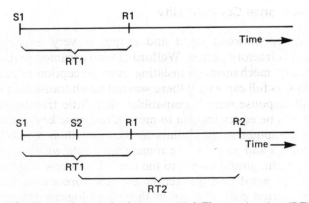

FIG. 5.3 The psychological refractory period. The reaction time (RT) to a second stimulus (S2) is increased by the interval between the second stimulus (S2) and the first response (R1).

signal occurs before the response to the first has been made then the reaction time to the second is lengthened by the interval between that signal and the response to the earlier one (see Fig. 5.3).

Legge and Barber (1976) have described this result as being a bit like a doctor's waiting room. If it takes five minutes for a consultation with the doctor then you will emerge after five minutes if there is no one before you. But if someone else goes in to see the doctor just as you arrive then you have to add their five minutes to yours. You will be delayed by the length of time between your arrival and the end of the previous patient's consultation. In the same way, the response to the second signal cannot be prepared until the first one has been completed. In many experiments in the 1950s and 1960s it was found that the delay in the second response time was not influenced by practice, that the delay occurred when one signal was visual and the other auditory and when the two movements were made with different hands. It was concluded that there was some central decision-making channel, which was limited in that it could only make one decision at a time (Welford, 1968).

The decision that was thought to occupy the central channel was of a specific type. An increase in reaction time did not occur if a response to the first signal was being made and a new instruction required that the response should be speeded up (Vince & Welford, 1967). That is, the pattern of action already being planned simply had to be intensified, not changed. The kind of decision that did increase the second reaction time, and so limited people doing two things at once, was one which initiated a fresh pattern of action or changed the relationship between input and output.

Stimulus–response Compatibility

The relationship between input and output is very important for the psychological refractory period. Welford (1968) assumed that the decision or "translation" mechanism (translating from perception to action) would be used below its full capacity if there was not much translation to do. If the stimulus and response were "compatible" then little translation would be required. It will be easier for you to move a response key to the right if an arrow on a computer screen points to the right than it will if the word *elephant* appears and you have to remember a rule which says "elephant means to the right, giraffe means to the left." The arrow and the action are compatible, the word and the action are not. Greenwald and Shulman (1973) investigated compatibility in the psychological refractory period. When the first response was to move a switch in the direction of an arrow and the second was to say "one" when the word "one" was heard, there was no refractory period at all. Subjects were able to do these two things at exactly the same time. However, if the second task required a translation from stimulus to response (hear "A" and say "one") then a longer reaction time appeared. It was therefore not just the change of response from key pressing to talking that made the improvement in compatible conditions, but the relationships between input and output.

However, just making the relationship between input and output more direct does not necessarily get rid of refractoriness. It is much easier to move a finger which has just been touched than it is to move a finger in response to an instruction or because a light has come on (Leonard, 1959), yet Brebner (1977) found refractoriness when he used touch stimuli on the fingers of the right and left hands. Simple compatibility did not remove the "only one thing at a time" principle when the two responses involved the two hands.

In many of the earlier studies it was thought that using different hands for the two responses was enough to show that the limitations were based on a central waiting period, not on the execution of the movements (Davis, 1956). However, we now know that moving the two hands requires very similar sorts of motor instructions and it is possible that the nature of the response systems involved is causing limitations that are not due to any central waiting period. We used the Posner and Boies (1971) experiment earlier in the chapter to show that there were times when people were able to do a second task and times when they were not, just as you might expect from driving and talking. However, McLeod (1978) altered one aspect of the Posner and Boies task and produced quite different results. He asked his subjects to decide whether two successive letters were the same or different and to press one key for "same" and another for "different." Also, instead of having to use the other hand to respond to an auditory probe (which made a "bip" noise) some subjects were asked to say "bip" when they heard the tone. These subjects showed no interference between the letter matching and responding to the tone, no matter when the tone was presented. The overall limitation on the ability to decide whether two letters are the same or different and to make another response at the same time did not exist if the response systems were separated.

The number of things we can do at one time can be limited by the relationships between our limbs, which makes it difficult to move them totally independently unless we are highly skilled. There are also limitations on the number of decisions we can make at once, but these only occur if the relationship between the input and the output is not a direct one, or if the same response systems are being used for each task. We will refer again to these issues later in the chapter, but first we will consider more fully the idea that there is a general limitation on our ability to do two things at once.

ATTENTION AND CAPACITY

So far in this chapter we have ignored the term "attention" but some readers may think that what happens when we do two tasks is simply that attention has to be shared between the tasks, and there is a limit to attention. This view has been held by many psychologists, some of whom have also shared the ordinary view that sometimes we can do one thing automatically while attending to another. This view of attention is linked to our everyday experience that we can attend to, or be aware of, only a part of the potentially available information from the outside world. This is clearly a perfectly accurate account of our experience, but it may not be a good explanation for what we experience. We started by considering some of the findings when people do two things at once because we want to emphasise that we are not trying to explain what people are aware of, but what they can do. If we use attention to explain our failures to do two things at once, there is a danger that we can ignore response factors altogether, and forget that we are interested in the whole system which links our perception, our thoughts and memories and our actions, not just in perception alone.

Some of those who studied attention in relation to perception argued that there was a bottleneck somewhere in the information processing system because we often only perceive a part of what is available in the world around us (Broadbent, 1958; Deutsch & Deutsch, 1963). There has been considerable dispute over the stage at which the bottleneck might occur, and Welford's view that there is a limit on the number of decisions relating perception to action that can be made at one time is a kind of bottleneck model. Welford accepted that there could be many limitations in the processing system, including early perceptual filters or gates, but he was chiefly concerned with the links between perception and action, and with the way in which these could change over time. Many of the other workers who looked for a bottleneck at some stage in the system did not agree that there could be more than one stage, yet evidence for any one particular stage was not totally convincing as some experiments supported one stage and some supported another.

Treisman and Geffen (1967), for example, asked subjects to listen to words that were played into one ear and to repeat them aloud, while at the same time other words were played into the other ear but were not to be repeated aloud. The task of repeating speech aloud as you hear it is known as "shadowing." In addition to shadowing the message that came in on one ear, subjects were asked to press a button if a particular word target appeared in either ear. The results showed that subjects could push the button when they heard targets in the message they were repeating aloud but that they could not do so very often if the targets were in the message they were not repeating. This result was interpreted to mean that the subjects had filtered or blocked the words they were not repeating so that they were not allowed into awareness, and that this happened before the words were recognised. If you don't know what a word is you can not push a button in response to it. McKay (1973), on the other hand, showed that when people repeated aloud ambiguous sentences like: "They threw stones at the bank yesterday" and at the same time the word "river" was presented on the ear that was not being shadowed, the subjects did not remember hearing the word "river," but they remembered that the sentence was about throwing stones at the river bank, not about throwing stones at the money bank. This experiment suggested that subjects did know what the words on the unshadowed ear meant, even though they could not remember them, so McKay argued that some selection of items which are allowed into awareness must happen after words have been recognised.

One way to deal with this conflicting evidence was to reject the idea of a block in a particular part of the system, which restricts how much we can do. Kahneman (1973) suggested that instead of a particular restricted stage there was a general limit on our ability to do mental work. This can be thought of as a limited supply of power or resources. If all the domestic ovens linked to the natural gas system in one area are turned on at the same time, the gas pressure goes down. This happens regularly at Christmas when everyone tries to cook a twenty-two pound turkey at the same time as everyone else. The gas supply is normally sufficient to meet the demand, but if the demand is increased then either everyone's supply is decreased or there are selective changes so that high-priority users get more gas than others. Kahneman's theory of a limited amount of mental power may be compared to this. If two things have to be done at once then performance will deteriorate on one or both when the two together go over the limit for mental power. If they don't, there is no deficit. If one task is more important then it can be given more power or resource so that performance in that task stays high, whatever happens in the other.

Most of Kahneman's account of how we do things at once was concerned with general resources. However, he also realised that there were times when tasks used the same particular resource, that is, they interfered with each other because they used the same structures. As we have already seen, tasks that use the same kinds of response may interfere whereas those that use different responses do not. Kahneman proposed that there would be some interference when two tasks were performed together, even if they did not share any perceptual or response mechanisms, so that even if there were no structural interference there would be a general lowering of performance.

Problems with Attention and Capacity

How can we tell whether there is a general limit to our processing capacity or not? If two tasks use less than the total capacity they can be done at the same time, but unfortunately the only way that we could know that they did use less than the total capacity would be to see if they could be done at the same time (Allport, 1980). Although it is possible to determine whether two tasks interfere or not, it is very difficult to test the basic notion that there is a limit to overall resources (Navon, 1984). In addition, if we have both specific and general resources, how do we tell whether one task is interfering with another because it uses general capacity or because it uses a specific resource? The Posner and Boies (1971) result was taken by Kahneman to support the notion of general limitations on capacity. When subjects were deciding whether two letters were the same or different, they did not have any spare resource for the response to the probe task, so reaction time increased. When McLeod's subjects had to say "bip" when they heard a tone there was no interference, but it is not clear whether we should say that the two tasks no longer required the same central resource or that they now use different structural resources. There is a limitation, but we do not know why it occurs, and we cannot use that limitation as evidence for a general limitation on mental capacity.

One prediction made by general resource theory is that increasing the difficulty of one task should make it harder to carry out two tasks simultaneously because there is more strain on the general resource. Allport, Antonis, and Reynolds (1972) asked pianists to sight-read music they had never seen before, and at the same time to shadow prose that they heard over headphones. Subjects thought that the sight-reading task was quite difficult, and shadowing someone else speaking at 150 words a minute is also difficult. Yet after a single thirty-minute practice session subjects were able to play the piano and shadow aloud, and even to understand some of the content of the passage they were repeating. At first there was some tendency for the rhythm of the music to appear in the subjects' speech, but this did not last. When the difficulty of the sight-reading task was altered in the second practice session there was no change in shadowing. In this situation difficulty did not lead to interference.

As you might expect, subjects sometimes made mistakes in the sight reading. When this happened the performance of both tasks was interrupted. This does not necessarily mean that correcting an error requires more resources and that there is an overall limit on capacity. When an error occurs, analysis of it and choosing and implementing a response to correct it may require different processes from those already in use in the task. Checking for and correcting errors could be a specialised type of processing which both tasks have to use, so the limitation is specific to what is actually being done at the time. It is probably more useful to consider the circumstances in which one task interferes with another and when it does not, than to assume that there is an overall non-specific limitation.

Disconnecting Perception and Action

If specific patterns of interaction and interference are more useful than notions of general limitations then we should be able to return to the experiments by Treisman and Geffen (1967) and McKay (1973) and consider why interference has occurred in one case but not in the other. To do this we first have to analyse the tasks to see how they differ. In Treisman and Geffen's experiment subjects had to shadow (repeat aloud) a message that they heard on one ear while another message was played to the other ear. They also had to push a button when they heard a target word, whether it came up on the shadowed ear or the non-shadowed ear. When two different streams of words are arriving in the two ears and only one stream is repeated, both inputs are closely linked to the output, but one message has to be cut off from the output system while the other is allowed access to it. The subject has to decouple one link between input and output, while retaining another. Allport (1980) argues that it is this competition for the output which makes selective shadowing so difficult and that decoupling the speech input from vocal output also decouples that input from other outputs. In McKay's experiment, on the other hand, no response to the words on the unshadowed ear is required, but the change in meaning is shown up in a memory test. Overall, the suggestion is that people cannot physically produce two streams of speech simultaneously, so when they are hearing two streams they have to distinguish between them and allow one to have access to speech production, and prevent the other from doing so.

McLeod and Posner (1984) have suggested that shadowing is a special activity because there is a "privileged loop" in the cognitive system between what a word sounds like and how to say it. They asked subjects to carry out a letter-matching task and to respond to a probe that appeared during it, just as Posner and Boies had done in 1971 and McLeod in 1978. As can be seen from Table 5.1 they used slightly different versions of both tasks. The first combination of letter-matching and probe tasks in Table 5.1 is the same as that used by McLeod (1977). Subjects decide whether the letters are the same or different and make a movement response. During the matching task they hear an auditory probe (a spoken word, "up" or "down") and they respond by saying the same word. In this

TABLE 5.1

Combinations of Letter-matching and Probe Tasks Used by
McLeod and Posner (1984)

	Matching Task	*Probe Task*
Combination 1	Visual input	Auditory input
	Movement output	Vocal output
Combination 2	Visual input	Auditory input
	Vocal output	Movement output

situation there is no interference. In the second combination subjects match the two letters and say either "same" or "different." The auditory probe is also a word ("up" or "down") and the response is to move a switch in the appropriate direction. In this case interference between the two tasks does occur, although the input systems are different and the output systems are different. However, the link between hearing a word and saying it has been broken. Subjects hear one word ("up") and at around the same time they are about to say another word ("same"). The link between hearing one word and saying another one is so strong that having to say a different word leads to an increase in reaction time. This result extends our earlier conclusion that it is important not to use the same response system if you are trying to do two things at once. It is also important to consider the relationship between the input and the response for both tasks.

Typing and Talking

The tasks we have been considering give us some insight into how we do two things at once but they are quite far removed from ordinary experience. We can, however, think of the real-life skill of typing as being a situation in which people read words and make the appropriate movements (copy typing), or hear words and make the appropriate movements (audio typing). Do you think that a typist could read aloud while audio typing or shadow words while copy typing? In both cases there are two verbal tasks to be carried out at the same time and a string of vocal responses is combined with a string of manual responses, so it might seem that typists should be equally good or bad at both combinations. However, Shaffer (1975) found that typists could copy type and shadow, although there was some decrement in performance, but they could not audio type and read aloud. McLeod and Posner's results on the simple task can help us to understand the performance on the more complex ones. If in audio typing subjects hear one stream of words while they speak another, they have to disconnect the tendency to speak the words they hear, which leads to interference and increased difficulty. On the other hand, when copy typing and shadowing, the words that are heard have an easy route to speech.

WHEN ARE TWO TASKS INDEPENDENT?

When we say that two tasks are carried on independently we could mean that changes to one do not affect the performance in the other, and this is what Allport, Antonis, and Reynolds (1972) found when they varied task difficulty. It is possible, however, that although tasks are independent there is a general decrement in performance when they are combined. This has been shown in several laboratory studies. Peterson (1969) found that subjects could read letters aloud and add digits that were presented auditorily at the same time, and that changing the difficulty of one did not change the performance on the other. Both tasks were performed less well together than they were separately. McLeod (1977) asked subjects to combine a continuous tracking task with responding to a probe. In the tracking task subjects had to watch a light spot on a computer screen. The spot tended to drift away from its centre position on the screen and subjects had to move a lever to adjust its position and keep it in the centre. This is a continuous task which requires lots of small movements to be made in response to visual input. In the second task subjects had to say "high" or "low" when they heard a high or low tone. McLeod looked very closely at the times at which movements were made in the tracking task and found that tracking movements were just as likely to occur at the same time as a probe response as they were to occur at any other time. That is, the times at which events occurred in the two tasks were totally independent. Nevertheless, there was a slight overall drop in accuracy in the tracking task when the subjects knew that a probe task would also be present.

These results make it clear that "interference" between two tasks can mean more than one thing. We can consider overall level of performance on two tasks and look at whether they are done less well when combined than alone. We can alter the difficulty of each task and look at whether this affects performance on the other task. We can look at the time at which events occur in one task and see if there are events in the other that are related in time. Each approach may give us a different answer if we simply ask "Is there interference?" In order to understand the organisation of the processes involved we need to look at all of these questions and the pattern of results they produce. The evidence we have reviewed suggests, rather oddly, that it is possible to do two tasks independently, in that events and changes on one do not affect the other, yet there is still some decrement in overall performance when both are performed at once. Indeed, Shallice, McLeod, and Lewis (1985) have gone so far as to suggest that if the performance decrement is small (around 10 per cent) when tasks are combined, then the tasks are using different structures.

There are several ways in which we can explain this decrement. If the detection of error is separate from the execution of each task, then two tasks may compete for this function when they do not interact in any other way. The person doing two things at once has to keep the goals of the two tasks active, and this may be more difficult than keeping one goal active, or there may be more uncertainty about which stimulus and response links are to be used, which will also lead to slightly poorer performance (Duncan 1980). Rather than use Kahneman's (1973) explanation that there is an overall general limit on what we can do, we find that tasks may be carried out independently, yet have secondary aspects that can affect each other (Navon, 1984).

PRACTICE AND AUTOMATICITY

In the experiment of Allport, Antonis, and Reynolds (1972), subjects could play the piano and shadow prose but only one subject showed no decrement in her comprehension of the passage being shadowed. This subject was the most skilled pianist in the experiment and her comprehension performance while sight reading was as good as other people's when they only listened to the passage. The level of skill in sight reading reflects the amount of practice the subject has had, and these two factors are an important determinant of when things can and can not be done at the same time.

Earlier in the chapter we discussed the ways in which practice altered movement control and allowed creation of new linkages in the motor system. Practice also affects the perceptual system and the development of links between perception and action. In our account of the refractory period we mentioned that practice did not decrease the tendency for a second response to have to wait for the first to be finished. This was the established view put forward by Welford in 1968. However, practice in this context did not link particular stimuli to particular responses, but was practice on repeated presentation of different stimuli and responses (Hick, 1948). Links between input and output were not improved, so independence could not develop.

There are many occasions when it is very difficult for people to stop a response being produced, even when they try. Many of our language processes are so well practised that we cannot stop ourselves from using them even if we don't need to. A good example of this is the Stroop task, in which two kinds of information are present in one stimulus pattern. In a well-known version of the task a colour name (*red*) is written in coloured ink (*green*). The task is to name the colour of the ink. This takes longer to do than it would if the written word was also the name of a colour (Stroop, 1935). The increased time to respond suggests that it is very difficult to stop the word being read aloud so that the colour of the ink can be named. This effect can also be found when line drawings of objects have a name written inside them (Rayner & Posnansky, 1978), or when the spoken words "high" and "low" are said in either a high- or a low-pitched voice and the task is to name the pitch of the voice (Cohen & Martin, 1975). In tasks like this, one component has to be prevented from controlling output with which it has very strong links.

Schneider and Shiffrin (1977) and Shiffrin and Schneider (1977) carried out an extensive investigation of the role of practice in the development of automaticity by asking subjects to search for target letters among other letters in briefly presented displays. The targets were consonants from the first half of the alphabet and the background items were consonants from the second half. Subjects simply had to detect whether a target was present or not. Performance in this task was not very good at the beginning of practice. Subjects made many mistakes and they responded quite slowly. After 1500 trials performance was much more accurate than it had been initially and the reaction times to find a target on any trial decreased. At this point the number of targets that had to be searched for at the same time did not affect the reaction time, nor did the number of non-targets that had to be searched. Subjects were able to respond to targets without having to consider all the other alternatives. In a second phase of the experiment Schneider and Shiffrin reversed the target and the non-target items. Now subjects had to search for consonants from the second half of the alphabet in a background of consonants from the first half. For the first 600 trials in this phase of the experiment performance was worse than it had been at the beginning of the experiment, and after 2100 trials it was still not as good as it had been at the end of the first phase.

This experiment created a kind of Stroop effect in which the first set of targets were identified even though they were no longer targets and subjects could not stop this happening. Just as in the Stroop task, responses to the first set of targets had to be inhibited, or actually occurred as errors. This effect of practice only occurred if the subjects practised with the same target set in the first phase of the experiment. If the target and non-target sets were changed at every trial the discrimination of target from background had to be different on each trial. Shiffrin, Dumais, and Schneider (1981) showed that subjects could detect targets they had seen before if the background was changed and they could detect new targets if the background remained the same. That is, what they had learned to do was to detect targets and to ignore irrelevant items.

Shiffrin and Schneider's results have been used to suggest that practice leads to a completely different kind of processing. After extensive practice, processing is said to become "automatic." This is a term we use in everyday accounts of our activities so it has some plausibility as a description of changes with practice. Most of us can walk and chew gum at the same time because we do them "automatically." However, if two of these well-practised search tasks are combined there are small but consistent deficits (Schneider and Fisk, 1982; Hoffman, Nelson, & Houek, 1983), just as there were in the independent tasks we discussed earlier. This could mean that we could walk more efficiently if we didn't chew gum, or it could mean that both "independent" and "automatic" refer to particular patterns of non-interference, rather than a different kind of processing.

What does it mean to say that responding to the items in a search task is automatic? Shiffrin, Dumais, and Schneider (1981) have put forward two rules for automatic processing. One is that an automatic process should not reduce the capacity for doing other tasks, and the other is that automatic processes are unstoppable, or mandatory, so that they cannot be influenced by what you intend to do. The first rule is a part of general limited capacity or resource theory that we discussed earlier, and the second follows from tasks like the Stroop and practised search.

The criteria for automaticity proposed by Shiffrin et al. have been widely accepted and sometimes extended (Jonides, Naveh-Benjamin, & Palmer, 1985), but there are several problems with their use. One is that practice could build up strong relationships between patterns of input and the correct output, without the process becoming mandatory or compulsory. A copy-typist is not compelled to type the letter *t* every time *t* appears, but if that typist were transferred to a keyboard with a new layout it is very likely that the old response would sometimes appear. The mandatory, or compulsory, nature of the processing of some information is an important topic, particularly for perception and language. Fodor (1983), for example, argues that we cannot help hearing words in a language we know as words, even if we are trying to do something else like respond to the sounds which make them up. Low-level detection of the features of objects may also be automatic in this sense (Treisman & Gelade, 1980). However, the explanation of how people do two tasks at once needs a careful account of what it is that changes with practice.

Cheng (1985) has argued that there are changes in the way people organise tasks as they learn them, which makes them simpler, but this does not mean that they are automatic. She has used a simple analogy to make this point. If you are asked to add ten twos you could do it by adding two to two, getting four, then adding two and getting six, then another two to get eight, and so on. It would take you some time do this in your head, and you might forget how many twos you had added. Of course, if you have a little arithmetical knowledge you may know that adding ten twos is equivalent to multiplying two by ten, you have the answer to the multiplication stored in memory, so you can produce the correct answer in just one step. You will now be able to produce the correct answer very quickly, without any effort and it would seem that you have added ten twos "automatically." However, what has changed is not the speed at which you carry out the same operations, but the very operations themselves.

Cheng argues that the results in the Shiffrin and Schneider studies are due to category strategies that enable subjects to restructure the task. For example, in some experiments subjects could be using features of the stimuli to distinguish between the target items, as a group, and the background items, as a group, rather than identifying each item separately. Instead of doing the same kind of searching but in a different way, subjects are actually doing something different. "Automatic" and "without awareness" could mean that there is a difference in the kind of processing being carried out.

Reading and Writing at the Same Time

You may feel that your everyday assumption that you do some things automatically is being reduced from whole tasks to little parts of tasks, and that these are difficult to put together into reading, or driving a car. The tendency to break tasks down has not always been found in research in this area. In the late 1800s two researchers at Harvard trained themselves to read stories while writing to dictation and noted how they felt the tasks were carried out (Solomons & Stein, 1896). They reported that the writing was performed without awareness while they carried on being aware of the material they were reading. So, automaticity for them was the subjective experience of lack of awareness of carrying out the task. However, subjects' awareness of one of two tasks rather than the other is not a very reliable way of establishing how tasks are being performed, as Spelke, Hirst, and Neisser (1976) found when they trained two subjects to write dictated words while they read stories. They found that after 20 weeks of practice the subjects could comprehend the stories and write the words and could even write down the name of the category to which a word belonged rather than the word itself. However, the subjects sometimes said that they thought clearly about a word before they wrote it and at other times they said that they were unaware of writing. It is for this reason that psychologists have devised many of the measures of performance that we have discussed throughout this chapter, rather than depending on what performance felt like to subjects.

Spelke, Hirst, and Neisser argued that whereas writing down a word without understanding it could be called automatic, making sense of the world is not a routine activity. Comprehension and understanding involve so much complex processing that they should never be considered to be automatic. This position was extended in a later study in which Hirst, Spelke, Reaves, Cahavack, and Neisser (1980) also asked subjects to practise reading while writing to dictation. The dictation was not of single words but of short sentences. After extensive practice their subjects could write the short sentences while reading aloud, they could also answer complex comprehension questions about the passage they had read while copying, and they recognised as familiar sentences that were close in meaning to the ones they had copied, so they must have understood the meaning of the copied sentences. This seemed to mean that they were doing two comprehension tasks at the same time.

It is possible to argue that subjects who can read and write at the same time are really alternating very quickly between the two tasks. In normal conversation we can follow what is being said even if we do not hear every word because language is often redundant, and training might help subjects to exploit this redundancy more efficiently. Hirst et al. investigated this by training some subjects to read stories while they wrote dictation, but training other subjects to read encyclopaedia articles, which are much less redundant than stories. After subjects became skilled at reading and writing at the same time with one kind of reading material they were switched to reading with the other. Hirst et al. found that subjects were just as good at reading, writing, and comprehending with new material as they were with old. They concluded that their subjects were not alternating between the two tasks, and they were not doing one automatically in the sense of having no understanding of it, but rather they had restructured the task by learning new stimulus patterns and new patterns of action.

Although Hirst et al. attempted to use redundancy to show that subjects were not alternating between tasks, it is not really possible to say exactly what was going on. Subjects were tested for comprehension after they had finished reading, and there was no way in which the times at which words were presented to eye and ear could be controlled. It is possible that probing the tasks while they were being carried out would give us more information about the restructuring that is occurring but this would break up the naturalness of the tasks. Although we may have some reservations about exactly what is going on in these tasks, the evidence suggests that new kinds of skill in reading and writing do not involve carrying out the same processes in a different way, but rather that the processes themselves are different ones.

PRACTICE, KNOWLEDGE, AND SKILL

The changes that occur with practice are the development of skill, and there are many kinds of skill as well as many changes with practice. Skill can be perceptual and perceptual-motor—that is, we can become better at selecting relevant information from the world, we have stronger links between patterns of input and output, and we can control the movements of our limbs in a different way. However, skill can also involve changes in memory, and in the ability to use improved memory in problem-solving tasks like playing chess. Simon and Gilmartin (1973) have calculated that an expert chess player has 50,000 units of knowledge of positions in chess, which have been developed over years of practice. These units are organisations of chess pieces rather than the individual pieces themselves and they enable experts to recognise chess positions and to produce responses without having to go through all the possible options open to them. This means that acquiring new rules that organise incoming information in a different way may be just as important as building stronger links between input and output patterns which we already know. We discuss the reorganisation of knowledge further in the next chapter.

Is it possible that with increased practice and skill we can do as many things as we like at the same time? The answer is probably "no." Very few of us want to spend the time and effort necessary to develop independent systems for running two or more tasks, and even if we did there are some situations in which practice may not get rid of interference because the amount of practice that has already occurred with one combination of input and output is so great that the links cannot be broken. Typists who cannot audiotype and speak at the same time have spent many years building up the relationship between the sound of words and the production of them. They would probably have to spend many more years practising audiotyping and speaking together before we could say whether independence was possible or not. For a normal level of skill in two tasks we can predict that interference will occur if the two tasks involve the same kind of operations or response processes, or if the input from one already has links to the output of another. We also know that without high levels of skill two movements will not be independent if they have timing or rhythmic components in common or if they make use of the two hands separately. Most of us can talk and make other movements at the same time but we cannot read a book and talk about something else at the same time and we cannot correct novel errors in one task while carrying on with another.

SUMMARY

In this chapter we have considered some of the constraints on our abilities to do two tasks at once. Some of the most basic limitations are imposed by the motor system, which is organised so that timing patterns between the limbs are co-ordinated, although these patterns can be altered with practice. Making a response to a stimulus involves making a decision and there may be a delay in doing one task if another is not finished. However, this can be reduced if the stimulus and response are compatible, or if different response systems are used for the two tasks. A limit on decision making between perception and action would be a general limitation on what we can do, similar in some ways to the concept of a limited amount of attention that we can allocate to tasks. Explanations for attentional limitations can also be given in terms of specific problems, particularly when well-established links between perception and action have to be broken. It is not easy to say what it means for tasks to be independent, and this is also true of the use of the term "automatic." Automaticity is thought to develop with extended practice on a task. However, increased speed and efficiency in processing can result from reorganisation of the tasks, as well as the strengthening of the perception–action links. We continue this discussion in Chapter 6 when we discuss the effects of practice on working memory.

Further reading on the links between perception and action can be found in two chapters by Allport in G. Claxton (Ed.) (1980), *Cognitive Psychology: New Directions*. Ulric Neisser's (1976) book *Cognition and Reality* presents a well-written but polemical argument that there is no limit at all on what we can do. Modern accounts of attention, mostly concerned with selectivity in perception, can be found in M. I. Posner and O. S. M. Marin (Eds.) (1985), *Attention and Performance XI*.

6 Doing Mental Arithmetic: Holding Information and Operations for a Short Time

The experience of performing some kind of mental arithmetic is a common one, even if calculators are making it less necessary. If you want to decide whether a tube of toothpaste that costs 33 pence for 50 ml is better value than a tube that costs 79 pence for 125 ml, you could try to find the equivalent cost for 25 ml in each tube. If you want to buy enough paint for the walls and ceiling of a room that measures 7 feet 11 inches from floor to ceiling and has floor dimensions of 20 feet by 14 feet, the calculation becomes more complicated. It says on the can that one litre of paint will cover about 14 square metres. You try to work out how much paint you need. "That's a 20 by 14 ceiling, making 280 square feet . . . 7 feet 11 inches . . . call that 8 feet . . . 20 by 8 that's 160, and 14 by 8, that's . . . 132, no 112 . . . add to . . ." you've forgotten! If you turn to a shop assistant however, the answer could be different: "20, 14, 8 . . . say, 8 or 9 hundred square feet . . . 2 coats . . . three $2\frac{1}{2}$ litre cans should do it." This answer is approximate but it is about right. The shop assistant probably does not have a better memory for numbers than you have, so perhaps experience can help with these calculations. The ordinary customer gets lost in the complexities of partial results, trying to remember the general plan and where the plan has go to. Even with pencil and paper, errors can still occur when we try to keep a general plan in the head while recording parts of the results on paper.

Now try the simpler example of adding 325 to 146 in your head. If you had a piece of paper you could set one number above the other, start at the right, add 6 to 5, write 1 in that column, carry one, add 1 to 2 to 4, write 7 in that column, and so on. If you do it in your head your probably find that you break up the sum in exactly the same way and you may create an image of the numbers written as they would be set out on a piece of paper. As long as you remember the answer to each sub-component, remember where you are in the calculation, and remember the bits of the answer as you go along, the whole answer will be produced correctly. Errors can occur if the answers to parts of the problem (e.g. $7 \times 9 = 63$) are not retrieved correctly, if you cannot break up the problem into the correct or most useful pieces, if you cannot keep your place in the problem, and if you cannot hold the list of digits which you have to speak to give the answer.

Two of the reasons for error given above relate to knowledge held in long-term memory (how to break up sums and the knowledge that 7×9 is 63), and two relate to immediate memory or working memory (keeping place and holding the list of digits). We discuss the relationship between knowledge held in long-term memory and the ability to use immediate memory later in the chapter, but first we consider some of the limitations on immediate memory, that is, on our ability to hold information and use it to solve problems.

The limitations of immediate memory are apparent in a wide variety of experiences, not just in mental arithmetic. You have just checked your shopping list of four items. While considering where the first item should be purchased, one or two of the items are forgotten and the list has to be consulted again. Someone tells you a new telephone number. You are securely repeating it to yourself and dialling the number, when someone asks who you are 'phoning, and some of the digits seem to disappear. Searching for the right word in a sentence you are constructing as you speak to a group, you forget precisely what it was you were going to say. Many of the tasks discussed in other chapters of this book could be used to demonstrate our capacities and limitations in immediate processing, but they vary considerably in the balance of activities involved. In reading a book, for example, we can pace the input to match our understanding and desired level of analysis. Witnessing an unanticipated event in the street is very different; information about people, faces, dress, actions, voices, and who-said-what flows thick and fast and we cannot deal with all of it. (The role of memory in these activities is discussed in Chapters 9 and 10.)

Mental arithmetic illustrates a particular mix of the processes involved in many other activities, but it has special features of interest to us at this stage. The inputs to the task are well defined. The procedures for doing arithmetic are usually well understood and at least some of the things we do in our head probably owe much to the way in which we have been taught to do sums. The focus of the activity is to achieve a result here and now by immediate processing rather than to remember something for ever. But we can not do any very intelligent immediate processing, like mental arithmetic, unless we have some knowledge of numbers stored away somewhere. First then, we sketch just a small fraction of the evidence and ideas that led researchers to make a distinction between a short-term memory store and a long-term memory store.

SOME BASIC PHENOMENA

Suppose you were asked to add 73,441,958 to 62,597,113 in your head; it is very doubtful that you would be able to hang on to more than about one-third of these digits, let alone to start adding them up. Like the telephone example given earlier, there seems to be a basic limitation on how many items we can hold. The experience of losing information when there is rather too much of it, or when it arrives too quickly, is so common that we should not be surprised that there has been a stream of laboratory studies since the turn of the century which have investigated how many items can be held for short periods.

Immediate memory for digits, letters of the alphabet, and words, was investigated extensively in Wundt's laboratory at Leipzig at the end of the nineteenth century. If you were to hear a string of letters read to you just once at a rate of 2 letters per second, how many items would you recall? Wundt (1905), like many later workers, found the number of items that could be recalled in the correct order, the *span* of immediate memory, to be about 6 "simple impressions." The repeated finding in a variety of studies that people could recall between 5 and 9 items whether an item was a letter, or a digit, or a word led Miller (1956) to argue that the span of immediate memory was, typically, 7 plus or minus 2. We need to clarify what units are implied by "7 plus or minus 2." We could say "items" again, but Miller called them "chunks." Obviously, if you can only remember 5 or 6 letters you will have difficulty with a string of 25 letters, but if they are organised into words so that you have to recall a sequence like "table, camel, paper, plate, grape," then the words become the items. If the words form short and simple sentences, then sentences might become the items. The term "chunk" acknowledges that definition of the units of information depends on what the subjects in our experiments make of the information. This interaction between our ability to hold information in immediate memory and what it means to us will be referred to again, but for the present we shall assume that we are dealing with relatively independent items.

Another sighting of our limited capacity is given when subjects are asked to read or listen to word-lists of various lengths and then to recall as many of the words as possible, but in any order. This style of experiment is often referred to as "list learning with free recall." The responses produced in immediate free recall are examined for their correctness, and, when correct, for their position in the list as originally presented. Using groups of subjects and several different lists of words, the relationship between the probability of correctly recalling a word and its serial position—1st, 2nd, 3rd, and so on—in the original list can be examined. Murdock (1962) carried out systematic studies of this type in which he varied list length and the rate of delivery of the words. Figure 6.1 shows his principal findings.

For all list lengths the first few items presented are well remembered but decreasingly so with serial position. This has been called the *primacy effect*. It is as though items presented early in the list benefit from primacy in processing; they suffer less competition for time and space in immediate memory from other items. The last few items show an increasingly higher

CA-E*

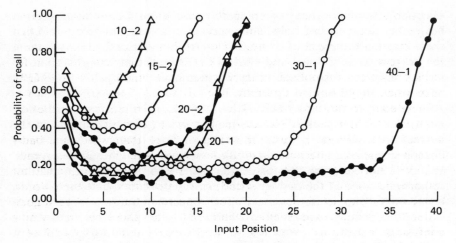

FIG. 6.1   Serial position curves for different list lengths (10, 15, 20, 30, and 40 words) and presentation times (1 or 2 seconds per word). Based on Murdock (1962).

success rate with serial position. This is termed the *recency effect*. Items that have most recently entered immediate memory are most readily recalled, at least by subjects who have had a little practice at the task. For items intermediate in the presentation order, there is low plateau of recall success, as though each item has only a small chance of being processed to sufficient depth for it to be recalled. The primacy effect is enhanced and the middle-order plateau is raised somewhat when the words are presented at a slower rate (compare the curve for 20–1 with that for 20–2), again suggesting that some kind of limitation in the capacity for processing is a key factor.

A great deal of attention has been given to the differences in depth or kinds of processing during list learning that might account for the primacy and recency effects. Many studies have shown that delaying the moment for recall, or requiring the subject to engage in other mental activities before recall, can markedly reduce recall of the last few items, yet a primacy effect persists.

This somewhat informal account has assumed that a shift in processing style has occured as between earlier items received and the later ones. Recall that our central interest is in what happens when we take in information for immediate use. Take a *quick* look at the following list of letters, look away, and then say them out loud in the order in which you read them:

BTGDPC

Did you get some of them mixed up? Conrad (1964) asked his subjects to remember sequences of consonants, visually presented, and he found that they often made errors by substituting letters that sounded rather similar to the correct ones. Conrad and Hull (1964) found that memory span for strings of letters was poorer if they were similar sounding, like *DCBTPV*, than when they sounded different, like *LWKFRT*. Like you perhaps in your attempt to reproduce *BTGDPC*, subjects often recall several letters from the "similar sounds" condition, but fail to reproduce them in the correct order. We do better with strings of digits than with some badly chosen letter strings because digits are less confusable in how they sound.

It will not surprise you to learn that there is much evidence for "phonemic coding" (coding by sound) of digits, letters, and even words, when we have to act immediately upon input by outputting them in good order to a waiting experimenter. Similarly, some phonemic or rhyming confusions appear as responses to words presented at the end of a sufficiently long list, whereas some similar meaning or semantic substitutions more commonly occur for words from the beginning of the list. For example, it is easy to get confused between *huge, big, great*, and *large* if some of these are part of a list you have learned well—processed "deeply", let us say. If the list contains words like *green, screen, preen*, and *spleen*, then phonemic coding could lead to confusions among these words if they are presented at the end of the list. But free recall of these words if they are presented at the beginning of the list could well be strengthened by phonemic plus semantic codings, since subjects can use "sounds like" as an additional retrieval cue. Speculatively, we are more likely to make "sounds like" errors in the early stages of learning a poem, because of the natural emphasis on getting the rhythm and sound just right. For random words presented in a list, however, the words at the beginning of the list are likely to be deeply or semantically coded, and for the last few items there is likely to be a switch to phonemic coding. In general then, immediate or short-term coding was thought to be phonemic, whereas long-term coding was semantic.

Phenomena and ideas such as these reinforced the distinction increasingly being made in the 1950s and 1960s between two components of memory, between some kind of short-term store (STS) and a long-term store (LTS). In addition to the laboratory studies of verbal learning in normal subjects, several studies of amnesic patients supported the distinction. Zangwill (1946) reported that amnesic patients who could not learn new material, such as lists of word-pairs that were to be associated together, had no difficulty repeating series of digits or letters. Similarly, the patient HM studied by Milner (1970), whose amnesia resulted from an operation on the temporal lobes of the brain and the hippocampus, showed an unimpaired digit span coupled with an inability to remember what happened yesterday. There are also patients with impaired digit spans and normal long-term retention, such as the patient KF studied by Shallice and Warrington (1970). How can we explain these findings?

MODELS OF MEMORY

The things that we can and cannot do with our memories under a variety of conditions give us clues about how our memories are organised or structured. The research on learning lists of items suggested that we have a memory system in which a short-term store acts as a holding device, a buffer store, until our long-term store of well-established memories can be accessed in some way. If the long-term store cannot be accessed quickly enough, information is lost from the short-term store. If routes to our long-term store are somehow impaired, we can repeat digits held in the short-term store but not learn them. The "information processing models" developed from this kind of thinking were much influenced by analogies with the workings of computers.

The Computer Analogy

Computers deal with streams of input. Computers also deal with output to printers and displays as well as inputs, so we are reminded here that emphasising how we take things in may not be enough. We also need to consider how we hold output before we make it.

A typical computer can be thought of as having three major parts, namely, a central processor, a fast random access memory store, and various input and output devices. Each input device has its specific properties. A key press on a keyboard generates a signal, which is encoded by circuitry into a computer symbol. The central processor may be in one of three states: (1) it may be wholly attending to the keyboard and ready to receive the next symbol; (2) it may be busy with some other task but this task may be automatically interrupted when the keyboard signals that it is receiving information; (3) it may be busy with some other task but programmed to check the keyboard device for any activity from time to time.

The keyboard device in a computer may have its own storage space or buffer, such that a limited number of symbols can safely be held locally, even if the central processor pays it no attention and this buffer is one kind of short-term store. But the keyboard might be pressed at too high a rate for it to detect, code, and store the distinctive symbols; or the central processor might fail to attend to the signals in time to avoid overflow in the keyboard buffer. Or, the central processor may be programmed to perform the minimal task of emptying the keyboard buffer of symbols from time to time, so that it never overflows, and of storing these symbols away in some part of memory—a more central form of buffer store—for later attention. In this latter case the computer's memory, perhaps a defined amount of space for storing keyboard input, could fill up with symbols, and even overflow if they are not attended to in time. Output devices, like visual display units, robotic operators, and printers, can also interact with a central processor via local or central buffers.

The analogy between the input, output, and central processing of information by computers and the management of information by people became increasingly influential in the 1960s and 1970s. The notions that incoming information could be held in one or more buffers, that it could be part-processed in several stages and that these processes are subject to time–space constraints were particularly attractive for research on memory.

A Three-store Model of Memory

The studies of primacy and recency, different memory codes in immediate recall and long-term recall, and neuropsychological evidence, all suggested a functional distinction between two kinds of memory. This, along with computer analogies which illustrated possible mechanisms, led to the development of models of a three-store memory system, of which the version put forward by Atkinson and Shiffrin (1968) was very influential. Their model is shown diagrammatically in Fig. 6.2.

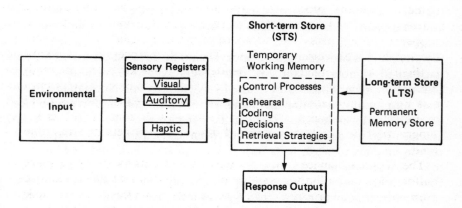

FIG. 6.2 The Atkinson–Shiffrin model of memory. Taken from Atkinson R. C. & Shiffrin R. M. (1971). The control of short term memory. *Scientific American*, *225*, 82–90. Copyright 1971 by Scientific American, Inc., and reprinted by permission.

The first kind of storage is one of a number of sensory information stores that register incoming signals, holding them for a second or two in a primitive form which is readily disrupted by further signals in the same sensory channel. The second is a short-term store (STS), the contents of which we are partially conscious, as when we hold on to a telephone number while we dial, or when we hold on to the last few words from a list read out to us. The third store is a long-term store (LTS) from which we retrieve well-established memories and in which we store well-processed new information.

In the Atkinson–Shiffrin version of STS, data received from the various sensory registers are subject to a number of control processes. *Rehearsal* is a process that requires a transformation of the (selected) incoming information into a rehearsable form such as a phonemic code for verbal material. Although maintenance rehearsal is enough for some tasks, we usually need to hold information so that something may be done with it. For one thing, we usually need to engage in further *coding* of the information by retrieving some aspects of its previous meaning to us from the LTS. The different purposes for processing information—answering a specific question, following a conversation, performing mental arithmetic, learning paired-associates in a memory experiment—are each likely to require different *search and retrieval strategies*. Another control process in the Atkinson–Shiffrin model is concerned with *decision-making*. Decisions might include shifting the direction of a search, abandoning an item, or determining that sufficient has been retrieved for one item.

Several questions arise from this model. Wherein lies the limited capacity for holding items? How automatic are the control processes? Do the operations being performed on the contents of STS take up some of the limited capacity? These questions will occupy us for the remainder of the chapter.

Early studies of immediate memory span had focused on the notion of the limited number of data slots or registers available for holding items. This notion is emphasised, for example, by Lindsay and Norman (1977) in their account of performing mental arithmetic tasks. Most of us experience no difficulty in multiplying two single-digit numbers like 5×9. We can assume that we retrieve the answer from LTS. But 65×9 requires a certain amount of work to be done. We can speculate that STS must at some stage hold something like the following items: 65, $\times 9$, 45, 6×9, 54. Exactly how many slots this takes up is debatable, but the fact is that many of us can, with some effort, manage the task. The multiplication of two two-digit numbers, such as 89×37, is probably at or beyond the limit for most of us. That is, the number of items that have to be held in some arithmetic problems might be said to be larger than the number of slots available.

A task that has frequently been used to estimate the number of registers in STS is the digit span task referred to earlier as part of Wundt's work. The task is used, for example, as a sub-test of the major intelligence tests employed in educational and clinical diagnostic settings. The assumption had been that the immediate recall of random digit sequences is largely unaffected by the contents of LTS—at least in those who are familiar with digits. Variations among us in digit span correlate moderately well with some tasks that demand immediate mental work upon paced inputs; but the very incompleteness of the correlation is a challenge to our view of STS functioning. What else is STS doing? Beyond holding items, there are the control processes referred to in the Atkinson–Shiffrin account which might take up mental space. In the study of mental arithmetic we can count the items that might occupy slots in STS and some partial answers may be rapidly retrieved from LTS, but the management of the whole problem, decisions about how to proceed, the memory for "next step," and so on, might be less automated control processes and might add to the pressure on the limited capacity. How automatic are the processes? We now look at just one decision process.

Current Operations in Immediate Memory

Sternberg (1966, 1969) studied the speed with which subjects could make decisions about items held in immediate memory. In one study, he presented them with strings of between 1 and 6 digits, allowed 2 seconds for rehearsal and followed up with a probe digit. The subject, armed with "yes" and "no" levers, had to decide as quickly as possible whether or not the probe digit was in the presented string.

The reaction-time data showed the same linear increase in decision time with increasing size of the set of digits for both "yes" and "no" decisions. Decisions took about 40 msec more for each extra digit in the set held in memory whether the subjects decided "yes" or "no." It was evident that subjects were performing a serial search rather than a parallel search of the digit string held in memory because otherwise varying the size of the set would not have had such a strong effect. Further, since both "yes" and "no" decisions were increased by a similar amount of time for additional digits in the set, it was as though subjects searched the whole set before indicating their decision. If subjects can respond as soon as they find a match for the probe digit, then "yes" decisions would on average be made after only half the list has been searched, whereas "no" decisions would require a complete search. The data indicated that subjects performed an *exhaustive search* before signalling either decision rather than a *self-terminating search* in the case of "yes" decisions.

Sternberg and others explored many variations of this task. Similar data result when fixed sets of digits are used and each set is probed over several trials. Other types of item also gave similar findings. These studies seem to give us one indication of the operation of a non-interruptible automatic control process at work in STS.

Some studies, however, have given somewhat different results. For examples, decisions for probe digits used more often than others are faster; decisions for digits repeated in the initial sequence are faster than for non-repeated digits; and decisions for sequences of consecutive digits (e.g. 2–3–4–5–6) are faster for digits in the middle of the set than for those at the set boundaries (see e.g. Baddeley, 1976, p. 145). It is clear than when the items to be held readily lend themselves to deeper encoding, as when repeated digits or consecutive digits are present in the set, the scanning process is somehow less automatic and more flexible than when a set of random digits are routinely to be rehearsed and scanned. The purest kind of maintenance rehearsal may be useful for some laboratory tasks and for remembering telephone numbers while we dial, but we usually do more than this. In terms of our simple computer analogy, the processes that code inputs into a rehearsable form sometimes do more than just stacking the items in a buffer.

Problems for a Unitary Short-term Store

Successful as it was in capturing much of the existing data, a number of phenomena fail to fit comfortably in the framework of an Atkinson–Shiffrin type of model. One problem concerns the variety of input and output modalities that people have to manage. If we consider only the verbal medium, we can read and listen and we can speak and write. Are all these activities mediated through a single short-term store? Perhaps, like computers, different buffers are used at some stage in the operation? Murdock and Walker (1969) found that the free recall serial position curves for visually and aurally presented words differ somewhat, aural presentation giving an enhanced recency effect over visual presentation. Is this because auditory coding is the more natural medium of STS and visual codes take extra processing to become auditorily represented there? Next, errors in recall often show evidence of the input modality, visual form and auditory sound errors showing up according to the type of input in several studies. Recall modality—spoken or written—can similarly give differential results. Margrain (1967) simultaneously presented two lists of four digits, one list visually and the other aurally, and called for either spoken or written recall. Aural presentation with written recall gave the highest recall performance, whereas the "visual–spoken" input–output combination gave better performance than "visual–written." If STS is a unitary store, then how can we account for this variety of input–output coding effects?

A further challenge to the view of a unitary STS concerns the variety of tasks that we can engage in at the same time. If the recency effect in list learning is due to the activity of a unitary STS and digit span uses the same store, then if we are using the store for one of these tasks we should be unable to do another task which requires the use of the same store at the same time. Baddeley and Hitch (1977) asked subjects to listen to a sequence of unrelated words and to watch digits appear on a screen. They were asked to write down the digits one at a time, in groups of three, or in groups of six. They also had to remember the words. The effect of adding the load of holding up to three or six digits on the recall of the words can be seen in Fig. 6.3. Although a load of six digits makes recall more difficult, it does not affect the recency portion of the curve. Baddeley and Hitch (1974) had earlier shown that remembering up to six digits did not prevent subjects from comprehending sentences or doing verbal reasoning tasks, and they concluded that memory span and other aspects of immediate memory were not using the same processes. So, either digit span is not a good indicator of the use of short-term memory, or else Atkinson and

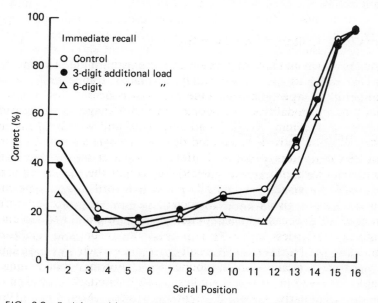

FIG. 6.3 Serial position curves with 3-digit and 6-digit additional short-term memory loads and with zero additional load ("Control"). Taken from Baddeley, A. D. & Hitch, G. J. (1977). Recently re-examined. In S. Dornic (Ed.) *Attention and Performance VI*. London: Academic Press. Copyright 1976 by Academic Press and reprinted by permission.

Shiffrin were wrong to suppose that the only route to long-term memory was via the short-term system.

De Renzi and Nichelli (1975) investigated two kinds of memory span. One was for auditorily presented digits and the other was the Corsi test of spatial position span. In this test the experimenter taps out a sequence of positions on a set of spatially dispersed wooden blocks and the subject has to repeat the sequence exactly. Normal span is about six blocks. De Renzi and Nichelli found one patient who had a very short digit span, about three items, and a normal spatial span, yet other patients with normal digit span could remember only two or three spatial locations. If there are short-term stores, there must be more than one; or there must be marked individual differences in the speed with which the different kinds of input are coded. Either way, the simpler conceptions of STS and its role in holding limited numbers of items are called into question.

Another problem concerns the relation of STS to LTS. Recall that Miller had referred to "chunks" of information and that items vary in their ease of coding. Recall also that in some variants of Sternberg's studies it was found that the processes that code inputs for maintenance rehearsal can recognise the more economical codings that exist when patterns are to be found in the original items. In general, we need to recognise the interactions that occur in immediate memory between short-term operations and long-term memories. In the example given at the beginning of the chapter, we hesitated to assume that the assistant in the paint shop had a better or bigger short-term memory than the customer. We turn then to consider the ways in which experts in handling mental calculations and in remembering digits might differ from the rest of us.

Expert Immediate Memory

If we have an ability to remember a set number of "chunks" of information, we still have to consider what a chunk might be. At the beginning of the chapter we pointed out that in order to do mental arithmetic at all we have to have knowledge in long-term memory as well as in immediate memory. Multiplication is very difficult if you have not learned that $7 \times 8 = 56$ and $8 \times 9 = 72$, and so on. You also know how to break up calculations in order to execute one part at a time. If you were asked to multiply 123 by 456 you would know how to break it up into components and the answers for all the sub-calculations, but you would require too many slots to hold the parts of the problem. However, when Hunter (1962, 1978) asked Professor A. C. Aitken to multiply 123 by 456, Aitken was silent for two seconds and then produced the answer, 56,088, giving the digits in their natural left-to-right order starting from 5. Hunter (1978) gives this quote from Professor Aitken's comment:

I do this in two moves: I see at once that 123 times 45 is 5535 and that 123 times 6 is 738; I hardly have to think. Then 55,350 plus 738 gives 56,088. Even at the moment of registering 56,088, I have checked it by dividing by 8; so 7011 and this by 9, 779. I recognise 779 as 41 by 19; and 41 by 3 is 123, 19 by 24 is 456. (p. 341).

Professor Aitken, as you will gather, is rather special in his ability to perform mental arithmetic. He is one of a small group of virtuoso mental calculators who have been studied by psychologists. Aitken enjoyed numbers, he liked to think about numbers and calculations for their own sake, and over time he developed a very large store of knowledge about numerical equivalents (e.g. 123 multiplied by 45 is 5535) which most of us do not have. In addition, he has a store of methods for dividing problems up into sections which make calculations easier. For a calculation like the one given above, there is very little strain on immediate or short-term memory. This is not because immediate memory is larger but because there is still a comparatively small number of steps.

If a short-term store may be characterised as having a fixed number of storage registers, then individuals can vary markedly in the size of item that can be accommodated in each register. The size of the "chunk" of input—the number of input items—that can rapidly be coded and held as one unit of information depends on how readily LTS can supply a coding principle or a unifying coding. Professor Aitken and other individuals with surprising memories may be different from other people in more ways than just their capacity to do mental arithmetic. Can we take an ordinary person and change their ability to remember large numbers? This was the question that Ericsson, Chase, and Faloon (1980) asked when they asked one person to spend 200 hours spread out over 18 months remembering lists of digits. By the end of the 18 months this subject, known as SF, could listen to a list of 81 digits read to him at one digit per second and repeat them back perfectly. To do this he had developed a series of strategies for coding groups of digits into one unit. One of these strategies developed from the subject's interest in running. He had a wide knowledge of times for running different distances at different standards, so when he heard 3492 he could recode it as "3 min 49.2 secs, close to the world record for the mile."

This strategy uses a specific kind of knowledge in long-term memory; it does not improve span performance in other tasks. Memory for a list of letters, for instance, stayed at six even though the span for digits was very large. This strategy requires the active use of a rich encoding system that changes lists of digits into something else. The time to create these rich codings, given enough practice, is very short and does not prevent the subject from dealing with the rest of the digits as they continue to be read out. To check this interpretation Ericsson et al. later taught SF's technique to a student volunteer who was not a runner, and they successfully increased his "digit span" after months of practice. Simple maintenance rehearsal of the original input items can play little part in such a skill, but the encoding strategies may be only very advanced versions of procedures available to all of us when we notice meaningful groupings within seemingly meaningless material.

Under pressure from studies of encoding processes, the "capacity" of immediate memory is seen to be very much a matter of how speedily and richly the subject can elaborate, by search and retrieval, the characteristics of the stimuli, a process which in turn depends on the prior knowledge of the subject and his or her approach to the task. The "chunks" of information presumed to exist in earlier studies undoubtedly exist but are ultimately definable, especially for everyday memory, only in terms of the particular knowledge a person brings to the task set for the experiment.

WORKING MEMORY

The problems for the conception of a unitary STS are: (1) that different inputs and outputs may use different processing routes and data buffers; (2) that some immediate operations do not seem to occupy or to compete for the same space; and (3) that the coding of information for use in STS depends on the view that LTS takes of the information. Next, we shall recall that Atkinson and Shiffrin did not propose that STS was just a store, a space for holding items, but that it also executed control over a number of activities in immediate memory. Their idea of a "working memory" could be more appropriate than the idea of a passive store which simply holds partially processed material until some other part of the system is ready to deal with it. Using the term "working memory" rather than "short-term store" implies that the information is held for use, and not just because it has not yet been processed enough to get into long-term memory. The information in working memory at any time is already in long-term memory in one sense. In the case of span tasks, for example remembering the telephone number 651342 you already know the digits 1 to 6; what is important is that they have to be kept in a particular order to carry out this task. If you are asked to remember 123456789 your span will appear to have increased because the order information is available as an economical coding from long-term memory, as well as the digits themselves.

If some uses of working memory involve processing and holding items in order, can we show that some elements of real tasks are like those which have been studied in traditional short-term memory experiments? Hitch (1978) used mental arithmetic to look closely at the relationship between operations and storage. He gave people addition problems in which a three-digit number was added to a two- or three-digit number to give a three-digit result. Some problems required a carry from one column to the next. The subjects did not have the answers to questions like "What is the sum of 347 and 52?" already in memory so they had to deal with each column in turn, often using the units–tens–hundreds sequence which they might have learned at school. To complete the "tens" stage of the addition of 476 and 23 the subject has to retrieve 7 and 2 from temporary or working storage, retrieve the sum $(7 + 2 = 9)$ from long-term memory, and either write that bit of the result or put it back into working storage. If the answer is written down in the normal hundreds–tens–units order then the early part of the calculation has to be held in storage until the "hundreds" column is finished. However, if subjects are asked to write the digits in the reverse order each digit is written as it is calculated. Hitch found that subjects made more errors with the "tens" and "units" when they had to hold these items until the end of the calculation than they did when they could write them down as soon as they calculated them. The partial results that are entered into working storage are forgotten quite quickly as a function of the number of intervening steps so that errors occur. Forgetting is virtually complete after 60 seconds have elapsed or after 30–40 processing steps have occurred.

The Articulatory Loop

Baddeley and Hitch (1974) argued that the importance of working memory was not that everything had to be held in a system that was used for digit span before it could get into long-term memory. After all, if we remember the patient KF, it is possible for people to have a very short digit span yet manage to get access to long-term memory. Baddeley and Hitch asked subjects to remember a series of digits (e.g. 523 or 638294) while carrying out a reasoning task in which they had to judge the truth of statements like: "A is not preceded by B" in relation to "AB." They found that the time to complete the reasoning task increased when more digits had to be remembered, but the task was, nevertheless, completed. Baddeley and Hitch argued that if there were just one phonetically based store involved in holding the material for both tasks then it should not be possible to rehearse 638294 and do the reasoning task as well.

They proposed that the limited-capacity working memory consists of a "central executive" and an "articulatory loop." The executive deals with control processes, rather like those envisaged in the Atkinson–Shiffrin model, including a general responsibility for short-term retention. The articulatory loop is a storage device available to the executive which is especially useful for rehearsing articulatable codes, such as words or verbal reference codes for "chunks." The analogy with a loop of audio recording tape is a useful one because the articulatory loop is thought of as being able to maintain a limited number of items in sequence without requiring any processing by the executive. But is it the *number* of items which is critical?

Baddeley, Thomson, and Buchanan (1975) investigated the role of the articulatory system in memory span by asking subjects to remember short lists of words of different lengths. Word length, measured by number of syllables, was strongly related to the number recalled. However, when subjects were asked to remember lists containing words like *Friday* and *harpoon* they tended to remember fewer than if they had to remember lists containing words like *bishop* and *wicket*. These words are matched for the numbers of phonemes and syllables and they are also matched for frequency of occurrence in English. The words differ in the length of time it takes to say them. So, if they are put on to a short "tape loop" which holds than in a form like that used for speech, fewer of the *Friday* and *harpoon* group with their longer vowel sounds will be able to get on the loop. In general, memory span for words was found to be more directly related to the rate at which they can be read—the speed of articulation—than to the other indicators of memory load.

Can we identify the articulatory loop with some of the working storage used in mental arithmetic? The argument is that the capacity of the loop is affected by how long it takes to say the words being held. So, if there is a language in which digits take a long time to say, then digit spans will be shorter than they would be in a language in which digits take a short time to say. Ellis and Hennelly (1980) looked at children who spoke both Welsh and English. They found that it takes longer to speak digits in Welsh than in English, and that bilingual children actually had shorter digits spans in Welsh than they did in English. When the children were asked to produce irrelevant sounds to suppress articulation while they remembered the digits, the difference between the two digit spans disappeared. More interestingly, the children made more mistakes in arithmetic when they did it in Welsh than when they used English, even though Welsh was their first language. This suggests that they did indeed use the articulatory loop to hold digits while they calculated.

But is the articulatory loop, and the articulation time effect to which it is subject, solely responsible for memory span performance? Baddeley, Thomson, and Buchanan (1975) also asked subjects to count repeatedly up to six while words were presented. Memory span was impaired as might be expected, but more importantly the word-length or articulation time effects seemed to disappear. If we assume from this that the articulatory system, including the articulatory loop, is well occupied by the activity of counting up to six, then the central executive must have some short-term memory capacity of its own, or access to some other subsystem, for holding some kind of codes for the words. As we have suggested before, memory span cannot be regarded as a simple index of a unitary capacity in short-term memory.

The concept of the articulatory loop has not remained a simple one. Salame and Baddeley (1982) asked subjects to encode visually presented items for immediate recall while at the same time listening to irrelevant speech. They found that this led to interference when the words that were being listened to were phonemically similar to those being remembered. However, there was no effect on memory if the words which were heard took longer to say. Salame and Baddeley suggested that the irrelevant speech was not articulated (the process responsible for word-length effects), but that it did get access to a different store which is specially for the phonological characteristics of speech (what speech sounds like) and that this is the origin of the phonemic similarity effect. They therefore divided the articulatory loop into two components: a passive phonological store which is linked to the perception of speech and an articulatory process which is linked to the mechanisms of speech production.

The mechanisms for speech production and perception have been studied in considerable detail. For example, Broadbent (1984) argues that there are separate stores for speech input and speech production, rather than two aspects of one system like the articulatory loop and the phonological store; but these arguments take us away from our interest in this chapter and are discussed more fully in Chapter 8. Many of the findings related to holding verbal material for a short time probably do reflect the involvement of temporary storage which is specialised for the representation of different aspects of language use. However, there are very many attributes of language to be represented and there may be many language-specific stores (Monsell, 1984). These speech-specific stores may not all be available for use in problem solving or reasoning or other tasks that utilise other aspects of working memory, although some systems may link up to allow rehearsal to take place.

Visual and Spatial Working memory

It sometimes seems that psychologists are obsessed with words. Unless you can read it, say it, or repeat it to yourself, they are not going to be interested. Fortunately, this is not quite true and some attention has been paid to other aspects of immediate or working memory. If we return to mental arithmetic, Professor Aitken, whose skilled calculations far outstrip our ordinary mental arithmetic, reported using imagery during calculation (Hunter, 1977). Hayes's (1973) subjects reported that they "move" images of symbols and that some use images even for simple operations like addition. Hayes also found that presenting a problem in an unfamiliar format made it more difficult to solve and increased computation time.

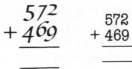

FIG. 6.4   Arithmetic problems differing in visual characteristics but not in spatial form.

If we see words or digits we can translate them into a verbal code of some kind in order to maintain them, but we can also maintain a visual representation that will last for several seconds (Phillips & Baddeley, 1971). It is also possible that purely visual information can be rehearsed (Kroll, Kellicut, & Parks, 1975) although this may be due to the construction of a different kind of code which is spatial rather than visual. The distinction between visual and spatial memory can seem a little difficult at first. In Fig. 6.4 the numbers are the same, the spatial relations are the same, but the detailed visual characteristics of the digits are quite different. It would be possible to remember the spatial arrangement without the visual characteristics. When people report imagery associated with mental arithmetic in which digits are moved about, the important element is the spatial relationships, not the actual appearance of the digits.

Could we be taking some of the strain in mental arithmetic by using a totally non-verbal system to maintain parts of the problem? The answer would depend on whether we could show that spatial processing was independent of verbal processing. This independence has been shown in a series of studies by Brooks (1967, 1968), who was concerned with the manipulation of information and not just its storage. Brooks asked subjects to imagine a block capital letter like that shown in Fig. 6.5. They were then

FIG. 6.5   A block printed 'F', similar to the letters used by Brooks (1967).

asked to start at one corner of the letter and to evaluate each corner in turn, deciding whether it was a top or bottom corner or not. Subjects responded in different ways. In the one, they responded verbally by saying "yes" if the corner was on the top or bottom and "no" if it was not. A second response method was pointing at either a Y or an N in a spatial array of Y's and N's. The time to do the task and the errors both increased when the response was spatial pointing. In a second condition subjects were asked to remember a sentence like "A bird in the hand is worth two in the bush" and then to evaluate each word and categorise it as either a noun or not a noun. Again the responses were saying "yes" and "no" or pointing to a spatial array of Y's and N's. With this task, time and errors both increased when the response was verbal. Brooks argued that there was interference between verbal processing and verbal responding and between spatial processing and spatial responding, but that the control processes for using spatial information were different from those involved in using verbal information.

Of course, the interference in Brooks's task might be visual rather than spatial, possibly because it is hard to hold an image when seeing new input. However, a purely visual perceptual task does not interfere with an imagery task. Baddeley and Lieberman (1980) asked subjects to do a spatial task while detecting changes in the brightness of a patch of light and found no interference; but when the second task was an auditory spatial one, in which subjects had to track the path of a moving sound source, then interference did occur. We can summarise the results by saying that a spatial visual task was not interfered with by a non-spatial visual task, but it was interfered with by a non-visual spatial task. Of course the non-spatial visual task in this study was a very simple one. We cannot conclude that there is no visual component to having an image but rather that using an image can require the same kind of control processes as are used for other spatial tasks. Baddeley (1983) has suggested that the mental uses of images involves an analogue of eye movements, so that when you look round an image you behave as if you were moving your eyes, just as when you speak a sentence to yourself, you use parts of the speech output system.

How does memory for spatial relations differ from memory for visual patterns? Phillips and Christie (1977) showed subjects patterns of squares in which some squares were filled in and others were not. Subjects were shown a series of these and then asked to recognise the ones they had seen. On immediate test the final pattern was remembered best and this was interpreted as evidence for a short-term active visualisation of the details of the last pattern. The memory for the last item was not affected by subsequent visual stimulation which subjects did not have to act upon, but it was affected by activity such as adding digits before the memory test. Memory for the earlier patterns was not affected in this way. Phillips and Christie (1977) took the view that adding digits was not a visual task and hence they argued that the two tasks interfered because they shared the same general processes. But since imagery can be involved in adding numbers, it is also possible that the two tasks share some aspects of a special process, perhaps both using a visuo-spatial store, a visuo-spatial "scratch-pad" as it is referred to by Baddeley and Leiberman (1980).

These results have been extended to show that visualisation tasks disrupt other visualisation tasks but that judging phonemic similarity does not affect visualisation (Phillips, 1983). However, they also make us aware of how easy it is to assume that because we can do something we must have a special system for doing it.

While the relationship between spatial immediate memory and visualisation is not yet clearly understood, there is evidence that visualisation processes are different from those involved in verbal memory span. If you remember from our earlier discussion, Margrain (1967) presented two lists of digits at the same time, one visually and the other aurally, and found that when recall was spoken, visual items were remembered best; but that when it was written, aural presentation was remembered best. This suggests that the digits do not have to be recoded in to a phonemic form, but can be held visually. Frick (1984) investigated this by presenting a set of digits visually followed by an auditory set, and asking subjects to try to visualise the first set and to rehearse the auditory one at the same time. He found an increase in span in the mixed conditions, which suggests that some of the digits presented visually were held long enough to be recalled. Overall, we can conclude that the visuo-spatial processes in immediate memory are different from those used for verbal materials.

Overview of Working Memory

We have come a long way from the simpler views of the use of a short-term store for the immediate recall of strings of letters and digits and for recalling lists of words. While the Atkinson–Shiffrin model provided a focal summary of earlier views, they also emphasised the expression "working memory" and gave attention to control processes. Baddeley and others developed a view of working memory with its central executive and the specialised subsystems, the articulatory loop and the visuo-spatial "scratch-pad." Other specialised subsystems and their control systems, particularly those for receiving and producing speech, seem to be required. The picture of immediate processing has become quite complicated in recent times, but it should be admitted that several writers over the years (e.g. James, 1890; Broadbent, 1958; Miller, Galanter, & Pribram, 1960) had speculated that we have such special systems for particular purposes.

Certainly our initial attempt to account for our difficulties in performing mental arithmetic in terms of a simple view of a limited-capacity immediate memory store comes to grief. When SF recalls 81 digits that he has just heard, he cannot be recalling 81 articulated items from a short-term articulatory store; he has performed a great deal of on-line processing, reduction coding and storage as the digits arrived. Similarly, Professor Aitken's speedy recognition of the deep properties of many numbers and his speedy retrieval or development of memory-efficient procedures show ways in which our system can, admittedly with much effort and practice, learn to cope with extraordinary loads and tasks. Of course, even Professor Aitken met calculations that were outside his capacity and, like the rest of us, he reached for pen and paper or for a calculator. The overall point is that whether the task is a nominally simple one like a memory span task or whether it is evidently more complex like mental arithmetic or, as we shall see in later chapters, listening and speaking, our working memory involves a very complex set of processes handling a variety of inputs, selecting, retrieving, storing, planning and preparing outputs, probably using a number of subsystems adapted for special purposes.

When we think about the way our immediate memory is limited, we have to recognise that people had these limitations before they started to do mental arithmetic. However, they have always needed to extract order and structure from events that occurred over time. This may be one reason why working memory is partly parasitic on speech systems. If we were able to take everything we perceive and put it straight in to memory, that is if we had virtually infinite capacity to hold new information as it arrived, we would have all the sounds produced by a lecturer "taped" in long-term memory. But we would not understand the lecture until we had run the tape and we would not be able to find items in memory which were actually there in the lecture. Without processing incoming information we would have a lot of memories and no knowledge. We need to be able to respond to events as they happen, yet to take in enough information to make sense of the world. Limitations on our input systems reflect a trade-off between these requirements.

SUMMARY

In this chapter we have focused on the immediate processing of inputs to the cognitive system. Beyond the recognition processes discussed in Chapters 1 and 2, this chapter has discussed what happens when the inputs arrive too quickly and, relatedly, what happens when the operations we wish to perform on the inputs strain our capacity to hold on to all the bits we need successfully to complete the task. Doing mental arithmetic comes close to illustrating these problems.

We began by describing a few phenomena and sketching some ideas from early studies of memory. The Atkinson–Shiffrin model marked a phase of consolidation of what many researchers thought about the memory system. New experiments were provoked by this type of theory, new phenomena were brought to light, and old evidence was re-interpreted. Immediate memory, conceived as "working memory," came more certainly to be seen as a current processing activity, as an interaction of the analysis of perceptual inputs, long-term knowledge, preparation for output, and overall task management.

Our story is necessarily incomplete. Memory and its role in immediate processing lie at the core of every activity in which we engage, but Chapter 8 in particular takes up some of the issues raised here. Chapters 6–9 of A. D. Baddeley (1976), *The Psychology of Memory*, give a deeper coverage of the topics most directly dicussed here.

7 Popping the Question: Planning and Producing Speech

The subject matter of the present chapter is the cognitive processes involved in speaking. For our scenario we are willing to give the reader a choice of backdrop. It could be a table for two in a chic French restaurant; it could be the stand-up bar of a fast-food hamburger joint. What matters is what you are there for—you are there to "pop the question." We make no assumptions about the sexes of the addresser and the addressee: All that matters to us is that you have something you very much want to say. We are interested, that is, in the cognitive processes involved in translating thoughts into speech. The real-world activity of speaking is both the example we use to illustrate the problems and the topic of the chapter as well.

Speech production is not an easy skill to study in the laboratory, and the psychologist who wishes to investigate speaking has to exploit rather devious and perhaps indirect sources of evidence. Chief among these are the distribution of hesitations in spontaneous speech, the occasional, involuntary slips of the tongue to which all speakers are prone, and the patterns of language disorder that can occur following brain injury. We shall use these sources of evidence to follow a thought through its translation into language to its external realisation as a sound wave and shall discuss in some detail the influential model of speech production developed by Merrill Garrett.

IDEAS AND CYCLES IN SPONTANEOUS MONOLOGUE

The food was good and the drink better. The time has come. You take hold of your partner's hand and gaze imploringly into her/his eyes. "Will you be mine?" you ask. "Why should I?" comes the reply, like a bolt from the blue. You hadn't expected this. Suddenly and without forewarning you are asked to present a coherent and reasoned argument for why your partner should accept your proposal. In Table 7.1 we have invented a transcript of the reply you might give. Read it now because we shall use it to illustrate various points about speech production later in the chapter.

TABLE 7.1
A Simulated Transcript of Spontaneous Speech

Why should you marry me? Er, well . . . I hadn't expected that . . . but there are lots of reasons . . . er . . . like . . . well, for a start think of the savings on fuel bills we'd make. We'd only have to heat one flat instead of two, so it's worth it on economic grounds. And then, well . . . I suppose mm . . . well, when we get jobs—er, if we get jobs—we'll pay less tax as a married couple than we would as two singles. Wouldn't we? So that's two reasons why you'd make a big killing if you married me.

Oh! and there must be lots more reasons . . . not just economic . . . I mean, yeah, well, we'd be company for each other, wouldn't we? Someone to sit next to while we watch *Dallas* or the big match on t.v. Someone to cook and clean the house for— I mean, *with* . . . oh, we'd have a very equal partnership—share the cooking, ironing decorating, fixing the car, all that sort of stuff.

You want more? . . . Well, er, I suppose looking a *long* way ahead, er, there's kids you know. We would *have* kids eventually I guess; I mean, genes like mine can't be lost to posterity can they? Of course, they're bound to inherit my tennis prowess. I could give 'em that vital early coaching I missed out on. Only thing that stopped me making it as a pro. Neither of us would have to stop work if we didn't want to—we could always hire a . . . oh, you know, one of those foreign girls who comes over and helps around the house . . . not housemaid . . . a French word *au* something-or-other . . . *au pair*, that's it. Well, anyway, we could get one of those.

That enough reasons for you? I could, of course, mention my good looks, charm, wit, intelligence—the fact that my father's a merchant banker—that sort of thing, but modesty forbids. Well . . . will you?

Butterworth (1975) studied some of the properties of this kind of unplanned, extemporary monologue. Rather than asking speakers to justify a proposal, he asked them to "make out the best case they could" either for or against a social or political proposition (*There is no room for a monarchy in a modern society*, for example). The eight speakers were allowed to talk uninterrupted on their topic until they had no more to say. The transcripts of what they had said were then typed up and given to eight new subjects whose task it was to "read through the whole text and then divide it into ideas." Although the experimenter remained deliberately vague as to precisely what an "idea" was, it was possible to find locations in the transcripts where five or more subjects agreed that there was a boundary between one "idea" and the next. Not surprisingly perhaps, conceptual boundaries between ideas also tended to be grammatical boundaries between sentences or clauses in the text.

In addition to locating idea units, Butterworth also looked at the occurrence of fluent and hesitant phases in the speech. He noted a common pattern of alternating hesitant and fluent stretches of speech which he called "cycles." The duration of these cycles ranged from 10 to 40 seconds, with a mean of 18 seconds. Idea boundaries tended to fall at points where a fluent phase ended and a hesitant phase began. What appears to be happening is that when a speaker is given a proposition to speak on immediately and without rehearsal, he or she will begin rather slowly and hesitantly to articulate the first reason but become more fluent as that reason is worked out and becomes clear. Once it has been articulated there will be another hesitant phase while the next reason is formulated, then it too will be expressed fairly fluently, and so on in the sort of cycles Butterworth describes.

We can see these cycles in the (admittedly fake) transcript in Table 7.1. Challenged to say why the intended partner should accept the marriage proposition, the proposer is at first somewhat at a loss for words. A reason (idea) dawns, however (the potential savings on fuel bills) and the initial hesitancy is replaced by greater fluency. The fluency declines as the benefits of fuel economy are exhausted, but picks up again as the speaker thinks of the tax allowances. The boundary between idea 1 (fuel) and idea 2 (tax) would probably be located between "grounds" and "And then"—that is, between a fluent phase and a new hesitant phase heralding a new cycle and idea. Idea 2 runs out at the end of the first paragraph to be replaced, hesitantly at first, by idea 3 (company). Whether job sharing counts as a new idea (idea 4) or as a continuation of "company" is a moot point, and illustrates the sort of problems that probably prevented Butterworth's raters from reaching total accord. Finally, idea 5 (kids) is the last to be fully worked out, though others are briefly alluded to at the end.

PLANNING UNITS AND PLANNING LEVELS

The Sound of Silence

We have seen how speech sometimes goes through alternate hesitant and fluent phases. It is important to note, though, that the words spoken in a hesitant phase are not articulated any more slowly than the words in a fluent phase. What distinguishes hesitant from fluent speech is the amount of time spent *not* talking. When Goldman-Eisler (1968) asked subjects to give impromptu talks on selected topics, the amount of time occupied by pauses ranged from 35 to 67 per cent. Interviews were rather more fluent, with the amount of utterance time taken up by pauses varying from 4 to 54 per cent. So it is quite normal for spontaneous speech to contain between one-third and one-half of silence.

Why is speech so full of silence? One reason may be that when you have said what you want to say you naturally fall silent (or most people do, anyway). In conversation—arguably the most natural context for speech—the moment when a speaker falls silent is often the appropriate point for another conversant to being talking. So pauses serve a social role in conversational management. Do they in addition play a cognitive role? Speakers could pause at random points in speech simply because they run out of breath and need to inhale, but it is also conceivable that some pauses in speech occur because speakers are planning what to say next. That is, speakers may sometimes finish saying one thing before they have planned and prepared the next. If speech follows a pattern of plan–execute–plan–execute, and if at least some hesitations are indicative of planning in progress, then pauses in speech should not occur at random, but should occur at the beginnings of planning units.

We have already seen that speech is hesitant at the beginnings of large-scale "idea units," which are candidates for planning units at the very highest level. But the pattern of distribution of pauses within these high-level units suggests a role in planning for smaller, more local linguistic units.

Most natural, spontaneous speech is comprised of a sequence of reasonably grammatical sentences. Deese (1980) examined samples of speech taken from the deliberations of committees, academic seminars, business meetings and the like, and found that 98 per cent of the sentences spoken were grammatically correct. Studies of the distribution of pauses in spontaneous speech (where a pause is typically defined as a silence of 250 msec or more) have found that pauses within idea units tend to cluster at the boundaries between one sentence and the next (Goldman-Eisler, 1968; Ford & Holmes, 1978), thereby implicating the sentence as one unit of speech planning. But pause analysis has also revealed another smaller unit: the clause.

A clause is a group of words centred grammatically on a verb. Suppose our proposer were to say, "We could both work for a while, then we'll be able to afford a house in the country, and one of us could take a few years off to raise a family." That is all one sentence but contains four verbs (*work*, *afford*, *take . . . off*, and *raise*), and thus four clauses:

1. We could both work for a while
2. then we'll be able to afford a house in the country
3. and one of us could take a few years off
4. to raise a family.

Work on pause distributions (summarised by Butterworth, 1980a; Garrett, 1982) shows that pauses within sentences tend to cluster at clause boundaries. In the above example, our proposer would tend to pause (or say "um" or "er") before or after "then", "and," or "to". We say "after" as well as "before" because another way to signal that a pause does not imply the end of a conversational turn is to say the first, conjoining word of the next clause before pausing. The speaker might thus say, "We could both work for a while then . . . er . . . we'll be able to afford a house. . . ."

Slips of the Tongue

Another independent line of evidence implicating the clause as an important planning unit comes from analyses of involuntary and unintentional speech errors or "slips of the tongue." Imagine that our proposer is half-way through the list of reasons why the proposal should be accepted. He or she intends to say "we'll be able to afford a house in the country," but what actually comes out is "we'll be able to afford a country in the house." The speaker is merely embarrassed by the slip, but at the next table a psycholinguist pauses in mid-chew, smiles ruefully, takes out a little pocket book and writes the error down. Later, after amassing quite a large collection of errors, the psycholinguist sits down to examine them. It soon becomes clear that they fall into several distinct categories, and that different types of error have rather different properties.

Garrett (1975, 1976) collected and reported just such an analysis of a corpus of around 3400 slips of the tongue. Ninety-seven of these were word exchanges like our proposer's slip, or like the following (where *I* denotes what the speaker intended to say, and *E* denotes the error):

I:　"I've got to go home and give my *back* a hot *bath*."
E:　"I've got to go home and give my *bath* a hot *back*."

I:　"She'll have my *guts* for *garters*."
E:　"She'll have my *garters* for *guts*."

I:　"one *spoon* of *sugar*."
E:　"one *sugar* of *spoon*."

Garrett observed that all of his word exchanges involved two words from within the same sentence, and that 85 per cent came from within the same clause. Another type of exchange error found to respect clause boundaries was the "morpheme exchange error." Examples of this type of error are:

I:　"Is your *whisky finish*ed?"
E:　"Is your *finish whisky*ed?"

I:　"The *hill*s are *snowy*."
E:　"The *snow*s are *hilly*."

I:　"The *prong*s of a *fork*."
E:　"The *fork*s of a *prong*."

In these errors the "roots" of the words (*whisky*, *finish*, *hill*, *snow*, *prong*, and *fork*) have become detached from the "inflections" to which they should be attached (-*ed*, -*y* and -*s*). The roots exchange positions while the inflections remain "stranded" in their original, intended positions. On examining the grammatical distributions of these errors, Garrett (1975) found that 42 of his 46 morpheme exchanges (91 per cent) involved two words from the same clause. Again the significance of the clause as a planning unit is apparent.

FINDING THE RIGHT WORD

We have discussed hesitations at the onset of idea units, and hesitations at the onset of sentences or clauses. There is, however, one other location (and cause) of pauses in speech that we must mention. In our "transcript" of speech in Table 7.1 the speaker has problems at one point remembering the word *au pair*. The speaker knows the concept to be conveyed ("a foreign girl who comes over and helps around the house"), and knows it is a French word, but is momentarily trapped in one of those tantalising "tip of the tongue" states. William James—brother of the novelist Henry James, and one of the founding fathers of psychology—captured the subtle agony of a tip of the tongue state in the following famous passage (James, 1890):

> Suppose we try to recall a forgotten name. The state of our consciousness is peculiar. There is a gap therein; but no mere gap. It is a gap that is intensely active. A sort of wraith of the name is in it, beckoning us in a given direction, making us at moments tingle with the sense of our closeness, and then letting us sink back without the longed-for term. If wrong names are proposed to us, this singularly definite gap acts immediately so as to negate them. They do not fit its mould. . . . The rhythm of a lost word may be there without a sound to clothe it; or the evanescent sense of something which is the initial vowel or consonant may mock us fitfully, without growing more distinct [p. 251].

From a psychological perspective, tip of the tongue (TOT) states are valuable for the way they help us appreciate the distinction between a concept and the verbal label (word or phrase) used to denote it. A speaker in a TOT state knows full well the concept that is to be communicated but cannot recall its label. The victim can give a paraphrase or definition of the sought-for word, and can bring to mind related words (like "housemaid" in our example), but knows them to be incorrect. Brown and McNeill (1966) managed to induce TOT states in subjects by reading them definitions of uncommon words and asking them to supply the word. The signs of a TOT state, they say, were unmistakable. The subject "would appear to be in a mild torment, something like the brink of a sneeze, and if he found the word his relief was considerable." The subjects could often offer words similar either in meaning or sound to the target. Thus, the definition, "A navigational instrument used in measuring angular distances, especially the altitude of the sun, moon and stars at sea," for which the correct response is "sextant," induced the similar-meaning attempts "astrolabe," "compass," "dividers," and "protractor," and the similar-sound attempts "secant," "sextet," and "sexton." Subjects were sometimes so close to the target as to be able to say how many syllables it had, or what letter or sound it began with. This latter information was presumably the basis upon which the similar-sound attempts were constructed.

A tip of the tongue state clearly reflects some form of memory failure—the failure to retrieve the word that matches a concept. But what is the nature of the memory store which lets the speaker down, albeit only temporarily, since the elusive word usually comes to mind eventually? Psychologists usually refer to the memory store for words as "the mental lexicon." There are reasons, however, for believing that the mind may contain more than one word-store, for example separate stores for the production and recognition of spoken and written words (see Allport, 1983; Morton, 1979), so we will be cautious here and refer to the store from which words are retrieved in speaking, and whose failure causes TOT states, as the *speech output lexicon* (see Chapter 2, pp. 25–45).

A feature of TOT states is that they are normally only induced by words the speaker uses rarely. *Au pair* might induce a TOT state; *girl* never would. The ease with which a word can be retrieved from the speech output lexicon seems therefore to be related to its frequency of use by the speaker. Experiments by Oldfield and Wingfield (1965) and Wingfield (1968) support this conclusion. They studied the ease of either recognising or naming pictures of objects. Whereas the frequency of use of an object's name had only a slight effect on the ease with which a drawing of it could be identified after a brief presentation, word frequency exerted a strong influence on the time taken to retrieve and articulate the name, with low-frequency (rarely used) names taking much longer than high-frequency (commonly used) names. Similarly, Beattie and Butterworth (1979) observed in an analysis of natural spontaneous speech that hesitations attributable to word-finding difficulties were precipitated more often by low- than by high-frequency words.

Certain types of slip of the tongue also seem attributable to problems in or around the speech output lexicon. The *word blend* is one such example. Here there are two words in the speaker's lexicon which could be used equally well to communicate a particular concept. What emerges is a blend of the two. In the following examples the two blended words are shown in brackets after the error.

"You can't *swip*" (swap + switch)
"It's blowing a *gizzard*" (gale + blizzard)
"Just the *poo* of us" (pair + two)
"I'm not that *dick*" (daft + thick)

Semantic word substitutions occur when a word is produced which is similar in meaning to the intended target word:

I: "You'll find the ice-cream in the *fridge*."
E: "You'll find the ice-cream in the *oven*."

I: "Can you wriggle your *ankles*?"
E: "Can you wriggle your *elbows*?"

I: "Do you want me to *leave* all my belongings?"
E: "Do you want me to *take* all my belongings?"

In word substitutions, the intended concept seems to activate the wrong word in the speech output lexicon, rather in the way that concepts whose names are on the tip of your tongue can activate related names. In word blends, two candidate labels for the same concept are activated simultaneously and emerge as a compromise formation. Beattie and Butterworth (1979) found that pairs of words involved in blends tend to be closer in terms of frequency of usage than pairs involved in substitutions, and that in substitutions the intended target word tends to be of lower frequency (less common) than the word that replaces it. These findings clearly fit our earlier claims about frequency of use of a word determining the ease with which it can be retrieved from the speech output lexicon.

Finally, a type of slip of the tongue that we have discussed already has implications for theories of how words are stored in the speech output lexicon. The slips in question are those involving the exchange of two root morphemes. The fact that, for example, *hill* can exchange with *snow* in the error "The snows are hilly," leaving the *-s* and *-y* stranded, has been taken to imply that root morphemes and some of the "bound morphemes" that can be tacked on to them may be stored separately in the lexicon (Henderson, 1985). Slips like the following, in which incorrect bound morphemes have been attached to roots, carry the same implication:

I: "He *understood* it"
E: "He *understanded* it"

I: "*most heavily*"
E: "*heaviestly*"

I: "... *made* him so popular"
E: "... *maked* him so popular"

THE SOUND LEVEL

The Reverend William Archibald Spooner was born in 1844. In 1867, at the age of 23, he became a Fellow of New College, Oxford, and was appointed Warden in 1903. He taught ancient history, philosophy, and divinity. He died in 1930 and is buried with his wife close to the poet William Wordsworth in the beautiful Lake District village of Grasmere.

If that were all there was to say about the Reverend Spooner, his name would probably have disappeared quietly into history by now, and he would certainly not feature in a textbook on cognitive psychology. But that is *not* all there is to say about the Reverend Spooner because he made—or is reputed to have made—large numbers of speech errors of a sort which have come to be known as spoonerisms. He is said, for example, to have rebuked a student by telling him, "You have *h*issed all my *m*ystery lectures" (*I*: "... *m*issed all my *h*istory lectures"), and informed another that, "I saw you *f*ight a *l*iar in the back quad; in fact you have *t*asted the whole *w*orm (*I*: "... *l*ight a *f*ire ... *w*asted the whole *t*erm").

The truth is probably that very few of the errors attributed to Spooner were actually made by him, and that the majority were invented by the Oxford wags of the time (Potter, 1980). Spooner was a shy man, and not at all proud of his reputation as an errorsmith, but the name has stuck, and "spoonerism" is now the term widely employed to refer to slips of the tongue which involve the exchange (reversal) of two phonemes. Examples taken from the Appendix to Fromkin (1973) include:

I: "*l*eft *h*emisphere"
E: "*h*eft *l*emisphere"

I: "*h*eap of *r*ubbish"
E: "*r*eap of *h*ubbish"

I: "be*d* bu*g*s"
E: "bu*d* be*g*s"

I: "You *b*etter stop for *g*as"
E: "You *g*etter stop for *b*as"

The properties and characteristics of genuine spoonerisms have been closely studied (Fromkin, 1973, 1980; Cutler, 1982). The picture that emerges is that both consonant and vowel phonemes can exchange, but consonants only exchange with consonants (as in the first two of the preceding examples) and vowels only exchange with vowels (the third example). Reversing phonemes come from so-called "content" or "open class" words (nouns, verbs, and adjectives) rather than from "function" or "closed class" words like *through*, *from*, *to*, *then*, or *such*. The exchanging phonemes tend to be similar in sound, so that /p/ will be more likely to exchange with /b/ than with /s/, and they tend to come from similar locations within their respective words and syllables. Finally spoonerisms never cross sentence boundaries, and Garrett (1975, 1976) found that 93 per cent of the errors in his corpus occurred within a clause.

It appears, then, that speech planning in roughly clause-sized units extends from higher conceptual and syntactic levels right down to the level at which the individual phonemes of words are activated and readied for articulation. Spoonerisms show that words being planned are not spelled out as phoneme sequences one at a time. In the last of the four examples the word "gas" must already have been retrieved as a phoneme string from the speech output lexicon at the time the speaker wished to say "better," otherwise the /g/ of *gas* would not have been available to exchange with and replace the /b/ of *better*. In Lashley's (1951) words, spoonerisms are "indications that prior to the internal or overt enunciation of the sentence, an aggregate of word units is partially activated or readied."

If an "aggregate of words" is to be partially activated as phoneme strings, then the sound level must be equipped with the necessary storage capacity to hold them ready for articulation. Following Morton (1970), Ellis (1979) argued that this storage capacity might be what subjects draw upon when they are asked to repeat random sequences of letters, digits, or words in psychological experiments on "short-term memory." Others have argued that such short-term storage involves memory stores more closely linked to the perception and comprehension of speech. We return to this issue in Chapter 8.

Articulation

We cannot leave our speaker quite there, with everything planned and readied but nothing yet spoken (or only errors anyway). Phonemes must be articulated: they must cause the lips, tongue, and teeth to move in a co-ordinated manner while air is expired and the vocal cords vibrated so as to produce that communicative perturbation of the air that we call speech.

What kinds of targets do phonemes set the articulatory apparatus? One theory proposed by MacNeilage (1970) was that the targets are *spatial* ones which specify the positions the articulators must achieve in order to produce a particular sound. The motor system would then need to compute the movements necessary to realise the next target position from the present one (since the movement to a /t/ target would be different after, say an /e/ than after an /s/).

This theory, however, soon ran into problems when Folkins and Abbs (1975) showed that if movement of the lower lip is suddenly impeded during a lip closure (as when producing a /p/ or /b/), the upper lip compensates rapidly with a greater than normal lowering. We can now see this as an example of the general phenomenon discussed by MacNeilage (1980) that different articulatory configurations may be used on different occasions to produce the same sound. To account for this fact, MacNeilage (1980) revised his earlier view and proposed that the targets set by phonemes are not spatial ones but are *acoustic* targets. That is, a phoneme specifies a *sound* that the articulatory system must produce, and the system then computes a movement from the range of possibilities available. This way we can begin to understand how it is possible to produce intelligible speech while holding a pipe between your teeth or while maintaining a fixed smile for the cameraman.

Pre-planning in speech extends to the articulatory level where it is revealed in the phenomenon of *co-articulation*. Try saying the word "get." Now try "got." Feel how the lips, which are not involved in producing the /g/, take up positions at the start of the word in anticipation of the vowel. In "glaze" and "glue" the same happens though there are two phonemes to be articulated before the vowel. Co-articulation of this sort can extend across word boundaries. Try saying "tickle you." Toward the end of "tickle" the lips already begin to form the rounded shape necessary for the /u/ vowel of "you." Again such planning would not be possible if aggregates of words were not planned as groups.

GARRETT'S MODEL OF LANGUAGE PRODUCTION AND THE APHASIAS

Perhaps the most comprehensive model of language production from ideation to articulation has been developed by Garrett in a series of papers (e.g., Garrett, 1982, 1984). The model is built on three primary lines of evidence. The first two—pauses and slips—are familiar to us already. The third line of evidence is the cognitive analysis of those language disorders (*aphasias*) which can occur after brain injury such as a stroke or missile wound. We shall begin by briefly summarising Garrett's model, then show how some of the different forms of aphasia can be interpreted within it.

The model has four separate *levels of representation*; that is, four successive stages that speech must pass through in the planning process

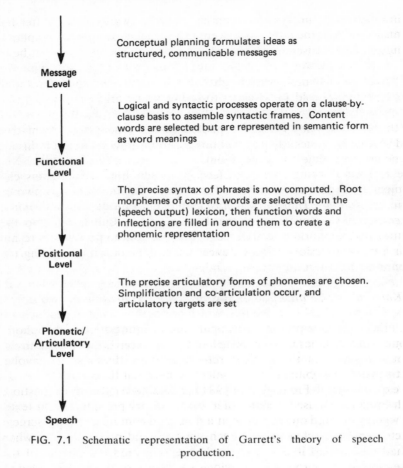

Conceptual planning formulates ideas as
structured, communicable messages

**Message
Level**

Logical and syntactic processes operate on a clause-by-
clause basis to assemble syntactic frames. Content
words are selected but are represented in semantic form
as word meanings

**Functional
Level**

The precise syntax of phrases is now computed. Root
morphemes of content words are selected from the
(speech output) lexicon, then function words and
inflections are filled in around them to create a
phonemic representation

**Positional
Level**

The precise articulatory forms of phonemes are chosen.
Simplification and co-articulation occur, and
articulatory targets are set

**Phonetic/
Articulatory
Level**

Speech

FIG. 7.1   Schematic   representation   of   Garrett's   theory   of   speech
production.

(see Fig. 7.1). Cognitive processes of one sort or another translate between
the levels to shape the utterance from ideation to articulation.

First comes *conceptual planning*, which formulates the abstract,
conceptual plan of the gist or meaning of the utterance the speaker intends
to say. That conceptual plan constitutes the first, *message level* of
representation. *Logical* and *syntactic processes* then work on the message
level plan to create, clause by clause, the second, *functional level* plan. The
content words (nouns, verbs, and adjectives) that will communicate the
important elements of the utterance are chosen now, but they are here
represented in *semantic* form as meanings. The syntactic processes indicate
the relations which will exist between the content words—which noun is to
be the subject of the clause and which the object; which adjective qualifies
which noun; and so on.

The need for syntactic relations to be coded at the functional level is obvious when we consider sentences in which the content words occur in different positions to very different effect, for instance:

The fierce lion chased the timorous mouse
The fierce mouse chased the timorous lion

The same elements are involved in these two sentences—there is a lion and a mouse, one is fierce and the other timid, and one is chasing the other—but by changing the word order we have dramatically altered the nature of the scenario described. In English, relational information of this sort is largely carried by word order, and in Garrett's model it begins to be spelled out and to control the growth of a sentence structure at the functional level. Word-exchange errors, which usually involve pairs of content words and which occur primarily within clauses, occur in the process of assembling a functional level description, as does the occasional mis-selection of the semantic form of a word, resulting in meaning-based word substitution errors.

At the functional level a growing sentence is still represented abstractly as a set of meanings and relations between them. The impending sentence becomes more concretely defined in the creation from the functional level plan of what Garrett calls the *positional level* of description or representation. The positional level is what we have earlier called the sound level; that is, the level at which words are represented as strings of phonemes. Garrett sees the positional level not as being created instantly, but as growing gradually under the guidance of the information coded at the previous, functional level.

Initially the root morphemes of content words are retrieved from what we have called the speech output lexicon. The detailed syntax of phrases is computed at the same time, specifying the appropriate locations of inflections (*-s*, *-ed*, *-ing*, etc.) and function words (*and*, *of*, *the*, *in*, etc.). These are then retrieved from the lexicon and slotted into place around the existing root morphemes. This two-stage process permits explanation of some of the slips of the tongue mentioned earlier and of some of the phenomena associated with them.

First, a mislocation of two root morphemes will result in morpheme exchanges like "the forks of a prong." The fact that the inflections are added at the second stage explains why they remain stranded in their original positions. Also, the precise form an inflection takes can vary according to the root to which it is attached. The plural *-s*, for example, is pronounced three different ways in the words "ropes" (/s/), "robes" (/z/), and "roses" (/iz/). In "prongs," the intended plural in the above slip, the inflection takes the /z/ form, but in the error "forks" it becomes /s/. This *accommodation* of the inflection to the root morpheme it has become erroneously attached to is, according to Garrett, made possible by the two-stage assembly of the positional (sound) level.

Garrett believes that spoonerisms also arise in the process of assembling the positional level. Because they typically involve pairs of phonemes from the root morphemes of content words, the first of our two stages must be the principal culprit. And assigning spoonerisms to that stage permits explanation of another way in which accommodation to errors can occur. Consider the following pair of errors, the first taken from the Appendix to Fromkin (1973) and the second from Garrett (1980):

> *I*: "*an* ice *c*ream cone"
> *E*: "*a k*ice ream cone"

> *I*: "*a l*anguage acquisition problem"
> *E*: "*an* anguage *l*acquisition problem"

In fact, neither error is a complete spoonerism—the first is an anticipation of the /k/ of "cream" to the front of "ice" making "kice," and the second is a perseverative shift of the /l/ of "language" to the beginning of "acquisition" making "lacquisition"—but such phoneme translocations show the same properties as spoonerisms and thus seem attributable to the same processing stage. What is important is what happens to the "a" or "an" in each error. In the first example, it would have emerged as "an" if the utterance had been produced correctly, but when the /k/ shifts the speaker does not say "*an* kice ream cone" but instead says "*a* kice ream cone." Conversely, the intention in the second example was "*a* language acquisition problem," but the /l/ is shifted so that what emerges is not "*a* anguage lacquisition problem" but "*an* anguage lacquisition problem." The point to realise is that such accommodation of the indefinite article (*a/an*) to the error could not occur unless the form of the article were selected *after* the phoneme mislocation had occurred. This again supports Garrett's suggestion that function words, of which *a/an* is one, are slotted into the positional level *after* root morphemes of content words have been retrieved from the speech output lexicon and *after* spoonerisms and similar phoneme errors have occurred.

Garrett's fourth and final stage is the *articulatory/phonetic level*. Here the phonemic representation of the positional level is prepared for articulation. Co-articulatory processes of the sort discussed earlier operate at this level, as do the motoric processes which compute and execute the articulatory movements necessary to achieve spatial or acoustic targets.

The Aphasias

Garrett's theorising was based in part on the patterns of language disorders—aphasias—that can follow brain injury. Imagine that Garrett's four levels and the processes which translate between them are all quite independent one from another both cognitively and in the organisation of the brain. It should be possible if this were the true state of affairs for brain injury to damage one level or process while leaving the others unimpaired. That is, it should be possible to find patients whose problems lie exclusively (or at least primarily) with the conceptual formulation of a message level, the translation of that into a syntactically structured structural level, the retrieval of word-forms from the speech output lexicon, and so on. Discovering patients whose symptoms could be interpreted in this way would lend support to the model. Patients whose pattern of disorder did *not* comply with the model's predictions could lead to a change in the theory of normal processing (since a fundamental tenet of the cognitive neuropsychological approach espoused by Garrett is that all disorders should be interpretable in terms of impairment to one or more of the elements of a theory of normal cognitive processing).

The more cognitive neuropsychologists study aphasia, the more they realise that language impairment can take a wide variety of forms (Ellis & Young, in press; Saffran, 1982). On reflection this is perhaps to be expected. The ultimate "true" theory of language use will contain a great many processes, levels, etc., and if these can all be affected separately or in combination, then the number of possible patterns of disorder will be correspondingly large. It is impossible here to cover the whole spectrum of aphasias, so we must settle for discussing just a few, showing how they can be explained by Garrett's model.

Syntactic Deficits.   We shall begin with a *syntactic deficit*. Syntax, it will be remembered, refers to those processes which take a conceptual message-level input and create a structured sentence frame which expresses correctly the relationships exisiting between those elements which appear as the "content words." Patients with syntactic disorders should know the message they would like to communicate, should be able to retrieve the appropriate content words, and should be able to articulate them fluently and without error. They should have difficulty, however, in assembling the grammatical sentences in which to order those content words. Such a patient was described by Saffran, Schwartz, and Marin (1980). Shown a picture of a woman putting clothes into a washing machine, this patient said, "The lady . . . the lady launders the . . . the lady puts the washes . . . wash on . . . puts on the wash with the laundry." A picture of a woman kissing a man elicited the attempt, "The kiss . . . the lady kissed . . . the lady is . . . the lady and the man and the lady . . . kissing." All the necessary content words are here in these efforts ("lady," "launder," "wash," "kiss," "man") but the syntactic structure is inadequate, pointing to a deficit between Garrett's message and functional levels.

Anomia.   Semantic processes which specify the meanings of content words also operate between the functional level and the message level. Impairment to semantics alone should result in a patient who can construct sentence frames but has difficulty accessing the content words to place within the frame because semantic descriptions of sufficient detail to single out words in the speech output lexicon cannot be formulated. When the patient reported by Allport and Funnell (1981) was asked to describe a picture of a kitchen scene, he produced the following attempt (where the words in square brackets are Allport and Funnell's attempts to guess what he was trying to say):

> Well, it's a . . . [kitchen], it's a place, and it's a girl and a boy, and they've got obviously something which is made . . . some . . . [biscuits], some . . . made . . . . Well . . . [the stool] it's just beginning to . . . [fall] go and be rather unpleasant . . . . And . . . this is the . . . [mother?] the woman, and she is [pouring?] putting some . . . [water] stuff . . . [p. 405].

That this patient's underlying deficit is semantic was indicated by his performance on other sorts of task. If he was shown a picture of an object and two written object names, the patient could select the correct name provided that the two names were not close semantic associates. For example, he would have no difficulty selecting *nail* to match to a picture of a nail if the second "distractor" name was *bird*. But if the "distractor" was *screw* he would have great difficulty. It was not that he did not know the difference between a nail and a screw, because he could use the two objects appropriately, taking a hammer to the one and a screwdriver to the other. In Allport's (1983, p. 77) words, "it appears that his disability must be located in the processes that translate *between* the word-forms and their underlying conceptual representations." In Garretts' terms this is between the functional and message levels.

Neologistic Jargonaphasia.   The speech output lexicon is involved in the translation of the functional level into the positional level. It is the memory store from which words are retrieved as strings of phonemes. Ellis, Miller, and Sin (1983) described a patient whose form of aphasia they attributed to a problem in retrieving the full phonemic forms of words from his speech output lexicon. In normal speech he would produce what appeared to be well-formed sentences in which some words would emerge as incorrect approximations (for example, *scout* mispronounced as "skut," *bull* as "buk," *chasing* as "cherching," and *tent* as "tet"). Ellis, Miller, and Sin argued that the patient could often retrieve only some of the phonemes of a sought-for word and had to guess at the rest.

This patient generally pronounced commonly used words correctly, including function words like *the*, *and*, *for*, etc., and high-frequency nouns like *boy*, *tree*, *paper*, and *man*. His problem lay with lower-frequency words, supporting our earlier contention that frequency of usage is an important determinant of ease of access of items from the speech output lexicon. Additionally, if patients of this type attempt, say, a plural noun but only manage to produce an approximation to it, the plural morpheme will still be produced and will adapt ("accommodate") itself to the error. Thus if the target was "bulls" where the plural takes the /z/ form, an error form "buks" would be pronounced with the appropriate /s/ form. This supports the proposal that inflections may be retrieved separately from the lexicon and be added to root morphemes in the second stage of assembling the positional level.

These are just some of the qualitatively distinct patterns of disorder that can afflict speech production (Ellis, 1985b). Other patients, for example, have problems at the sound level and make frequent errors that resemble the occasional spoonerisms of normal speakers. The simple fact that so many different forms of aphasia can occur, each with a different pattern of impaired and intact abilities, strengthens our belief that speech is made possible by the interaction of several separate but intercommunicating cognitive subsystems. Each subsystem can be independently damaged, giving rise to its own distinctive pattern of aphasic symptoms.

SUMMARY

Extensive monologues tend to consist of alternating stretches of hesitant and fluent speech, with the onset of a hesitant phase marking the beginning of a new "idea." In addition to revealing high-level planning units, pause patterns in speech also suggest a role for the sentence and the clause as lower-level planning units. Evidence from the distribution of slips of the tongue also supports this claim—misordering errors almost always involve two elements from within the same sentence, usually from within the same clause. Hesitations occurring *within* clauses often signal word-finding difficulties which in severe form leave the speaker in a "tip-of-the-tongue" state. Some slips of the tongue are attributable to word-finding errors and give insights into the operation of the lexicon from which spoken word-forms are retrieved (suggesting the separate representation of certain morphemes).

Garrett's four-stage model of speech production is based on data from hesitations and speech errors, but also on analyses of the different forms of aphasia that can occur following brain injury. These various qualitatively distinct patterns of disorder are accounted for in terms of impairment to one or more of the components of the information processing model.

Speech production begins with high-level planning. A speaker must make decisions about what points to make in what order, what to infer about the listener, and so on. There are thus links to be drawn with our treatment of decision making and the drawing of inferences in Chapters 12 and 13. We discussed the nature of human concepts in Chapter 3. Concepts are, of course, the very building blocks of speech production: Without the appropriate concepts a thought can be neither formulated nor uttered. At the final stage of articulatory planning and execution we find links with the psychological study of other motor skills discussed in Chapter 4.

The end of speech production is the beginning of speech perception and comprehension. The formulation of speech is likely to be moulded by the receptive capabilities and limitations of the listener, so a better knowledge of language understanding (see Chapters 1, 8, and 9 in particular) is likely to lead to a better understanding of language production and vice versa. In short, although it is convenient to isolate speech production as a topic, it soon becomes clear that as with so many other topics, a full understanding will require contributions from many other, related areas of psychology.

A broader introduction to speech production encompassing cognitive, social and neuropsychological perspectives can be found in A. W. Ellis and G. Beattie (1986), *The Psychology of Language and Communication*. More advanced treatment of various aspects of speech production can be found in B. Butterworth (1980b, 1983), *Language Production* Vols 1 & 2.

8 Listening to Speech: Perceiving, Understanding, or Ignoring a Spoken Sentence

Language in one form or another recurs as a topic of investigation over and over again in cognitive psychology. In Chapter 7 we emphasised speech production. Here we deal with the cognitive processes involved in perceiving, comprehending, and also ignoring spoken sentences. These are such commonplace activities that we hardly need to illustrate their use: having a conversation, listening to the radio, attending to a talk or lecture—all of these involve spoken sentence processing. And it is not uncommon to find yourself in a situation where there are two competing speech messages, one of which you wish to attend to and the other of which you wish to ignore (e.g., trying to hold a conversation while the DJ on the radio rambles on).

We shall begin by considering theories of how individual heard words are recognised and how the context within which a word occurs may influence its perceptibility. We shall then move up a level to investigate the cognitive processes involved in extracting the meaning from whole sentences. This leads us naturally to the question of the short-term storage capacities necessary for efficient speech comprehension. Our final section is concerned with what happens to a speech signal that is actively ignored. Is the subjective experience of understanding none of the meaning of an ignored sentence accurate, or can something of its meaning be shown to have percolated though below conscious awareness?

RECOGNISING HEARD WORDS

It is useful when thinking about speech perception to contrast the situation faced by a listener with that faced by a reader (cf. Chapter 1). If you cut a printed word out from a book or magazine, the word continues to remain perfectly recognisable. The same is not true of spoken words. Lieberman (1963) recorded speakers saying phrases like "A stitch in time saves nine" or "Neither a borrower nor a lender be." The phrases were all perfectly intelligible when played in their entirety. However, words spliced out of these phrases and presented in isolation with no supporting context were much less easy to make out. The word "nine" was correctly identified only 50 per cent of the time, "borrower" 45 per cent of the time, and "lender" a mere 10 per cent.

These results can only mean that listeners utilise the contexts in which words occur to assist in their recognition, and there is no shortage of experimental evidence to support such a claim. Miller, Heise, and Lichten (1951) presented listeners with either single words or sentences embedded in a background of hissing "white" noise, and found that words in sentence contexts were identified much better than words in isolation. Marslen-Wilson and Tyler (1980) asked subjects to listen out for target words in three types of two-sentence "passage." The first type was normal, coherent prose; the second was "anomalous" prose which was grammatical but nonsensical; and the third was "scrambled" prose which was both ungrammatical and nonsensical. Examples of the three types, in which the target word "lead" is italicised, are:

1. Normal prose:
   "The church was broken into last week. Some thieves stole most of the *lead* off the roof."
2. Anomalous prose:
   "The power was located in great water. No buns puzzle some in the *lead* off the text."
3. Scrambled prose:
   "It was great power water the located. Some the no puzzle buns in *lead* text the off."

Although the subjects' task was simply to press a button as quickly as possible when they heard the target word "lead," reaction times were nevertheless faster in the normal prose condition (305 msec) than in either the anomalous (373 msec) or the scrambled (364 msec) prose conditions. The difference between the last two conditions was not, in fact, statistically significant, which suggests that the facilitating effects of normal context are mostly due to its coherence of meaning rather than its simple grammaticality. The later the target word occurred in the normal passages, the greater was its advantage over targets in comparable positions in anomalous or scrambled passages. This shows that the beneficial effects of context increase as more information becomes available to guide the predictive processes.

We argued in Chapter 1 that skilled readers faced with clear print probably make relatively little ongoing use of context to aid word recognition, but that context may be used when stimulus conditions are poor (brief exposure, degraded print, etc.). Poor readers, whose stimulus-driven recognition processes may be somewhat inefficient, also appear to use context more. The situation in normal, everyday speech perception seems close to that experienced by poor readers or by skilled readers with unclear text: The stimulus quality is sufficiently poor, and stimulus-driven recognition sufficiently error-prone, that it is worth the cognitive effort involved in utilising context to aid ongoing word recognition.

Models of Auditory Word Recognition

Models for how context and stimulus information may combine in word recognition have been proposed by Morton (1969) and Marslen-Wilson (1980, 1984) among others. As in Chapter 1, each word in a listener's vocabulary is represented by a different unit or node (or "logogen" in Morton's terminology) in a word recognition system. A word is recognised when the level of activity in its unit reaches a certain value. Incoming stimulus information from a word being heard obviously contributes to that level of activation, but so too does context, via comprehension of what has already passed. Thus context is used to increase activity in the recognition units for likely next words so that less stimulus information is necessary to effect recognition. It is important to note than in very few models is context used to actively predict *single* likely upcoming words: In the view of most psycholinguists that would not be a viable way of organising a recognition system. Rather, context is used to increase activation levels in a *set* of likely word units. Thus after the context "He went to the shops for some . . ." a large number of units would be partially activated (bread, meat, sausages, stamps, etc.), making any of that set easier to recognise. An unlikely continuation ". . . for some windows" would still be perceptible, but activity in the unit for "windows" would have to rise from zero, so recognition would take fractionally longer.

Marslen-Wilson's "cohort model" of word recognition exploits another crucial difference between reading and listening. In reading, all the letters of a word are seen simultaneously and are probably identified in parallel. Heard words, in contrast, are strung out in time, with speech sounds (phonemes) impinging sequentially upon the auditory system. Marslen-Wilson and Welsh (1978) argue that the first sounds of a heard word serve to activate the recognition units of all likely words beginning with those sounds. This set is known as the "word-initial cohort." The function of subsequent sounds is to eliminate words from the cohort which do not contain those sounds in those positions. Suppose, for example, that you have just heard the initial sounds of a word beginning "tre." Assuming there is no context to help rule out any possibilities, the speaker could be in the process of saying any one of the 21 words in English that begin "tre" (trek, trellis, treasure, treble, etc.). If the next sound is "m" then 17 of that cohort can be eliminated, leaving just 4 candidates (tremble, tremolo, tremor, and tremulous). If the fourth sound is "b" then you know that the word being spoken is tremble (or one of its variants like trembles or trembling).

In one study described in Marslen-Wilson (1980), subjects were asked to listen to a passage of text and press a button as rapidly as possible when they heard a target word. The average duration of the target words was 370 msec yet the average time to press the button as measured from the onset of the target word was only 275 msec. That is, the button had normally been pressed when the word was only three-quarters finished, and if we bear in mind that it takes time to execute a button-push, then we realise that the target words were being identified after only about half of their length. According to Marslen-Wilson (1980) a word is identified after just enough of the word has been perceived to specify it completely and exclude all other members of the cohort.

Visual Aspects of Listening

Next time you have the opportunity, try this simple experiment. Switch your television on to a news or similar programme where there is someone talking straight to the camera. Have the volume set quite low. Now turn on your radio and tune in between stations so that it produces a hissing noise. Turn the radio's volume up until it begins to be difficult to make out the words being spoken by the television announcer. Now observe the effects on the intelligibility of the speech of either looking at the face of the person who is talking or closing your eyes. If you have got the set-up right you should find that the speech is much easier to discern against the hissing noise coming from the radio, and seems much clearer, when you have your eyes open and are looking at the speaker than if you have your eyes closed. That is, visual information from the speaker's lips and face, seems to aid the perception and recognition of words in the sound wave (Dodd & Campbell, 1986).

Cotton (1935) provided an early demonstration of this phenomenon. He sat a speaker in a soundproof booth and relayed his speech via loudspeakers to listeners seated outside. The speech was made harder to understand by removing high frequencies and adding a buzzing noise. When the light inside the booth was switched on, so that the listeners could see the speaker's face through a window, the listeners could follow the speech, but with the light off and the speaker no longer visible, the speech was unintelligible. Cotton interpreted this finding as indicating that "there is an important element of visual hearing in all normal individuals."

If the speech wave provides a noisy signal, and if the movements of the speaker's lips and face provide useful supplementary information regarding the words being spoken, then it would seem useful to combine the two sources of input when engaged in natural, face-to-face interaction. Evidence provided by McGurk and MacDonald (1976) suggests that this combining occurs very early on in the processing of the two signals. They made a videotape of someone simply saying "ba-ba-ba. . ." over and over again. They then replaced the sound channel with the synchronised voice of someone saying "ga-ga-ga. . ." The face and lips were thus indicating one syllable (ba-ba) and the voice another (ga-ga). If you closed your eyes, you heard "ga-ga" clearly enough, but if you opened them and looked at the face you heard neither "ga-ga", nor "ba-ba", but "da-da". Presented with two conflicting signals, one visual and the other auditory, the perceptual system resolves upon a compromise—in this case/d/, which is intermediate between /b/ and /g/. This striking illusion shows that visual and auditory information combine at a point *before* any conscious percept is formed, and demonstrates also that what we consciously perceive is the end-product, not the starting point, of extensive cognitive processing.

PROCESSING SENTENCE STRUCTURE

Explaining how we recognise heard words is an important and difficult task for cognitive psychology, but words themselves participate in the higher-level, rule-governed linguistic units we call sentences. There are intermediates too. A sentence like "John ate his tea then he switched on the television" can be divided into two clauses (after "tea") and a larger number of phrases. The words themselves are made of syllables and sounds, so the sentence can be seen to contain a whole hierarchy of units at different levels and of different sizes, each of them playing a role in speech production and comprehension.

We have seen that you do not wait until all of a word has been spoken before you start to process and identify it. So it is with sentences—listeners do not wait until a speaker has finished a sentence before beginning to process and comprehend it. The context experiments discussed earlier illustrate this since they show that listeners will use the meaning of the initial portion of a sentence to help them identify words later in the sentence. Another illustration of our efforts to make sense of sentences continuously as we hear (or read) them is provided by sentences like the following:

1. "The man pushed through the door fell."
2. "I told the girl the cat scratched Bill would help her."
3. "The old dog the footsteps of the young."

In these sentences there is a strong tendency to construe the early portion in a way which the later portion shows to be incorrect. They are known in the literature, for obvious reasons, as "garden path" sentences. In sentence 3, for example, the tendency is to interpret *dog* as a noun qualified by the adjective *old*, whereas the end of the sentence makes it apparent that *dog* here has to be interpreted as a verb. This would not happen if the interpretation of a sentence was deferred until it had been heard or read in its entirety, but because we try to process the sentences as we perceive them word by word we are all too easily "led down the garden path."

Sentence Structure and Sentence Meaning

Consider a simple sentence like *The cat chased the mouse*. It is unlikely you will have any difficulty understanding that sentence and forming a mental picture of what is going on. But what are the elements of the sentence from which you derive its meaning? There are the key words *cat, chase*, and *mouse* which tell you who the participants are and what activity is going on. You learn who is chasing whom, however, not from the words themselves, but from their *arrangement* in the sentence. This is readily demonstrated by the fact that we can retain all the same words but arrange them in a different order and change the meaning of the sentence, as in *The mouse chased the cat*. Note that only certain arrangements are permissible: *Chased mouse the cat the* is not a sentence in English and is quite uninterpretable (though if a foreigner with a weak grasp of English came up to you and said it you could have a guess at what was meant; of which more later).

The rules that determine which strings of words are legal sentences, and which enable us to use the information provided by the arrangements of words in sentences, are called the *syntax* of the language. To understand a sentence we must make use of both the meanings of the individual words it contains and their syntactic arrangement. To describe the syntax of a sentence it is necessary first to assign each word to one of a small set of grammatical categories. In the above example *cat* and *mouse* are nouns, *chased* is a verb, and *the* is a determiner. Other categories include adjectives (e.g. *fierce, timorous*) which "qualify" nouns, adverbs (e.g. *hurriedly, yesterday*) which qualify verbs, pronouns like *we, her* or *it*, and prepositions like *above* or *until*.

The next step is to group the words together in a hierarchical description which captures the overall syntactic structure of the sentence. In our cat-and-mouse example this would involve identifying *The cat* as a noun phrase with *cat* as the subject of the sentence, and *chased the mouse* as a verb phrase containing the verb *chased* (in the past tense) and another noun phrase (*the mouse*) where *mouse* is the grammatical object of the sentence. We can represent this structure diagrammatically as in Fig. 8.1.

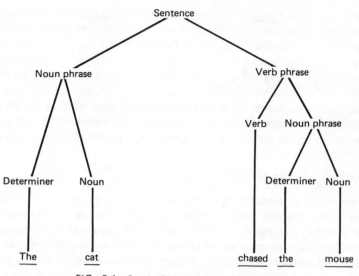

FIG. 8.1   Syntactic structure of a sentence.

In psychological theories of language processing, the cognitive component that is given the job of describing a sentence's syntactic structure in this manner is referred to as the *parser* (to "parse" a sentence is to assign a structural, syntactic description to it). If the human parser is to keep up with speech being heard and words being recognised, then it must constantly be making the best guess from the information it already has as to the structure that should be assigned to the words in the sentence. When it makes a mistake, as in garden-path sentences, it must be able to go back and reparse the sentence differently. Modern theories assume that the parser uses a set of *strategies* in its attempts to describe sentence structure (Pullman, 1986). So-called "function words". like *a, the, to, at, because,* or *when* play an important part in such strategies. The determiners *a/an* and *the* usually signal the beginning of a new noun phrase, while auxiliaries like *is, was, were,* and *have* signal the beginnings of verb phrases. Words like *which, because,* or *since* often mark the onsets of new clauses, and so on.

These strategies are not foolproof. Garden-path sentences, for example, are ones which are prone to be mis-parsed by such strategies. But these are, of course, precisely the sorts of sentences that mislead us, suggesting that we do indeed operate with fallible parsing strategies rather than foolproof rules. We have hinted at how some of these strategies might conceivably work, but there is no current concensus regarding details. We shall limit outselves here to brief considerations of two questions that have attracted considerable research attention, namely, "Is the human parser a separate cognitive component from those responsible for processing the meanings of words and sentences?" and "If it is, can its operations nevertheless be *influenced* by the processes that deal with meanings?" Our tentative answer will be "Yes" to both questions.

The Separateness of the Parser

There is no a priori reason why sentence structure should be processed separately from word and sentence meaning. Computer programs have been built which do not make this assumption and run with some success (e.g. Schank, 1975). Nevertheless, there are reasons for thinking that the human parser might operate independently from meaning. One line of evidence comes from a particular disorder of language processing that can arise as a result of brain injury.

Brain injury can affect language in many different ways. In one type of disorder, commonly known as Broca's aphasia, the patient appears to lose the capacity to process sentence structure while retaining the capacity to identify word meanings and formulate hypotheses as to sentence meanings. Caramazza and Zurif (1976) asked their patients to match sentences to a choice of two pictures. Some of the sentences were of the type: *The apple that the boy is eating is red*. Suppose you could understand the "content words" *apple, boy, eat*, and *red* in that sentence but could make no use of word order or of the function words *the, that*, and *is* (i.e. no use of syntax). Despite your handicap you would probably arrive at the correct construal because other construals (e.g. an apple was eating a red boy) are nonsensical. Caramazza and Zurif found that the Broca's aphasics interpreted over 90 per cent of these sentences correctly.

Another class of sentences used by Caramazza and Zurif (1976) depended, however, on syntax for their correct interpretation. These were sentences like *The cow that the monkey is scaring is yellow*. Armed only with the meanings of *cow, monkey, scaring*, and *yellow* and without any syntactic skill, you would be at a loss to know whether the sentence was about a yellow monkey scaring a cow, a yellow cow being scared by a monkey, etc. Caramazza and Zurif found their Broca's aphasics to be quite unable to select correctly between pictures depicting such alternatives, though normal subjects and aphasics suffering from other sorts of language disorders performed well.

The behaviour of the Broca's aphasics is consistent with the hypothesis that they have an impairment of syntactic parsing mechanisms. They can still understand content words, however, and can use what they understand to guess at what a sentence they are hearing might mean. It is surprising how effective that strategy is. Until quite recently the sentence comprehension of such patients was thought to be intact, and fairly subtle tests like those of Caramazza and Zurif were needed to reveal their deficit.

Nevertheless, the deficit exists, and its importance in the present context lies in the fact that it is hard to see how a selective impairment of syntactic parsing could occur unless the parser were a discrete cognitive component, separate from the processes which handle meanings and which remain intact in Broca's aphasics.

Higher-level Influences on the Parser

Our second question was directed at whether the parser, even if a distinct component, might nevertheless be influenced by other linguistic processes. How might we set about answering this question? Psycholinguists who have addressed themselves to the issue of interaction have asked whether the meanings of the words a sentence contains can influence the ease with which subjects can parse the sentence syntactically.

Crain and Steedman (in press) studied the influence of both sentence content and preceding context on subjects' tendency to be misled by garden-path sentences. On the issue of sentence content, they showed that subjects were much more likely to misparse sentences like 1 below than sentences like 2:

1. *Teachers taught by the Berlitz method passed the test.*
2. *Children taught by the Berlitz method passed the test.*

These two sentences are identical on all but the first word and are indistinguishable syntactically (*teachers* and *children* are both nouns and occupy the same grammatical roles in their respective sentences). The correct construal of both sentences is along the lines of "Teachers/children [*who were*] taught by the Berlitz method passed the test." Listeners are used to the idea of children being taught, and naturally parse sentence 2 in that way. In so doing they avoid the garden-path effect induced by sentence 1 in which the listener's first tendency is to suppose that the teachers were doing the teaching rather than being taught.

In a second experiment Crain and Steedman showed that sentences preceding a potential garden-path sentence could bias the likelihood of subjects misparsing. Consider the following pair of sentences:

3. *The psychologist told the wife that he was having trouble with her husband.*
4. *The psychologist told the wife that he was having trouble with to leave her husband.*

The two are identical up to the word *with*. The ending of sentence 3 (. . . *her husband*) makes it clear that the clause *that he was having trouble with*

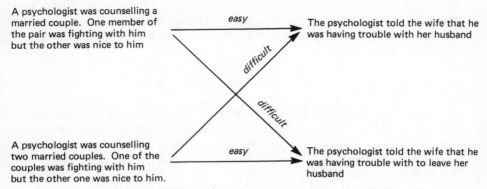

FIG. 8.2   Illustration of the design of Crain and Steedman's (in press) experiment showing that preceding context can affect subjects' tendency to be misled by "garden-path" sentences.

belongs with the verb *told*. In sentence 4, however, the ending . . . *to leave her husband* signals that the clause in question modifies *wife*.

The ingenuity of Crain and Steedman's experiment lies in the way they were able to devise contexts which rendered both of sentences 3 and 4 either easy to parse or difficult (because of the tendency to misparse). Their design is illustrated in Fig. 8.2. The two "opposite" combinations of context and test sentence were easy because the meaning of the context biases people towards the appropriate parsing. The two "diagonal" combinations, however, were difficult because the context leads people initially to prefer the inappropriate (garden-path) parsing of the test sentences.

The importance of this experiment lies in its demonstration that the meaning of what has already been heard or read, and the meaning of the sentence currently being processed, affect the moment-to-moment decisions of the syntactic parser. We now consider another aspect of sentence processing in which a similar interaction between structural and conceptual processing has been demonstrated.

Anaphora

If you hear a sentence like "John finished writing the letter then he went to bed," you have no difficulty knowing to whom the pronoun *he* refers: There is only one candidate in the sentence, namely John. The phenomenon whereby an expression like *he* can take its meaning from some other part of the text, or from the nonlinguistic context, is known as *anaphora*. In the sentence just quoted, *he* is an anaphoric pronoun referring back to John. Anaphor can also point forwards as in "After he had finished writing the letter John went to bed." An example of anaphora pointing out of the discourse to people or events in the world might be:

Q: "Are you coming round tonight?"
A: "No, they've told me I've got to stay in and work."

Here the pronoun *they* points to people (parents perhaps) whom the second speaker assumes the first will be able to infer with the aid of his or her general knowledge about the speaker.

The task of working out the referents of anaphoric expressions can sometimes become quite complex: To what, for example, do the two *its* refer in the sentence *The dog that most deserved it won the prize that it had been entered for*? How did you work it out? An issue relating to the resolution of anaphoric reference concerns the situation where there are two or more expressions in a sentence that are candidates for being the referent of a pronoun. An example might be:

5. *Karen poured a drink for Emily. She then put the bottle down.*

When the sentence-processing apparatus encounters the anaphoric pronoun *She*, how does it decide which of the two women referred to in the previous sentence is the correct referent? Does this process involve activating both possibilities before selecting between them?

An experiment by Frederiksen (1981) addressed itself to this question, though Frederiksen used visual rather than auditory presentation of texts. Texts were presented one sentence at a time on a computer display screen. Subjects were instructed to read each sentence and press a button when they had understood it. Pressing the button triggered the display of the next sentence. This procedure provides a measure of the time needed to process each sentence. Embedded within the text were pairs of sentences in which an anaphoric pronoun in the second sentence referred back to an antecedent in the first sentence. Sometimes the first sentence contained another irrelevant term (like Emily in example 5); sometimes there was just the relevant antecedent in the first sentence (e.g. Karen alone).

Frederiksen found that subjects took significantly longer to read the sentence containing the anaphoric pronoun when there were two potential antecedents in the preceding sentence than when there was just one. Frederiksen concluded that when readers encounter an anaphoric pronoun the set of alternative referents is retrieved and then the most likely one is selected.

If this is the case, what sort of information is employed to select among alternative referents of a pronoun? Winograd (1972) showed by simple but ingenious demonstrations that syntactic information and information about the meanings of individual words are not sufficient to permit anaphoric resolution among rival alternatives. For example, to what group does the word *they* refer in the following two sentences?

6. *The city councillors refused the protestors a licence because they advocated violence.*
7. *The city councillors refused the protestors a licence because they feared violence.*

Most people take *the protestors* to be the referent of *they* in sentence 6, but *the city councillors* to be the referent in 7. Winograd (1972), from whom this example is adapted, noted that this is only because peoples' knowledge of the world tells them that protestors are more likely than city councillors to advocate violence, whereas city councillors are more likely than protestors to fear it. The involvement of general knowledge in anaphoric resolution takes anaphor out of the capabilities of the parser which operates on syntactic information and places it in the domain of high-level conceptual integration.

RETENTION AND LOSS OF SURFACE STRUCTURE

In Chapter 7 we noted several lines of evidence that together point to the importance of the grammatical clause as a unit of sentence formulation. A significant proportion of hesitations, for example, occur between one clause and the next, and certain categories of slip of the tongue occur within but not between clauses. If speakers package conceptual messages into clause-sized units then it would seem likely that listeners will also employ those units in their attempts to reconstruct the speaker's message within their own minds.

This possibility was tested in an experiment by Caplan (1972). His design is best illustrated by example. Subjects heard sentences which could be like either 8 or 9:

8. *Now that artists are working in OIL £ prints are rare.*
9. *Now that artists are working fewer hours £ OIL prints are rare.*

In these sentences £ marks the position of the clause boundary. The reader will note that the endings of these two sentences are the same but their construction is such that the word *OIL* occurs at the end of the first clause in sentence 8 and at the beginning of the second clause in sentence 9. It is, however, the fourth from last word in both sentences.

After hearing a sentence, the subjects in Caplan's (1972) experiment were presented with a "probe" word. Their task was to decide as quickly as possible whether or not the probe word had occurred in the preceding sentence. For sentences 8 and 9, the probe word would be *OIL*, the word which occurs the same distance from the end of both sentences but in the first clause of sentence 8 and the second clause of sentence 9. Caplan found that "yes" responses were significantly faster for probe words in the second clause then for probe words in the first clause.

Jarvella (1970, 1971) had subjects listen to lengthy passages of text. Occasionally, the text was interrupted and the subjects asked to write down, word for word, as much as they could of the passage immediately preceding the interruption. The interruption was always timed to come after a sequence of three clauses. In one condition of the experiment the first two clauses formed one sentence and the third clause another, for example:

"The document had also blamed him for having failed to disprove the charges, Taylor was later fired by the President."

In the other condition of the experiment the first clause stood alone as a sentence with the second and third clauses combining into another sentence, for example:

"The tone of the document was threatening. Having failed to disprove the charges, Taylor was later fired by the President."

It will be noted that the second clause ("having failed to disprove the charges") is the same in both conditions. However, a sentence boundary stands between the clause and the point of interruption in the first condition but not in the second. Jarvella found 54 per cent correct recall of the crucial second clause where it was part of the most recent sentence, but only 21 per cent recall when a sentence boundary had intervened. The presence of the third clause seems to have caused some loss of the verbatim form of the second clause, even when the two are combined in the most recently heard sentence. This supports Caplan's (1972) claims about the importance of clause boundaries in sentence comprehension. But the additional sentence boundary intervening in the first condition has led to yet more loss of "surface structure" information about the precise wording of the text.

In Chapter 9 we shall see how the end-product of text comprehension is typically an abstract representation of the gist of the text. Surface structure (verbatim) information is only occasionally retained in long-term storage. The results of Caplan (1972) and Jarvella (1970, 1971) suggest that surface structure is retained in some literal but temporary form of storage while a clause or sentence is being parsed and comprehended, but that the surface structure is then normally lost fairly rapidly as the products of comprehension are woven into the developing representation of the meaning of the text as a whole. Before advancing to those higher levels, however, we take a little time to look at the role of temporary storage or "short-term memory" in linguistic and other modes of cognitive processing.

Short-term Storage in Language Processing

The German psychologist Ebbinghaus (1885) studied his own capacity to memorise lists of meaningless "nonsense syllables" (*keb, pif, lut*, and so on). He observed that there was a limit of about seven or eight on the number of syllables he could repeat correctly after a single presentation and considered this limit to be ". . . a measure of the ideas of this sort which I can grasp in a single unitary conscious act." The English philosopher Jacobs (1887) similarly studied his own ability to repeat random sequences of letters or digits and asked: ". . . as to what is the exact power of the mind which is involved in reproducing these sounds . . . It may be described as the mind's power of taking on certain material . . . We clearly cannot take in without first taking on, and the mental operation we have been testing thus seems a necessary preliminary to the obtaining of all . . . material."

Ebbinghaus and Jacobs thus seem to have believed that the mind is limited in the number of things it can take in at one time, and that this limitation can be measured by discovering the point at which people break down in attempting to repeat progressively longer strings of randomly ordered items. This notion of memory span (as we would now call that limit) as a general restriction on the uptake of material persisted for a long time, cropping up half a century later in influential models of memory such as those of Miller (1956), Waugh and Norman (1965), and Atkinson and Shiffrin (1968) (see Chapter 6).

We now know that the limited-capacity store (or stores) revealed in immediate recall situations is not some general way-station for all incoming stimuli. Neuropsychological evidence once again was used in arriving at this conclusion. Shallice and Warrington (1970) discussed a patient (KF) who, as a result of brain injury, had a severely restricted memory span (limited to just one or two digits or letters). If the short-term mental store were responsible for entering material into longer-term storage and possibly retrieving it out of storage, then KF would surely be expected to have some difficulties with forming or retrieving long-term memories. No such difficulties appeared on testing—KF's ability to learn and recall word lists and other material was entirely normal.

A further observation regarding KF helped narrow down the role of the short-term store underlying memory span, namely that whereas his immediate recall of auditorily presented letters, digits, and words was greatly reduced, his immediate memory for meaningful environmental sounds (e.g. a cat mewing, a telephone ringing, a whistle blowing, etc.) was normal. His memory span limitation was for verbal material only, causing Shallice and Warrington (1974) to propose that the limited capacity store underlying memory span for random sequences of digits, letters, words, and so on should properly be termed "auditory-verbal short-term memory."

There are further lines of evidence pointing to the conclusion that the store under consideration is speech-based. First, immediate recall of similar-sounding letters or words is worse than immediate recall of different sounding items, and errors typically involve the substitution of similar-sounding items (Conrad, 1964). Second, the memory span for long or slow-to-articulate words is worse than for short or quick-to-articulate words (Baddeley, Thomson, & Buchanan, 1975). Third, memory span is reduced if subjects are required to articulate aloud or silently while the material is being presented (e.g. repeatedly saying "the-the-the"). With written material this concurrent articulation also removes the effects of similarity of sound and of word length, suggesting that subvocal articulation (or "inner speech") is necessary in order to convert written material into a speech code (Baddeley, Thomson, & Buchanan, 1975). With auditory input, in contrast, although concurrent articulation reduces memory span, the effects of word length and sound similarity remain, suggesting that heard material enjoys more direct access to the speech-based store.

Work on short-term memory has, therefore, revealed the existence of a speech-based temporary store with a limited capacity. It has also taught us something about that store's properties. What it has *not* taught us as clearly, however, is the purpose of the store—what function it serves in everyday cognition. Immediate recall of random sequences of items is not something we are often called upon to do. The example repeated over and over again is that of holding a telephone number in your head in the interval between looking it up in a directory and dialling it, but given that the widespread use of telephones is a twentieth-century phenomenon it is most unlikely that Nature has equipped us with a short-term store designed primarily for that purpose.

Can we tie auditory-verbal short-term memory into speech comprehension? Hitch (1980) did this by noting that the evidence of Jarvella (1971), Caplan (1972), and others suggests temporary storage of the sentence or clause currently being processed with fairly rapid loss of information upon completion. Hitch proposed that subjects called upon to repeat random sequences of letters, digits or words may make use of an input store whose everyday function is to preserve in a speech-based form the "surface structure" of sentences which are in the process of being parsed and comprehended.

That proposal is reasonable and quite possibly correct, but as Morton (1970) and Ellis (1979) pointed out, speech *production* also has its temporary storage requirements. In Chapter 7 we discussed evidence that whole clauses or sentences may be planned before the articulation of the first word begins. Such pre-planning introduces the need for speech-based storage on the output side. Hitch (1980) and Monsell (1984) have raised the possibility of two speech-based short-term memory stores, one tied to perception and the other to production, and have attempted to delineate some of their properties.

Monsell's (1984) view is that cognition is sustained by many different processors, each performing its own specialised operations. Some of these processors will require the aid of dedicated short-term "buffer stores." Alternatively, they may themselves demonstrate temporary storage in the way they are able to keep active the material they are currently engaged in processing. The cognitive system will therefore have the capability to demonstrate temporary storage or activation of visual, acoustic, lexical (word-based), syntactic, semantic, phonological (sound-based), and other sorts of information or code. The particular demands of the current task will determine which sorts of temporary storage are employed.

Ultimately, therefore, we may have to acknowledge the existence of many distributed short-term stores of which the speech-based stores we have considered are just two. The work on anaphora that we discussed earlier in this chapter, for example, points to the active maintenance in a more conceptual form of recently mentioned participants in the actions described in a text.

IGNORING SPEECH

In all the situations discussed so far, the listener is faced with only one incoming speech signal. But it is not uncommon to be in a situation where two or more speech signals are competing for attention. You may, for example, be trying to listen to the news on the radio while other people in the same room are holding a conversation.

The questions we shall address in this section are, first, how are you able to attend to one input and ignore another? and, second, what is the fate of the ignored signal? Research on how people cope with two rival speech signals has tended to be pigeon-holed as "selective attention" rather than "speech processing." In Chapter 5 we looked briefly at aspects of people's performance on a task in which they are required to monitor two incoming speech signals and respond to them in some way. There we were concerned with possible limitations on people's capacity to do two things at once: Here we approach the same literature from a different position, that of trying to discover what happens to speech which is actively ignored.

Cherry (1953) inaugurated research into how people cope with two competing speech signals. He called it the "cocktail party phenomenon" after the way one can attend to the conversation of a nearby group of people at a party and ignore that of your own group. Cherry's (1953) subjects wore headphones, with one message being presented to the left ear and another to the right. The subjects' task was to "shadow" (repeat continuously) one of the messages but ignore the other (the so-called 'dichotic listening task").

This is relatively easy to do if the two signals are perceptually different, being in two different voices or languages, or presented at two different locations. It is also fairly easy if the signals are conceptually different passages on different topics. It becomes very difficult, however, if perceptual and conceptual cues are removed. Cherry and Taylor (1954) constructed two passages from strings of cliches (e.g. "I am happy to be here today to talk to the man in the street. Gentlemen, the time has come to stop beating about the bush . . ."). When the two passages were presented at the same location in the same voice, subjects found it almost impossible to shadow one and ignore the other because all of the cues which might normally enable a listener to keep the two signals apart had been removed.

It would seem that attention can act at a peripheral, perceptual level or at a central, conceptual level to select one signal or message and ignore another. In most normal situations the rival signals will be coming from two different speakers with two different voices in two different locations. We might expect that under such circumstances one signal can be blocked out completely while the other is attended to. That is certainly what it feels like: Cherry's (1953) subjects claimed to be utterly unaware of the content of the neglected message, often failing to notice when it switched from normal English either to German or to English played backwards, and showing virtually no recall of the content of the ignored message at the end of the experiment.

Treisman and Geffen's (1967) subjects shadowed one of two auditory messages, but were asked at the same time to listen out for key "target words" which could be presented to either ear. If they heard a designated target word they were to tap on the table in front of them. The detection rate for targets in the message being shadowed was 87 per cent, whereas detection of targets presented in the message being ignored was a mere 8 per cent. This result quantifies dramatically people's apparent unawareness of the content of ignored speech.

But how reliable are people's conscious introspections under such circumstances? There is now a considerable body of evidence showing that although speakers may have little or no *conscious* awareness of the unattended message, something of its meaning can be shown to have been registered. Lackner and Garrett (1972), for example, had subjects attend to, and then paraphrase or interpret, sentences presented to one ear while ignoring sentences presented to the other ear. Some of the sentences they had to interpret were ambiguous. For instance, in the sentence "The spy put out the torch as our signal to attack", "put out" could be taken to mean either "switched off" or "made visible." Although subjects, as usual, claimed to have been largely unaware of the content of the ignored sentences, they nevertheless interpreted "put out" more often in the first sense when the accompanying, ignored sentence contained the word "extinguished," and more often in the second sense when the accompanying sentence contained the word "displayed." The significance of this finding is that this sort of biasing of the interpretation given to the attended message could only occur if the unattended (ignored) message was processed for its meaning, even if that meaning never entered consciousness.

Other findings using somewhat different experimental designs point to the same conclusion. Lewis (1970) and Treisman, Squire, and Green (1974) found that the time to shadow a word presented to the attended ear was slowed if a synonym of that word was simultaneously presented to the unattended ear (though, as usual, subjects claimed no awareness of the unattended channel).

How do we relate these findings on the meanings of the words of which listeners are unaware to the research on recognising and understanding speech which we discussed earlier in the chapter? According to the theory outlined earlier, a word is recognised when the level of activity in its unit reaches a certain value, and that level of activity is affected both by stimulus information and context. So, if you are following one message, a set of likely units will be activated as a sentence progresses and words will be recognised quickly if they fit the context. If at least some of the words that are *not* being attended to also activate their recognition units then the effects which we have described would result.

We can take the Lackner and Garrett (1972) result as an example. Here a word that is clearly heard has more than one meaning, so several units and several meanings could be activated. However, the unattended word adds to the activation of one of those meanings, so that comes to be the dominant one.

The finding that a synonym presented to the unattended ear increases the time to say the word on the attended ear is probably best explained in terms of the activation of an output unit as well as a recognition one. Both of the words presented fit the context and so they are activated to the same degree, but only one is to be produced. The difficulty is deciding which output unit to activate, although the person is not aware that the units have been activated. If partial activation is occurring in some of the unattended tasks and complete activation occurs in others, but there is competition for the required output, then dichotic listening or dichotic ignoring fits quite well into the current theories of word recognition and production.

This would also accord with the work on visual word recognition, which appears to have established that meanings can be activated by words that are presented so briefly that the subject is not aware of having seen anything at all (e.g. Allport, 1977; Marcel, 1983a,b). However, as complete activation of a recognition unit should mean that a word is perceived consciously, it is possible that in the dichotic listening task the activation which is available from the unattended channel is less than the normal amount, although it is not entirely clear how such attenuation would happen (Broadbent, 1971).

Work on the fate of the unattended signal has been limited to word and meaning recognition. We do not know whether listeners can process the sentence structure of an unattended speech signal, or whether syntactic analysis is confined to the attended channel. Studies of simultaneous comprehension reported in Chapter 5 suggest that some high-level analysis is possible after extended practice, but for normal perception it seems likely that the complexities of the analysis required make it impossible to perceive two streams of speech at the same time. Context and coherence guide the resolution of ambiguity and lead to selection of one input from other possible ones.

SUMMARY

Most current theories of speech perception regard word recognition as involving the activation of a permanent stored representation of the word (a "recognition unit" or "logogen"). This is similar to the accounts of the recognition of written words and familiar faces and objects discussed in Chapters 1 and 2. As in those cases, context could exert its influence through an effect upon the level of activity in particular recognition units. Although speech perception is commonly thought of as an exclusively auditory process, visual information from a speaker's lip and face movements can be shown to be an important additional cue.

It is probably fair to say that theories of how we process speech at the sentence level and above are less well developed than theories of word-level processing. It seems likely, however, that the cognitive component which assigns structural descriptions to sentences (the "parser") exists as an independent subsystem, though its operations can be shown to be influenced by the results of the interpretation of word and sentence meanings. Some aspects of sentence processing, such as determining the referents of pronouns like *he*, *she*, or *it*, can be shown to have access to, and be influenced by, a listener's general knowledge of the world.

The interpretation of an early portion of a sentence can be influenced or determined by a later portion. For this and other reasons, listeners must store the form of a sentence at least until it has been fully decoded. Short-term memory capabilities have evolved for this function, though they are also employed in the performance of other cognitive tasks, as we saw in Chapter 6. Ignoring one of two competing speech signals is an aspect of doing two things at once (Chapter 5): Our interest in it here was primarily for the evidence that meaning can be at least partially recovered from an ignored source, even though the listener may have no conscious awareness of, or memory for, that meaning.

Finally, language comprehension does not stop at word meanings and sentence structures. In Chapter 1 we examine how lengthy texts are understood and remembered. In so far as high-level comprehension includes and requires the solving of problems and the drawing of inferences, there are additional links between this chapter and Chapters 12 and 13.

Two recent textbooks that provide more detailed coverage of speech perception and sentence processing are A. Garnham (1985), *Psycholinguistics: Central Topics*, and A. W. Ellis and G. Beattie (1986), *The Psychology of Language and Communication*. More specialised coverage of particular aspects can be found in H. Bouma and D. G. Bouwhuis (1984), *Attention and Performance X: Control of Language Processes*.

9 Reading a Book: Comprehending and Remembering Text

In Chapters 6 and 8 we looked at the processes that go on when we hear or read and make sense of single sentences. In ordinary life, however, it is rare for us to hear a single sentence on its own. What we hear are conversations, stories, jokes, lectures, and so on. They all involve many sentences which each convey some pieces of information that the listener needs to abstract and integrate into the full message that the speaker is seeking to convey. Similarly with written material, we read articles, stories, chapters, etc. In doing so we have to put together the meaning of the full message from the individual sentences. Furthermore, it would be wrong to imply that this happens only for written and spoken language. It is a general aspect of our lives that we have to construct the more general meaning of what is happening from the continuous flow of our experiences. To do this we must draw upon the information that we have stored in memory. Using it and the new information from our current experience we have to interpret what is happening, draw inferences about what is implied but not explicitly stated, and develop a coherent understanding of the situation.

In this chapter we take the specific example of reading a book. As with the other chapters, however, we are using this merely as an example. The processes that we discuss will normally apply equally to what we hear as to what we read. Indeed, they apply to most of our experiences.

We consider first the way in which stories are structured. Then we look at the use of our past experience in guiding our comprehension and memorising of a story. Next, we turn to the way in which a new story may be integrated with connections made between the elements involved. Finally, we turn to the types of mental representations that may be stored as the result of reading a new story.

Have you ever looked at a book written in a foreign language? Can you remember the blank feeling? Can you compare it with the experience of reading the most interesting book which you have ever encountered—the one that kept you engrossed for hours. Marks on paper that are quite incomprehensible if you cannot read the language, are capable of stimulating your cognitive system to occupy you completely for hours on end. How? What is going on?

We made a start on this question in Chapter 8 when we discussed how we read individual sentences. In this chapter we will go further. We will be asking how passages from a story are comprehended, how they are built into a mental representation of what is going on in the book, and how this determines what you can remember. There are two important questions. Firstly, what part does our memory of past experiences play in our understanding of both real events and stories? Secondly, how much of our comprehending of real and imaginary events involves inferences and deductions that we make automatically using the knowledge we already possess? Following these questions, we can ask how authors take into account our use of past experience and our making of inferences.

Consider the following short paragraph.

As evening approached the road became icy. John yawned, but forced himself to concentrate. Suddenly, ahead of him a truck swerved out of control. John saw a car being rammed onto the embankment.

This is not a work of any great literary merit, but it is quite comprehensible. Now, look again and notice how many assumptions and inferences you made, based on your past experiences. You probably assumed that the road became icy because it got colder, which often happens in the evening. It *might* have got icy for several other reasons. For example, it could have been freezing all day, but only just have snowed. A pipe might have burst. A tanker might be leaking. No doubt you could invent many other examples. But you were not puzzled about why it was icy because you assumed, without conscious thought, that the most likely explanation would be a change in temperature. Here are some other inferences that you probably drew: (1) that John was the driver (he could have been a navigator, or merely a passenger trying to stay awake); (2) that the truck skidded on the ice; (3) that the truck, rather than some other vehicle, rammed the car; and (4) that the car had been on the road. You probably drew other inferences, but those listed so far should be enough to illustrate how inferring and constructing, on the basis of prior knowledge, is a fundamental aspect of reading connected prose. So, how are these inferences made, and what implications do they have for the way a book is written?

Every author assumes that readers make these sorts of assumptions and inferences. Given how our cognitive systems function, that is a relief! Few of us could bear to read many pages of a book which took nothing for granted. You could try imagining how long the example passage would be if most of the assumptions were eliminated! Few of us could bear to read more than a page or two of such stuff.

You may wonder why a passage in which all the assumptions are spelt out should be boring. It is so because we read, as we do most other things, for a purpose, and whether we continue reading depends on our motivation and the success with which reading supplies our requirements, both for knowledge and entertainment. Questions about what determines our interests and needs are outside the scope of this book. In this chapter we are concerned mainly with what goes on while you are reading a book that you do find well written and interesting.

COMPONENTS OF STORY COMPREHENSION

What is happening when you read a story? You are comprehending the meaning of each sentence, you are drawing inferences and making deductions. But is there more involved? Is a story more than a collection of sentences? If so, how does this influence our cognitions? In this section we will first explore these higher-level aspects of the structure of a story. Then we will return to a more detailed discussion of the processes underlying the comprehension of the story.

When we read a story we must make sense of each sentence, but that is only a beginning. In a story, each sentence is part of an episode. Most episodes are in the story for a purpose. Each episode must be constructed and understood in the wider context of the story's plot. A story has a structure, with each sentence contributing towards an episode which will, in turn, move towards a resolution of the plot. Think about a familiar story, perhaps a fairy story like *Goldilocks and the Three Bears*. Can you identify how the story builds in episodes towards its resolution? Several cognitive psychologists have emphasised this structure within stories. They have suggested that, just as sentences have a syntax, irrespective of their meaning, which can be described by a grammar, so well-written stories can be analysed has having a "story grammar." Rumelhart (1975) analysed the structure of folk fables and Thorndyke (1977) applied Rumelhart's story grammar to the learning of short stories. Figure 9.1 illustrates a simplified version of their story grammar. As with the grammars that describe the construction of sentences, this story grammar consists of rules (Table 9.1) which can be used to generate a branching structure as each higher-order component is rewritten into several new components, eventually reaching the structure of the story itself.

As will be seen from the set of rewrite rules, this grammar analyses a story into a goal, one or more episodes, and a resolution of the situations. Episodes involve the setting of subgoals and attempts to achieve the resolution of the subgoal. The idea of a story grammar becomes clearer if you imagine that you are reading a short story. You will want to identify early on what the story is about; in other words, you will want to know the goal towards which the story will work. In much romantic fiction it is the girl getting the boy, in a detective novel it is the resolution of the murder.

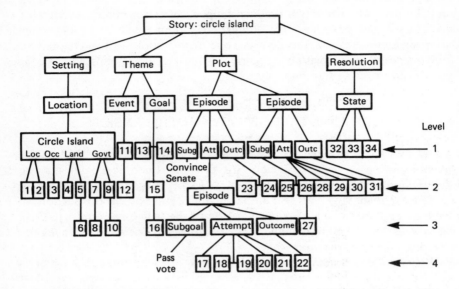

(1) Circle Island is located in the middle of the Atlantic Ocean, (2) north of Ronald Island. (3) The main occupations on the island are farming and ranching. (4) Circle Island has good soil, (5) but few rivers and (6) hence a shortage of water.(7) The island is run democratically. (8) All issues are decided by a majority vote of the islanders. (9) The governing body is a senate, (10) whose job is to carry out the will of the majority. (11) Recently, an island scientist discovered a cheap method (12) of converting salt water in fresh water. (13) As a result, the island farmers wanted (14) to build a canal across the island, (15) so that they could use water from the canal (16) to cultivate the island's central region. (17) Therefore, the farmers formed a procanal association (18) and persuaded a few senators (19) to join. (20) The procanal association brought the construction idea to a vote. (21) All the islanders voted. (22) The majority voted in favour of construction. (23) The senate, however, decided that (24) the farmer's proposed canal was ecologically unsound. (25) The senators agreed (26) to build a smaller canal (27) that was 2 feet wide and 1 foot deep. (28) After starting construction on the smaller canal,⁄ (29) the islanders discovered that (30) no water would flow into it. (31) Thus the project was abandoned. (32) The farmers were angry (33) because of the failure of the canal project. (34) Civil war appeared inevitable.

FIG. 9.1 Analysis of a short story. The number in each box refers to the proposition in the story. From Thorndyke, P. W. (1977) Cognitive structures in comprehension and memory in narrative discourse. *Cognitive Psychology*, 9, 77–110. Copyright Academic Press. Reproduced by permission.

TABLE 9.1
Thorndyke's (1977) Grammar Rules Used in the Analysis of the
Story Presented in Fig. 9.1.

Rule number	Rule		
(1)	Story	⟶	Setting + Theme + Plot + Resolution
(2)	Setting	⟶	Characters + Location + Time
(3)	Theme	⟶	(Event) + Goal
(4)	Plot	⟶	Episode
(5)	Episode	⟶	Subgoal + Attempt + Outcome
(6)	Attempt	⟶	Event / Episode
(7)	Outcome	⟶	Event / State
(8)	Resolution	⟶	Event / State
(9)	Subgoal / Goal	⟶	Desired State
(10)	Characters / Location / Time	⟶	State

On the way to this goal you will expect several episodes. The characters will have subgoals that they need to achieve before the main goal is reached. So, for example, a detective story requires the murder to be committed, the murder to be discovered, the brilliant detective to become involved, and so on.

Here we do not need to dwell for too long upon the particular story grammar described, nor should it be assumed that a grammar for all stories can be easily generated. What we want to point out is that a story can be legitimately thought of as consisting of component goals and activities which make up the plot. The readers must comprehend these relationships if they are to understand the story. Understanding a story requires far more than the comprehension of the sentences of which it is composed; it also involves the construction of the whole story, including the identifying of goals and the analysing of what is happening in the light of the ongoing construction.

COMPREHENSION AND MEMORY

So far we have illustrated how inferences are drawn and a representation constructed at several different levels when a story is read. It is now time to ask more detailed questions about these processes. How do we

The procedure is actually quite simple. First you arrange things into different groups. Of course, one pile may be sufficient depending on how much there is to do. If you have to go somewhere else due to lack of facilities, this is the next step; otherwise you are pretty well set. It is important not to overdo things. That is, it is better to do too few things at once than too many. In the short run this may not seem important, but complications can easily arise. A mistake can be expensive as well. At first the whole procedure will seem complicated. Soon, however, it will become just another facet of life. It is difficult to foresee any end to the necessity for this task in the immediate future, but then one never can tell. After the procedure is completed, one arranges the material into different groups again. Then they can be put into their appropriate places. Eventually they will be used once more and the whole cycle will then have to be repeated. However, that is part of life.

FIG. 9.2   Passage for comprehension and recall. From Bransford, J. D. & Johnson, M. K. (1972) Contextual prerequisites for understanding: Some investigations of comprehension and recall. *Journal of Verbal Learning and Verbal Behavior*, *11*, 717–726. Copyright Academic Press 1972. Reproduced by permission.

comprehend an individual sentence? How do we use our experience to help make sense of what we are reading? How does this process of comprehension influence what we are subsequently able to remember from the story? As an introduction to these questions, read through the passage in Fig. 9.2 and then try to recall it to yourself. Did you find it hard to understand the passage? Was it then very difficult to remember what was in it? Why should this be?

If we now tell you that the passage was about washing clothes, and you re-read it, you should find it much easier to understand and then to remember. Bransford (1979) has shown in several experiments that once readers can comprehend a passage they find it far easier to remember.

But why was the passage hard to comprehend initially? Presumably because you were not able to find a suitable theme from your past experience that you could bring into play. Once the idea of washing clothes was suggested, all your past experience of washing was made available to help the comprehension of the passage.

Comprehension and memory are interwoven. Comprehension involves recalling information from memory and interpreting and predicting what is experienced under the guidance of those memories. In turn, what is stored in memory as a record of a particular act of comprehension will depend on the activities involved and the particular construction of the event that has been formed in the cognitive workspace (see Chapter 6).

Let us consider a specific example. What happened when in our earlier example, you read the sentence *As evening approached the road became icy*? Each word triggered a recognition unit, which itself triggered the retrieval of stored knowledge about evenings, roads, and ice. From these, your cognitive system was able to construct a representation of what was going on. As you read farther you discovered that the passage was about driving on the road, and this will have activated stored information and expectations about that particular activity. These expectations will allow you to make the appropriate inferences and to select the necessary information from the next input. The expectations will guide your comprehension. A record of the construction that you have made will be entered into memory. Where expectations have been fulfilled these will be strengthened. Where they have not been fulfilled a record will be made of the failure. If you failed altogether to comprehend the passage you will be left with disjointed memories of sentences and little that you can easily retrieve. This is just what happened for the subjects of Bransford and Johnson (1972, 1973) when they were read the "washing clothes" passage of Fig. 9.2 without knowing its title. Most of them rated it as incomprehensible, and, when they were asked to recall the passage, they could remember, on average, only 2.8 of the 18 idea units it contains. Another group of subjects had one slight difference in their experience of the passage; they were read the title "washing clothes" first. To these subjects the passage made good sense, and what is more, they could recall an average of 5.8 of the idea units. Bransford and Johnson also tested a third group who were given the title after they had heard the passage but before their recall attempt. These subjects did not benefit from knowing the title at that stage. Both their ratings of their comprehension of the passage and their recall matched that of the group who never heard the title.

Of course, we do not often have such a vague passage to read as that deliberately composed by Bransford and Johnson, but their results do tell us a lot about normal comprehension and memory. Where their subjects were able to draw upon their knowledge of the activity of washing clothes they could easily make sense of what they heard. In general, comprehension involves interpreting new input in terms of what we already know about the world. The Bransford and Johnson results show that it is necessary to have recognised the framework and to have activated the appropriate memories at the time the new material is encountered. Later revelation of the title was no help.

Finally, notice how comprehension and recall went hand in hand. This may reflect a more integrated entry into memory when the subject of the passage was known, or it may be that knowledge of what the passage was about helps to guide recall. Probably both occur.

CA–G*

SCHEMAS AND SCRIPTS

The Bransford and Johnson (1972, 1973) experiment illustrates the use of stored knowledge in the comprehension of new experience. When do we need to use such knowledge? In what form will the stored knowledge need to be to enable us to comprehend what we read? In recent years cognitive scientists have been forced to consider in great detail the type of stored knowledge that is required for comprehension because they have been trying to program computers to understand human language. Taking on such a task is a very valuable incentive to our understanding of the processes underlying comprehension because all of the processes must be faced up to and programmed into the machines. It is no longer possible to overlook some aspects because we take them for granted and to ignore others that seem difficult to solve. When faced with this problem of programming a computer to understand a short story, it soon became apparent that the computer needed to be equipped with a vast array of expectations of what was likely to happen in a given situation. Several cognitive scientists began to develop models of the representation and use of this knowledge about the workings of the world. Minsky (1975) wrote of *frames*, Schank (1982) and Schank and Abelson (1977) of *scripts*, and others, more generally, of *schemas*. We have already met the term "schemas" in Chapter 4. Thorndyke (1984) discusses the essential similarities underlying these terms.

The common set of ideas underlying these theories are that they assume that there are organised structures of knowledge in memory. These are derived from past experience, and can be retrieved to guide comprehension and recall. These schemas provide the framework for the interpretation of the new experience. They specify what to look for in the input, and they indicate what is likely to happen next, which allows inferences to be drawn.

One of the best known examples is the script for "eating in a restaurant" developed by Schank and Abelson (1977). By equipping their computer program SAM with expectations about the routine of going to a restaurant they were able to produce a program that could interpret simple stories about restaurants and answer simple questions. The following is an example from the script scene for ordering in the restaurant:

Ordering
Customer picks up menu
Customer looks at menu
Customer decides on food
Customer signals waitress
Waitress comes to table
etc.

One advantage of such script knowledge is that it allows the person or computer to fill in gaps left by the story teller. So, if there is no mention of the customer deciding on her food, or of the waitress coming to the table, but the story picks up the script further on, it can be inferred that these steps have taken place.

Bower, Black, and Turner (1979) explored the psychological basis of such scripts. They found that most people give similar accounts of activities such as going to a restaurant. Bower et al. went on to explore how these expectations of what will happen in a familiar situation will influence subsequent memory of stories based on the script.

What sort of errors would you expect in the recall of a story based closely on a script for a familiar event such as going to a restaurant, a lecture, or a doctor? As you might have guessed, either when recalling, or when being tested on recognition of sentences from the stories, by far the most common error was to import statements that were implied in the general script. So, for example, people might mention paying the bill in the restaurant or going into the doctor's surgery, even though neither was specifically mentioned in the original story. Perhaps the subject had deduced these steps in the script when comprehending the story. Alternatively, when using the script to guide retrieval, the subject may have been unable to discriminate whether or not the statement had been in the story. Bower et al. also found that there was a strong tendency for events that they had deliberately moved from their normal place in the scripts either to be forgotten or to be shifted back to their normal position.

How do scripts influence reading? One way is in helping to specify what should happen next; they provide expectations to direct our reading. Often, what interests us are situations where the normal expectations are *not* fulfilled. What, asked Bower et al. would this do to our memory of the story? To find out, they introduced non-script actions into the stories. For example, the normal running of the restaurant script might be disrupted by the wrong food being brought or the dishes being dropped.

A story that is purely based on a script with nothing unusual happening is a very boring story; in fact, Brewer and Lichenstein (1981) found that people rate such passages as barely being stories at all! The only point in telling a story is to acquaint the listener with something they do not already know, to go *beyond* the knowledge that is represented in their scripts. Bower et al. investigated the effect of two types of deviations from conventional scripts. One was merely to introduce irrelevant statements with no essential place in the causal flow of the events (e.g., describing the waitress's hair). The other type of script deviation broke the smooth flow by introducing an obstacle (e.g., you cannot read the menu because it is in French), an error (e.g., you are brought snails when you ordered soup), or a distraction which temporarily suspends the running of the script (e.g., the waitress spills soup over you). Bower et al. found that obstacles, errors, or distractions were especially well remembered by their subjects, who, on average, remembered 58 per cent of such interruptions, compared with 38 per cent of the script actions. Irrelevancies were the poorest recalled (32 per cent). So, one role of the script was to specify what was interesting by helping to identify when normal expectations were not immediately fulfilled. We look for what is new in any story. It is the interruptions in a scheme that make the story worth telling, and it is these that are most attended to and recalled.

Schemas, therefore, help to guide and structure our interpretation of new information. They assist in identifying what is and what is not important, and this is reflected in our memories of what we have read. So, for example, when we read a story or watch a film, we can analyse and identify the goals of the individuals involved. These goals are usually the important aspects of which we are experiencing and it is the goals that tend to be remembered. Lichenstein and Brewer (1980) either gave their subjects stories describing someone setting up a projector or writing a letter, or showed them a video film of the same events. The actions involved could be classified as goals in the overall task (e.g., typing, painting out an error); as goal-directed, that is, as steps to achieving a goal (e.g., opening the typewriter, getting out the correction fluid); or as non-goal directed items (e.g., putting down a pencil, moving a pad to one side). Lichenstein and Brewer instructed their subjects to recall every move the person made. They found that goal actions were the best recalled. From the letter-writing video, for example, 96 per cent of goal actions were recalled compared with 66 per cent of goal-directed actions and only 44 per cent of non-goal directed actions.

Many different schemas will be activated all our waking moments. The culture shock experienced by someone moving to a different society reflects the lack of suitable schemas, and the activation of their old, inappropriate schemas. The use of a schema when reading a book is just one example of schemas in action.

Schank's Model of Dynamic Memory

How are scripts retrieved from memory? How do they develop through our experience? How are they modified to meet our needs? Is there just one type of script, or should we think of a more complex structure to the knowledge that we use when we process a new experience?

We have already described how Schank and Abelson (1977) argued that much of our knowledge is organised into structures, which they called scripts, that help us to comprehend and carry out predictable and relatively common activities such as going to a restaurant, or a lecture, or a dentist.

Schank (1982) extended his earlier work on scripts. He became dissatisfied with the limitations of the script concept. He suspected that many of the past experiences that aid our understanding do not seem to be of the frequently experienced, highly predictable type. For example, people have expectations about what will happen in many situations that they have never experienced, such as earthquakes and breaking off diplomatic relations. Can they have scripts available in memory for these events? Then there are the sorts of mistakes that people make when they confuse memories of going, say, to a doctor and a dentist. In the original formulation of the script concept there should be a separate one for dentists and for doctors. How could such errors come about? Schank argued that such errors would occur only if the memories shared some higher-level properties, but this led to many problems with generalised scripts. The whole point of a script is that it gives you specific expectations for a given situation. If you did not have separate dentist and doctor scripts, you would have problems over what to expect from each. For example, in Britain, you have to pay dentists but not doctors. Your doctor would be surprised if you lay down on his couch with your mouth open, and your dentist would think it odd if you sat in an ordinary chair waiting to be asked what was wrong with you. It would, therefore, be difficult to make up a script that applied to both doctors and dentists.

Schank tackled these problems by examining instances where our memories are stimulated and one event reminds us of another. For example, someone told Schank of an occasion when, while waiting in a long queue at a post office, they noticed that the person ahead had been waiting to buy just one stamp. This reminded Schank of people who buy only a dollar or two of petrol at a petrol station. Clearly, there was something about both occasions which transcended the scripts being run and which led to the one event reminding Schank of the other.

By analysing many examples of reminding, Schank was led to the view that memory is dynamic and failure-driven. It is when something goes wrong in our predictions that we must modify our memories so that they will be more likely to cope in the future. Schank suggests that we store the details of the scene in which a failure occurred. With further failures the memory will be modified and elaborated to make prediction more accurate.

At any one time, Schank argues, more than one level of memory structure will be activated. In the lower levels there will be *scenes*. These are general structures that describe how and when a particular set of actions take place. When going to a doctor's, for example, there will be reception scenes, waiting-room scenes and surgery scenes. Scenes organise specific memories. These represent, as Schank (1982) says (p. 96), a kind of *snapshot* of one's surroundings at a given time. The scenes need not be physical scenes; they can be, for example, *societal scenes* which have a social setting as their common thread and the actions comprising the interaction between two or more people define the scene. Each scene defines a setting, a goal, and actions in attempting to reach the goal. Scenes can point to scripts, which are now defined as stereotyped actions that take place within a scene. Scripts provide the specific details.

Scenes are then, according to Schank, organised into what he calls "memory organisation packets" (MOPs). These consist of a set of scenes directed towards the achievement of a goal. Each MOP has one major scene whose goal is the essence or purpose of the events organised by the MOP. Finding the appropriate MOP in memory enables one to predict which scene will come next.

According to Schank's model, several MOPs may be active at one time. These will usually reflect the physical, social, and personal aspects of the current activity. So, for example, Schank suggests that a visit to a dentist will activate at least three MOPs, which he calls M-HEALTH PROTECTION, M-PROFESSIONAL OFFICE VISIT (M-POV), and M-CONTRACT (Fig. 9.3). The first represents the personal aspects of keeping fit, the second the physical activity of visiting the dentist, and third the social contractual obligations (e.g., to pay the dentist). Notice that the same scenes can be linked to different MOPs.

Schank suggests that MOPs are themselves organised by meta-MOPs into higher-level structures, representing, for example, trips. The meta-MOP "mM-TRIP" can deal, for example, with the stages in a visit by activating MOPs such as M-AIRPLANE, M-HOTEL, M-MEETING.

Beyond MOPs there are other structures dealing with more abstract information. These are "thematic organisation points" or TOPs. They allow us to be reminded of abstract principles that are independent of a

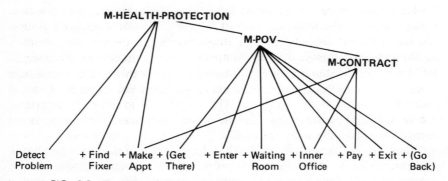

FIG. 9.3 Example of the interconnection of three memory organisation packets (MOPs) in the structuring of the scenes (bottom line) for a visit to a dentist. From Schank, R. C. (1982) *Dynamic Memory*. Cambridge: Cambridge University Press. Reproduced by permission.

particular context. So, for example, when a city council gives way to a big businessman we may bring to mind the effect of the appeasement of Hitler over Munich. The principles we abstract are sufficiently similar, even though the actual events have no other features in common. It would be inconceivable that we should remember the potentially useful knowledge about appeasement if there were not some high-level process abstracting and retaining it.

Schank's (1982) full account of the structure of memory is more elaborate than we can do justice to here. However, from the foregoing description it is possible to envisage the rich and elaborate hierarchy of memory structures that will be activated when we read a story about a familiar activity. Specific scenes will cue appropriate scripts to analyse and predict the events; MOPs will supply higher-level similarities and coherence to the events. TOPs will introduce abstract principles. New memories will be laid down when the scripts fail. These new memories will be linked to the higher-level units, and, if necessary, they will form the basis of new structures if future experiences show that a new script, scene, MOP, or TOP is required.

One important feature of Schank's model is the relationship between the planning and interpretation of actions, and the memory laid down. We will return to this in later chapters. In Chapter 10 we argue, as Schank does, that memories are the by-products of making sense of our experience and of the tasks in which we indulge in interacting with the world.

CONSTRUCTING A NEW COHERENT REPRESENTATION

So far in discussing schemas and Schank's (1982) model, we have been concerned with the interpretation of large sections of stories. Obviously, the schemas that are activated are important to the overall interpretation of the text. But how is a story comprehended, sentence by sentence, to build up an understanding within those general frameworks? On what basis does our cognitive system construct a new coherent story from the individual sentences that we read? The schemas from our past experience aid in this new construction of the novel experience, but how is the construction actually accomplished?

When we read a story we know that the message of the story is coherent and meaningful. How do we identify the links and structure of the message? One way this is achieved is through references to common objects, people, or concepts. From these a coherent representation is constructed in memory. One result is that it is often difficult for someone to remember exactly in which way they acquired this information. Anderson and Bower (1973), for example, showed that their subjects who had read:

George Washington had good health

and

The first President of the United States was a bad husband

would claim to recognise:

The first President of the United States had good health

as a sentence they had met earlier. To do this they must have inferred that "George Washington" and "the first President of the United States" were the same person and then constructed in memory a single entry representing the two facts that had been mentioned.

In the process of reading, a person is continually analysing the text for connections. The reader will very quickly use references to the same thing to develop a representation of what is happening. Where the connection is not made immediately obvious by the same object being named, the reader will try to infer a link. Such inferences take time to devise, but are an essential part of reading. Without them most stories would be incomprehensible.

A sentence is interpreted and understood in the context of its preceding sentences. Haviland and Clark (1974) give the example of the sentence *George thinks vanilla*. By itself this appears to be nonsensical. Suppose, though, that it were the answer to the question *What kind of ice cream does Vivien like*? Then it would read perfectly sensibly.

Haviland and Clark (1974) argue that a speaker or writer identifies what the listener or hearer apparently already knows, which they call *given information*, and also what the audience does not know, which Haviland and Clark term *new information*. The listener or reader has to identify the given information, which is used as a cue to information already stored, and then must integrate this with the new information.

Consider the following pairs of sentences:

1. (a) *We checked the picnic supplies.*
   (b) *The beer was warm.*

2. (a) *We got some beer out of the truck.*
   (b) *The beer was warm.*

In 2 "beer" is mentioned in both sentences. Having read 2(a), when reading 2(b) the reference to beer provides the given information for linking the new information that the beer was warm. In 1, however, the link is far less obvious. The reader has to infer that the beer was part of the picnic supplies before the information that it was warm can be incorporated. You may have been conscious of a slight delay in your reading of 1(b) while working out how it was connected to 1(a). Haviland and Clark found that having read sentences of the 1(a) and 2(a) types, subjects took markedly longer to indicate that they comprehended the second sentence if the pair was of the 1 type, where inferences had to be made.

Once inferences have been made they are incorporated into the representation that the individual is creating. Bransford, Barclay, and Franks (1972) found that after subjects had read that:

There is a tree with a box beneath it.
A chair is on top of the box.
The box is to the right of the tree.

they tended to claim they had read:

The tree is to the left of the chair.

since this fitted with the representation they had formed.

Many statements in stories are linked by causal relations rather than just by mentioning the same object or event. Haberlandt and Bingham (1978) found that people were quicker to read triplets of sentences linked by causal relationships. It appeared that, where no causal relationships were involved, the readers paused and searched for them. Memory is also improved if statements are easily linked. Black and Bern (1981) found that memory for pairs of statements was much better if they were linked by causal relationships. So, for example, the pair:

The child was pulling at a bottle.
It fell to the floor and broke.

was much better remembered than a pair where "pulling" was replaced by "looking."

Statements can also be linked on the basis of the motivation or goals interpreted in the actions of the characters. The more that motivational steps need to be inferred, the longer it takes the reader to comprehend a pair of statements. So Smith and Collins (1981), for example, showed that it takes longer to read:

Rita was having stomach pains.
John got out the telephone book.

than:

Rita needed a doctor fast.
John got out the telephone book.

The former involves the extra step of realising that a doctor is needed.

MEMORY REPRESENTATION

We have argued that comprehension is heavily dependent on memories of past experience which make available knowledge about what to expect and what to look for in a given situation. Such information, in the form of schemas, can guide the construction of the representation of what has occurred. On the more detailed level, shared objects and events, and causal and motivational links all contribute to the construction of a mental representation of a story.

What form does this representation take? What type of information is normally retained in our memories after reading a story? How is the information interconnected and related to our other memories? Almost anything that we experience *can* be stored in our memories. We can recall, for example, how things looked, smelt, tasted, or the exact words of songs and quotations. Memory is very flexible. As is argued in Chapter 10, what is stored in memory is a product of the processes of making sense of the input from the world, and depends on the particular task that we are undertaking at the time.

In some situations it is valuable to remember exactly the words in which a message was conveyed. On such occasions the detailed wording may be remembered (e.g., Wanner, 1968; Kintsch & Bates, 1977). However, when we read a story we are not usually concerned with the exact words used, but rather with the message that the author is trying to convey. The words are a means of transmitting the message, but the same message could usually be sent in another way. You could use different words, or, if both you and your listener knew another language it would be possible to say the same thing in that language. It is the *meaning* of the message that is important, not the particular way in which it is conveyed. The meaning of a message is often described by philosophers in terms of *propositions*. Propositions are the fundamental elements of meaning, which are either true or false and which are independent of the way the message is transmitted. The same propositions underlie my saying "I love you" in English, "Je t'aime" in French, or "t'amo" in Italian. For someone reading a story it is the propositions that they need to identify and build into a representation. The exact wording of the story is often not very important.

The result is that, when trying to recall a story, we normally find that we have forgotten the exact wording, except for the telling or unusual phrase which especially attracted our attention beyond our processing of it for the message it conveyed.

When Whipple (1912) summarised early German research on the recall of passages he described it as:

> ... a progressive abbreviation of the anecdotes; the story becomes less definite and more general in phrasing; each report deviates in two or three points from the preceding; the errors are confusions, substitutions, alterations of temporal and spatial setting; names and dates suffer particularly [p. 267].

Later, Bartlett (1932) emphasised the "effort after meaning" reflected in the recall by his subjects when they tried to reproduce either a story from another culture, or to pass on the disjointed attempt at recall made by another subject. Bartlett noted how the style and details of the original were lost. Gomulicki (1956) found that it was hard for subjects to distinguish attempts at recall, from précis written with the passage available at the time. All this suggests that what is normally stored in memory after reading a story is the essential meaning of the text but not the details.

So, people are usually quite good at recognising if the meaning of sentences they are shown are different from those they saw earlier but they are not normally good at spotting if the structure of the sentence itself is different; if, for example, it has switched from active to passive (Mary kissed John; John was kissed by Mary) (e.g., Sachs, 1967).

NETWORK MODELS OF MEMORY

We have a rough outline of what seems to be stored in memory after reading a story. It will be in terms of episodes constructed from the basic message that the story was conveying. The encoding will be modified by the individual's particular schema, and further details at a higher level, reflecting the main themes of the plot, will also be stored. Indeed, these higher-level representations often appear to be the best recalled (Thorndyke, 1977).

Can we go beyond these generalisations and try to produce a more detailed model of the sort of information that is stored in memory after reading a story? Several psychologists have tried to devise such models. The most elaborate model has been developed by John Anderson and refined and applied over many years. The first version, known as HAM (human associative memory) was proposed by Anderson and Bower

(1973). This was later replaced by ACT by Anderson (1976) and extended and modified over subsequent years (e.g. Anderson, 1983, 1984). Others have devised related models (e.g. Kintsch, 1974; Norman & Rumelhart 1975).

Underlying these models is the assumption that what we experience (e.g., read or hear) is analysed for its underlying propositional contents. Then a record of this contents is built up by linking together related propositions. The end result is an integrated representation of an episode which has lost the details of the original wording of the story but still contains the fundamental message.

All the models assume that what is read is analysed for its propositions. As we described earlier, a proposition is the smallest unit of knowledge that can be sensibly considered true or false. They involve a *relationship* (such as giving, hitting, being beautiful) and *arguments* to which the relations apply. Relations usually correspond to the verbs and adjectives in the story, and the arguments correspond to the nouns. Relations like *hit* will always have three arguments, since there must be someone doing the hitting, someone or something being hit, and something being used for the hitting. So the sentence *John hit Mike with the stick* would be interpreted as one proposition, with "hit" as the relation and John, Mike, and the stick as the appropriate arguments.

Longer sentences or passages can be broken down into propositions. Take the sentence *The girl broke the window on the porch*. This consists of two propositions: (1) *The girl broke the window*, and (2) *The window is on the porch*. Figure 9.4 represents propositions (1) and (2) in the system used by Anderson (1985). The representations in Fig. 9.4 are for the two separate propositions, but, of course, it is the same window that is referred to. Hence, someone reading the sentence *The girl broke the window on the porch* would combine the two representations as in Fig. 9.5 via the entry for "window".

Suppose that a person reads or listens to the following sentences:

1. *The girl broke the window on the porch*.
2. *The girl who lives next door broke the window on the porch*.
3. *The girl who lives next door broke the large window*.

These sentences are made up of four simple propositions: (i) *The girl broke the window*: (ii) *The window is on the porch*; (iii) *The girl lives next door*; (iv) *The window is large*. No sentence contains all these propositions, but, to understand what was being said, we can assume that the listener will attempt to construct a representation integrating all the propositions. They can do that in a way that would be written:

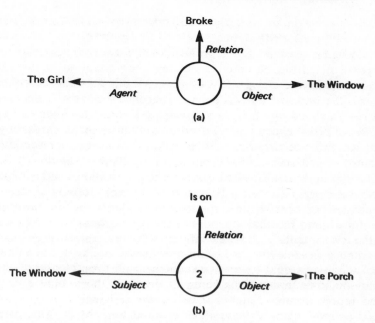

FIG. 9.4   Propositional network representations of the sentences *The girl broke the window* and *The window is on the porch*.

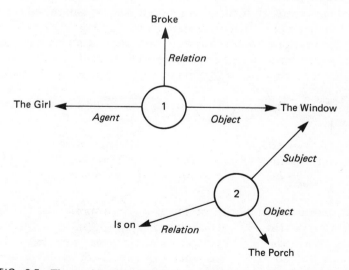

FIG. 9.5   The combination of the two propositions in Fig. 9.4 into a single network.

4. *The girl who lives next door broke the large window on the porch.*

This can be represented in the propositional network by Fig. 9.6.

Several things can be noted about this representation of the episode. First, it contains the essence of what occurred but does not record the way in which the information was derived. Second, the same structure could have been formed in many different ways, through listening to any of a large set of possible combinations of the sentences. Afterwards, however, *which* sentences occurred cannot be deduced from the representation.

Bransford and Franks (1971) showed subjects the sentences 1–3 along with similar ones that repeated some of the propositions, and combined to tell a short story. Afterwards Bransford and Franks tested the recognition of sentences composed from various combinations of the four propositions. What they found was that the more of the propositions were incorporated into the test sentence, the more confident were the subjects in claiming that the sentence was one they had been shown earlier. So that, when they were shown sentence 4, that sentence was the one most confidently reported as an old one, even though it had not actually been shown before. Since the stored representation matches most closely sentence 4, that is the one judged as most likely to have been encountered before. This particular result depends on the way the experiment is carried out (see Bransford, 1979) but under some circumstances, when people have been encouraged to process the implied story and when superficial clues are not available, the readers or listeners seem to base their recognition on the extent to which the new sentence matches the stored representation.

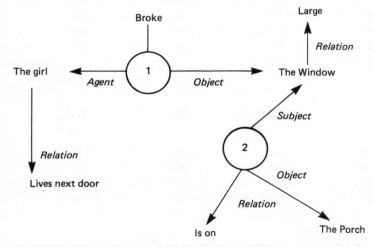

FIG. 9.6   Representation of the sentence *The girl who lives next door broke the large window on the porch.*

Answering Questions via the Semantic Network

The example just given illustrates the development of a semantic network in memory, and one way in which such a network might be used. What other uses might it have? One might be to retrieve information when answering questions. For example, when a question is read, it could be composed into a new network which matches one stored already in memory. This could then make available that stored information and any additional, connected information in memory (e.g., Anderson & Bower, 1973).

Is this the only way that a network could be used when answering a question? Some models of inference and comprehension (e.g., Collins and Quillian, 1969; Collins and Loftus, 1975) have assumed that questions can be answered by tracing routes through an existing network in memory. Early experiments by Collins and Quillian (1969) found that the more links and relations in a network that would have to be crossed to find the connection to answer the question, the longer the response took. So, for example, it took longer to confirm that a robin is an animal than that it is a bird. This was as expected, since it was assumed that to get between the entry for "robin" and "animal" the search would have to cross through and go beyond the "bird" entry. Unfortunately, later results caused problems for simple network models. For example, it takes longer to say that a bat is *not* a bird than to say that a far more dissimilar animal, such as a cow, is not a bird. Since the networks should only record what *is* the case, not negative information, at first sight one would expect questions about bats and cows being birds to take an equal and probably a comparatively long time to answer. The issues raised by these problems are dealt with further in Chapter 5. Network models can be developed to cope with these problems (Anderson, 1984; Collins & Loftus, 1975), but so can alternative frameworks (see Cohen, 1983).

EPISODIC AND SEMANTIC MEMORY

We have discussed how stored information from past experiences can be used to help in the construction of a new entry in memory. In this final part of the chapter we spend a little time considering the types of memories that we have. Are all our memories the same? What memories might be evoked when reading a sentence such as the following:

As Carol steered her bicycle through the streams of Cambridge undergraduates she looked up to see the outline of King's College Chapel.

To anyone who has never learned to ride a bicycle or who has never seen King's College, Cambridge, the sentence will still be perfectly understandable. They will know what riding a bicycle looks like, that Cambridge is a famous old university town, and what chapels often look like. Such a person knows about these things as relatively impersonal facts. Someone who can ride a bicycle has additional knowledge. They know how it is done and what it feels like. It is not something that can be easily described and it is not a piece of propositional knowledge. That is, it is not something that can be thought of as either true or false; it is something that you do—something for which you have the procedural knowledge to know how to carry it out.

Suppose, also, that you have been to Cambridge and seen King's College Chapel. The mention of it may bring to mind a memory of the way it looked when you saw it. Here, you are remembering not a fact that you have learned but an event that has happened to you—an episode from your own life.

In Chapter 10 we will be concerned with memories for such events. Tulving (1972, 1983) has argued that there are important distinctions between our memories for facts, our memory for events that have happened to us, and our knowledge of how to carry out skills such as riding a bicycle. The first distinction that he draws is between procedural and propositional memories. *Procedural* memories are the results of the improvement in skilled performance, such as learning how to knit, to tell wines apart, and to read music, or English. We have dealt with such skills in Chapters 4 and 5. Tulving is more concerned with what he calls *propositional* memory. This is memory for information: for knowledge. It is the sort of information that we have been concerned with in this chapter.

So far we have assumed that whatever information enters the memory system, it is stored in similar ways. Tulving, however, pointed out that if we think about the sort of memories that we use, there seem to be two different sorts. There are personal memories of the events of our lives, and there are stored "facts" which are not specific to the experiences that we have had. Compare your memory for your last day at school with your memory that the name of the first President of the USA was George Washington. These two memories seem quite different. The one is of an episode from your life, perhaps rich in visual images. The other seems to be a fact that lacks any connection with when or how it was learned.

Tulving suggested that there are two types of memory for propositional knowledge. One of these is in the form of episodes of personal experience, and he called this *episodic* memory. The other is a collection of the facts about the world. He called this *semantic* memory. Tulving (1983) lists 28 ways in which he believes episodic and semantic memories differ in the information that they store, the way they operate, and their applications.

The episodic memory, Tulving believes, stores memories of the events from our lives. The units of storage are the events. Temporal relationships between the events are used as the basis for their organisation in memory and as the way by which they can be retrieved. For retrieval cues to be successful they must specify the time and place at which the memory occurred. Your last day at school may be a fairly distinctive example, but any personal memories will be episodic memories. Much of the experimenting that has gone on in memory research had been on episodic memory (though of a not very interesting kind of experience), because for many years the study of memory was devoted to subjects learning lists of words or nonsense syllables. All they had to do was to learn and remember the particular words they had experienced at that particular time. In other words, they had to remember an episode from their lives, albeit a rather boring and readily confusable one.

In contrast to episodic memory, semantic memory is concerned with storing facts and concepts. What is stored is independent of when or how the experience was encountered. The purpose of the memory is to aid the comprehension of the world, and details of the time and place in which the knowledge was acquired are normally irrelevant. Tulving argues that semantic memory will be organised and interlinked to make the retrieval of its knowledge as successful as possible.

Tulving's distinction is a useful one in helping us think about the nature of our memories. There is no doubt that the two types of memories represent very different types of experience that are important to our lives. To many people, remembering is recalling from what Tulving would describe as episodic memory. It is the recollection of experiences from the past, often with images and memories of the emotions involved. On the other hand, our memories of past experience are central to our ability to understand the new situations in which we find ourselves, and to plan and carry out actions. Much of the knowledge upon which this comprehending of the world is based is knowledge that is retrieved independently of the way in which it was acquired. We all know what dogs, trees, and tables are, even though we cannot remember our first experiences of them. Coping with tables, dogs, and trees in everyday life calls for the rapid retrieval of knowledge about the way such things look, act, and the uses to which they can be put. This must be derived from experience, but will not be best stored in terms of the time and place at which our experiences of them occurred.

Although it is useful to recognise the types of memories that we have, it may not be necessary to think of there being two separate systems. Or perhaps there should be more than two systems in our models? Tulving has highlighted important distinctions in our types of memories, but other researchers have not found it necessary to build into their models special ways of coping with the two systems. So, for example, the network models discussed earlier seem to be models of episodic memory, since they relate to the storing of a record of the scene that the person has just experienced. These models do not normally have different entries for events from one's life and those representing facts such as the name of the first President of the USA. On the other hand, there is a recognition of the need to easily access the meaning of a word, which is one of the arguments for a separate semantic memory. This is accomplished by having a separate node known as the *type* node, which is linked to the details that define the meaning of the concept it represents. Then, each time that concept is referred to in the building up of the memory network, an entry known as a *token* is laid down which does not itself contain the information that defines the concept, but which is linked back to the type node so that it is easy to retrieve the defining information if it is required.

It may not be necessary to think of there being two different systems. However, it is useful to note that our memories have to record and supply information on a wide range of topics, and that two very important areas where information from memory is necessary involve the interpretation of what we read and hear, and the remembering of events that happen to us. These aspects are sufficiently similar for the memory systems to share much in common, but there are distinctive aspects to remembering the events that happen to us. For this reason, we turn to those events in the next chapter.

SUMMARY

In this chapter we have tried to show how the interpretation of a story that we read is a complex process. It draws upon much of our past experience, so that the psychological questions of this chapter have become ones about how past experience is organised and recovered from memory. We have pointed out that interpreting a story involves more than just understanding what has been written. There is an implicit agreement between the reader and the writer. The writer assumes that the reader will make many assumptions and will be able to deduce much that has happened. If the writer did not do so the result would be grindingly boring for the reader. The writer is able to exploit the reader's knowledge of the world and uses this in structuring the story. Stories are only regarded as stories when they begin to diverge from how the world would normally run its mundane course. A story is a divergence from such conventions, but a divergence that is itself usually understandable in terms of rules and schemas to which stories usually abide. From the study of story comprehension we have been able to recognise the full complexity of storage and structuring that is required for us to be able to understand what we read, and, more importantly, what we experience in our daily life. We must constantly retrieve past structures developed from our experiences of the regularity of life, modify them when they fail, and search for their implications and their relevance to our goals and plans.

We discussed how new memories of the stories we have read might be formed. The meaning of the story will be abstracted and constructed into a representation that retains many of the propositions of the original while losing the details of the original wording. Such representations might resemble semantic networks that could be searched to retrieve information. We hope that it is clear from this chapter that reading a story, however relaxing we may find it, is a demanding and dynamic task for our cognitive systems.

Many of the issues discussed in the chapter are considered further in chapters in J. R. Anderson and S. M. Kosslyn (Eds.) (1984), *Tutorials in Learning and Memory*. Chapters of particular interest are those by P. W. Thorndyke, J. B. Black and J. R. Anderson. Schank's model of dynamic memory is described in R. C. Schank (1982), *Dynamic Memory*. A fuller introduction to network models of memory will be found in J. R. Anderson (1985), *Cognitive Psychology and its Applications*.

10 Witnessing an Accident: Remembering and Recalling Events

In Chapter 9 we suggested that it may be worth distinguishing between our memories for factual information and those for events that we have experienced. In this chapter we concentrate on our memories for episodes from our lives, that is on episodic memory. To illustrate such memories we have chosen an example of witnessing an accident. The purpose of the chapter is, however, not to explore all that is known about eyewitness testimony but rather to indicate the general principles that govern what gets encoded into memory and the conditions under which it will or will not be retrieved.

A useful distinction will be that between encoding, storage, and retrieval. All three are logically necessary stages for anything to be remembered. The event must leave some trace, cause some change within the cognitive system, and this we call encoding. That change must remain over time, and later, something must activate the record in the system for the individual to recall the event. These latter are the storage and retrieval stages. When considering our memory for events, it will be useful to discuss separately the factors that will influence the encoding, storage and retrieval of the details of the event and the chapter will be structured in this way. All three must take place efficiently if we are to remember accurately. How will each stage be affected by the conditions in which they occur? We will look separately at each stage in the following sections.

WITNESSING AN ACCIDENT

You are walking home along the road that leads to your house. Suddenly a white car swerves out of a side street and, without slowing down, cuts across the oncoming traffic. There is a squeal of brakes and a red car that was travelling along your road has to swing away. It skids and crashes into a lamp-post. The white car accelerates off. The driver of the red car climbs out, swearing, and comes over to you. "Did you see that?" he shouts, "I was only doing 30 miles an hour and that stupid woman just cut out without looking." A policeman appears. You agree that you did see what happened. The policeman asks you about the white car. Did you get its number? What was its make? How fast did it come out of the side street? Did it stop at the Stop sign? Could you describe the driver? How many people were in the car? How fast was the red car going? Did the white car try to avoid the red car? You answer the questions as best you can. The policeman draws up a statement that you sign and you continue home, rather shaken, and thinking over the few seconds of the incident. You expect to be called as a witness if the driver of the white car is charged. What will you say?

As you think about the crash you find that you have a series of vivid mental images of the events. You can see again the white car swinging out and the red car swerving. You can see the white car with two occupants racing away. You remember the look on the face of the driver of the red car as he climbed out. However, there are lots of things that you cannot remember, and some of these seem odd to you. You can "see' the white car, but you cannot "see" it clearly enough to read any of the letters on its number plate. You think that it was a woman driving, that is what you told the policeman, but you are not really sure. The driver of the red car was sure, and he ought to know. You feel it probably was a woman. You know that there is a common view that women are worse drivers' than men, but also that women are more cautious than men. Would a woman have driven out so recklessly? Or was it especially reckless? Did the white car slow down at the junction? Was its view obscured by another car? You saw the whole thing, but you find that you cannot really remember. The policeman was very tolerant with the way you couldn't give all the details that he hoped for, but you feel a fool for not being able to answer questions such as the make of the car. You wonder what sort of witness you will appear to be if you are faced by a good lawyer who will highlight the gaps and uncertainties in your evidence. At least you feel that you are certain of some things. You can vividly remember the sight of the two people in the car as it drove away.

ENCODING

The Importance of the Processing Task

In Chapter 9 we discussed how the activity that goes on when we comprehend a story determines what is encoded. We discussed how the active, ongoing processing triggers related information that is stored in the long-term memory and makes it available to aid the current activity of making sense of the particular situation we are in. Is this specific to reading a story? Clearly not. All the time our cognitive systems are actively working towards fulfilling whatever current task we have been set.

As in most of the situations studied in Chapter 9, this may be merely the comprehension of what we are hearing or seeing, but in other circumstances it may be more specific and more or less demanding. How does this apply to our witnessing example? In that example the demands are very low, the task is merely to walk home without accident, and this task, with its well practised components (walking, avoiding other pedestrians, etc.) makes few cognitive demands. Indeed, it is very likely that we will be doing other things at the same time. We may be thinking over events that have happened to us, we may be daydreaming, but whatever we are doing, not much processing of the world around us will be necessary. In other situations we may have a far more complicated task to carry out. Crossing a busy road requires far more analysis of the world around us.

How do the processing tasks influence our encoding into memory? The answer appears to be that they are very important. The experiments that we will shortly describe show that what is encoded seems to be a by-product of the processing that has taken place. If the processing has required the careful analysis of some item or event, then a richer code recording that analysis will be laid down in the memories. On the other hand, if the current tasks determining the activity in the cognitive workspace are such that very little analysis is required then the resulting record that is encoded will be sketchy. What is more, what is encoded will be not just a record of the specific processing, but will include other details from the current cognitive activity. It will record details relating to the time, the place, the emotional state we are in, and so on.

Poor Memories of Familiar Objects

What evidence do we have for our claim that the type of task is so important to encoding? One source of evidence is that we often have very poor memories for highly familiar things that we see and use everyday. Nickerson and Adams (1979) for example, tested the memory that American adults have for a US "penny." Only one person (a coin collector) in the 20 they tested could recall all the eight main features of the penny (the writing, the direction the head faces, etc.) and locate them in their correct places. On average, people can correctly recall and locate only three of the eight features. Nor was this poor memory merely the result of testing by requiring the subjects to draw the coins. When Nickerson and Adams asked their subjects in a later experiment to pick out the correct drawing of the coin from among 14 incorrect drawings, only 15 of their 36 subjects selected the accurate drawing as the one they thought most likely to be correct. In an unpublished study of 100 first-year British undergraduates, one of the authors (Morris) found even poorer

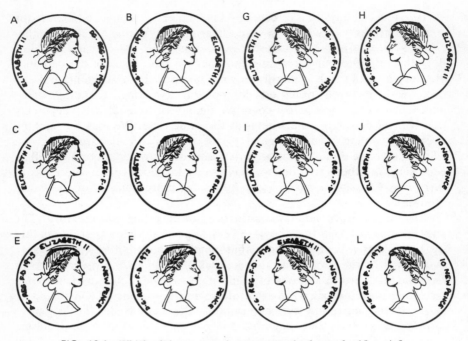

FIG. 10.1   Which of these correctly represents the front of a 10p coin?

recognition of the correct appearance of a 10p piece. Only 15 per cent of those tested were able to identify the correct design from a set similar to that shown in Fig. 10.1. Try it yourself.

Why are people so bad at recognising or describing something that they use every day and may have known all their lives? The most likely answer is that they do not need to attend to the details of the coins when they are using them. Highly skilled perceptual tasks develop so that only those features relevant to making the necessary decisions are processed. Normally, we select coins from among change made up of quite distinctive sets of coins and there is no need to process them for the details of their wording. We need only distinguish the coins by shape, colour, and size. If the tasks do not demand a careful processing, the memory that is laid down at encoding will also be crude.

Evidence for the poor memory of objects used every day is not restricted to memory for coins. In the days when British telephones had the alphabet as well as the ten digits on the dial, Morton (1967) found that none of his 50 subjects could correctly recall the locations of all of the numbers and digits on the dial. When telephoning, the letters and numbers are available in front of the person and there is no need to process exactly where they are placed. It would be possible to learn these placings in a matter of minutes if that was a task set for a subject in a psychology experiment, but in everyday life it is the task set by the demands of the world which determines what is processed, and what is processed determines what will be subsequently remembered.

The experiments of Nickerson and Adams (1979) and Morton (1967) demonstrate that to memorise something it is necessary to do more than just encounter it, however frequently that encounter may occur. The very important conclusion to be drawn from these experiments is that good memory is not just a function of the number of times we have seen or heard the item to be remembered. In a similar way, Bekerian and Baddeley (1980) showed that a saturation advertising campaign to acquaint listeners to a new set of wavelengths for radio broadcasts led to an almost complete lack of precise learning of the new wavelengths. Craik and Watkins (1973) illustrated that the simple repetition of words over and over again does not lead to any appreciable increase in their ease of recall. They had their subjects learn lists of 12 words, with one group of the subjects required to repeat out loud the last four words in the list for 20 seconds before recalling the list. On that immediate test, the subjects could remember those four words well, but at a test a few minutes later, the subjects who had spent the extra time repeating the last four words were no better at recalling those words than were the subjects who had a mere 3 seconds to learn each word. In general, it has been found that the strategy of just repeating what one wants to learn, with no other attempt to analyse the meaning leads to especially poor encoding (cf. Morris, 1979).

How does this research apply to our witnessing example? In that example we imagined that you were walking home; a familiar task with little to demand attention to your surroundings. All the time, every day, cars will be passing. There is no reason why your cognitive system should process the fact beyond ascertaining that the cars were not about to do something dangerous such as mount the sidewalk and threaten to mow you down. Until something special occurred there was no demand on your system to do elaborate processing, and the result will have been that, although you will have been aware of the white car before it swung into the main road, the details of it that you will have encoded will be few and sparse.

Factors Leading to Good Encoding

What then will lead to good encoding? To answer this question we must consider the problems faced by any system which has to record large amounts of information to be used in the future under conditions that at the time of encoding are not clearly known. The efficiency of encoding is inextricably linked to the information available at the time when retrieval is required. The appropriate information must be selected from among the other that is stored, and to allow for this a sufficiently specific record must be laid down at encoding. Most of us keep books or files of some sort, and these give an idea of the problems of encoding and retrieval that have been faced during the evolution of the cognitive system.

Suppose that you are looking for a book on a single shelf. If the shelf is reasonably small, it does not take too long to look at every book, seeing if it is the one required. Equally, we may need to have available little information about the book to be able to find it. Knowing that it has a blue cover will be enough if it is your only book with such a cover. However, as we acquire larger libraries, we find that the serial searching through every book becomes extremely inefficient. What is more, we need to know more about the book that we are searching for before we can locate it. Now we have many blue books, and need to know the title or the author. In a large library a serial search through the stock would be ridiculously inefficient. It becomes necessary to examine each book as it is purchased by the library and to make a record of special distinctive features of the book. Libraries classify books according to their subjects, their titles, and their authors. It would, in theory, be possible to classify them in other ways also. Their colour, size, and date of publication might be other ways of specifying each book. When the book is required it is quite easy to find it so long as one knows the appropriate piece of information on which the book was classified when it was placed in the library. Notice two things here. First, that one needs to know the right information. Knowing the size and colour is no help unless they were used to code the book when it was first shelved. Second, that the ease of access (retrieval) depends on the work done when the book is entered (encoded) into the library. Suppose that you went to a library to look for a book knowing only its colour and date of publication; another time you go knowing the name of the author; another time only the name of the second of two authors; another time knowing the book's size and subtitle. In most real libraries only your second visit would be successful. However, it would be possible for a very keen, efficient library to provide records of all its books on the basis of date of publication, size, etc. By themselves these would not, perhaps, specify just one book, but, taken together, these records could allow you to locate the book you sought. The point of this example is that the more details that are encoded when a new book (or memory) enters the system, the more likely it is that at some time in the future, with only selective and scrappy information you will be able to locate the book (or memory) again. What is more, the more distinctively the information you possess identifies one and only one book (or memory), the more easily that item will be distinguished from the rest, and retrieved.

This example suggests that encoding into the human memory system will be most efficient when what is laid down is a record with much richness and elaboration that is as distinct as possible from other memory entries. Such a memory trace has more opportunities to be retrieved because of the many facets of its encoding and is less likely to be competing with alternative memories that might be located with the same retrieval information.

Elaboration of Encoding

What evidence is there that the more details that are processed, the better will be the subsequent recall? Several research programmes have accumulated considerable evidence to support the view that more elaborate and distinctive encoding leads to better recall. Craik and Tulving (1975), for example, had subjects judge whether nouns would fit within sentences that they had already been given. The sentences themselves were varied to be either short and simple, such as "she cooked the . . . ." or complex, such as "the small lady angrily picked up the red. . . ." The words that the subjects were shown either did or did not fit into the sentences. Craik and Tulving found that (when the words did fit the sentence), recall of the words, when subsequently tested, was far better when complex sentences had been used. This effect was especially strong, with twice the recall with complex sentences, when the sentences themselves were provided as cues to the recall. By processing the word in a context of an elaborate and complex sentence, the subjects had produced an elaborate and distinctive memory trace that could be easily located, especially when the sentence itself was available as a recall cue.

Notice how in the Craik and Tulving experiment the ease of recalling the same items was strongly influenced by the particular encoding task. Johnson-Laird, Gibbs, and de Mowbray (1978) illustrated how it is the processing that is carried out upon an item to be remembered, not just the nature of the item itself, which determines the likelihood of future recall. They showed their subjects a series of names of things that could be classified as liquid or solid and consumable or non-consumable; words such as milk, cheese, petrol, and coal. The subjects' task was to indicate which items met a given specification. For one group of subjects it was consumable liquids, for another, consumable solids, so that for each of the possible combinations of the properties a different group classified the same word list. Subsequently, the subjects were asked to recall the list of items. Johnson-Laird et al. found that about 50 per cent of those items were recalled which, in a particular subject's list, possessed *both* of the properties on which the list was being classified, whereas about 21 per cent of those items with just *one* property were recalled. Of those with *neither* of the properties only about 11 per cent were recalled. One important point to notice here is that the same words were being tested with each group, but that the probability of a given word being recalled varied from .5 to .11 depending on whether both or neither of the properties of the word matched the classification given to the classifying group of subjects. Where neither property was possessed by the item, then, when the subjects searched their memories for their knowledge of the terms to be classified, they were able to stop their processing when it had been ascertained that one of the two properties was not possessed by the item. If both were possessed, then further processing was necessary to determine that both were indeed true for the item. So if, for example, the subjects' task was to identify non-consumable solids, they could stop processing "milk" as soon as they had identified *either* that it was a liquid *or* that it was consumable. On the other hand, for "coal" they would have to identify not only that it was a solid but also that it was not normally eaten.

Levels of Processing

Can we go further in specifying how different processing tasks will influence encoding, and develop a theory of what leads to good encoding? Craik and Lockhart (1972) emphasised that what is encoded is a by-product of the ongoing perceptual processes. They therefore tried to predict the amount that would be remembered on the basis of their theory of the nature of the perceptual processing that might be activated by different tasks. They initially proposed that a given item might be processed to different *levels* within the processing system and that the level would determine the ease with which the item would be recognised or recalled subsequently because of the resulting elaboration of encoding of the particular entry in memory that had occurred. They suggested that superficial levels of encoding would involve just the physical appearance of the word, but deeper levels would progressively involve the sound and the meaning of the item. However, what makes one level "deeper" than another? How can the "depth" of processing in a particular instance be measured? The theory ran into considerable problems over how one can specify the depth to which an item has been processed and over the model of perceptual processing which it seemed to incorporate (cf. Baddeley, 1978; Eysenck, 1979; Nelson, 1977). Nevertheless, it did highlight the importance of the type of task in which the individual is engaged and the influence of this on subsequent recall. Prior to Craik and Lockhart's (1972) paper much research on memory was more concerned with trying to identify the structure and capacities of short- and long-term memories, and too little attention had been paid to the importance of the particular processing task and the individual's choice of a strategy for memorising.

By how much can variations in processing task change the amount subsequently remembered? A good example is provided by Craik and Tulving (1975) who showed that the probability of later recognising a noun such as "table" as having been previously presented varied from about ·85 to less than ·20 depending on whether the subject's task was to decide if the word fitted a given sentence (e.g. *He sat down to eat at the* . . .), or to decide if it was shown in capital letters. These sorts of differences remained even when the subjects knew that a test of their memory would follow the experiment, suggesting that it was the task itself rather than the subjects' wish to learn that determined the quality of the encoding. Research on mnemonics (e.g. Morris, 1979) shows how people can dramatically alter the amount that they remember by adopting appropriate strategies. This is brought about by the individuals, in effect, setting themselves a task that will lead to good encoding.

The Influence of Expertise on New Encoding

So far we have dealt only with things like coins or common words with which everyone is familiar. However, in Chapter 9 we emphasised how new encoding depends on the existing knowledge (e.g. in schemas) that is activated by the current situation. Surely people differ in the knowledge they possess? How will this influence what they encode? For example, in our witnessing example we assumed that you did not remember the make of the car. Perhaps we were unfair. Perhaps you are very knowledgeable about cars and think that you would have remembered what type it was. You would be assuming that experts on some topic, in this case makes of cars, will be more likely to remember new information on their favourite topic than will novices. Is this true? Perhaps experts might have poorer memories? They will have many similar instances encoded in memory if they spend their time dealing with one specialist type of information. Perhaps this will make it *harder* for an expert to learn and remember a new piece of information about their special topic. How will experts and novices differ?

An expert on the makes of cars will be able to encode the fleeting glimpse of a car more easily than will a novice. Perhaps that is not an aspect of memory, although it will lead to the expert remembering the make whereas the novice will have to say that they do not know. However, research has shown that the activities of the expert in processing a new example from their favourite topic will lead to better memory.

The best known examples of experts showing far superior memory to novices come from chess. De Groot (1966) found that when shown a five-second glimpse from the mid-game of a chess match, chess masters could reproduce 20 or more of the positions of the pieces on the board.

Novices could manage to correctly position only 4 or 5 pieces. If, however, the pieces were arranged randomly, rather than in a realistic position from an actual game, the superiority of the chess masters disappeared and they could perform no better than the novices. What is more, the experts described the experience of trying to reconstruct a random arrangement as disturbing. The relationships of the pieces and their positioning broke the well-established rules that were so much a part of the chess master's life.

How do chess masters achieve their superior memory of the board? With the real position from the game, they can draw upon two sources of their expertise to help them encode and remember the arrangement. First, they may recognise the position as one from a particular type of game. Simon and Gilmartin (1973) and Chase and Simon (1973a, b) followed up de Groot's research and studied the recall of chess positions by experts and novices. They concluded that chess masters have memories of up to 50,000 chess positions from games, which they can bring to aid the classification of a given board. So, for the chess master in this case, what is encoded is not the individual positioning on the board, but the memory that the board represents, for example, "move 16 in the Sicilian Defence." Second, even if the expert does not recognise the actual position from the game, the way that the expert perceives the board differs from the novice. To the novice they are simply pieces on the board. To the expert they represent attacks, threats, defences, and common arrangements such as the king, rook, and pawn pattern that follows castling. The expert sees the board from a real game as an integrated battleground with far fewer independent units than are seen by the novice.

Other Encoding Benefits From Expertise.   What evidence is there for expertise leading to better recall in other circumstances? What will be the reasons for such better memory? In recent years there have been several demonstrations of better recall by experts in several areas of expertise. However, the reasons for the better memory will vary from situation to situation. For example, Spilich, Vesonder, Chiesi, and Voss (1979) showed that knowledge of baseball predicted the recall of stories describing episodes from a baseball match. In this case the terms used are quite technical and the experts probably benefit from being able to comprehend what is happening, whereas novices may get lost in a collection of poorly understood terms.

In other situations, the better performance of the expert may have a different basis. Morris, Gruneberg, Sykes, and Merrick (1981) looked at the recall of soccer scores that were broadcast during the experiment. They found that there was a very close relationship between the number of these new scores that any subject could recall and that subject's knowledge about soccer measured by a questionnaire. Soccer "experts" could not predict the scores in advance any better than novices, but they acquired them much more easily. Morris et al. argued that this was probably because the experts processed the implications of the results and produced a much richer encoding.

In a subsequent study, Morris, Tweedy, and Gruneberg (1985) showed that the soccer experts had better memory than novices for real scores but not for simulated scores, even though the simulated scores were composed to be indistinguishable in form from the real scores. The experts had however been informed that they were simulated.

As Fig. 10.2 shows, for the quarter of the subjects who knew least about soccer, the recall of the real and simulated scores was identical. However, as football knowledge increased, so did the superiority of recall of the real results over the ones that had been simulated. This suggests that the experts do not automatically process better anything that seems like a soccer result. Rather, they must know that the result has real implications before their expertise comes into play.

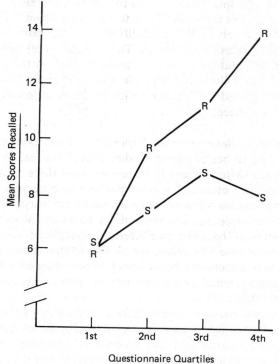

FIG. 10.2   Recall of real (R) and simulated (S) soccer scores as a function of the level of knowledge about soccer measured by questionnaire.

Morris et al. (1985) also found that the liking and disliking of the teams involved was a good predictor of the recall of real scores. They argued that the salience of the results for the subjects was an important component in their superior processing.

STORAGE

Decay

What happens to our memories between the time they are encoded and the moment when their retrieval is desirable? "Change and decay in all around I see" wrote H. F. Lyte in his hymn "Abide with me," and it would certainly be odd if the human memory system was the only exception to this generalisation. However, it is impossible to prove that a memory has been irrevocably lost. For this reason many psychologists have been tempted to adopt the working hypothesis that no memories are actually lost during the storage stage. Loftus and Loftus (1980) questioned 75 psychologists and found that 84 per cent believed that once information is entered into memory it remains there permanently. Nevertheless, despite the problems in providing evidence of change and decay in the memory store that would convince the more determined sceptic, it remains the case that the human body with its brain is a biochemical system, continuously in the process of decay, modification, and renewal, and it would be surprising if the aspects of the brain responsible for retaining our memories did not change and decay over time, perhaps losing the quality of the encoding originally laid down.

Possible Evidence for Memory Decay

Is the loss of information from memory simply a matter of it decaying? It is easy to find evidence that seems to fit neatly with this assumption. In one of the first experimental studies of memory, Ebbinghaus (1885) tested how long it would take him to relearn lists of nonsense syllables after delays of from 20 minutes to a month. Nonsense syllables are syllables composed of a consonant, a vowel, then another consonant, which do not form a meaningful word (e.g. *hax*, *fet*). Ebbinghaus found that the "savings" in the time to relearn was quite considerable after 20 minutes, but declined with a curve suggesting exponential loss of the information over time (see Fig. 10.3(a)).

This decline in the amount that can be remembered, as time passes, is demonstrated in many different situations. The graph in Fig. 10.3(b) shows the relationship between the number of words recognised and the length of

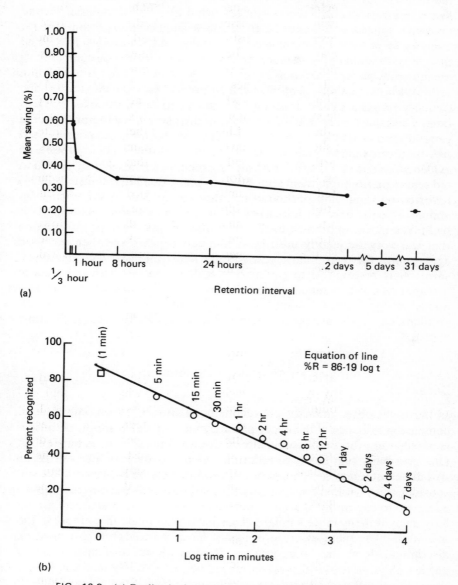

FIG. 10.3 (a) Decline in the time saved when relearning a list of nonsense syllables, as a function of the delay before testing (Ebbinghaus, 1885). (b) Decline in recognition over time (Woodworth, 1938).

the delay in testing summarised by Woodworth (1938). Evidence for the loss of information over time is not restricted to artificial material such as nonsense syllables. Boreas (1930) found a similar information loss for memory of poems, and more recently, Squire and Slater (1975) showed that people's ability to remember the names of television programmes or of racehorses who won famous races declines steadily over time. Linton (1982), who kept a record of two "salient events" for each day for 6 years, similarly found a steady decline in her ability to recall the events across time. There have been a few exceptions in the psychology literature to the generalisation that the longer the interval since encoding, the poorer recall will be. For example, Bahrick, Bahrick, and Wittlinger (1975) found no evidence for a decline in the recognition of school friends who appeared in old school photographs even after 30 or so years. Similarly, Bahrick (1984) reported no significant decline in memory for Spanish by Americans for about 25 years, once an initial period of forgetting lasting about 3 years had taken place. In both cases the memories are for semantic information that was very frequently used for a number of years and then not used again until the test many years later. Such information does seem surprisingly resistant to forgetting, but it does contrast with the mass of research on episodic memory over the last 100 years where performances almost always show a decline over time. In our example of witnessing an accident we would expect the memory to become less accurate as time passed.

Retrieval Problems as an Alternative Explanation to Decay

Is the usual observation of poorer memory after a longer time interval convincing evidence of the decay of the memory trace? It is not, because it is possible to propose plausible alternative accounts of what is happening. One possibility that needs considering is that the memory may not decay with time but it may be changed when new information is encoded. We will consider this possibility shortly. Secondly, the same retrieval cues may be adequate to cue retrieval after a short delay but may be inadequate after a long delay if many more similar entries have been made in memory in the meantime. The memory trace need not have changed, but if it must be discriminated on the later occasion from many more similar memory entries, then its retrieval may no longer be possible. By analogy, with a single bookshelf we can retrieve a book on the basis of its colour alone. If ten more shelves are then filled with an assortment of new books (analogous to new memories) then there may be several books of the same colour and our original means of retrieving the one that we wanted will no longer succeed.

There is a third possibility. This is that the way that we interpret a given situation will change with time. Our schemas are modified and updated, as we have changed in our interests and knowledge. Consequently, even though the obvious, external conditions at the time of attempting retrieval may appear the same, the way they are processed and the cues that our cognitive system actually supplies to the memory system may have changed and may no longer adequately match the stored entry in memory.

All of the accounts given above are plausible reasons why the amount that we recall declines with time, whether or not the memory trace does itself decay. What is more, there has been considerable research to show that these types of influences do play a major part in what is remembered. Consequently, although it remains plausible that our memories may decay with time, we show in the rest of this section that there are enough other reasons to explain why we forget, even if our memories do not decay.

Are Stored Memories Modified by New Entries? The idea that subsequent learning may modify the memory trace of an earlier memory was suggested by Webb (1917) and especially championed by Melton and Irwin (1940) and Barnes and Underwood (1959). Melton and Irwin (1940) showed that the more lists of nonsense syllables their subjects learned, the harder they found the relearning of their first list. For Melton and Irwin, the important thing was that when the original list was relearned, the number of mistakes that the subjects made by giving, incorrectly, nonsense syllables that they had learned in the intervening lists also *declined* as more intervening lists were learned. Melton and Irwin argued that if the poorer relearning of the original list was to be explained by subjects retrieving syllables from the intervening list and having problems in telling whether or not they came from the original list, then the number of such intrusions should *increase* as more intervening lists were learned. This, as we have just said, was not so. Melton and Irwin therefore attributed the forgetting to *unlearning* of the original list during the learning of the new lists.

Barnes and Underwood (1959) gave their subjects the opportunity to recall two responses learned to each of eight nonsense syllable stimuli. They found that as their subjects had more trials on the second pairing their ability to recall the first pairing that they had learned declined. Again, this was attributed to the unlearning of the association of the nonsense syllable stimulus and the adjective response as a result of a new adjective being learned as a response to the original stimulus.

Despite the evidence of the Melton and Irwin and Barnes and Underwood studies, the case for unlearning was not especially convincing. The argument was that unlearning must occur because there was no evidence of the other major explanation of forgetting then current, the competition of other learned responses. Many psychologists were not convinced that forgetting was best conceptualised in this simple way and since there were alternative explanations of the Melton and Irwin and Barnes and Underwood findings (cf. Baddeley, 1976), it was not necessary to accept their conclusion. For example, as the second list in the Barnes and Underwood (1959) study is better and better learned, it may become harder to retrieve the first list because the second list is always found first, automatically terminating the memory search. In other words, allowing for retrieval as Barnes and Underwood did does not mean that retrieval will be possible, even though the entry remains in store.

Recent Evidence on Memory Modification. More recently, the idea of changes in the memory where information has been stored has been raised again by Elizabeth Loftus and her associates. Loftus and Palmer (1974) demonstrated that the evidence given by subjects who saw a film of a traffic accident could be distorted by the inclusion of questions about the accident which added further "information" to the subjects. When asked how fast the cars were going when they *smashed* into each other, not only did subjects give higher estimates of the speed than if asked how fast they were going when they *contacted* each other, but they were twice as likely to agree (wrongly) when questioned later that they had seen broken glass. The idea of the cars smashing into one another not only distorted the speed estimate, a phenomenon familiar from earlier work on leading questions, but also changed the recall of other events. Loftus, Miller, and Burns (1978) followed up the distorting effects of questions by showing a series of photographs which together as a sequence depicted a traffic accident. Before the accident a car was seen beside either a Stop or a Yield (Give way) sign. In questions to the subjects, one group were asked about the car at the road sign. However, for them, the sign mentioned in the question was *different* from that actually seen. Loftus et al. found that in a subsequent test when the subjects had to choose between the actual picture shown and one with the sign mentioned in the question, 80 per cent of the subjects erroneously chose the one referred to in the question.

In subsequent experiments Loftus and her associates went on to demonstrate that the biasing effect of the questions was *not* the result of their subjects giving the results which they guessed Loftus was seeking. Subjects were offered payments of up to $25 for correct answers, but went on making the same errors.

Loftus (1981) varied the time at which the misleading information was given to the subjects, and found that it was most effective the longer the interval since the original exposure to the event and the shorter the time before recall was required. Loftus (1983) also found that the biasing questions were most effective if the misleading information was not the central theme of the questions but slipped in as an assumption within a complex question. So, for example, the reference to the loan sign in the question "Was the woman who was sitting at the desk with the loan sign biting her fingers?" led more subjects to report having seen a loan sign than did the more direct and simpler leading question of "Was the loan sign knocked off the desk by the robber?".

Loftus and Loftus (1980) argue that the memories of the original event were actually *changed* by the misleading questions, which became incorporated into the memory entry. Like Barnes and Underwood (1959), Loftus (1979) tried to see if her subjects still had memories of the correct details. Perhaps, for example, the confident assumption of the alternative details made in the misleading questions had led them to doubt what they could recall? In this new experiment a key character was seen reading a green book. Misleading information given subsequently implied that the book was yellow and, interestingly, the first guesses at the book colour tended to be a compromise colour combining the original with the one suggested in the misleading question. Loftus then asked her subjects to make a second guess at the possible book colour. This second guess, however, turned out to be no better than chance guessing might have been.

There is no doubt that Loftus's findings have important implications for predictions of what will be recalled by eyewitnesses. However, there is a fundamental problem, which Loftus and Loftus (1980) themselves acknowledge. This is showing that the memory entry has been changed. Could it be that what is recalled by the subjects is a construction from both the original and the misleading information? Or that although the new, misleading information is all that can be recalled (in the situations examined by Loftus), there may still be ways in which the old memory, so far unfound in memory, but there nevertheless, may be retrieved in the appropriate circumstances? Bekerian and Bowers (1983) were able to show that the original memory was still available and that the problem in the Loftus experiments was that the conditions at recall led to the retrieval of the misleading information. They replicated the Loftus experiment with the Stop and Yield signs, but then changed the testing procedure. Loftus had tested by randomly ordering her test pictures. Bekerian and Bowers argued that this did not give the greatest opportunity for memory of the original to be cued. They tested recognition of the pictures from the story in the order they had been originally shown, so that the representation of the story would help retrieve what had been stored. In this condition they found that the Loftus effect of misleading information did not occur, and the subjects were able to select the correct picture which they had seen when the story was originally shown. It does, therefore, appear that Loftus's research, although very important when considering the reliability of eyewitness testimony, has not shown that the old memory entry is irrevocably lost.

As yet, there is little convincing evidence that what is stored in our memories is actually changed by new events, rather than being added to or supplemented by further entries. Even so, there would be attractions in a memory system that was able to replace out-of-date information with a more appropriate substitute. There would be less storage capacity required, and no possibility of recalling the old rather than the new items. Such a memory system would be especially useful in storing our intentions to do things (see Chapter 4).

To return to the example with which we began the chapter, Loftus's research suggests that your accuracy as a witness may have been reduced by the comment you heard from the angry driver or the assumptions that the policeman made during his questioning. Perhaps you did not really see a woman driving but were influenced by the way the driver assumed that it was a woman driver? You would probably doubt this since you can retrieve an image of the woman in the driving seat. Would you be right?

RETRIEVAL

The most efficient encoding and storage system is worthless unless the stored information can be retrieved when it is needed. As emphasized in the section on encoding, it is the information that was stored at encoding that must be used to discriminate one memory from another. To retrieve the information, however, appropriate cues must be actively being processed in the cognitive system.

Retrieval as an Automatic, Continuous Process

When does retrieval take place? It is tempting to think of retrieval as an occasional, deliberate process because in everyday life we only occasionally make a deliberate effort to search for something we have stored. However, if we consider what memory is *for*, we recognise that it is for making sense of what is *currently* happening to us and for predicting what is *likely to happen* in the future. Since we continuously need to understand what are the implications of our present experiences, we need to probe memory constantly for suitable information to help us make sense of what is going on. If we can retrieve high-level schemes that organise and clarify what is going on, if we recall similar situations and their implications, we can be much more efficient at coping with the world. Consequently, memory systems are necessary for the continuous process of comprehending the sensory input (see Chapter 9) and we should expect the memory system to make available automatically any suitable information that resembles the current active processing going on in the cognitive system. One way to conceptualise retrieval processes is as a continous matching of what is currently active in the processing system with the stored memories. If the active elements that are being processed sufficiently match a stored entry in memory then that memory becomes potentially available for recall. It is only potentially available because òther memories may also be activated and the system be able to select one or none of them. Also, the current plan being processed in the cognitive system may be one which, because of its capacity demands or for some other reason, does not allow the activated memory to be actually read out from memory.

Matching and Mismatching with Current Cognitive Activity

Suppose that, while on holiday, you return to a viewpoint which might remind you of happy memories of an earlier holiday. You may not retrieve such memories if you have too many of them stored with this single context as the retrieval code. Nor will such memories recur if at that moment a car comes dangerously round the bend and you have to occupy yourself with more important actions of steering to safety. At any particular moment there are three possibilities for the matching of the processes active in the cognitive system with those previously stored in memory. One is that no entry in memory will match sufficiently for it to be made available; the second is that one entry will be activated with sufficient strength and to a degree that sets its activation clearly above other partially activated memories; the third is that several entries in memory are all activated but none to a sufficiently greater extent than the others to make it clearly discriminable from its competitors. Nothing would be recalled in the first condition, in the second condition the memory entry would normally be read off into the working memory, and in the third condition no item would be sufficiently clearly appropriate to be read off. It is worth pausing over this third condition. As will become clear shortly, the evidence on retrieval and retrieval problems suggests that when competing memories are activated then none of them will be recalled unless one is far more strongly activated than the others. Nevertheless, this assumes certain properties of the retrieval system which might well be otherwise. It assumes that the system does not or cannot make a random choice between the competing memories and that there are limitations of the number of memories that can be read out at one time. Perhaps neither of these is surprising. A random choice between competing memories would frequently lead to an inappropriate choice with considerable harm to the accuracy of the resulting construction composed in the workspace. Evolution has probably selected for conservativeness in the retrieval of information since it would often be impossible to construct a suitable interpretation of the situation if memories from very different past situations were introduced into the working memory.

Interference Explanations for Forgetting

From the 1930s to the 1960s much of the study of memory was based on the investigation of how the learning of similar material interfered with recall. A good illustration of interference is the experiment by McGeoch and MacDonald (1931). They first taught their subjects a list of 10 adjectives, until the list could be recalled through once without an error. Then, in the next 10 minutes, the subjects either rested or learned a new list. The new lists were constructed to vary the similarity between them and the original list. For example, one list consisted of three-digit numbers, another of unrelated adjectives, and another of synonyms of the words in the first list. When they were retested on the first list, the amount that the subjects could recall decreased as the items learned in the intervening period increased in similarity to the original adjective list. On the first trial after the intervening period, subjects who had rested could recall, on average, 45 per cent of the adjectives in their correct positions; those who had learned the digit list could recall 37 per cent, those who had just been learning unrelated adjectives could remember only 22 per cent; and those who had learned a synonym list could recall only 12.5 per cent. The explanation would seem to be that, for these different groups the entries in memory differed in their distinctiveness. For those subjects who had rested there were no competing entries in memory. For those who learned the lists of numbers there were entries of those numbers which were coded as having been memorised in the experiment, but the memory entries for the numbers were sufficiently distinctive from the entries for the adjectives for them to be discriminated and be quite well recalled. However, the entry for the synonyms must have been very similar both in the record of the time and context of the learning and the nature of the words themselves. Consequently, it was very difficult for the subjects to recall the correct words.

McGeoch and MacDonald's experiment illustrates the problem for retrieval created by the entry in memory of similar items to those to be remembered at a time after the learning of the items to be remembered. The interference of these items with recall is known as *retroactive interference*. Items learned before those to be recalled can also cause retrieval problems and such interference is called *proactive interference*. Underwood (1957), for example, showed that the more lists a subject had previously learned, the less could be recalled of a new list when it was tested 24 hours later (see Fig. 10.4).

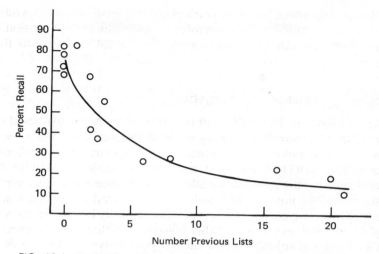

FIG. 10.4   Decline in amount remembered from a list of nonsense syllables after 24 hours, as a function of the number of similar lists learned previously (Underwood, 1957).

Traditionally, the explanation of interference effects involved a combination of the unlearning of the memory and problems in discriminating between competing learned memories. In recent years there has been a greater recognition of the need for appropriate retrieval cues at recall.

Context, State, and Mood Dependent Recall

In our sketch of the retrieval process we pointed out that retrieval depends on the currently active information in the cognitive system activating entries in memory. Obviously, the closer the current processing is to the original conditions under which learning took place, the better should be the retrieval of the information. Support for this conclusion comes from research on context, state, and mood dependent learning. The general finding of this research is that the closer the recall situation resembles the learning situation, the better the recall.

Godden and Baddeley (1975) illustrated the influence of the context of learning on recall when they had divers learn and recall lists of words either under water or on land. Recall was tested in either the same context (above or below water) or in the reverse condition to that in which learning took place, i.e. divers who had learned the lists above water were tested under water and vice versa. Recall of the words in the same context as when learning had taken place was 47 per cent better than when the context was switched. Of course, the contexts above and below water are very different.

Merely changing from one room to another does not alter the context so dramatically. Nevertheless, powerful effects of context have been reported where both the room and the way in which the material to be learned was presented were made markedly different (e.g. Greenspoon & Ranyard, 1957).

There are many anecdotes about drunks who forget what they have done when they sober up, only to recall again when drunk once more. Research upon the influence of drugs such as alcohol and marijuana, which influence the state experienced by the subjects, has supported these stories. In general, with alcohol and many other drugs, recall is better if the state in which learning took place is re-created at the recall stage. Material learnt while under the influence of alcohol tends to be best recalled when similarly inebriated (Eich, 1980).

We have considered examples involving quite gross changes in the context of learning and recall, or the influence of drugs. What about less dramatic changes? Even differences in our moods can influence what we recall. Bower (1983) manipulated the moods of his subjects either by hypnosis or other techniques such as the reading of statements designed to induce happiness or sadness. He found that recall was as much as halved if the mood state was switched between learning and recall. In work with manic-depressive patients, Teesdale (1983) has shown similar dependencies of memories on the mood state at the time of encoding. One implication of this research is that an aspect of depression is the self-sustaining nature of the state. Once someone is depressed they will find it easier to recall depressing memories than happy ones, and this will deepen the depression.

Encoding Specificity

The results of the experiments on context, state, and mood dependency are examples of the *encoding specificity principle* (Tulving and Thomson, 1973; Tulving, 1983). The principle asserts that retrieval depends on the compatibility of the stored information and the retrieval information. Recall requires appropriate retrieval information, information that is suitable for the particular memory trace that has been stored at the time of encoding.

It is not just the context in which information is encoded that can vary and so influence the conditions required for retrieval. The ways in which words and concepts are interpreted when they are encoded will determine what makes an appropriate retrieval cue. This is illustrated in an experiment by Barclay, Bransford, Franks, McCarrell, and Nitsch (1974). They manipulated the properties of objects that were emphasized by the sentences in which they were mentioned. Two example sentences are: *The student spilled the ink* and *The student picked up the ink*. The first sentence is likely to remind the reader that ink is messy when spilled, the second that it is kept in a bottle. Barclay et al. read 10 such sentences to two groups of subjects, one group having sentences emphasising other properties. Then both groups were given a list of 20 cues to recall: 10 were relevant to the properties emphasised to one group, 10 to the other group. For example, the list included the cues *something in a bottle* and *something messy*, the former being appropriate to the group who had the sentence about picking up the ink, the latter to those who heard about the ink being spilled. Subjects wrote the noun of which they were reminded by the cues. On average, 47 per cent of the target words were recalled to the appropriate cues and only 16 per cent to the inappropriate cues. At encoding, only some aspects of the objects were considered and interpreted when the sentences were comprehended. At the recall stage, only the processing of information related to those aspects encountered during comprehension made the subsequent retrieval possible.

Retrieving Increases the Likelihood of Future Recall

Does retrieving an item from memory have an effect on the memory itself? The act of retrieval is in itself a processing event and the result will be to alter the ease with which the item can be recalled again. Retrieving something from memory increases the likelihood that it will be remembered again in the future. This has been known from research on list learning of words, where the act of testing recall of the list can be as effective as showing the list again (Cooper & Monk, 1976). It is also known from everyday experience, where, especially among people who have little opportunity for fresh, interesting experiences, such as the infirm elderly, the same stories repeatedly come to mind and are retold.

It is likely that at least two processes lead to the strengthening of memories when they are recalled. One has already been suggested. In effect, a new entry in memory is made when the old memory is recalled since the system will make a new record of the use to which the memory is put. The other factor relates to the old memory itself. After a memory has been activated it is likely that the amount of input necessary to reactivate the memory in the future is lowered (Brown, 1968; Rundus, 1973). In the future, less specific information will be required before the memory is made available. This concept of a lowering of the threshold for activation is a common one for cognitive models (see for example the models of word and face processing, Chapters 1 and 2). The lowering of the threshold may be especially marked immediately after retrieval and may decline with time.

Memory Blocked by Other Recalled Items

The result of making a memory easier to activate can be interesting and leads to some apparently odd memory phenomena. Being reminded of part of what you have been asked to remember can make remembering the rest harder! Brown (1968) asked two groups of subjects to recall the names of the states that make up the USA. He provided one group with the names of 25 of the states. These subjects were actually *poorer* at recalling the names of the remaining 25 states than were those subjects who had to try to recall all 50 states. Reading the names of the 25 states activated those states' entries in the memories of the subjects and made them more likely to be re-activated when the subjects searched their memories for the names of the States of the Union. The result was that competing names kept being recalled by the subjects and in turn this recall would strengthen the memory and make it even more likely in the future that the competing names kept being recalled instead of the name of the states as yet unrecalled.

Have you experienced this phenomenon of an unwanted response repeatedly coming to mind when trying to remember something such as a name of a friend or a place, or the exact word in a crossword? Reason and Lucas (1984) had subjects keep diaries of occasions when they had such memory blocks, and they found that the persistent recalling of an unwanted word (which Reason and Lucas called a "blocker") happened on over 50 per cent of occasions where a tip of the tongue (TOT) state was eventually resolved. The proportion may be much higher in unresolved TOT states.

In such situations where a word feels on the tip of one's tongue but cannot be retrieved, the common advice is to wait a while and it will come. The sense of this can be seen, since waiting allows the threshold of the competing response to increase while a new attempt at recall in the future will be in a context of rather different current activities in the cognitive system, so that another set of features will be activated in memory and the blocker may no longer be the one which is most highly activated.

RECONSTRUCTING AND INTERPRETING

The Function of Memory

Because memory logically involves encoding, storage, and retrieval and because it is easy to illustrate such processes with examples of the storage of real objects, such as books, there is a temptation to think that memory is analogous to the storing of objects. A book is put on a shelf, kept there, and later the same book is taken down and used again. It is important to remember that this analogy when pushed this far may be inappropriate for memory. Encoding must take place, but that encoding is merely some change within the system which could in the future be "read out" again. The use of magnetic tape for the recording of video or audio cassettes is a good example of storage where the result of the encoding, the magnetic changes made on the tape, is clearly different from the original input, but from which, given the right system, the original can be retrieved again when required.

We should not expect encoding to be such that the readout will exactly resemble the original experience, although it may do. The memory system is involved in making sense of the world, in predicting the future and in supplying components to aid in the planning of future actions. Exact readout may not be the best aim of such a system; what will be best will be some compromise between ease of access and usefulness. We have already seen, in Chapter 9, that what is encoded may be the *interpreted* meaning of the input rather than the *exact* form of words (or whatever) in which the input was received.

Just as encoding is rarely a copying of the original input, so retrieval is unlikely to be merely the simple readout of what has been stored in memory. Again, it is worth remembering what the memory system is principally for; it is to provide minute-by-minute information to help interpretation and prediction; it is not a video or tape recorder. Our memories have not evolved specifically to cope with the reproduction with great accuracy of large amounts of past experience, but rather to provide quick answers to implicit questions such as "What does this mean?" and "What will happen now?" Consequently, when we use our memories to try to give a detailed account of a whole series of events or of a story, what can be retrieved from memory rarely provides enough information by itself. As in the witnessing example with which we began, our memories of events are often a collection of stills and highlights. This may be because little more was encoded, or it may reflect the inappropriate nature of the retrieval cues available.

Memory in Non-literate Societies

It is sometimes assumed that people in literate societies have lost much of their powers of memory. It is assumed that in non-literate societies, where there are no written records to rely on and no books or computers, people would make far more use of their memories and would be more accurate in their recall. In particular, it is often assumed that in such cultures there would be accurate, word perfect recall of such important oral traditions as the genealogy of the king or the words of epic songs or folk tales. Hunter (1979, 1985) has studied the literature on such oral traditions and concludes that what he calls "lengthy verbatim recall" is not a feature of the performance of those who retain the verbal traditions. The wording of stories and genealogies change with telling. What are valued are other aspects of the performance: the poetry, the singing, the placing of the king as a descendant of all the important and often mythical characters in the tradition. Where no opportunity to compare a performance with a verbatim record has existed, not surprisingly, the skill of exact recall has not been valued. It is in literate cultures where the accurate learning of religious and artistic works has been valued that lengthy verbatim recall has been achieved. The performance of the transmitters of oral tradition in non-literate societies is structured by the demands of the situation. Our own recall is also structured by a mixture of the memories we can recall, the higher-level plan into which we would expect the recall to fit, and our other knowledge that we bring to the situation. Recall, at least as it is written or spoken, is very much a process of reconstruction.

Role of Expertise During Retrieval

When Bartlett (1932) presented his subjects with an Indian folk tale ("The war of the ghosts") they, as Cambridge undergraduates, found it difficult to understand. Bartlett observed that the recall attempts by the subjects reflected an "effort after meaning." The stories reflected an attempt to make sense of what could be remembered, often at the expense of the insertion of details that were not in the original. Some of these errors may reflect mistakes in encoding, but many can be interpreted, as Bartlett did, as evidence for memory being a reconstructive process. Bartlett wrote of the influence of schemas, the "active organisation of past reactions, or of past experiences," which he believed directed the reconstruction. To him:

> Remembering is not the re-excitation of innumerable fixed, lifeless and fragmentary traces. It is an imaginative reconstruction, or construction, built out of the relation of our attitude towards a whole mass of organised past reactions or experience, and to a little outstanding detail which commonly appears in image or in language form [p. 213].

It is not always easy to tell whether the influence of past experience and prior knowledge is upon the initial encoding or the retrieval of the information, and it is quite likely to be upon both. The prior knowledge will help in the initial interpretation of the new experience and will also provide a framework to guide retrieval. It helps to ensure the matching of encoding and retrieval conditions which we have identified as of such importance in effective recall. So, for example, when Bower, Clark, Lesgold, and Winzenz (1969) gave their subjects hierarchical lists to learn such as that in Fig. 10.5 they found that these could be learned more than

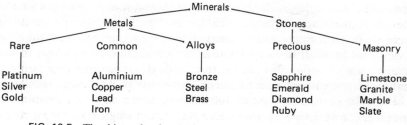

FIG. 10.5   The hierarchy for "minerals" from the list of Bower et al. (1969).

four times as quickly than when the words were randomly placed in the layout. Here the structure probably helped the subjects at encoding by emphasising related properties of the words and aided recall by supplying a suitable framework within which recall could be attempted.

Anderson and Pichert (1978) were able to show the influence of prior knowledge upon the recall stage in the following way. They had their subjects read a story about two boys who stayed at home instead of going to school. Prior to reading the story the subjects were instructed to read it from the perspective of either a burglar or a housebuyer.

The story contained 72 ideas, some, such as the mentioning of the leaky roof, being important to a housebuyer but not to a burglar; others, such as reference to a collection of rare coins, being interesting to a burglar but not a buyer. Both groups of subjects recalled what they could of the story and were tested again after a short delay. On this second test they were either asked to recall from the same perspective or from the other one that they had used when reading. The switch in perspective led to the subjects now recalling more while those who used the same perspective recalled slightly less. Changing perspective changed the retrieval conditions and gave a different framework to recall.

Imagery and Confidence During Recall

In our original example we suggested that you would be confident that there were two people in the car because you can recall a mental image of them as they drove away. Could you be wrong? Just because something is retrieved from memory when we try to remember it does not mean that what we recall is accurate. Mental images are especially convincing since they seem to be a snapshot from the past. For particularly emotional moments in our lives we can often remember a lot of details, with mental images of the scene. Brown and Kulik (1977) called these "flashbulb memories" and showed that many people can give considerable details about what they were doing when they heard of a famous event such as the assassination of President Kennedy. Much earlier, Colegrove (1899) had collected similar anecdotes of memories of the news of Lincoln's assassination. One issue here is whether special processes of encoding or retrieval need be postulated to account for flashbulb memories, or whether they are recallable because the context is highly discriminable and the memories frequently retrieved. For our purpose here, however, we should ask if the memories are accurate. Neisser (1982) gives examples of flashbulb memories which cannot be accurate. Linton (1975) for example, while studying memories of Kennedy's assassination, had a subject assert that they knew that Linton had told them herself. Linton was able to check that she could not have been in the same place as the subject on that day.

Bartlett (1932) had commented that mental images give a confidence that is unjustified. Morris (in press) examined the accuracy and confidence related to mental images of scenes from video films. He found that questions about the film were far more accurately answered when subjects reported having a mental image of the scene. However, subjects were significantly more confident of answers which were actually wrong but to which they had images than they were to answers which were *correct* but *not* accompanied by images.

MEMORY IMPROVEMENT

Improving Encoding

What can be done to improve retrieval of information from memory? Many mnemonic techniques exist which will help make the most of encoding (see e.g. Morris, 1979; Morris & Hampson, 1983). These seek to encourage elaborate, distinctive, integrated memories and provide good cues for retrieval. Often, however, especially in everyday life, we either do not recognise that a special effort must be made at the encoding stage, or we do not want to expend the necessary effort. There was little that could have been done to improve encoding during the witnessing example that we have used.

Improving Retrieval

The object of retrieval techniques must be to re-create the type of processing that occurred when the event was originally encoded. One initial problem is that if an attempt at retrieval fails, memory search may be abandoned. Searching memory is a complex activity, and more than one line of search may be followed at a time. Evidence suggesting that retrieval will be unlikely can lead to a search being abandoned. If you are asked to recall Charles Dicken's telephone number, you will quickly recall enough about Dickens, telephones, and your other knowledge about telephone numbers (that you do not remember even those of some of your friends) for you to rapidly classify the questions as unanswerable, if not silly. If I ask you what you were doing on Monday afternoon in the third week of October two years ago, you will probably respond by refusing to try once you have recalled what the words mean and constructed what is implied. Lindsay and Norman (1977), however, claim that if you can be persuaded to try, you will probably go through a problem-solving routine of gradually reconstructing the context of two years ago using what you can remember. One problem is that you may remember what you *think* are details from the day, but what if they are memories from another day, recalled because you are so determined to recall something that your criteria for acceptance are lowered? Read and Bruce (1982) had people try over a long period of time to recall the names of classmates from their school days. The result was a steady and dramatic increase in the number of false names offered.

Hypnosis.   Every so often there is a report in the press of a hypnotist enabling a witness to remember something they were unable to recall without aid. There is no doubt that during hypnosis several useful aids to retrieval will occur. The individual may be more relaxed and able to genuinely attempt recall, they will try for some time, and it has long been known that reminiscence, the recalling of information not recallable on earlier attempts, is common even after many recall attempts. Perhaps most importantly, the hypnotist will attempt to reconstruct the events, in so far as they are known, in the imagination of the subject. All this probably provides the source of the anecdotes on hypnotism, since some recall will take place under hypnosis that did not occur earlier. Nevertheless, from the many studies of hypnosis as a means of improving the accuracy of eyewitnesses there is no evidence that it improves the accuracy of recall (see Loftus & Loftus, 1980; Wagstaff, 1985). It does seem to increase the number of false items "remembered," which is, of course, particularly dangerous in witnessing where there is often no external check on accuracy.

Reconstructing Context.   If the context in which the events to be remembered took place is known, it is possible to improve recall by, for example, supplying photographs of the scene (Smith, 1979). Alternatively, witnesses can be carefully led through a reconstruction of the events in their imagination. Malpass and Devine (1981) arranged what appeared to their subjects to be an act of vandalism and then interviewed them five months later. One group were reminded of the events with a detailed interview which explored their feelings, memories for the room, and immediate reactions. When these subjects tried to identify the vandal they were more accurate than control subjects who had not received the preceding reconstruction of the events. It is important, however, that these efforts prior to recall should reconstruct the appropriate conditions. Loftus, Manber and Keating (1983) showed their subjects a highly stressful film of a fire in a hospital. Some subjects were reminded of events early in the film, prior to the fire, and shown slides of the hospital as it appeared then. These subjects had poorer recall, and Loftus et al. speculated that this might be because the emotions associated with the non-stressful early part of the film were not appropriate to the stressful part on which the questions were based.

Morris and Morris (1985) argued that the best recall would be obtained if the ordering of questions best matched the structure of information as it had been entered in memory and if what was initially tested by the questions could serve as good retrieval cues for the later recall. They used the same set of questions to test recall of short video sequences that had been taken from TV police thrillers. The questions were ordered (1) randomly, (2) in the order of the time sequence of the film, (3) beginning with the main characters, or (4) beginning with the main event (a car chase). Using the time sequence or beginning with the main characters turned out to lead to the more accurate recall.

SUMMARY

Let us return to our original example and apply what has been discussed subsequently in the chapter. We have argued that what is encoded into memory depends on the processing demands at the time. For a simple task like walking home you need do little processing of the surrounding world, and it is not surprising that what you remembered from the early stages of the accident was vague and sketchy. We have suggested that what can be recalled depends on the extent to which the current processes in the cognitive system match those which took place when the memory was encoded. Your memory of the scene will depend on how well you can re-create the situation for yourself. We have also pointed out several ways in which your memory may be distorted. The comments of the policeman or the other driver, or later your friends, lawyers, and so on, in so far as they seem to imply knowledge of what took place, may be entered in memory and subsequently retrieved to distort what you recall. You felt confident that at least the part of your memories that were supported by mental images were accurate, yet, although it is the case that such memories are likely to be more accurate than others, they tend to give a misleading sense of confidence. Finally, we pointed out that our memory systems have evolved to supply information in answer to specific situations where we need to know what is happening and what will take place next. They have not evolved to act as video recorders, storing away exactly what we perceive. We should neither expect our memories to supply exact photographic recall nor feel ashamed that they do not. Rather, we should be impressed that we have evolved a system that can so quickly and readily supply information to prevent the world seeming like the world which William James assumed greeted the newborn infant; a booming, buzzing confusion.

Good discussions of many of the topics mentioned will be found in M. Eysenck (1984), *A Handbook of Cognitive Psychology*. A simple but knowledgeable treatment of many of the issues is given by A. D. Baddeley (1983), *Your Memory: A Users Guide*. The more historical aspects are described in M. M. Gruneberg and P. E. Morris (1978), *Aspects of Memory*, and A. D. Baddeley (1976), *The Psychology of Memory*.

11 Arriving in a New City: Acquiring and Using Spatial Knowledge

Imagine you are visiting a strange town or city for the first time. You are met at the airport or the railway station by a friend who drives you through unknown streets until you have no idea where you are. You don't know how to get back to where you started from and you don't even know if you are north, south, east, or west from that point. You know that you went past a large church and some civic buildings, you noticed a demolition area, a couple of fruit-market stalls, and two men having a fight in the street. You also had a conversation with your friend. Later, when you realise that you have to go out and find your way about, you start to panic. It's easy to get lost and you could be late for important appointments if you take a wrong turn, find yourself outside the wrong building, or catch the wrong bus.

After you've lived in the same town for a few months you can drive or walk confidently from your home to your friend's home, to the office, to the theatre. You don't know everything about the city but you have a rough idea of the direction of places with which you aren't acquainted: You know many ways to get from place to place and you can invent new routes if familiar ones are obstructed. The new knowledge you have obtained is related to the spatial characteristics of the environment and it is this spatial knowledge which concerns us in this chapter. The ways in which psychologists and others have thought about the representation of large-scale space has many things in common with ordinary experience, so we can start to think about the spatial knowledge in our heads in much the same way as we think of spatial information that someone gives to us when we arrive in a new place. We spend a major part of this chapter dealing with the development of large-scale spatial knowledge and then relate that to more theoretical questions about how we store and use spatial information in general.

ROUTES AND MAPS

Imagine again that you are on your first visit to a new town. Your friend tells you how to get from the house where you are staying to the bus station. If you were visiting Lancaster, for example, the instructions for how to get from Dale Street to the bus station would be something like this:

> When you leave the house turn right and walk along the road. The road swings to the left at the Moorlands pub and you follow it. Keep going straight downhill. When the road levels out there is a right turn. Don't take that one. After that turn there is the back of the Town Hall. Pass that and then turn right at the main road. Walk along that road, past the edge of a square with a statue of Queen Victoria, and then downhill. At the bottom of the hill the main road swings to the right. You don't go that way, but at that point you turn left. The bus station should be in sight. It is to the right, after the left turn.

This set of instructions contains a list of commands which link up various sights and even feelings. There is some emphasis on landmarks—pub and Town Hall, for example—and there are instructions to change direction, to keep going straight, and extra information such as that the road goes downhill. Basically, your friend has given you a route to follow.

Of course, your friend could just give you a map and let you work it out from there. Look at the map in Fig. 11.1. This is a representation of part of Lancaster and it contains roads, landmarks, and directions to travel, some of which are in the form of verbal labels like names, whereas others have a more direct relationship to the town. This map may be more difficult to use while walking than a list of actions would be, but it allows you to go back along a route, it allows you to use one of several routes to get to the bus station, and to construct a new route if an old one goes wrong.

When we look at the knowledge of the environment which we build up with experience we find that sometimes we use route information, which we can think of in terms of links between conditions and actions, and sometimes our knowledge has more of the characteristics of a map. These include reversibility—knowing how to get from A to B implies knowing how to get from B to A; transitivity—knowing how to go from A to B and from B to C allows you to go from A to C; and flexibility—the ability to take more than one route from A to B. These three kinds of operations that can be performed on real maps can also be performed on our internal representations of the environment (Pick & Lockman, 1981), and it is because we can take detours, reverse journeys, and put components of journeys together that the name "cognitive map" has so often been applied to our knowledge of the space in which we live.

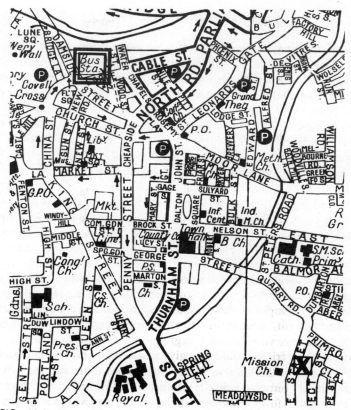

FIG. 11.1   Part of a map of Lancaster, from Lancaster Centre Plan
published by Geographia Ltd. X (lower right corner) represents the starting
position for the walk to the bus station (upper left).

Because maps are a way of representing the real environment on paper it
is easy to use them as analogies for our mental representations, but we
have to be quite careful about the analogy. On a printed map, like that in
Fig. 11.1, there are several ways in which things are represented. The label
"Town Hall" has only an arbitrary relationship to the object it stands for
and the label doesn't have any qualities resembling those of the building
itself. On the other hand, some information on a map does have a similarity
to what is being represented. For example, one can tell that the Town Hall
is closer to the Police Station than it is to the bus station and this is true
both for the map and for the world it represents. When we study our
cognitive representations of space we also find different ways of dealing
with the complexity of real-world knowledge. However, the term "map" is
used as an analogy, and we are not necessarily implying that we store
pictures of the layout of the world in our memories.

ORIENTATION IN THE WORLD

The use of the term "cognitive map" became important in psychology through studies of other animals, not humans. The important part of representing space is being able to get from one place to another, not being able to talk about it. Early observations of the spatial behaviour of rats indicated that they learned where places were rather than chains of responses that would take them from one place to another. Tolman (1948) proposed that the animal learns something like a field map of its environment. It is this map "indicating routes and paths and environmental relationships," as Tolman put it, which determines what the animal will do.

There is also evidence from wild animals that the flexibility of using short-cuts and going back as well as forward along a route is not confined to humans. Peters (1973) suggests that wolves hunting in packs must have a map-like organisation of space as they can take short-cuts, split up and regroup at distant points, and return to base from any direction. It is possible that this use of space is dependent on the sense of smell, which is a more important source of positional information for other animals than it is for humans.

Some of the most dramatic examples of animal orientation are homing and migration in birds. Birds *could* navigate in ways that did not require the use of spatial knowledge. For example, they could fly from landmark to landmark, or they could head in a particular compass direction when they start off and they would arrive at the destination, provided they weren't blown off course. However, homing pigeons actually use different routes when returning home from the same release site so they do not simply use landmarks. In addition, they can navigate correctly, provided they can use the position of the sun and the earth's magnetic field. That is, they seem to have both an overall spatial map, and the ability to orient within it, like the ability to use a compass with a field map.

It has been suggested that people may also use compass directions within a spatial framework when they navigate over large areas. In a famous account of navigation across long stretches of open sea, Gladwin (1970) has described how people from the Puluwat atoll in the South Sea Islands use different kinds of information to ensure that they arrive at the right place. This involves learning a spatial map of the area which locates the islands and major landmarks, and which relates them to a superimposed sky map of the area. The islanders then have to remember the star patterns that link one island to another. The stars and the sun are used during navigation to maintain direction, but this is in combination with a system for calculating distance, so that directional information can be used correctly. Distance is calculated by thinking of the canoe as stationary with the world moving past it. For each voyage between islands there is a reference island, out of sight to one side of the course. The navigator calculates the movement of this unseen island in relation to the star map to arrive at a judgement of distance. It might seem curious to hold the boat stationary when it is clearly moving, but Hutchins and Hinton (1984) have shown that this is the easiest way to make the required calculations without any external aids. Obviously, the maps used by the islanders need not derive from their own individual experience. They are cultural products, learned from other members of society. The way in which the map is used also has to be learned. This does not mean that individuals do not also learn from their own experience, but rather that we have many ways of developing spatial knowledge of our surroundings.

It has sometimes been suggested that people, like pigeons, can orient within their environment using the earth's magnetism. Pigeons flying under overcast skies are unable to fly in the correct direction if magnets are attached to their heads so that their perception of the earth's magnetic field is distorted. Baker (1982) has suggested that people also make errors of orientation if they cannot see a route and wear electromagnets on their heads. Unfortunately, Baker's results have not been replicated (Fildes, O'Loughlin, Bradshaw, & Evans, 1984) and there is not a great deal of support for the view that humans do use geomagnetism to help them orient.

A Sense of Direction

Although there is little support for the view that people can orient using geomagnetism, it is very common for individuals to describe themselves as having or not having a good sense of direction. Early research on the "sense of direction" looked at how people developed the ability to point in the direction of the points of the compass (Smith, 1933), but the ordinary meaning of the term includes more general orientation skills such as the ability to find one's way back to the car park, say, or to point to the shopping centre when it is out of sight. Kozlowski and Bryant (1977) found that people who rated themselves as having a good sense of direction were better at pointing to places on their college campus and to nearby locations, but that they were no better at pointing to North than anyone else was. Kozlowski and Bryant thought that their subjects with a good sense of direction might have been more active at exploring the campus and surroundings than others were, so the difference might have been one of experience at using the environment rather than a superior skill. To investigate this they took subjects with good and poor senses of direction into the service tunnels under the university and walked them through a "maze." At the end of the route subjects had to indicate the direction of the starting point. Both groups were equally bad at this on the first trial but those with a good sense of direction improved over subsequent trials while the others did not.

When you walk along a route with someone else guiding you, you are not actively exploring but you may be actively trying to remember the turns of the route, or you could simply follow without making an effort, so even in Kozlowski and Bryant's experiment it is possible that ways of approaching the task contribute to success in direction finding. The "sense of direction" is probably a complex group of abilities and preferences, and those who have a good sense of direction may be more active in their environment, they may try to remember new details, explore to find new routes and attempt to construct a more detailed representation, as well as being more efficient at using the representation in directing their movement in the environment.

The ability to point to the position you started from when you have changed direction a few times is often studied within a laboratory environment which has little or no relationship to the knowledge the subject has of the larger spatial context (Howard & Templeton, 1966; Book & Garling, 1981), or in a maze which minimises the use of external information, such as that used by Kozlowski and Bryant (1977). In these environments the directions tested occur within the maze itself. In such a situation continuous backward counting while walking along a route affects the ability to point accurately to earlier positions (Book & Garling, 1981). Counting backwards is a fairly demanding cognitive task, and it seems to prevent subjects from making the spatial inferences that would allow them to maintain orientation. This detrimental effect occurs even when subjects move through a new route which is located within a well-known environment and are asked to point to landmarks in that environment which are out of sight (Smyth & Kennedy, 1982). However, Smyth and Kennedy found that some subjects could point accurately to external landmarks but could not give an accurate account of the route travelled, whereas others who could not point accurately were able to give an accurate account of the route. That is, the route knowledge and the orientation do not necessarily go together. Some people may update their position within an overall frame of reference (such as a town or campus) every time they make a turn but do not remember the turn itself, whereas others attempt to do both, or to use the accumulated memory of the turns taken to update position after a series of turns has occurred.

DEVELOPING A REPRESENTATION OF THE ENVIRONMENT

When you move to a new town or to a new university campus you have many sources of information available to you. Some will come from instructions, some from maps, and some from moving around in the environment. We will look at the way we use external maps in a later section, but first we consider the overall changes in knowledge of the environment that occur with experience.

At the beginning of the chapter we presented a list of instructions and a map and compared them as ways of understanding the environment. The most general change in our spatial knowledge with experience is probably from a sequential route-based type of representation to a more flexible one like the survey map. Siegel and White (1975) argued that routes are important units within an overall cognitive map and that development of the general structure or schema for a route starts with the knowledge of landmarks, with little about the spatial relations between them. This then changes to a sequential ordering of landmarks followed by knowledge of spatial relations between the landmarks and an overall grasp of the layout of the route. With several routes through an area we can eventually combine them into one map.

There has been some dispute over this suggested order of development, both over the movement from landmarks to routes and the movement from routes to maps. Appleyard (1976) found that people who had lived in a city for less than a year drew sketch maps which showed routes, whereas those who had been there longer emphasised boundaries of areas and landmarks, so had a more integrated approach. Devlin (1976) also found that routes were very important in the early stages, with the landmarks more important later. However, it is not always clear what the function of a landmark is in a map. Evans, Marrero, and Butler (1981) found that adults who had lived in a town for a year produced more interconnecting links and pathways between landmarks, but that the landmarks themselves were the same as those used by people who had been in the town for a short time. That is, the landmarks, which originally function as places on a route, become positioned in a space that can be crossed by many routes, and so become a major part of the organisational framework for the map of the town.

Studies of whether routes are the key developmental units within a representation have tended not to use a map-drawing approach. Some have used artificial presentation of a route in order to investigate the way in which subjects create a coherent unit. Jenkins, Wald, and Pittenger (1978) showed subjects slides that simulated a walk across a campus which was unfamiliar to them. Afterwards, the subjects were shown another set of slides and asked to judge whether they had occurred in the original sequence or not. It was found that subjects could recognise slides which they had seen and could reject slides which did not belong to the route at all. However, they tended to recognise slides which did in fact belong to the route, but which they had not actually been shown in the first series. Jenkins et al. suggest that subjects are developing a general representation of the route itself, which is not a memory of the individual slides. There are some similarities between this and work on comprehension of sentences, discussed in more detail in Chapter 9. Bransford and Franks (1971), for example, have found that subjects recognised sentences that fitted with the meaning of a series of sentences they had read previously, even though this meant they sometimes "recognised" sentences they hadn't actually seen.

When we travel in a new environment we do not use only one route, and it is likely that some routes will intersect so that one landmark could be on two routes. If routes are the basic unit of representation, then that landmark will exist separately in two schemas and the relationship between the two routes will not be developed until after the routes themselves are established. It is, of course, also possible that the developing schemas are based on a more complex unit that connects the routes from the beginning. Moar and Carleton (1982) investigated this using the presentation of slides of two different but intersecting routes through an unfamiliar area. Subjects later judged distances and directions between pairs of places within routes and between routes, and there were no differences in accuracy between these judgements, which suggests that the routes were not being maintained separately. However, with a few presentations of the routes subjects made more errors when they judged the distance and direction between two slides which were presented in the direction opposite to that of travel along the route. That is, they knew how far it was from A to B, but they didn't also know how far it was from B to A. The early presentations of a route seem to be chained together in one direction and do not yet have map-like reversibility. Even if routes are not basic separate elements of a map, they are different from maps in important respects.

To investigate the role of experience in the development of cognitive maps we can ask people to use their knowledge in a laboratory situation, by drawing maps, for example, or we can try to present new artificial routes to them in order to control their activity within the areas they are learning about. We can also take people out into the environment and ask them to do things that will expose their knowledge. Kirasic, Allen, and Siegel (1984) asked university students to make judgements about the direction and distance to well-known places from an experimental room. Students who were in their first year on campus were less accurate in their judgement when the room had no windows, but there was no difference between them and second- and third-year students when they had extra cues available to them through a window. This does not mean that there is no functional difference between the knowledge of a first-year student and a later one, but rather that the "realistic" situation provides enough cues to enable them to carry out this particular task. The experienced students had a more stable cognitive map, in that the relations between the distances and directions they gave were more accurate, and they can also be said to be more flexible in that they could use the information in a wider range of situations. "Realistic" tests of spatial knowledge may not allow such differences to appear.

Are Cognitive Maps Like Survey Maps?

When we draw maps of the world we can choose to emphasise some aspects of the surface and ignore others. For example, in the London Underground map, stations are often marked in straight lines and equidistant (see Fig. 11.2). However, if you take the High Barnet branch of the Northern Line from Camden Town you do not actually travel straight north, and Kentish Town and Tufnell Park are actually closer together than Archway and Highgate, although the distances are shown to be the same. Of course, the traveller needs to know how many stops there are to travel rather than the absolute distance, and the map would be very hard to follow if all the lines wriggled about as they actually do underground. This kind of map is called a "network map" and is very useful when specific information is needed. In a "survey map" on the other hand, the distance and direction between two points are accurate—a distance which is twice a particular distance on the map is also twice that distance on the ground, for example. Using our real maps as analogies again, we can ask whether the geometry of our mental representation is the same as that of the world itself, or more schematic, like a network map.

Many of the experiments we have mentioned indicate that people do become very good at judging the distance and direction of one place from another, but how good do we have to be before we can say that the knowledge is like a survey map? Byrne (1979) asked long-term residents of a town to estimate the length of several routes. He found that estimates tended to be longer for routes in town centres and for routes with changes of direction. As a result, he argued that the number of landmarks and turns contributed to the judgement of distance, so the stored information was similar in some ways to a network map in which the number of places, or nodes, on a route is more important than their overall spatial relations. Byrne also found that if people were asked to draw the angles at which roads joined they tended to err towards 90 degrees, which also suggests that mental maps are more like network maps than survey maps.

In the experiment discussed earlier, Moar and Carleton (1982) found that interconnecting routes were linked into a network from the beginning. With more experience the network is expanded and becomes more detailed. However, it is difficult to judge whether a map is *more* like a network map than a survey map because we cannot always tell whether there are some zones which are more like a network than others, because

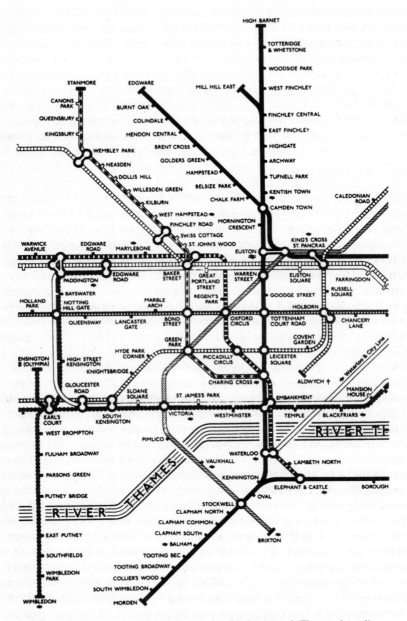

FIG. 11.2   Part of the map of the London Underground. The northern line is in solid black. This is a network map in which distances and directions are not an accurate reflection of the actual spatial arrangement of the underground lines.

they are less well known. Byrne's subjects tended to overestimate some distances and to move angles closer to right angles. This might mean that all cognitive maps are of this form, or that beyond a certain level increased survey knowledge is not useful for most purposes, or that such knowledge is not acquired without a great deal of experience of the area. Another way to look at this problem is to ask what happens when people make judgements of real space or judgements based on actual maps and see if these err in the same way as judgements of cognitive maps. Are the errors due to the stored spatial knowledge, or to the way that knowledge is used?

Using Real Maps and Cognitive Maps

When people make judgements about distances within their mental maps, they may be doing something quite similar to the way in which they judge actual distances. Baum and Jonides (1979) investigated this by asking students to estimate the distance between familiar locations on their university campus—from the library to the student union building, for example. However, the interesting part of the experiment is not the accuracy with which they made the judgements, but the time it took to make them. Baum and Jonides found that it took students longer to answer the question when the actual distance was longer; in fact, they found that the time taken to answer the questions was linearly related to the distance between places.

Why does it take longer to estimate the length of a longer route? Baum and Jonides suggested that subjects used a mental measuring tape and that it took longer to "unroll the tape" for longer distances, just as it would if the measurement were being carried out in the real world instead of in the head. But what is the relationship between real and memory representations that have more places on the route? There is evidence that when adults and children are asked to judge the distance between two objects, they tend to report that the distance is longer when a barrier is put between the objects (Kosslyn, Pick, & Fariello, 1974). That is, the way people judge a real distance can be affected by items within that distance. Thorndyke (1981) argued that using cognitive maps is similar to using actual ones and that errors in distance judgement and the effects of distance and number of places might be based on the *use* of the representation, rather than the representation itself. He asked subjects to learn fictitious maps of roads linking several towns and cities and then asked them to estimate distances, by road, between pairs of cities. Both the distance between the two targets and the number of intervening places were varied. The results showed that distance estimates increased both with the number of intervening places and the actual distance on the map. Thorndyke thought that these errors were not part of the memorised map but occurred at retrieval when distance judgements were made, so he asked another group of subjects to judge the distances between pairs of cities while looking at actual maps, without memorising them. He found that yet again both the actual distance and the number of places between two points affected the distance judgements, although these effects were smaller than those in the memory condition. Estimating distances as being longer because there are more places between the two points is not necessarily based on errors in the map or representation itself, but in the way it is used.

Of course, we do not want to say that knowledge learned from maps and knowledge learned from moving around in the world is the same thing and is always used in the same way. When you learn about an area from looking at a map you view the map from above and your use of your memory representation will probably have the same perspective. If you learn a new area by walking along routes you will see places as you walk towards them or past them, not from above. With increasing experience your knowledge becomes more map-like, but does this mean that you use it as if you saw it from above?

It is not easy to disentangle the contribution of navigation and map learning in the development of one's knowledge of a new area. Thorndyke and Hayes-Roth (1982) took a group of people who worked in a complex building who had never seen a map of it, and compared them with people who had no experience of walking about in the building but had seen a map of it. They asked subjects to indicate the direction of one place from another, the straight-line distance between them, and the distance of the route between them, and they also asked them to indicate the position of one place on a piece of paper which already had two other places marked on it. They found that map-learning subjects were better at estimating straight line-distances than route distances, whereas those who had walked around were better at route estimation. With greater experience of using the building, straight-line distance judgements became as accurate as those made by people who learned maps, and the route estimates improved even more. Walking around in an environment provides an accurate representation of the segments of routes, which can be added together to give an overall distance, but it also leads to a map-like representation of straight-line distances.

Subjects who had learned a map in this study were good at putting locations on paper in relation to other locations, but poorer at judging the direction of one place from another, whereas subjects who had experience of walking around judged direction more accurately than location. This suggests that making a judgement of the direction of one place from another requires map-learning subjects to take a different perspective than the one they had used previously. For subjects with experience of the building, judging direction is more like seeing along a straight line of sight through translucent buildings than looking down on a map from above.

With 12 month's experience in the building, subjects who had not seen a map were better than map-learning subjects at orientation between points and they were also just as good at putting places in their locations. That is, their knowledge now had all the good points of a map-like representation as if seen from above, but they also maintained their ability to take a perspective from inside the building looking straight through the walls at where they knew a target position to be. The "cognitive map" involves knowledge that is within, rather than above the world which is represented.

So, what have we learned about cognitive maps by comparing them with the use of real maps? The first thing is that we cannot always be sure that errors in judgements of distances in memory are the result of errors in what is stored, as both real map judgements and cognitive map judgements can show some of the same types of mistake. However, this does not mean that the cognitive map of an experienced person is just like the well learned memory of a real map. Just as the two have been learned in different ways, so they are used in different ways. Distance judgements of routes in both cases will involve the connecting of route segments but the map acquired from experience uses more accurate segments from within, rather than above the route.

VERY LARGE MAPS

Some of the information we have about geographical space has not been learned directly as we walk or drive around but is derived from instruction and from maps. In ordinary life it can be difficult to tell what comes from environmental experience and what comes from other sources, but some questions require the use of knowledge that could have only been acquired in one way. For example, if you are asked "Which is further west, Reno, Nevada or Los Angeles?" or "Which is further west, Bristol or Edinburgh?" you are unlikely to answer on the basis of your own experience of the land surface of the USA or the UK, but you *can* answer. If you are becoming suspicious of the kinds of questions asked in psychology books you would be right to be so in this case. Many people will answer that Los Angeles is further west than Reno, or that Bristol is further west than Edinburgh. Both answers are wrong. In Britain people seem to answer the question by using the information that Edinburgh is near the east coast of Scotland and that Bristol is near the west coast of England; they reckon that Scotland is due north of England, so Edinburgh is further east than Bristol. In the USA people tend to reason that California is further west than Nevada, Los Angeles is in California, while

Reno is in Nevada, so Los Angeles is further west than Reno (Stevens & Coupe, 1978).

When we try to remember the positions of places we use heuristics or strategies which make the task easier (Tversky, 1981). For example, up and down on a land area are taken to correspond to north and south, while right and left of the area may be aligned to be east and west. That is, in the absence of any other reference points that allow us to judge the alignment of a land mass such as Great Britain, we tend to square it up with the reference frame of the map itself by rotating its axis so that it matches the north–south line. This explains why Bristol is thought to be west of Edinburgh (Moar, 1979). A second general heuristic for solving geographical problems is to use a part–whole strategy within a hierarchical framework of countries, states, and cities, as Stevens and Coupe (1978) found with California and Nevada. It is not necessary to know the relationships between every place in Nevada and every place in California when the single piece of information that California is west of Nevada allows you to be right most of the time. A similar strategy is used within countries, so the Canadian and US border is straightened and all points in Canada are thought to be to the north of all points in the USA.

Tversky (1981) argues that the errors such as realignment and straightening of edges which occur when people make judgements about large areas, are not errors specific to mental maps. She considers that these errors are perceptual errors that occur in many situations when input is regularised and simplified to make it easier to deal with, and that maps may be stored in memory in an inaccurate form. However, the general heuristics are also used in inference when there are gaps in knowledge, and error can arise from such inferences. The spatial knowledge of countries, which is derived from instruction and from actual maps, can be organised hierarchically, can be regularised to provide a stable frame of reference, or can contain genuine spatial information. However, this knowledge may not be the same kind of knowledge structure as that developed for more local surroundings derived from experience of moving around.

MAPS AND PICTURES

We can set out to learn the spatial relationships between places printed on a piece of paper, we can listen to information about the relationship between places, and we can walk or drive around and develop spatial knowledge by navigation. Although we do not use the information derived from printed maps in the same way as we use that from navigation, it is easy to think that we must have something corresponding to a physical map in our minds. That is, we can imagine that using spatial knowledge means finding the current mental map, putting it on a mental "map table" and then "looking" at it. When you are asked "How many windows are there in the front of your house?" you can answer the question even though you may never have counted the windows. You may feel that you imagine the front of the house and then count the windows, so you feel you are using a mental picture which you "look at" in your mind.

This commonsense description of the mind's eye is one account of how we cognitively represent spatial knowledge. It can be attacked because it suggests that we have an extremely large number of stored mental pictures which are somehow unprocessed and so cannot be organised in memory. How then do we know how to find the relevant one? In addition, the evidence about error in mental pictures or maps suggests that when we forget information it is an organised feature or group of features that disappears, not a random fragment as would happen if you tore a piece off a paper map. So it is unlikely that we simply "photograph" information about the environment and then bring it out to make decisions about later. But if we don't have a large store of mental pictures, which include maps, how do we represent spatial knowledge?

The answers to this question are very complicated, and are usually discussed in the context of mental images, rather than mental maps. However, they are just as relevant here. There are two major alternatives. The first suggests that mental images are like percepts, not pictures. That is, they are interpreted knowledge, not undigested snapshots. So the information is coherent and organised in memory because it is the result of a great deal of processing. This view, put forward by Kosslyn and Pomerantz (1979), also suggests that images, including spatial representations of the world, are analogous to the things they represent. As we said at the beginning of this chapter, some aspects of survey maps maintain distance and direction between represented places which are like the distances and directions found in the world; that is, we can call them *analogue* representations. On the other hand, the word "church" retains nothing about the actual nature of a church, just as the word "left" only gives a spatial instruction if you speak English. Our general knowledge may be a mixture of analogue and non-analogue codes, but according to this view of images, spatial knowledge is analogue.

The opposing view, argued by Pylyshyn (1973, 1981), is that all knowledge is represented in the same way. The end product of all perceptual processing, whether reading the words on a map, or learning the spatial relations, is a non-specific, abstract representation. It is rather hard to understand what this is if we try to think of it being non-verbal *and* non-visual, but it can be thought of as the underlying meaning of a scene or map. Images or pictures stand in place of an aspect of the world. The abstract representations (called propositions) tell us what things are and

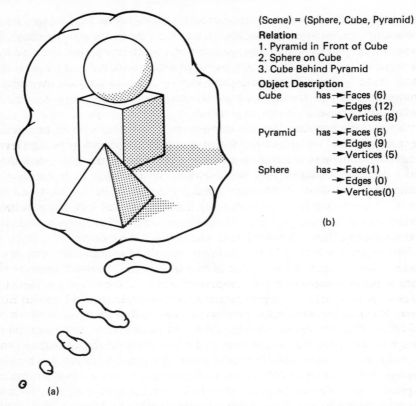

(Scene) = (Sphere, Cube, Pyramid)

Relation
1. Pyramid in Front of Cube
2. Sphere on Cube
3. Cube Behind Pyramid

Object Description

Cube   has→Faces (6)
            →Edges (12)
            →Vertices (8)

Pyramid   has →Faces (5)
            →Edges (9)
            →Vertices (5)

Sphere   has→Face(1)
            →Edges (0)
            →Vertices(0)

(b)

(a)

FIG. 11.3   (a): A simple pictorial representation. In some models this
surface image is constructed from an underlying abstract representation (e.g.
Kosslyn & Schwartz, 1981). (b) An abstract description (grossly
oversimplified). From Morris, P. E. & Hampson, P. J. (1983). *Imagery and
Consciousness*. London: Academic Press. Copyright 1983 by Academic
Press and reprinted with permission.

how they are related (see Fig. 11.3). Propositional models of how space is
represented suggest that what is important is not the experience of images
of stored spatial knowledge, but rather what happens when we use the
knowledge.

   Kosslyn (1980, 1981) has put forward a theory of imagery and spatial
knowledge which allows for both propositional and analogue information
to be stored in memory. He argues that the knowledge we have in
long-term memory is used to generate a surface representation which is
active while we carry out a task. It is this active representation that gives us
the experience of having things in "the mind's eye," but it is the underlying
long-term knowledge that is developed with experience. It is not clear

which of these two components is actually the cognitive map. Obviously, if we use the map analogy too strictly we can have difficulty with the idea that the permanently stored knowledge is different from the information we use to solve the problem, because a paper map has both roles. It is probably most useful to think of the long-term knowledge as the overall map of the environment, with the active representation containing the information necessary to solve a particular problem.

In Kosslyn's account, the long-term storage of spatial information could be propositional or analogue. When the information is to be retrieved searches could be made in both forms, but if the propositional system does not provide the answer then the analogue system will. So, for example, when you are asked "How many windows are there in the front of your house?" you could remember that the answer is "five" because you have counted them before, or you could create a spatial representation from the knowledge you have of your house and count the windows.

Kosslyn and Schwartz (1981) have investigated the active and long-term components of spatial knowledge in two ways. One of these considers the data or information which is in a representation and the other considers the structures that hold the representation. An example from Plato can help here. Plato, in the *Theaetetus* put forward a model of memory in which he said that memory was like a wax tablet and memories were written on it. The wax is the structure or medium and it can affect recall by being too soft to hold the message. The message itself (the marks on the wax) has a content (it could be about ducks, for example), and this content can be expressed in different formats. Words in English would be one format, words in Hebrew would be another, and pictures would be a third. What can we say about the medium in which spatial knowledge is held, and the nature of its content and format?

For the active representation of spatial information Kosslyn and Schwartz propose that the "visual" type space in which images are held while being used is limited in both size and shape. If you are asked to imagine an object and then mentally walk towards it, it seems to get larger and eventually overflows so that bits disappear. It is not possible to be very close and still have all the information available in the image space. In addition, the resolution, or the amount of detail in an image, is greatest at the centre and least at the edges (Finke & Kosslyn, 1980). If you are using environmental spatial information to walk through a route in your head, you will not be able to image all the surrounding areas in equal detail, even though you have such detail stored in your long-term memory for the area.

The content and format of the active spatial representation seem most relevant to issues involving spatial knowledge. If the representations are an analogue of the object in some way (like a drawing of a duck on a wax tablet) rather than a list of propositions (a list of a duck's visual characteristics), then answering questions about spatial knowledge should be affected by factors such as size and distance in the image. The distance from the duck's bill to its tail could be written in the list of characteristics, and so would have to be looked at only once whether the duck was big or little. On the other hand, if answering questions about the distance from bill to tail involves measuring that distance on an image, then the time to make the judgement will be longer if the duck is larger. This is just what we found when we looked at the time it took subjects to make judgements of distances in maps: The longer the distance, the longer it took to make the judgement. In addition, the increase in estimates of the distance between two places, which occurs when there are more places between them, happens on both real and mental maps and suggests that using a representation is more like looking at a real map than looking up a list of distances and adding them together.

Further evidence about the nature of the format of the active spatial representation comes from experiments on "mental rotation." In these studies subjects are asked to judge whether two two-dimensional pictures of three-dimensional objects are actually pictures of the same object which has been rotated to a new position, or whether one is different from the other (see Fig. 11.4). To do the task subjects have to change the orientation of one picture and then match the two (Metzler & Shepard, 1974). The time to make the judgement was longer if the object had to be turned further, which implies that the object was mentally rotated and that longer rotation took a longer time, just as it would if a real object were rotated. There have been criticisms of the conclusions of this study because the subjects could be rearranging only a small part of the image, not rotating all of it, or they could have arrived at the answer by a method that did not involve an image, but be mimicking what they know about the time it takes to turn real objects (Anderson, 1978).

If the format of spatial information in the active representation is analogue, what about its content? Is the image of a dog seen from a particular direction or is an image of a map seen from above? We have already considered the question of how we judge distance in a mental map and concluded that it may not be seen from above, but rather within, so that we can make direction judgements as if buildings were translucent. This contrasts with the results of an experiment by Keenan and Moore (1979) in which subjects were told to image two objects with one concealed within the other (e.g. a harp is inside the torch held up by the Statue of Liberty) or to image scenes in which both objects were visible (a harp is sitting on top of the torch of the Statue of Liberty). When one object was imagined inside the other, fewer details of the scenes were reported, suggesting that when the scenes were imaged the harp was not present when it was in the torch and so was not recalled later. The images

Rotate in picture plane for "SAME"

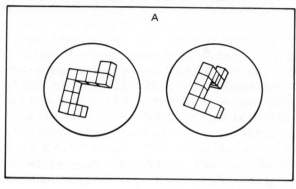

A

All rotations lead to "DIFFERENT"

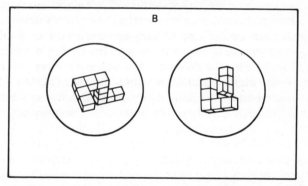

B

FIG. 11.4   Two-dimensional drawings of three-dimensional stimuli used in a mental rotation task. Subjects have to decide whether the two drawings are of the same object or different objects. Based on Metzler & Shepard (1974).

did not seem to contain all the pieces, because some covered others, and were not translucent.

The "translucence" in environmental knowledge is relevant only when judgements are being made about the direction of one place from another. It does not mean that the mental image you have when you imagine yourself standing outside the Student Union building has see-through buildings in it, but that you know a great deal from other experiences about what is behind the buildings you can see from the Union building. It may be that the research on cognitive maps can broaden the research on mental images because it is not concerned with one image only, but with the integration of what is learned from many encounters with the environment and the use of long-term structures to answer immediate problems.

Some of the debate about the fundamental nature of the representation of spatial knowledge may have confused the distinction between long-term memory and the active representation used to answer spatial questions, but much of the research has involved the active representation. It is possible to devise systems that can perform all the rotating and scanning of images which we have discussed, without having an analogue representation or image, but to do this we have to assume that the mental activities mimic the physical ones for no very good reason. Explanations that include images are simpler and may be preferred for that reason. No one has tried to deny that we have spatial mental experiences that we call images, but some theorists argue that they have no function. We would suggest that given the considerable evidence that perceptual judgements and imagery judgements are similar and that errors in using mental maps are similar to perceptual errors, it is reasonable to conclude that the internal representation used to make the judgements is analogue in some respects.

Research on imagery has tended to deal with the active component rather than the content and structure of long-term spatial memory. Although we can say that cognitive maps are long-term semantic memory representations of the environment (Garling, Book, & Lindberg, 1984) we do not as yet know how that information is retained. There is much still to be found out about what we remember about our world and how we use it, and it will probably be a very long time before we are close to understanding the basic elements which make up our spatial knowledge.

SUMMARY

In this chapter we have dealt with the process involved in building up and using knowledge of the environment, and then related this knowledge to the use of spatial knowledge in general. Orientation and the sense of direction are the products of our knowledge in use, and individuals with a good sense of direction may be those who are more active in attempting to understand their environment. In developing such understanding we build up cognitive "maps" which are derived from information about routes and landmarks but which eventually have the properties of reversibility and transitivity and which allow us to use routes we have never used before. The errors people make when they use their map knowledge suggest that that knowledge is like a network map rather than a survey map. However, people make some of the same mistakes using real maps as they make using mental ones, so errors may result from their use, not from their form. This distinction is also found when we consider very large maps in which knowledge is hierarchical and regularised.

The distinction between the form in which knowledge is held in memory and the form in which it is used is also important for all spatial processing.

In general, there is evidence that spatial knowledge is used in a similar way to information that is available for perception. There are links between the material covered in this chapter and spatial working memory which we mentioned in Chapter 6, and the issue of abstract representations or schemas in memory is dealt with in Chapter 9.

A wider introduction to the study of cognitive maps can be found in H. L. Pick and L. P. Acredolo (Eds.) (1983), *Spatial Orientation; Theory, Research, and Application.* P. E. Morris and P. J. Hampson (1983), *Imagery and Consciousness*, provides a much deeper account of the theories and data concerned with mental imagery than we could possibly do here.

12 Diagnosing an Illness: Uncertainty and Risk in Making Decisions

I experience abdominal, stomach and chest pains and a slight headache. I reflect upon the rather heavy meal I ate earlier this evening, the intense conversation, and the second bottle of wine we ordered. I take an indigestion tablet, but decide against taking an aspirin. The next day I feel fine. So it was simply indigestion. But then again, I recall that I have had this experience on several occasions over the past few months. I think that it has been happening more frequently recently. I recall friends or acquaintances who have had duodenal ulcers, bouts of sickness, mild food poisoning, stomach cancer, and pains in the chest that preceded a heart attack. Perhaps I had better visit the doctor? Wait—I had a heavy meal, the tablet worked, and so I was suffering from simple indigestion. But then I don't know what the other things feel like. Visiting the doctor is a bit of a nuisance and it would be embarrassing if she found nothing wrong with me. I will eat more slowly in future. I will visit the doctor next time. But I could be dying or need an operation and the problem might get worse if I leave it. But it would be very embarrassing just to be told to eat more slowly, to sit straight, and to try to relax when I am eating. No, it must have been simple indigestion: The tablet worked and—but I wonder how often the tablet would relieve the symptoms of the more serious conditions.

My doctor has more information than I do about the relationship of symptoms to diseases, but she too has problems in decision making. She has some models of diseases and the way in which they express themselves. She knows a lot about how often this causes that, how often it causes something else, and some cautionary tales of mis-diagnosis from her own and others' experience. But even she does not know everything and further investigations—X-rays, blood tests, calling in a consultant—all cost time and money, and may bring in their own risks.

All decisions involve an interplay between information, costs, and risk. There are many personal decisions, such as purchasing a house, selecting a mate, backing a horse, and crossing a busy road. Organisations also make decisions. A manufacturer steps up production and employs more sales staff in expectation of higher demand; a nation makes a military gesture and risks war; and a government raises interest rates and levels of taxation hoping to contain inflation. The organisations have information about what happened in the past and about the current state of affairs. They also lack information about many things, so they have to devise ways of making judgements that take into account what they know and the anticipated costs and benefits. In this chapter we consider decision making in general, using the example of medical decision making to illustrate some of the points. However, we also use many other decision situations, some of them artificial and some involving real-life choices.

One way to start studying how we make decisions is to look at situations in which people know about the risks and benefits and then see if they come up with the appropriate decision. There are a lot of complex factors in decision making, and ignorance or forgetting play a part. We need to start somewhere and there are some common situations in which decisions are made within a comparatively restricted setting. Gambling is one such setting. Real gambling, however, like betting on horses, is complicated by the fact that the punters often have information which they believe allows them to beat the bookmaker. The earliest development of theories of decision making looked at the purest instances of gambling, using coin tosses and similar well-defined events, in order to get some understanding of how people evaluate risks, and the costs and benefits when the odds of winning or losing are objectively defined. First, we look at the ways in which people deal with known probabilities and random events. A number of phenomena are described which point to some properties of cognition in the face of uncertainty which are not yet well understood and remain controversial. We conclude by looking at some alternative possible bases for rational decision making. We cannot yet expect, however, to gain anything like a complete understanding of the issues in decision making, a topic which remains one of the greatest challenges in the study of higher cognitive processes.

SIMPLE GAMBLES

Expected Value

Consider a simple gamble in which a friend invites you to stake 10p on the toss of a coin to gain 10p if it comes down heads, but you lose your stake if it comes down tails. If we can assume that the coin is unbiased and that it is tossed in a fair manner then we can say that it is just as likely to come down heads as it is to come down tails. As the two outcomes—heads and tails—are equally likely, the probability of getting one of them (say, heads), is one in two, or a half. Let us symbolise this statement as

$P\{\text{Head}\} = .5$ and $P\{\text{Tail}\} = .5$. If you know how likely one outcome is, and what it is worth to you, and how likely the other outcome is and what it is worth, then you can calculate the overall benefit or value of the gamble. To do this you take all the possible outcomes (such as Head and Tail), and for each outcome you multiply its probability by its value and then add the totals together over all outcomes. For the simple gamble suggested above the expected value, $E\{V\}$, of the gamble is

$$E\{V\} = P\{\text{Head}\}\cdot(+10\text{p}) + P\{\text{Tail}\}\cdot(-10\text{p})$$
$$= \cdot5 \times 10\text{p} + \cdot5 \times (-10\text{p})$$
$$= 0\text{p}$$

The calculation shows the obvious result, that with half a chance of winning 10p and half a chance of losing 10p the expected outcome is zero gain or loss. In general, the expected value of a gamble is

$$E\{V\} = P_1V_1 + P_2V_2 + \cdots ,$$

where the probability (P) and monetary value (V) for each outcome $(1,2, \cdots)$ are multiplied and summed over the possible outcomes. If the expected value is positive then the gamble is favourable; if zero, then it is a fair gamble; if negative, then it is an unfavourable gamble.

Do you want to play the above gamble? If you can choose either to play or not to play, we can consider the benefits of both options. These are displayed in the following *payoff matrix*:

| | *Outcomes* | |
	Head $P = .5$	*Tail* $P = .5$
Gamble 1	10p	−10p
Gamble 2	0p	0p

Gamble 1 is the one already discussed. Gamble 2 represents choosing not to play at all. Its expected value is, of course, also zero. Both gambles have the same expected value, so if what people do when they make decisions is to calculate expected values then the two should be treated exactly the same. (It is a bit odd to think of not playing as a gamble but, of course, it is a decision like any other.) Are we indifferent between Gamble 1 and Gamble 2? People will engage in Gamble 1 for fun—as though the game has some hidden positive value—and some will prefer not to play at all, in effect to choose Gamble 2. We can now add a third gamble in which you stake 10p with a one-in-ten chance ($\cdot$1 probability) of winning 90p; or a fourth gamble in which you stake £1 with a one-in-hundred chance ($\cdot$01 probability) of winning £99. The calculation of expected values for these gambles is as follows:

Gamble 3: $E\{V\} = \cdot 1 \times 90p + \cdot 9 \times (-10p) = 0p$
Gamble 4: $E\{V\} = \cdot 01 \times £99 + \cdot 99 \times (-£1) = 0p$

In all four gambles, the expected value is zero, yet some of us will prefer one gamble to another or, again, not to gamble at all. Why do we not treat the outcomes in the same way?

Some would regard this kind of calculation as true only *in the long run*. But, of course, we can never play such gambles in the (infinite) long run, and even if we could this particular game would not be worth playing, except as some kind of time-filler. Nevertheless, many of the studies of gambles of this form have assumed that expected value applied to a single decision in real life. It has been claimed that the expected-value type of calculation, combined with the expected-value rule—*choose the action (gamble) with the highest expected value*—leads to the best decisions, and in many cases this has been taken as a definition of what it means to act rationally. The sections that follow point to ways in which people depart from the rule.

Subjective Probability

A number of studies have demonstrated that probabilities and monetary values do have a strong influence on our preferences and our behaviour in a variety of circumstances but not always wholly in accordance with the expected-value decision rule. There are several possible reasons for this. The probabilities that a person perceives to be relevant may differ from the "objective" probabilities. For example, if you lost a coin-tossing gamble 10 times in succession, what would you think was going on? We may have a sneaking suspicion that Nature or the experimenter is being malevolent towards us even when a fair coin appears to be tossed in a fair manner. At other times we may feel that *we* can influence random events; or we may falsely infer that there are non-random rules at work from our observation of runs of outcomes. Other beliefs may intrude: "It is not my day today", "I am in luck today," and "I am overdue for a win" are all well-known expressions of human response to uncertain events.

Davidson, Suppes, and Siegel (1957), for example, offered subjects pairs of gambles like the following:

	Outcome		
	Heads	*Tails*	
Gamble 1	−5	+10	+ = win
Gamble 2	+10	−5	− = loss

Formally, it does not matter which gamble is chosen, but they found that over a series of trials subjects behaved as though heads and tails were not equally likely outcomes. The experimenters had to resort to use of a die, three sides of which carried one nonsense syllable (e.g. ZOJ) and the remaining three sides of which carried another (e.g. ZEJ). Even with this arrangement, subjects showed, for a variety of payoff matrices, that they were influenced by recent runs of wins or losses and by observing runs of one or other of the nonsense syllables. Choices on identical gambles altered somewhat from one occasion to another according to a localised or recent experience. In the main study, Davidson et al. resorted to the use of three such dice thrown in turn and subjects had to make batches of choices among gambles without immediate feedback of results.

Subjective Expected Utility

We do not maintain a clear perspective when dealing with random events even in the apparently simple case of responding to the equal probabilities of heads and tails. Perhaps also our subjective evaluation of money does not correspond to the public scale of money. For example, it seems reasonable to suppose that the personal value of gaining £250,000 may not be so great when you already have £10,000,000 as when you only own £10,000, or even just £100. This personal scaling of the objective cash values in terms of the usefulness of money to a particular person leads to the notion of *subjective utility*, and in turn to a modified decision rule based on maximising subjective expected utility.

Several studies have demonstrated that the laboratory gambling behaviour of *some* subjects can be made to fit the "maximise expected utility" rule when monetary values are suitably scaled. For these subjects, the utility of various amounts of money gained or lost varies in an orderly way such that a simple mathematical function expresses their personal scale of the value of money. For example, we can imagine someone so rich that it would take repeated doubling of his baseline wealth to achieve equal increments in his happiness. In general, however, it has been apparent since the early studies by Edwards (1956) that subjects do not typically follow the "maximise expected utility" rule either in choosing among notional gambles or in real gambling, even when the rule is explained to them (e.g. Lichtenstein, Slovic, & Zinc, 1969).

Tversky (1967) found fundamental departures from the expected utility model. The utility of a gamble varied with the level of risk involved, which implies an interaction of subjective probability and utility not permitted by the model. For example, some people might prefer to risk a small stake on a very small chance of winning a great deal of money and others might prefer to put a higher stake on a near certainty to win a moderate amount. These preferences can show some disregard for maximising expected utility. Alternatively, Tversky could explain the departures from theory by allowing that the activity of gambling itself had utility. That is, gambling was fun, or fulfilled a need which was not wholly expressed by the expected utility of the gamble. Even in the restricted worlds of the laboratory gamble or the casino gamble where probabilities and possible gains and losses are known, decision making is more complicated than subjective utility theory would suggest. There is no doubt that probabilities and monetary values, subjectively scaled or not, markedly influence our choices among gambles, but it is extremely doubtful that we find it natural to acknowledge the consequences of the detailed calculations specified by the model.

Randomness

The laboratory studies of gambling depend very much on how subjects cope with the randomness of events. Do we have any mechanisms for responding to events wholly beyond our control? Do we recognise that they are beyond our control? We next look at two phenomena which cast doubt on our readiness to acknowledge that sequences of random events, like coin tosses, do not conform to simple rules, at least not the ones we think they do.

Faced with a random sequence of events we are prone to the *gambler's fallacy*, the belief that a continuing run of heads on a coin, or of red on a roulette wheel, is increasingly likely to be followed by a tail or black. Imagine that you have 10 balls in a container each marked with a different digit from 0 to 9. Continue in your imagination, draw a ball and record the digit on it, write down the digit, replace the ball, draw again, until you have written down 20 digits. Now try an equivalent task in reality. Write the 10 digits on separate pieces of paper, fold the pieces of paper, put them in a container, shake it, and take out one piece of paper. Write down the number, return the folded paper to the container, and repeat until you have drawn 20 numbers. If you compare the two series—the imagined random sequence and the real random sequence—you may find that there are runs of the same number in the 20 digits which you drew from the container but few runs in the series from the imaginary experiment. You may also find that the set of 20 numbers actually drawn from the container does not include every digit, but that your imagined "random" set does.

Here are some unselected random sequences of 20 digits for you to examine along with some comments:

54196294948258024566	No 7's or 3's
55420851849493703680	49 recurs in the middle
12232219853307394049	1223221; no 6's
96284949371470246799	Five 9's; no 5's
09986420751840516059	86420; no 3's

Randomness certainly produces some funny looking outcomes. Yet these six sequences were found by sticking a pin in a table of random numbers.

The gambler's fallacy resides in the belief that even a short random sequence of equally likely events should be balanced, showing similar numbers of each event and not too many repetitions of the same event in sequence. Thus, our intuition dictates, a long run of reds on the roulette wheel must surely make black more likely at the next spin.

Probability matching is another response that we sometimes make to random events. Consider the following experiment: A bag contains 80 per cent red balls and 20 per cent green balls. A ball is drawn at random and you are to guess what colour it is. If you guess correctly you are rewarded. The ball is replaced in the bag, which is shaken, a ball is drawn and you are to make another guess. How do you think you would behave? (A better representation of the experiment would be to try it on a friend.) Which of the following patterns of guessing would you use?

1. RRRRGRRRRGRRRRGRRRRG ···
2. RGRGRGRGRGRGRGRGRGRG ···
3. RRRGRRRRRGRGRRRRRGRR ···
4. RRRRRRRRRRRRRRRRRRRR ···
5. RGRRRRRRGRRGRRRRRRRR ···

The long-run response to this task—to the real task and not to the intellectual exercise presented here—is to use a sequence rather like 3 or 5, or even 1, in which the relative frequency of red–green guesses matches the relative frequency of red and green events.

In these sequences, the guess "red" will match a red event about 80 per cent of the time that red occurs, but red only occurs 80 per cent of the time.

"Green" will match a green event 20 per cent of the time that green occurs, but green only occurs 20 per cent of the time. So the overall result is

$$P\{\text{Reward}\} = \cdot 8 \times \cdot 8 + \cdot 2 \times \cdot 2 = \cdot 68,$$

or only 68 per cent of rewarded guesses; whereas sequence 4, which is typically not selected, produces

$$P\{\text{Reward}\} = 1 \cdot 0 \times \cdot 8 + 0 \times \cdot 2 = \cdot 80,$$

or 80 per cent of trials rewarded. That is, if you go for red every single time you get 80 per cent reward, which is more than you achieve—unless you are extremely lucky—if you guess a sequence using a mix of reds and greens. In this kind of experiment we do reliably come to register the relative frequency of events in the environment after a period of training, but we do not readily come to maximise rewards.

Consider now how these factors might be represented in medical decision making. The records of a specialist clinic show that 80 per cent of the patients are diagnosed as requiring a serious operation and 20 per cent as requiring only mild medication or no treatment at all. On one particular day, the consultant finds that he has referred not one of the first half-dozen patients for the major operation. Is the next patient more likely to require it? Are the odds increasing against allocating a patient to the milder treatment? The experienced specialist may not be particularly aware of these localised or recent data, his database of experience being strong enough to resist the presumption that a particular morning's work should reflect the long-run probability. It is not only this probability that needs to be acknowledged but also the experience of *variability* in the proportion of referrals from one clinic session to another. The experienced clinician will have known days when no referrals arise and other days when all patients are referred. Nor can the consultant dodge the issue by referring everybody for the fullest investigation. That would cost a lot of money and unnecessary risk to those patients who do not need such drastic treatment.

Recency, we may speculate, is more likely to influence the less experienced decision-maker, or a novice gambler, desperately swinging to optimism and pessimism at the roulette wheel. Experience may sometimes give us ways in which we can overcome some local perturbations, but the laboratory "gambler" is unlikely to have a sufficient database. Another factor may be that people, and other organisms too, are natural seekers for patterns in their experience. As Simon (1979) wrote: "The urge to find order in the environment appears to be rather a deep-seated human drive [p. 260]." Probability matching may be something we do only when we refuse to regard events as beyond our control and understanding, when we are striving to find the rules as though we are tackling some concept-identification experiment. In decision-making tasks other than the simplest forms of gambling, perhaps we can call upon a strong long-term database of relevant experiences to steady our hands in face of uncertainty or a run of bad luck? We next look at studies of the use of knowledge in face of uncertainty.

KNOWLEDGE AND UNCERTAINTY

Subjective Probability and Representativeness

If we do not always accept the simple probabilities presented in coin-tossing, how do people make judgements about the relative frequencies of events in the real world? Consider the following questions taken from the work of Kahneman and Tversky (1982a):

Q1. All families of six children in a city were surveyed. In 72 families the *exact order* of births of boys and girls was GBGBBG.

What is your estimate of the number of families surveyed in which the *exact order* of births was BGBBBB?

Q2. Tossing a coin six times, which of the following sequences is the more likely to occur:
(a) HHHTTT; (b) HTHTHT; or (c) HTTHTH?

Many respondents to Question 1 choose a small number, certainly much smaller than 72. The exact order BGBBBB may seem to be less likely than GBGBBG, yet both by theoretical argument and by observation of human populations, the two sequences of births are equally likely. Certainly three girls and three boys is a more likely *combination* than one girl and five boys, but among *orders* of births the two sequences are equally likely. A similar phenomenon is often observed in response to Question 2. Subjects typically regard the three sequences of coins as having different chances of occurring, sequences (a) and (b) being thought to be less likely than (c); yet the chances of observing such sequences are, in fact, equal.

These and other observations of judgements about sequences of occurrences have given rise to the notion that we employ a *representativeness heuristic* in making some kinds of judgements. The use of heuristics and algorithms in reasoning and problem solving is also discussed in Chapter 13. Use of appropriate algorithm in the present case requires us either to generate all the possible sequences or to recognise that some formulae of probability theory are called upon by the question. Many subjects, even some of those having training in statistics, find it hard to resist taking a "cognitive shortcut"—a heuristic—to answer such questions. They seem to snatch at a partial insight and make a response. The sequence HHHTTT seems somehow special compared with one like HTTHTH; but arguments from theory, or trials with coins, an experiment which the theory would claim to represent, show that the sequences are equally likely. Somehow the sequence HTTHTH is more typical or representative of coin-tossing outcomes, we feel, than HHHTTT, even though careful and formal examination of the question as set shows that we are wrong. In general, if we know that the population has half males and half females we tend to expect the sample of babies to represent it.

Showing that the sequence HTHTHT is just as likely as sequence HHHTTT requires a little more detail on the theory of probability. We will continue to refer to this theory later in the chapter so we will describe three principles of probability, and call them "rules." First, the probability of an event (E) happening lies between 0 (never happens) and 1 (always happens). So:

Rule 1: $0 \le P\{E\} \le 1$

Second, the probability of throwing *either* a five-spot (E_1) *or* a six-spot (E_2) with a single throw of a die is equal to the sum of the probabilities of throwing a 5 and of throwing a 6. Getting *either* a 5 *or* a 6 accounts for one-third of the possible equally likely outcomes when you throw a single die; that is, the probability of throwing a 5, which is 1/6, added to the probability of throwing a 6, which is also 1/6, gives 1/3. Clearly, using one die, only one value—either a 5 or a 6—can be achieved on one throw. The second rule, given below, requires the events to be independent in the sense of this example, or else some amendment must be made to the formula to allow for the conjunction of events (E_1 *and* E_2) as shown in the alternative form.

Rule 2: $P\{E_1 \; or \; E_2\} = P\{E_1\} + P\{E_2\}$
$$or$$
$$P\{E_1\} + P\{E_2\} - P\{E_1 \; and \; E_2\}$$

Use of the second form of the rule can be illustrated by the question: "What is the probability of getting a 5 or a 6 at least once when throwing two dice?" Event 1 is now 5 or 6 showing on die 1 and event 2 the same on die 2. One such event is enough. If we use the first form of the rule we get the *wrong* answer (1/3 + 1/3 = 2/3) because we are double-counting on those occasions when both dice show a 5 or a 6 at the same throw. Some of the chances offered by one die are redundant when the other die is already showing a 5 or a 6.

The calculation of the term $P\{E_1 \text{ and } E_2\}$ requires the third rule. This will allow us to calculate that the probability of throwing two heads in consecutive tosses of a coin is equal to the probability of throwing a head on the first toss (E_1) times the probability of throwing a head on the second toss (E_2). If you get a head on a coin the first time you toss it, that is one of two equally likely outcomes (probability = 1/2), if you get a head the next time that is also one of two outcomes. However, before you toss the coin the first time there are a total of 4 equally likely ways in which the outcomes of the two tosses could combine (HH, HT, TH, TT) so the chance of getting any particular pair is 1 in 4, which is the answer produced by $1/2 \times 1/2$.

Rule 3: $P\{E_1 \text{ and } E_2\} = P\{E_1\} \times P\{E_2\}$

or

$$P\{E_1\} \times P\{E_2 \mid E_1\}$$

Looking for the present only at the first form of this rule, note that it can be used repeatedly to obtain the value of expressions like $P\{E_1 \text{ and } E_2 \text{ and } E_3 \text{ and } \cdots\}$. So, if you toss a coin six times then the probability of your getting HHHTTT is equal to the probabilities for the individual outcomes multiplied together, i.e. $1/2 \times 1/2 \times 1/2 \times 1/2 \times 1/2 \times 1/2$, and this is exactly the same for HTHTHT. You should now be able to use the second form of Rule 2 along with the first form of Rule 3 to calculate the correct answer to the question: "What is the probability of getting a 5 or a 6 at least once when throwing two dice?" The calculation is: $1/3 + 1/3 - (1/3 \times 1/3)$, and the correct answer is 5/9.

The second version of Rule 3 refers to the case when the events are not independent; that is, when one event is at least partially dependent on the other event. The occurrence of event 1 may alter the probability of event 2, so $P\{E_2 \mid E_1\}$ should be read as "the probability of event 2 given that event 1 has already occurred." This is referred to as a *conditional* probability. We shall use this form extensively later in the chapter and so its illustration will be deferred.

Consider now another example from Kahneman and Tversky (1982a):

*Q*3. Linda is 31 years old, single, outspoken, and very bright. She majored in philosophy. As a student, she was deeply concerned with issues of discrimination and social justice, and also participated in anti-nuclear demonstrations.

Which of the following statements about Linda is more probable:

(A) Linda is a bank teller;
(B) Linda is a bank teller who is active in the feminist movement.

Some 86 per cent of statistically naive undergraduates chose B as more probable. Even among the more statistically sophisticated psychology graduate students, 50 per cent endorsed that answer. Further, when the above two statements were embedded in a list of eight comparable statements about Linda, over 80 per cent of both groups endorsed B.

Statement B is less probable by the following argument. Represent the statements as:

(A) Linda is X;
(B) Linda is *both X and Y*.

The chances of Linda being *both X and Y* cannot be greater than her chances of being simply, X. At best, characteristics X and Y can be perfectly associated, in which case *"and Y"* does not further limit the chances and both statements are equally probable. Suppose that the probability of X is $\cdot 2$ and that Y always occurs whenever X occurs; then $P\{Y \mid X\} = 1$, and $P\{X \text{ and } Y\} = \cdot 2 \times 1 = \cdot 2$, using the second form of Rule 3. In other cases $P\{X \text{ and } Y\}$ must be less than $P\{X\}$. For example, if the events X and Y are independent and $P\{X\} = \cdot 2$ and $P\{Y\} = \cdot 6$, then $P\{X \text{ and } Y\} = \cdot 2 \times \cdot 6 = \cdot 12$. A conditional probability cannot be greater than an associated simple probability.

Subjects were given the statements: "the probability of a conjunction of X and Y cannot exceed the probability of X or the probability of Y." Some 83 per cent of statistically naive college students accepted this statement, yet only 43 per cent accepted the following equivalent argument in relation to Linda:

> Statement A is more probable than B because the probability that Linda is *both* a bank teller and an active feminist must be smaller than the probability that she is a bank teller.

Many of these subjects are committing an error of application of a rule which they correctly endorsed when presented in an abstract form. They know how to arrive at the decision in the abstract but they do not use that method in the real case. It is possible that statement B is somehow more representative of Linda, more to be expected in view of the details given about her. Linda is more likely to become a bank teller and feminist than a bank teller having no particular characteristic (anti-feminist; uninterested). Subjects seem to ask themselves: "Is B *more like* Linda than A?" This is not what Question 3 asks but it seems to be what is evoked.

Subjective Probability and Availability

Representativeness is one heuristic that can be used to make judgements about how probable something is. However, it is not possible to use it to answer all probability questions. Consider another question:

> Q4. The frequency of appearance of letters in the English language was studied. A typical test was selected, and the relative frequency with which various letters of the alphabet appeared in first and third positions in words was recorded. Words of less than three letters were excluded from the count.
> Consider the letter R. Is R more likely to appear in
> — the first position?
> — the third position?

By now you may have become alerted to the fact that our answers to these selected questions are often wrong. Many subjects say that R is more likely to appear in the first position than in the third. In fact, the letter R appears in the third position more frequently than in the first position. For example, you might note that in the question itself, the letter R comes third in 10 words and first in only 2 words. In response to such questions we may find ourselves attempting to retrieve words which begin with the letter R and those which have R in third position. After a little effort we find it easier to retrieve the former than the latter. For reasons that probably derive from the way we store words, words beginning with R are more *available*. The extent to which we can use our store of knowledge and experience when we are faced with a problem is limited by the restrictions on our ability to recall. The features of the situation, the specific stimuli involved, and retrieval strategies we may employ will all affect the success of memory retrieval (see Chapter 10). Rather than search through every single item in memory we retrieve a small subset of items which are easily found and use those. That is, we use an *availability heuristic* in judging the relative frequency of events in our experience.

Judging the relative frequency of words beginning with various letters of the alphabet may seem somewhat distant from risk judgement in general. However, Slovic, Fischhoff, and Lichtenstein (1980) have shown how the availability heuristic may operate to influence our perceptions of everyday events. In their study of the judged frequency of causes of death, there was a general tendency for subjects to overestimate the frequency of the rarer causes such as botulism, floods, measles, and tornadoes, and to underestimate the frequency of the more common causes such as strokes, various cancers, and diabetes. Combs and Slovic (1979) studied the relation between these perceptions of risk and the relative frequency of reported deaths in newspapers. Not surprisingly, it was found that the newspapers frequently featured homicides, accidents, and some natural disasters and markedly under-represented strokes, various cancers, and diabetes. The interesting finding was that to a large extent people's judgements of risk corresponded to the frequency of deaths reported in the newspapers, even when allowance was made for the extent to which both people and newspapers reflect some knowledge of the objective risks.

Perhaps we are better able to make these judgements when we experience events for ourselves or when the events are our professional concern. Fischhoff, Slovic, and Lichtenstein (1978) asked three groups of college students to estimate the relative frequency of major deficiencies that might cause a car to fail to start. One group was provided with a diagram of a "fault tree" showing details of the major groups of causes of "car won't start" shown in brief as follows:

1. *Battery charge insufficient*, e.g. faulty ground connection: paint, corrosion, dirt, loose connections.
2. *Starting system defective*, e.g. switches defective: ignition switch, starter relay, neutral start switch, solenoid.
3. *Fuel system defective*, e.g. insufficient fuel: car out of gas, clogged fuel line, leak.
4. *Ignition system defective*, e.g. coil faulty: cap cracked, electrodes corroded, improper point gap.
5. *Other engine problems* e.g. poor compression: leaking head gasket, cracked cylinder head, valve burnt.
6. *Mischievous acts or vandalism*, e.g theft or breakage of vital part, siphoning of gas, disruption of wiring.
7. *All other problems*

All headings were fully elaborated with possibilities, except the last category. Subjects were asked to examine the diagram carefully and to estimate how often in 100 trips which are delayed due to a "starting failure" those delays are caused by each of the seven factors and to make sure that the responses summed to 100. Two other groups were given "pruned trees"—fault trees in which a selection of only three of the major groups of causes plus the residual "all other causes" category was presented. If subjects were sensitive to the missing causes then the increased use of the "all other causes" category should reflect the proportions that would otherwise have been assigned elsewhere. The responses of the three college student groups are compared in the upper part of Table 12.1.

Fischhoff et al. took the first group's result as typical of what happens when all causes are mentioned. They argued that if the subjects in the "Pruned 1" group had been sensitive to the omitted causes, they might have been expected to assign 47 per cent (proportions $\cdot 39 + \cdot 08$ in Table 12.1) of causes to the "Other" category. Similarly, the "Pruned 2" group might have been expected to assign 61 per cent ($\cdot 53 + \cdot 08$) of causes to "Other." In fact, although the use of "Other" increased between two and three times in response to the omitted causes, it should have increased between six and eight times. Professional automobile mechanics

TABLE 12.1
Attribution of Starting Failures for Pruned and Unpruned Trees by
College Students and Experts: Proportions of Failures Assigned
to Causes[a]

Group	n	Causes 1,3,5	Causes 2,4,6	Other
College students				
Full tree	93	0.53	0.39	0.08
Pruned 1	29	0.86	—	0.14
Pruned 2	26	—	0.78	0.23
Experts				
Full tree	13	0.56	0.38	0.06
Pruned 1	16	0.79	—	0.21

[a] Adapted and rounded from Fishchhoff, Slovic, and Lichtenstein (1978).

("experts" in Table 12.1) shown the restricted list of causes similarly overestimated the prevalence of those causes when compared with the judgements made by fellow experts who used the full list. For both college students and experts, what was out of sight—not immediately available—was, in effect, out of mind. By contrast, the immediate availability of events featured in the media can create exaggerated perceptions of risk. Football attendance drops after a fire in a football stadium and recent aircraft accidents make people more apprehensive about flying. Advertisers, politicians, and insurance companies no doubt benefit from this phenomenon.

Another sign of the bias towards available information is seen by adding together the results for the "Pruned 1" and "Pruned 2" groups in accordance with Rule 2 of probability theory. It would seem that the probability of causes 1–6 (·86 + ·78) is greater than 1, thus breaking Rule 1. This phenomenon is not rare in human judgements. Formal systems like probability theory employ a strong notion of consistency. In school geometry, for example, if two lines are defined to be parallel at the outset then we would rightly be surprised if later in some proof or derivation they were found not to be parallel. In real probability judgements, however, a subject can apparently tolerate inconsistency, or at least not perceive it immediately.

People do not seem to use the three rules of probability theory when they make judgements. Instead they use cognitive short-cuts that are based on the way memory works. If an event or sequence of events is regarded as typical or representative it is thought to be more probable, and if events are easily retrieved in memory they are thought to be more probable. So, if I am deciding whether to visit the doctor about my pain which may or may not be indigestion, my judgement will be affected by information which does not actually alter the probability that I have indigestion. If a colleague at work has recently been diagnosed as suffering from a duodenal ulcer, and I have just heard that my neighbour's father has stomach cancer, then I will be more inclined to judge that I should visit the doctor. However, those two events, although available to me, do not change the probability that I have a serious illness.

Of course, I do not have much access to tables of statistics to tell me how probable it is that I have a serious illness. It is possible that I use a heuristic like availability because I do not have anything else. What happens if I am given the objective probabilities? Do I use them correctly once I have got them?

Base Rates and Updating Information

The availability and representativeness heuristics might well be employed for judgements when we are not aware of the objective frequencies of events in the world. When this information is available it has to be integrated with additional evidence from our current experiences. This integration, or updating, is not very easy to do.

Kahneman and Tversky (1973) showed subjects brief personality sketches of several individuals, claiming that they were drawn at random from a group of 100 professionals—a mix of engineers and lawyers. One group of subjects was told that the professionals were a 70 : 30 mix in favour of engineers. A second group was told that the 70 : 30 mix favoured the lawyers. These data provide the base rates, the prior information about the relative chances of coming across a lawyer or an engineer in the task at hand. A typical personality sketch was as follows:

> Dick is a 30-year-old man. He is married with no children. A man of high ability and high motivation, he promises to be quite successful in his field. He is well liked by his colleagues.

Subjects were invited to assess the probability that this description belonged to an engineer drawn from the group of 100 rather than to a lawyer drawn from the same group. Subjects in both groups produced essentially the same judgements, that the probability of Dick being an engineer was around ·5. The biographical and personal information does not help people to decided whether Dick is a lawyer or an engineer. However, the knowledge of the 70 : 30 mix in the group should have affected the judgements. That is, if the person could have come from either group then it is more probable that he came from the larger one. If the description of Dick had systematically biased subjects towards one or the other profession then the ·7 rate in one group and the ·3 rate in the other should both have been enhanced or both diminished. The subjects did not seem to use the prior probabilities or base rates in this situation. Yet it was observed that they were quite capable of using the prior or base rate probabilities when no additional information, such as the personality sketch, was supplied. Kahneman and Tversky (1973) concluded wryly: "When no specific information is given, prior probabilities are properly utilized; when worthless evidence is given, prior probabilities are ignored."

Some research suggests that the way in which we integrate what we know already with a new piece of information is more complicated than this. Phillips and Edwards (1956) showed that subjects who were asked to revise an initial judgement of probability given some new information, failed to revise the probability estimate sufficiently. That is, they kept closer to their own original estimate than was justified given the importance of the new information. So, when subjects were given prior information in Kahneman and Tversky's experiment they ignored it and when they were using their own estimates of prior probability they did not give full value to new information. Some of these differences may be due to the experimental situation. There may be no reason for subjects to pay any attention to the unexperienced and seemingly arbitrary information that there are 70 lawyers and 30 engineers in the group. Where base rates that have been experienced are challenged by new data presented in an experiment, subjects may be unlikely to make instant adjustments. Further, as Navon (1978) has pointed out, the new data we experience may not be wholly independent of prior knowledge and so would not deserve the degree of updating assumed for truly novel and uncorrelated data. The conservatism in adjusting the new data may result from the cautionary "drag" of the many connections that have been made among the old data. However, both the Kahneman and Tversky results and the Phillips and Edwards finding certainly indicate that integrating new information with old is not a simple matter.

Updating estimates of risk can be important in medicine. When physicians are considering a diagnosis, the initial data may give rise to an estimate of how likely it is that the client has a particular disease. The results of further tests may require that modifications be made to that initial estimate. A case in point is provided by Eddy (1982), who reviewed the problems of uncertain reasoning among physicians in the diagnosis of breast cancer. Women present themselves to a physician complaining of a "lump," an unusual mass of tissue. Following a general examination, the physician may have recourse to a mammogram, an X-ray examination in which cancer cells may be seen to absorb the X-rays differently from non-malignant cells. The result of this test is not always correct. The physician may further call for a biopsy, surgical removal of some or all of the tissue in the mass for microscopic examination. The latter procedure can be regarded as providing a definite answer but, of course, it can also be disfiguring to various degrees depending on the amount of tissue removed. Even a minor scar, along with the cost to personal or public resources and the nuisance and danger of an operation can be serious in a case where life turns out not to be at risk. Further, if the mammogram has any validity as a diagnostic stage then in some cases surgery should be avoidable even though there is some residual risk of incorrect diagnosis. Or, if surgery is to be employed in all cases then the mammogram is redundant.

Eddy asked physicians to consider the following data. From general examination of a particular case a physician estimates that the lump is highly unlikely—say, probability of ·01 or 1 per cent—to be cancerous, but orders a mammogram. The radiologist's report says "Positive: cancer suspected." What now should the estimate be of the chances of cancer? A simple answer would be to say that the estimate should be very high, to reflect what the radiologist reported. However, we have to ask how the original estimate (probability of ·01) has changed, given that the mammograph result is not always correct. The probabilities of positive (+) and negative (−) mammography reports when cancer is present (ca) and when cancer is not present (nc) are shown in Table 12.2. In particular, the data include values for the conditional probabilities $P\{+ \mid ca\}$ and $P\{+ \mid nc\}$. But these show the retrospective accuracy of a positive outcome to the test when the true nature of the cells in the tissue is known. What we need to find is the probabilities of cancer given the mammography reports, that is, the predictive accuracy of the test. We especially require a value for $P\{ca \mid +\}$.

The relation between the two kinds of data is given by Bayes' theorem, which calculates the probability that an hypothesis is true (this patient has cancer) given that a piece of evidence exists (the mammogram is positive). It can be derived most directly from Rule 3 (second form) of probability theory presented earlier. The theorem works for any hypothesis and any piece of evidence, but for this particular situation we can write the equation as

$$P\{ca \mid +\} = \frac{P\{+ \mid ca\} \cdot P\{ca\}}{P\{+ \mid ca\} \cdot P\{ca\} + P\{+ \mid nc\} \cdot P\{nc\}}.$$

To review: We are trying to find the revised probability for the hypothesis that the patient has cancer given that: (1) the physician originally thought that she probably did not have cancer $(P\{ca\}) = ·01)$; (2) the test gets it right 80 per cent of the time when there is a cancer $(P\{+ \mid ca\} = ·8)$; and (3) that the test gets it wrong 10 per cent of the time when there is no cancer $(P\{+ \mid nc\} = ·1)$. The remaining expression stands for the prior probability of not having cancer $(P\{nc\})$ which is equal to

TABLE 12.2
Probabilities of Positive and Negative Mammography
Reports given that Cancer is or is not Present[a]

X-ray Result	Cancer (ca)	No cancer (nc)
Positive (+)	0.8	0.1
Negative (−)	0.2	0.9
Totals	1.0	1.0

[a] Adapted (rounded) from Eddy (1982, p. 253); base data taken from Snyder (1966).

$1 - P\{ca\}$ or $\cdot 99$. So we fill in the values as follows:

$$P\{ca \mid +\} = \frac{(.8)(.01)}{(.8)(.01) + (.1)(.99)} = .075$$

The revised estimate is that there is now a 7 to 8 per cent chance of cancer. Many of the physicians studied by Eddy put the figure nearer to $\cdot 8$ or 80 per cent. They probably confused the accuracy of the test when cancer is known to be present with the predictive accuracy of the test. Because it is not very likely that the patient has cancer in the first place, the test result increases the probability by rather less than our intuitions would suggest in spite of the accuracy of the test. If this seems unlikely, check for yourself what the result would be if the test was 100 per cent accurate when cancer is known to be present $(P\{+ \mid ca\} = 1\cdot0)$. Remember that the test gives positive signs 10 per cent of the time that cancer is not present and that $P\{nc\} = \cdot 99$. Table 12.3 gives the full set of calculations using Bayes' theorem on the assumption that $P\{ca\} = \cdot 01$.

Eddy's review of decision making in medicine points to frequent misinterpretation of probability data in the medical literature. If we do not

TABLE 12.3
The Probabilities of Cancer or No Cancer Present Given That
the X-ray Report is Positive or Negative and That $P\{ca\} = 0.01$[a]

Clinical Outcome	X-ray Positive (+)	X-ray Negative (−)
Cancer (ca)	0.075	0.002
No cancer (nc)	0.925	0.998
Total	1.000	1.000

[a] Computed from Table 12.2 using Bayes' theorem.

find it easy to make well-judged use of probabilities when these are supplied, it is not surprising that the expected-value decision rule, which depends so strongly on the probability values employed, is not good at describing our decision-making behaviour even in simple gambles. However, several problems are left out of this analysis. First, our discussion of Eddy's review has left out any mention of costs. Although we know that physicians may sometimes estimate probabilities wrongly, they may nevertheless make sensible decisions in practice using some kind of compound of probability and costs. We should also recognise the base-rate data supplied in an experiment—such as $P\{ca\} = \cdot 01$—may not be as effective as data acquired by personal experience. So long as the physicians are not found to be referring every patient regardless of the outcome of preliminary tests, there is the possibility their decisions have some rational basis. To date there is no clear basis for adopting this more optimistic view; but we ought perhaps to suspend judgement until more work has been done on alternative bases for decisions.

OTHER BASES FOR DECISIONS

So far we have pointed to possible defects in our appreciation of probabilities and our failure to use probability theory. In addition, the expected-value decision rule, which has so dominated the research for some time now, is not easy to apply to situations beyond the simple gambles. We do not usually have enough data on probabilities and the utilities of outcomes for many real decisions; and when data are supplied we do not often seem to use the rule. We may also question the decision rule itself.

We should first note that millions of people gamble on horses, lotteries, football pools, the turn of a wheel at a casino, and the spinning of three wheels of symbols in the one-arm bandit. The expected value for the gambler of all these activities is surely negative since the organisers of these activities rarely go out of business, they maintain staff to run the place and take our money, they presumably pay some taxes, and make a profit. Similarly, insurance, viewed as a gamble, has negative expected value for those who buy it since the insurance companies plan to make a profit out of their business. Overall, people are bound to pay out more than they get back. Yet somehow it is regarded as rational to insure our houses, cars, and valuables, among other things. Some of the mismatches between the rule—maximising expected value—and what some people choose to do may be resolved by correcting their probabilities and utilities, in other cases by placing a value on the gambling activity itself or in avoiding risk, and in yet other activities may deserve quite a different conception of decision making. This is not to say that we shall be able to "rationalise" all those behaviours that appear to disobey the expected utility rule, but alternative conceptions and alternative procedures might come rather closer to explaining how real choices and risky decisions are made.

We get some clues even from the simpler studies of gambling. In his "portfolio theory" of risk, Coombs (1975) offered a new conception of the old problems of choosing among gambles. Although we do give some recognition to the probabilities, the utilities, and the expected values of gambles, these things only partially determine our choices. The perceived "riskiness" of gambles varies and we operate a preferred level of risk. Some of us might prefer a very small chance of winning a very high gain, say £250,000 in a repeated gamble at £1 a time; others might prefer to chance £100 on a 2-to-1 on favourite now and again. Strong preferences can exist among gambles with equal expected value. Higher or lower levels of expected value can be traded for less or more risk around an individual's most preferred or ideal kind of gamble. The notion of "risk" remains undefined, but Coombs's data show that subjects do indeed exhibit strong personal preferences for what amount to "styles" of gamble.

Kahneman and Tversky's (1979) "prospect theory" says that we are averse to taking risks when there is a sufficiently positive and certain outcome to be had; and where losses are necessarily to be suffered, some of us would prefer to limit our loss to a known and certain value rather than to risk higher loss even though the average or expected loss is lower. The principle of settling for a safe but less than maximum gain, or settling for a tolerable loss when greater loss is risked, comes close to illustrating a heuristic of wider applicability known as "satisficing." For example, one of the possible treatments for a disease might carry high risks of bad side-effects but the possibility of complete recovery; the other treatment might promise to alleviate the disease but not to resolve it completely. The patient might settle for a "sufficient" or "satisfactory" outcome rather than seek the more risk-laden best outcome. The old saying that "a bird in the hand is worth two in the bush" illustrates the same point.

In general, however, most of life's decisions have multiple attributes. When we are choosing a job, a car, or a house, the probabilities and costs are not well identified. We have to work at such choices, seeking out information, exploring many dimensions of the options open to us, and perhaps reflecting upon the alternative futures likely to be experienced. Hence, a recent trend in decision research has been to regard decision making as more akin to the process of solving a difficult problem, the moment at which a formula or rule may be applied being only a small part of the process. As we gather information and views about the alternatives, the structure of our knowledge may well shift dramatically, as when we achieve a new understanding in learning something. Also we cannot usually delay these decisions for too long. Job opportunities come and go, an old car is no longer safe, and desirable houses may be sold to others. A sufficient solution, knowing what we know and being unable to wait for more information, is what we must typically accept.

Similarly, the process of medical diagnosis, at least in the more difficult cases, is badly described if it is characterised as a simple matter of gathering evidence and making a decision. Rather, preliminary symptoms lead to some preliminary hypotheses. More evidence is sought in line with those hypotheses, further guesses are made, old evidence may be re-evaluated, and so on. This rather untidy process continues until a decision can be made with sufficient certainty, having regard to the, by then, elaborated structure of knowledge, risks, and costs. Some evidence of possible relevance may not be gathered, and some hypotheses may not be entertained. Studies reported by Elstein, Shulman, and Sprafka (1978) took a "process-tracing" approach to medical diagnosis. They found, for example, that physicians considered a limited number of hypotheses at any moment, they differed somewhat in how much information they extracted from the available cues, and they employed a number of heuristics to guide their search for a diagnosis. These are features of the broader arena of human problem solving which are discussed in the next chapter.

SUMMARY

Decision making has long been studied as a choice among gambles for which the probabilities of the various outcomes and the associated gains and losses are known. Rules based on expected utility theory that have been applied to such data are not wholly successful in modelling human decision-making behaviour, whether in laboratory studies of simple gambles or in more complex real decisions. In general, the research leaves one pessimistic about the descriptive status of expected utility theory in either its objective or subjective guises; but the extensive range of phenomena exposed in these studies raises a number of issues. For one, the probabilities we employ do not always correspond to the objective or publicly acknowledged values. Perhaps we do not reliably register the relative frequencies of events in the environment. Evidence is accumulating that we not only deviate from what probability theory and expected utility theory would specify as ideal behaviour but that we employ some short-cut heuristic principles and we exhibit some systematic biases. These heuristics and biases are sometimes interpretable as due to the way in which our memories work. Immediately available information naturally influences our thinking more readily than hard-to-retrieve information. We have strong notions from experience about the representativeness of sample events from variable domains. We do not seem to integrate base information with new information efficiently.

Against these doubts about the rationality of human decision making, there are doubts about the assumptions in some of this research. We do not commonly face the purest random devices, like coin tosses, in nature. Few of our decisions can be informed by clear probabilities and costs for simple options. We must treat with caution the view that the phenomena of availability and representativeness bias our judgements in some decision-making tasks; these heuristics must reflect the way our memories are organised so as to be sufficiently useful for many of the tasks we face. Decision making is also often concerned with complex sequences of information gathering and hypothesis testing—as in medical diagnosis—and to characterise only the moment of final decision by a rule may be to oversimplify matters and to overlook the problem-solving nature of reaching a decision. We take up the question of problem solving in Chapter 13.

Further reading, especially about the attempts to find the proper place of probabilities and utilities in human decision making, can be found in G. Wright (1984), *Behavioural Decision Theory: An Introduction*. A broad collection of papers, including several cited in this chapter, is provided by D. Kahneman, P. Slovic, and A. Tversky (Eds.) (1982), *Judgement Under Uncertainty: Heuristics and Biases*.

13 Investigating a Murder: Making Inferences and Solving Problems

Sherlock Holmes has examined the scene with great care. He turns to the police detectives, who admit that they have found no clues, and says:

> There has been murder done, and the murderer was a man. He was more than six feet high, was in the prime of life, had small feet for his height, wore coarse, square-toed boots and smoked a Trichinopoly cigar. He came here with his victim in a four-wheeled cab, which was drawn by a horse with three old shoes and one new one on his off fore-leg. In all probability the murderer had a florid face, and the fingernails of his right hand were remarkably long. These are only a few indications, but they may assist you. [*A Study in Scarlet*].

How did Holmes reach these conclusions? Some you can probably guess. Marks observed on the ground—perhaps in the soft surface of a driveway or depressions in a thick carpet—gave the basis for some inferences. Cigar ash or the smell in the room may have led to another. But the man's height, his "florid face," the state of his fingernails, and other details seem rather distant from what might reasonably have been observed. Unfairly perhaps, the reader of Sherlock Holmes stories does not know all the clues that are available to the great man. In many other detective stories, the readers have shared the clues with the fictional detective, but only later are they told how the crucial inferences are drawn.

Inferential processes were a focal topic in Chapter 9. Comprehension of stories is seen not merely to be a matter of looking up the meanings of words in some mental lexicon, but of constructing scenarios within which the sentences have some emergent and connected meaning, sometimes creating a tentative schema, referencing some familiar scripts and plans, inferring casuality, making attributions, and so on.

The real or fictional detective is said to work by careful observation and deduction. "Elementary, my dear Watson," said Holmes to his companion as he began to recount the links between observations and successful inferences, but most of us are just as impressed as Watson by Holmes's constructions and reconstructions of the evidence.

This chapter is about the role of inferences and their management on those occasions when we have to think a little harder, when we attempt to reason and when we attempt to solve problems. We start by considering what it means to make logical inferences. In what sense might Holmes, or a real detective, be regarded as an expert in deduction? What is the role of logic in human reasoning? Then we turn to consider what other skills might be required to solve problems that have greater variety than those found in the study of logical reasoning. To what extent are there general skills in thinking and reasoning, and to what extent do knowledge and experience play a part? To anticipate, our thinking skills depend very much on all the processes that we have described in earlier chapters.

LOGICAL INFERENCES

Categorical Reasoning

We make inferences when we move from what we already know to be the case, to something that follows from it. Deductive inferences are particular kinds of inference studied by logicians and their rules have sometimes been claimed to define "laws of thought." In the light of these rules many studies have been conducted in which people are given statements and asked to say whether something follows. For example, in the following argument, does the third statement follow from the first two statements when these are assumed to be true?

Some detectives are fictional characters	(Premise 1)
Some fictional characters are famous	(Premise 2)
Therefore, some detectives are famous	(Conclusion)

This is an example of the *categorical syllogism* first studied in depth by the Greek philosopher Aristotle some 2300 years ago. The first two statements are referred to as the *premises*, and the logician's concern is to determine whether or not the conclusion necessarily follows from the premises, whether it may be deduced from the premises. From this perspective the above argument is not valid although many of us would regard it to be so. Even though we might believe all three statements to be true and well-related to each other, it can be shown that the third statement does not necessarily follow from the premises. Indeed, no conclusion is logically necessary. It is logically possible that "No detectives are famous" or that "All detectives are famous." Remember that we are not discussing the truth of the supposed conclusion given all the things we know, but simply how it relates to the premises.

Logicians extract the *forms* of the valid arguments. In classical logic, four kinds of statement may take the part of a premise or a conclusion. Using symbols like *A*, *B*, and *C* to represent sets of things these are: *All As are Bs*; *Some As are Bs*; *No As are Bs*; and, *Some As are not Bs*. These may be combined, with *A* and *B* in one premise, *B* and *C* in another, and *A* and *C* in the third line, to produce the forms of all possible syllogisms, only some of which are valid.

The syllogism has been used by psychologists for some decades in the study of human reasoning. By and large, people are not very good at detecting logically valid and invalid arguments among the forms. You may already have found yourself struggling, with the examples just given, to distinguish the logicians' notion of the valid form of an argument from such things as the real-world truth of the statements, or your beliefs about them, and the general plausibility of an argument. There are other features which create difficulties for us and lead to wrong answers and long solution times. Some errors have been ascribed to the "atmosphere effect" first proposed by Woodworth and Sells (1935). This refers to the tendency of subjects to assert a particular "some" conclusion rather than a universal "all" conclusion when at least one premise is particular; and to include a negative "no" or "not" in the conclusion when at least one premise contains a negative. Terms like "some" and "no" are said to set the atmosphere for a style of conclusion. These tendencies seem to lead subjects to state some logically unjustified conclusions. Another possible source of error is the "illicit conversion" of premises. The premise "All *A*s are *B*s" could mean, but does not necessarily mean, that "All *B*s are *A*s." The premise "Some *A*s are *B*s" is even more rife with possible meanings for overlapping set memberships when one recognises that "some" for a classical logician means "at least one and possibly all."

More recently, Johnson-Laird (1983) has studied the "figural effect." To understand this, consider what conclusions might follow from the following pairs of premises:

(1) Some *A*s are *B*s   (2) All *B*s are *A*s
     All *B*s are *C*s   No *C*s are *B*s

The first turns out to be very easy and the second very difficult. Ignoring the all's, some's, and none's—those aspects which may generate atmosphere—the *figure* of a syllogism refers to the spatial arrangement of *A*, *B*, and *C* in the premises. In (1) most subjects readily favour conclusions of the form *A*–*C*, correctly eliminating the middle term, *B*, and making a connection between *A* and *C*. The valid conclusion in this case is "Some *A*s are *C*s." For the premises in (2) many subjects favour conclusions of the form *C*–*A*, drawing the invalid conclusion "Some *C*s are not *A*s" rather than the valid conclusion "Some *A*s are not *C*s." The middle term, *B*, is not easy to "eliminate" in this figure. The subjects' difficulties might be eased if they were to attempt whatever legitimate conversions of the premises are possible or to reverse the order of the premises to see whether that makes it any easier; but since Johnson-Laird and Bara (1982) required their subjects to perform orally, without use of pencil and paper, a significant additional mental load is created by such operations.

It is obvious that the subjects in these studies do not use knowledge of the formal rules of the syllogism. In any case, these are quite difficult to learn and it took professional logicians some time to develop them. Johnson-Laird (1983, Chapter 5) accounts for the difficulties in the following way. The subjects must gain mental representations of the premises as acts of comprehension, and they must integrate these and examine the implications. Let us suppose that we employ some kind of mental "tokens" like *D* for "detective," *C* for "fictional character," and *F* for "famous" to help represent the meaning of the premises "Some *D*s are *C*s" and "Some *C*s are *F*." In comprehending these premises and in combining them we might sequentially construct the following:

Premise 1	*Premise 2*	*An Integrated Model*
D = *C*	*C* = *F*	*D* = *C*
D = *C*	*C* = *F*	*D* = *C* = *F*
(*D*) (*C*)	(*C*) (*F*)	*C* = *F*
		(*D*) (*C*) (*F*)

The displays represent interpretations of the premises. In Premise 1, for example, the arbitrary number of tokens joined by the equals signs show that at least some *D*s are *C*s, and the unattached tokens in brackets show that some *D*s may not be *C*s and some *C*s may not be *D*s. Premise 2 has the same form in *C*s and *F*s. We can envisage that as its interpretation proceeds it rapidly attaches to Premise 1 to form the integrated model.

Now suppose that we were asked to say whether or not it follows that "some detectives are famous"; we would read off the answer from the integrated model and say "Yes"; and we would be incorrect. Recall that the logical question is: Does the conclusion *necessarily* follow from the premises? In fact the above premises can give rise to a number of different integrated models and to respond to the logical question we must test whether *any* model could exist which represents the premises and yet give a counterexample to the offered conclusion. The crucial counterexample is:

$$D = C$$
$$C = F$$
$$(D)\ (C)\ (F)$$

which while being consistent with both of the premises shows that there is no logical necessity for any detective to be famous.

The Johnson-Laird and Bara study showed that the numbers of incorrect responses were strongly related to the numbers of alternative models that would need to be constructed to test the necessity of any proposed conclusion. For example, the premises "No Bs are As" and "All Bs are Cs" require three models. None of the 20 subjects found the valid conclusion "Some Cs are not As." The mental model of the first premise is likely to be generated in a form that is not well suited to integration with the information supplied by the second premise, and the struggle to shuffle the symbols around increases the difficulty of considering all possible integrated models. We shall need to refer to these ideas again, but first let us look at the use of other logical problems in the study of reasoning.

Transitive Inferences

Performance on the so-called linear syllogisms has been studied in both adults and children. Consider the following:

1. Holmes is taller than Moriarty
   Moriarty is taller than Watson
   Who is tallest?

2. Jim is to the right of Amy
   Amy is to the right of Ben
   Who is in the middle?

3. Gerry is not as nice as Julie
   Susan is nicer than James
   Julie is not as nice as James
   Who is nicest?

The ability of children to make "transitive inferences," of the sort called for here, plays an important part in Piaget's theory of development, and is said to mark the transition from pre-operational thought to concrete operational thought. That is, children at one stage of development can not perform transitive inferences, but at a later stage they can. However, the picture is not as clear as it was when Piaget first described it. Firstly, Bryant and Trabasso (1971) have shown that children are capable, under careful training programmes, of making some transitive inferences at well below the ages at which Piaget would allow that the correct structures or schemas might develop. Secondly, adults do not find transitive inferences very easy.

Thirdly, studies have shown that both spatial and linguistic factors are implicated. From your own introspections in attempting the problems given above you probably found yourself arranging the characters in order in an imaged vertical or horizontal spatial array. "Taller than" and "to the right of" can obviously be coded in this way. Even in problem (3) you may have thought of "nice" as "up." Lakoff and Johnson (1981) have pointed to the spatial metaphors commonly implied by certain terms which have no necessary relation to space and orientation. For example, "control is up" as in "He is at the height of his power," or "She is on top of her job." In our example (3), "nice is up" is a likely coding.

Clark (1969) emphasised the role of linguistic factors in determining the difficulties arising in this form of reasoning. His principle of lexical marking suggests that certain "positive" adjectives like *good*, *long*, *nice*, *tall*, and *interesting* are stored in memory in a less complex form than the senses of their opposites. He terms the positive adjectives "unmarked" and the other poles "marked." The contrast can be observed by comparing the two questions "How good is the food?", which is usually an open evaluative question, with "How bad is the food?", which is not. If a purely logical perspective is taken, the questions can be regarded as equivalent in their call for evaluation of the food, but our language is not like that. Clark showed that in making transitive inferences it took additional cognitive effort to transform features of the surface structure of the sentences—the relational adjectives, the "not's," and the subject–predicate relations—into a form congruent with each other and with the direction of the question asked. Some forms of question make inferences more difficult that others. Changing a question from "taller than" to "shorter than" and adding a negative does not alter the strict logical form but it does affect how readily the inference is dealt with.

The study by Bryant and Trabasso showed that children can be trained to make some kinds of transitive inferences at an earlier age than Piaget had specified, but there seems to be no particular stage at which all transitive inferences become easy for children as though a core logical structure has become the major component of cognitive processing. Children and adults alike have to do a great deal of mental work on these problems, to code the initial linguistic forms and to recognise the possible transitivities. It seems likely that the credit for the correct solutions should be given to the achievement of suitable mental representations of the particular problem rather than to any logical form. If the emergence of logical form in development were the issue then we would have to admit that there is no clear stage at which all transitive inferences come to be operated by a unified logical structure. Later in the chapter we consider the question of whether generalised logical structures might operate in the mind, but first we have to consider a wider range of tasks.

Logical Connections

Words such as *if/then*, *and*, *not*, and *or* which link parts of sentences together in very different ways, can also be understood as logical connections between ideas. There have been many studies of how people understand these and the "selection task" which was devised by Wason (1966) and which is rooted in *if/then* has received a lot of attention over the years. Two forms of the task are illustrated here. You should attempt them before reading on, and record your answers.

Selection Task 1

Consider the following cards:

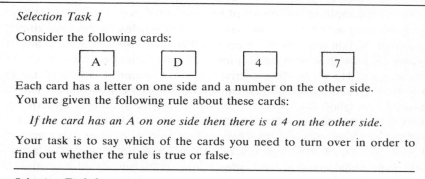

Each card has a letter on one side and a number on the other side.
You are given the following rule about these cards:

> *If the card has an A on one side then there is a 4 on the other side.*

Your task is to say which of the cards you need to turn over in order to find out whether the rule is true or false.

Selection Task 2

Consider the following cards:

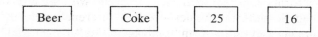

Each card has the name of a drink on one side and a number on the other, and each of the cards represents a person of a certain age drinking in a bar. The rule states:

> *If someone is drinking beer then that person must be over 21.*

Again, the task is to say which cards must be turned over to decide whether the rule is true or false.

In the selection task the rule may be characterised as "If *p* then *q*," where in Task 1 *p* stands for "there is an *A* on one side" and *q* stands for "there is a *4* on the other side." Over a series of experiments using university students, most subjects said that either the *p* and *q* cards (*A* and *4*) or the *p* card (*A*) alone must be turned over to find out whether the rule is true or false (Johnson-Laird & Wason, 1977, p. 145). These responses are incorrect, or at least incomplete.

In Task 2, most subjects realised that they should turn over the *Beer* and the *16* cards (Griggs & Cox, 1982). Obviously, people say, it does not matter what age someone is who drinks Coke and it does not matter what someone drinks if they are over 21 (in Florida, U.S.A.), but a 16-year-old should not be drinking beer in a bar. (In Britain a person must be over 18). So we should check the age of the person drinking beer and what the 16-year-old is drinking. It is quite unnecessary to check the other two cards. This real-world reasoning corresponds to the requirements of the logical form for which the correct answer is to turn over the p and not-q cards. Yet this is not the answer typically given by subjects in response to the more abstract Task 1.

If we carefully apply the beer–age argument to Task 1 with A, 4, D, and 7, we can see that the correct answer is that the A (p) and 7 (not-q) cards should be chosen. There is little doubt for subjects that the A card should be chosen: if there is not a 4 on the other side then the rule is clearly violated. It is quite unnecessary, against all our temptations, to inspect the other side of the card bearing the 4 because the rule does not say that only cards having an A on one side have a 4 on the other side. It is, however, essential to inspect the other side of the 7 card because if it shows an A then the rule is violated. Very few subjects want to inspect the D card: any number, including 4, could be on the other side without impinging upon the rule. A small number of subjects show "partial insight": they select cards A, 4, and 7 (the p, q, and not-q items), recognising that a not-q card might have p on the other side and hence could violate the rule, but they fail to eliminate the q card which, whatever was on the other side, could not violate the rule.

Many variants of this task have been studied in an attempt to pin down its difficulty for most subjects. Various alleged ambiguities in the task have been studied without adequately explaining its difficulty. Given a realistic content, the problem is solved more readily so long as the rule has been sufficiently experienced by the subjects and is not merely one clothed arbitrarily in concrete terms. However, the importance of the experience is that it should cue subjects to generate representations of the possible combinations and especially to those combinations which are *not* allowed. In many American States drinking alcohol in bars is not permitted unless the drinker is over 21. The rule for Task 2 may especially cue knowledge of this negative to help people solve the problem.

Berry (1983) found that a few sentences of explanation of the correct reasoning in a particular concrete but unexperienced case, followed by further experience and verbalisation of their reasoning by the subjects, was highly effective in improving performance on the immediate rule and this improvement transferred to an abstract version of the task that most subjects had failed earlier. That is, subjects can usually be persuaded to adopt the strictly logical interpretation of the task even if it is not their usual approach.

If the selection task can be carried out when it contains real-life rules, why is it not solved in the abstract version? After all, if people know enough to get the answer in a large variety of situations, they might be thought to have some knowledge of how the logical rule works. We can ask how useful it is to employ the logical formulation of *if/then* to all linguistic uses of *if* in ordinary discourse. Consider the detective entangled in the following network of "if's":

> A body is discovered with a knife protruding from its back. If the person is dead then he/she may be termed a "body." If a murder has been performed then the body may be termed "the victim's body." If the knife wound was the cause of death then a murder may have been committed. If the knife wound is not self-inflicted then someone else must have done the stabbing or an extraordinary accident must have occurred. If an extraordinary accident has not occurred and suicide can be ruled out then someone other than the victim is responsible. If someone intended harm to the person and stabbed that person then there is a crime of murder; but if there was unreasonable provocation or the person wielding the knife was in a peculiar mental state then the charge may not be murder. If a witness saw a person X with a(the) knife then a supposition that X stabbed the victim is supported. If medical evidence shows that the body had suffered a heart attack before the stab wound took effect then . . .

Although this—very incomplete—set of *if/then*'s is an expression of a reasonable set of professional rules, each having a logical interpretation, they vary markedly in their status in a reasoning process. Some are definitional, rather like "If a figure has three straight lines joined at their ends then the figure is (called) a triangle." Some refer to causation. Some assume commonplace definitions not supplied, e.g., stab, wound.

In many cases in which *if/then* statements are actually used, they bring other meanings with them. "If you confess, then I will go easy on you in court" conveys a promise as well as the special logical force of "If and only if." On the other hand, "If you don't confess, I will knock your block off" has more an emotional force, one would hope, than a logical one. In the detective's case, even if a complete set of *if/then*'s could be made explicit, it is doubtful whether misinterpretation of the logical *if/then* creates serious problems. Indeed, studies have shown that the *if/then*'s in a particular context are usually correctly interpreted from a logical point of view. The detective's skills and difficulties probably reside, not so much in the use of logical forms, but in deriving useful *if*'s, as hypotheses or suppositions, from a complex context and managing their relationships to any observations that have been or might be made.

Rips (1983) has given an account of performance on a more comprehensive range of propositional reasoning tasks in terms of the availability of natural deduction rules, the use of suppositions and a limited working memory capacity. Consider the following argument (Rips, 1983):

> If there is not both an M and a P on the blackboard, then there is an R.
> Therefore, if there is no M, then there is an R.
> Is this argument valid?

Subjects attempted a series of such problems, varying in the mix of logical rules required for their correct solution. Their performances were timed and noted as correct or incorrect. Rips found a degree of fit for a mathematical model for the times taken to achieve correct and incorrect solutions. The model supposed that subjects had available the deductive rules, such as "*not (p or q) = not p and not q*," which were required for a particular problem, but that they would not always retrieve them or apply them correctly. The difficulty of the problems corresponded to the number of component rules that had to be retrieved, which might be interpreted as showing the limits of working memory rather than simple ignorance of logical operations.

We have looked at reasoning using syllogisms, transitive inferences, and problems involving *if/then*. In general, people are not very good at these tasks, at least when the abstract forms are used. What does this tell us about the role of logic in reasoning?

The Role of Logic

Why are we so poor at logical tasks? One kind of general answer is that offered by Henle (1962), who argues that subjects may forget or misinterpret premises, or that they may make additional assumptions which are not explicitly part of the problem given, and that when we understand how they have interpreted the premises the subjects' answers are seen to be logical. She declares: "I have never found errors which could unambiguously be attributed to faulty reasoning." In essence she believes that we have logical competencies which for various reasons are not always exhibited in our observed performance. A problem with this view is that the errors in people's performance of the tasks remain to be explained. If poor performance can be explained in terms of linguistic factors, perceptual factors, real-world knowledge, or our limited capacity for holding and processing information in immediate memory, then we would have to assume that our capacity for "true" reasoning is marred by the ways in which we acquire knowledge and communicate it. If we could just get rid of these problems then logic would be shown to exist in the mind. Unfortunately this would be to discard many of the interests of psychology and to adopt a belief about the nature of mind which Johnson-Laird refers to as "the doctrine of mental logic."

Piaget likewise set great store by the emergence of logical operations in early adolescence, which are claimed to unify our approaches to classes of problems. Thus an early claim (Piaget, 1953) was that the period 11–15 years saw the emergence of: "the logic of propositions, which is both a formal structure holding independently of content and a general structure co-ordinating the various logical operations into a single system [p. 22]." These structures were specifically believed to be beyond linguistic forms. It has become increasingly difficult to hold to this view in the light of a variety of further data from studies of children, and especially in the light of the systematic failures of intelligent adults on logical tasks. Indeed, Piaget (1972) came to modify his views, accepting that the period of development must be extended to the range 11 to 20 years and that the hypothesised formal structures are not used in the same way in all cases.

Donaldson (1978) has offered a critique of Piaget's assumption that children learn to extract the forms of arguments and develop logical structures as the critical cognitive devices for their thinking. Donaldson's account of children's thinking points to the advantages and disadvantages of the process of abstracting the form of things in learning. "Disembedding," as she prefers to call the abstracting process, must be careful and selective. There are the dual dangers of the overgeneralisation of a form to inappropriate contexts and the overenthusiastic or premature extraction of form from limited experience. The use of general forms can be maladaptive when the situations in which they do and do not apply are not clearly identified. Further, she gives instances of naturally occurring events which show that children's thoughts can exhibit a correct logic in the absence of evidence that they employ any generalised form. For example, shown a wedding photograph, a young child volunteered that it could not be a wedding because there was not a man. In fact, the central pair in the photograph appeared to be of the same gender to the child because the bridegroom had long hair. We could construe the child's thinking as showing the following arguments: "If it is a wedding then there must be a man and a woman; there is no man; therefore, it is not a wedding." The child's apparent competence in constructing an argument which, when expressed in formal terms, adults often find extremely difficult, can hardly show the existence of the general mechanisms of logic as the basis for the child's inference.

Another possibility is that there are defects, from the psychologist's perspective, in the system of logic that is used to specify what the norms should be for human performance. Psychologists have used a limited range of logical forms like *if/then* and the syllogisms in their research with reasoning problems. The parts of logic adopted by experimenters are those which use special definitions, so that *some* and *if/then* have special meanings. Even terms like *and* and *or* do not have their full range of ordinary meanings in logic. Similarly, logicians may use *not* both to negate the truth of a proposition and of compound propositions in a way which does not carry all the ordinary inferences we make from ordinary language. For example, a murder suspect may say to the detective: "It is not true that I was not in bed at 11 p.m.". Logically this reduces to "I was in bed at 11 p.m.", but even in the absence of a more explicit context we can infer many things from the first statement that are not conveyed by the logically equivalent second statement. The meanings of *and*, *or*, and *not* in ordinary communication are usually made clear by the particular contexts in which they are used. Logicians usually wish to study the argument forms beneath their linguistic surface forms, but other aspects of this "surface" are essential for human inference in the broader sense of that term.

More generally, most systems of logic can only be derived from natural language after a considerable amount of work and some logicians would regard their logics, like mathematics, as having a separate existence from any particular relationships to the real world, linguistically represented or otherwise. For example, the logician might insist that the linguistic form *if/then* is not a proper representation of what in logic is called "material implication" and which is best expressed by the special symbol ⊃. The major purpose of formal logic is to examine the validity of arguments, not to describe how arguments are best developed or communicated in linguistic forms.

Meanwhile, psychological research has exclusively used linguistically expressed forms of classical logic as a source of reasoning problems. The status of that logic among other logics is something which we can leave logicians to argue about, but we can nevertheless ask whether something useful might be rescued from the evidence about reasoning that we have gathered so far. It is clear that we do not readily or reliably come to identify valid forms of argument for ourselves. Even training in classical logical forms is not very useful for helping people to solve reasoning problems.

We might conclude that there remains something to be explained, but it is not readily done in terms of logic, at least not logic alone. Is logic alone sufficient for the following problem? You should attempt it before reading on.

Murder Most Logical.   Lord Peter Wimsey was holding a fancy-dress ball in his country mansion. He had invited his friends Sherlock Holmes, Inspector Maigret, Inspector Alleyn, and Hercule Poirot to come early for a fictional detectives' convention, along with his favourite niece, Felicity Dunhill. She was, of course, a major beneficiary in his will. They all arrived in fancy-dress. At 4 p.m. a shot rang out from the study. Someone dressed as a burglar—striped jersey and mask—ran from the study to the staircase.

"His Lordship has been shot," announced the butler. "Please assemble on the lawn for tea in your normal clothes," was the message sent to all the bedrooms. The butler took charge.

"So one of you came dressed as a burglar and shot Lord Peter. Indeed, you all came dressed as someone else. The first arrived in a taxi at 3 o'clock and the rest followed at 10-minute intervals. The one dressed as Sherlock Holmes—how confusing—arrived at 3.20 p.m. I helped Inspector Maigret out of his Hansom Cab at . . . ."

"Don't give too much away," said Lord Peter emerging from behind a bush. "Let them work it out." Our characters smiled weakly, trying to look unsurprised as though they had expected a trick like this.

"Well, Hercule Poirot came on a bike dressed as a policeman and dismounted by himself," continued the butler, embellishing his story a little, "and Inspector Alleyn arrived in a helicopter just 10 minutes after the one who came dressed as the famous Chinese detective, who wasn't the first to arrive.

"You'd better tell them that Felicity arrived, dressed as Moriarty, just after Poirot."

"Oh yes, and one of them came on horseback."

"What was the motive?" said one of the guests. "Search the house and grounds," said another. "Question the servants," said another.

"You have enough information already," said Lord Peter. "The one who came dressed as a burglar must of course keep quiet. This requires no clever detective work. It is merely a matter of logic. Who was the murderer?"

This problem is fairly easy from a strictly logical point of view. Members of sets (fictional detectives, transport, fancy dress characters, times of arrival) have one-to-one relations, or exclusive connections, with members of other sets. There are no tricky logical operators like *and*, *or*, *not*, and *if/then*, and there are no ambiguities about *all*, *some*, and *none*. The task is more a problem of how we go about it, whether we persist sufficiently, how much we can hold in our heads and how clearly we represent the essential information when we use paper and pencil.

One method of solving the problem is to fit the several fragments of evidence into a matrix. First, *Taxi* is inserted at 3 p.m. under *Transport* and *"Sherlock Holmes"* under *Fancy Dress* at 3.20 p.m. The following three fragments are to be fitted into the matrix preserving the adjacency of the pairs of lines in 2 and 3:

1. Maigret   Hansom cab

   Chinese detective

2.

   Alleyn   Helicopter ("10 mins after")

Poirot   Policeman   Bike

3.

Dunhill   Moriarty   ("just after . . .")

Finally, *Sherlock Holmes*, *Burglar* and *Horse* fill out the remaining spaces without ambiguity, to complete the matrix as in Table 13.1.

In so far as this task has any "logical" difficulty, it is more a task of devising a sensible way of tackling the problem. In this sense, it is not easy to see how training in formal logic would help with the detective's task, fictional or otherwise. Whereas many inferences can be characterised as "deductive," much of the detective's task concerns those very factors that formal logics tend to ignore such as what to look for, who to ask, how they say it, what they are like and world knowledge generally. Formal logics have little or nothing to say about how we go about solving problems.

At this point, we can take another look at some of Sherlock Holmes's deductions. In *A Study in Scarlet* he said that the murderer was a tall man. Later he explains that 9 out of 10 tall men have a large stride, the murderer's footprints showed that he had a large stride which made it likely that he was tall. This was confirmed by the finding that a message had been written six feet from the floor, because a man will tend to write on a wall at eye level. What Holmes is doing here is not deduction at all. If he were, he would argue like this:

Some tall men have large strides
The murderer has a large stride
Therefore the murderer is tall

This argument is not a valid one, and neither is the argument:

Some men write on walls at eye level
The murderer wrote on the wall 6 feet up
Therefore the murderer's eyes are 6 feet from the ground

TABLE 13.1
Solution to the "Murder Most Logical" Problem

Time	Person	Fancy Dress	Transport
3.00	Sherlock Holmes	Burglar	Taxi
3.10	Inspector Maigret	Chinese detective	Hansom cab
3.20	Inspector Alleyn	"Sherlock Holmes"	Helicopter
3.30	Hercule Poirot	Policeman	Bike
3.40	Felicity Dunhill	Moriarty	Horse

What Sherlock Holmes is actually doing is much closer to the medical diagnosis discussed in Chapter 12. He is making probabilistic statements, basing plausible hypotheses on them, and making further inferences.

In another incident, when he meets Dr Watson he immediately "perceives" that the doctor has returned from Afghanistan (where British troops were involved in a war at the time). Later he explains that the doctor is browned by the tropical sun and holds his arm stiffly, so he must have been wounded. Afghanistan is the only place in which a British officer could get both brown and wounded, therefore Watson had been in Afghanistan. Put like that, it is clear that Holmes was imaginative and lucky rather than logical. Wounds, he assumed, occurred in wars, but they can occur in other ways, and suntans can be acquired in other places. Holmes's main achievements are observation and the application of knowledge to generate plausible accounts rather than the possession of any formal deductive powers. He recognised signs which other detectives ignored so that problems were seen quite differently; he interpreted what he saw against a wide background of knowledge and he did not get trapped into ruts as the fictional Scotland Yard detectives do. He can better be characterised as a skilled problem-solver rather than a logician.

PROBLEM SOLVING

Getting Stuck

Unlike Sherlock Holmes, Inspector Lestrade from Scotland Yard sometimes makes assumptions that prevent him from solving problems. His thoughts are blocked or misdirected. Investigations of factors that block or misdirect our thinking were a feature of many early studies of thinking. Maier (1930, 1931) showed subjects to a room in which two strings were hanging from the ceiling. The task was to tie the two strings together, but, holding on to one of the strings, a subject could not reach the other. The essence of the solution is to tie an object of sufficient weight on to one of the strings so that it can be caused to swing back and forth like a pendulum. Then holding on to the second string, the swinging string can be caught when it approaches. We can envisage subjects holding on to one string, reaching in vain towards the other string and looking puzzled. In one experiment, Maier offered hints to those failing to solve the problem. First, he brushed past one of the strings setting it in motion. To those who still failed to solve the problem, he handed a pair of pliers, saying: "With the aid of this and no other object there is another way of solving the problem." For some subjects, a pair of pliers remained an item which is used to grip things and not to act as a weighty object; that is, their thinking was blocked by seeing pliers in a particular way. Those who solved the problem following the first hint tended to do so rapidly and often without any awareness of what had caused the redirection in their thinking.

Among the several studies that followed Maier's work, Birch and Rabinowitz (1951) varied the subjects' previous experiences with the objects that might be used to weight the pendulum. All subjects were asked to complete an electrical circuit, one group using a switch and another group using a device called a relay. Both the switch and the relay were present when subjects were asked to attempt Maier's two-string task. Of course, many subjects required the redirective hint, the experimenter's "accidental" brush past one of the strings to set it in motion. All subjects eventually succeeded in the task, but all those who had fitted the relay to the electrical circuit used the switch as the pendulum weight, whereas most of those who had earlier fitted the switch to the circuit used the relay as the weight. This suggested that the recent use of an item in its normal role had made its other properties (e.g., weight) less available, whereas the unused item was freer to take on alternative functions. Duncker (1945) had termed this phenomenon *functional fixedness*, the "inhibition in discovering an appropriate use of an object owing to the subject's previous use of the object in a function dissimilar to that required by the present situation."

Subjects can be said to show various levels of functional fixedness in response to the following pencil-and-paper task. Try it before you continue. *You have two minutes to write down as many uses of a brick as you can*. Other common items like newspaper and paperclip can be used. Subjects typically begin their list with "build a house, build a wall, build a . . . ." Other responses may follow after a pause. Pauses became more frequent and some subjects became completely blocked well within two minutes, but other subjects may generate 50 responses. The marked individual differences found in this task do not in general relate very strongly to performances on other tasks which also purport to show fluency of ideas, flexibility in thinking, or, in general, creativity. Individuals who show an ability to overcome blocks in some situations are not necessarily those who are inventive in others.

Functional fixedness, and mental blocks generally, are clearly an aspect of prior experience that we bring to a new task. It is an example of what Wertheimer (1945) termed *reproductive* thinking (as opposed to *productive* thinking). He gave examples from the learning of mathematics in which pupils are liable to pick up specific routines, perhaps a particular formula, which may not readily transfer to new representations of the problem.

The classic, Gestalt studies of thinking tended to emphasise the negative effects of past experience, whether this is the experience of a particular function of something, like pliers, distributed over several years, or a concentrated recent experience, perhaps of success with a procedure, which creates a dysfunctional mental set with respect to new problems. Of course, it can also be demonstrated that our mental habits—the fixednesses and the mental sets—can be overcome in the right conditions. Maier (1945) showed that subjects who could be led to solve one unusual problem were more likely to be successful at another when sufficient features were shared between them. Cofer (1951) showed that a prior verbal learning task in which words like "rope," "swing," and "pendulum" were to be memorised facilitated correct solutions to the Maier two-string problem relative to the performance of control subjects who learned other words. Maier also, you may recall, found that "hints" were able to shift the direction for many of his subjects.

Positive or negative transfer, whether from diffuse past experience or from concentrated and highly recent experience, clearly depends on many factors. If problems appear to be similar this can facilitate solution where habitual ways of thinking are useful; but similarity of problems can sometimes be misleading. There is great risk of circularity here. The classical studies of thinking often focused on novel problems and although it would be attractive for us to show flexible and productive thinking in our responses to new problems, there is some question as to how useful it is to be ever alert to the possibility that our well-prepared habits will give the wrong answers to the next problem we meet. In most cases, when students learn to categorise geometry problems as requiring a certain sort of approach, they will be helping themselves to find the solution. However, for some problems we are alerted to the need for a change of approach by our self-evident failure to solve them and for these it would be well to have techniques to help us overcome the blocks and avoid the familiar channels in which our thinking runs. Unfortunately, however, it is not always so obvious that we fail at some problems and it is hard to see how we might derive general advice or guidelines for productive thinking from the results of the classic studies. Being in a rut must be useful most of the time because our life experience has given us sufficiently successful, if more-or-less habitual, ways of dealing with the many problems we meet, and it is difficult to specify those situations in which those habitual ways, the reproductive thinking ways, are likely to inhibit a satisfactory solution. It would be very odd if experience only hindered our ability to solve problems.

When modern detectives set out to investigate crimes they use a very wide range of routine activities such as questioning witnesses and searching the scene of the crime for evidence. In many cases the routine methods will lead to a solution. In some cases habitual ways of thinking—perhaps assumptions about the sort of person most likely or not likely to have committed the crime or which witness is to be believed—may inhibit solution. How do we strike a balance between the routine use of procedures which work much of the time and staying flexible, open-minded, and considering all possibilities that might lead to solutions on other occasions? Clearly we cannot restrict thinking and problem solving to any set of rules, whether logical or not. We have to create a model of problem solving which will encompass a wide range of approaches, abilities, and skills. We now consider a particular characterisation of problem-solving processes that has dominated recent accounts.

Problem Solving as a Search Process

One of the greatest difficulties facing the detective is to define what can be called the *problem space*, the range of possibilities—potential actors and action sequences—that might have led to the crime and which might now form the basis for enquiry, search, inference, and successful solution. Whereas the Gestalt psychologists discussed thinking and problem solving in such general terms as "restructuring" the problem, "redirection," and "insight," those developing the *information processing* approach in the 1950s and 1960s emphasised the need to make explicit the detailed mental operations and sequences of operations by which the subject solved problems. The terminology of Ernst and Newell (1969) has been widely adopted both for human problem solving and for problem solving by computer. To introduce the terminology, consider the following problem:

> Three detectives have captured three desperate criminals in the wilds and are taking them on foot through field and forest. Each criminal has his legs chained together to restrict his speed of movement. The detectives hold the keys to the leg-irons and the essential food supplies. The six men come to a river which they must cross. A rowing boat is available which will only take two men at a time. Two men can cross in the boat but one must row it back so that others can get across. The problem is that if at any time there are more criminals than detectives on a river bank they will overpower their guard(s), recover the keys to their leg-irons, take the food supplies, and escape with all speed. How is the crossing managed?

Table 13.2 gives a solution to the problem and illustrates the components of the problem space. The *initial state* of the problem is expressed by the diagram at State 1 in which all the detectives (*DDD*) and criminals (*CCC*) are on the left bank of the river, along with the boat. The *goal state* is that state achieved when all the detectives and criminals are on the right bank of the river and is shown as State 12. The *operators* are the set of permissible state-transforming operations. For example, from State 1 the

TABLE 13.2
Solution to the "Detectives and Criminals" Problem

State	Moves		
	Left Bank	River Operation	Right Bank
1	DDD CCC		
2	DDD C	CC →	CC
3	DDD CC	C ←	C
4	DDD	CC →	CCC
5	DDD C	C ←	CC
6	D C	DD →	DD CC
7	DD CC	CD ←	D C
8	CC	DD →	DDD C
9	CCC	C ←	DDD
10	C	CC →	DDD CC
11	CC	C ←	DDD C
12		CC →	DDD CCC

boat could carry the following alternative sets of passengers: DD, CC, DC, D, or C. However, some of these "boating operations" or journeys are not allowed to follow from State 1. Only journeys by CC, DC and C are permitted by the rules which say that the criminals must not outnumber the detectives on either river bank. The three permissible journeys transform State 1 into three different problem states. If the first journey is undertaken by CC then there is only one useful next move—in which a single C returns with the boat—if we are not to return to State 1. If the first journey is undertaken by CD then only the return of D is permitted within the rules. If C alone makes the first trip across the river, then there is only one possible operation and that is for C to return as he came, thus re-creating State 1. We can explore all permissible operations, moving from state to state, and looking ahead we can evaluate whether the move might be useful. The initial state, the goal state, and the set of operations or operators define the *problem space*. In fact the alternative paths through the problem space for this problem are extremely limited. There are some minor variants of the solution to this problem at the beginning of the sequence and towards the end. Nevertheless, this apparently simple problem allows us to illustrate some features of the information-processing approach.

First, we could attempt to solve this problem by trying all permissible moves from each problem state legitimately achieved. This would define the complete *search space* for the problem. A procedure which guarantees solution, as this one would for the detectives and criminals problem, is referred to as an *algorithm* or an algorithmic procedure. It is extremely unlikely that you found yourself using this approach when you attempted the problem. If you are like many of the subjects who have tried the equivalent "cannibals and missionaries" problem then you will have got a bit stuck in State 6, being somewhat reluctant to take two men back across the river, or even being blind to the possibility of this move. This, along with much other evidence, suggests that human search through the problem space is directed by *heuristic* principles. We met examples of heuristics in Chapter 12. In the present context it is suggested that we use the principle of attempting to increase the number of men who have crossed the river at each stage. It is as though we evaluate the possible moves in terms of which one takes us nearest to the goal state. This heuristic is referred to as "means–ends analysis." Another heuristic principle is "subgoal setting." You may have guessed that the problem is solved by taking all the criminals across first and that if this subgoal state can be achieved then the goal state proper might be more obviously in sight. Or you may have anticipated by working backwards that if State 9 can be reached then the goal state is certainly achievable.

The present problem is not too difficult, yet it gives us clues about the heuristic principles we might employ to guide a speculative journey of discovery through a problem space. Heuristic principles are devices for reducing the size of the "search tree" to be examined to a manageable number of branches which, hopefully, lead quickly to the goal state. The heuristic, path-reducing principles of means–ends analysis and of developing a hierarchy of subgoals were successfully implemented in a computer program called the General Problem Solver (Ernst & Newell, 1969), which solved a variant of the missionaries and cannibals problem, some problems in mathematics, and a number of other tasks. In many of these cases it would be possible to program a computer to examine systematically all possible branches in the problem space, one or several of which might lead from initial state to goal state. The program was regarded as successful, however, because it avoided such an approach and demonstrated the value of general heuristic principles even for fully determinate problems.

On the face of it, playing a game of chess is a well-specified problem. The initial state is well defined, the operators are clearly set out in the rules of the game, and the goal state ("checkmate"), although it can be achieved by a variety of patterns of pieces on the board, is also well defined by the rules. But the problem space is vast. Even the use of quite powerful computers does not allow "look ahead" for more than a limited number of moves. The "state-action tree" of possibilities grows very rapidly from most chess positions and programmers are led to use heuristic methods that may be akin to what human chess players use.

The problem space of the detective is somewhat diffuse. A murder has been committed. The "initial state" includes not only the body, the manner and time of death, and other matters which are obviously necessary starting data for the enquiry, but also a whole host of details that are available at the scene of the crime. Some of these details may take on the status of "clues" once the detective sees a possible relation to the "goal state." The goal state itself may not be sufficiently well defined at the outset, except perhaps in such general terms as "Find out who did it." Matters such as who found the body, when was the victim last seen alive and by whom, become part of the enquiry and are things to be determined, and these in turn provide subgoals that may define the next steps. Thus, the search space is not at all well defined in advance. The detective is, however, assisted by a set of professional heuristics. Two principal heuristics, familiar to detective-story buffs, are expressed in short form as "motive and opportunity": Who had a sufficient motive to kill the victim? Who had the opportunity? The weapon, if any, and its ownership is another line of enquiry obvious to the professionals. In following through these general guiding principles, the detective sets in motion one or more routine approaches. House-to-house enquiries, taking statements from all witnesses, interviewing the family, tracing the victim's movements, and many other lines are open to the detective.

Heuristics must be employed where no obvious algorithm exists. But which heuristics are to be selected from the many available in any complex situation? Definition of the search space and of the operators, and the selection of appropriate heuristics, so neatly separable in the case of well-defined problems, are much entangled in most real problems. In part at least, the nature of expertise lies somewhere in the effective management of search problems.

Expertise

Our detective is a kind of expert and Sherlock Holmes succeeds because he is more expert than other detectives. In what ways do experts differ from intelligent novices? Undoubtedly, they differ in the amount of practice and experience, but what is the nature of the difference? How are the effects of practice and experience expressed in the expert? One kind of expert that has been much studied in recent years is the master chess player.

The first difference between master and novice chess player is that the former encodes chess positions faster. Shown a chess position for only 5 seconds, masters reproduced it with 91 per cent accuracy whereas novices were only 41 per cent correct (de Groot, 1966). Masters and novices, however, are similarly poor at reproducing random arrangements of chess pieces (Chase & Simon, 1973a,b). It was clear from the way in which the subjects placed pieces on the board when reproducing a real board position, and from the frequency of their head movements when copying a position from one board to another, that the masters and novices differed markedly in the size of the "chunks"—groups of chess pieces in relationship—that are represented in their respective knowledge bases.

These studies give us warning that playing chess well is likely to require rather more than a "search all possibilities" strategy. Indeed, de Groot (1965) and Newell and Simon (1972) found that masters tend not to perform much of a search at all; masters and novices did not differ in the number of possible moves they considered nor how far they looked ahead. Rather we might suppose that the expert is faster to encode and to evaluate what for him would be stereotypical positions and moves, leaving more time for exploration of one or two novel points in the board position. In contrast, many of the early computer programs for chess focused on search and look-ahead methods for determining next moves. Although they came to outperform many human players, limits of advance towards grandmaster standards were reached. Currently, advances are being made in machine chess, not by extending their ability to search the problem space to greater depths, but by giving them knowledge of chess positions and of the "rules of thumb," or special chess-specific heuristics, for selecting a limited range of possible moves to be explored. Most importantly, the chess expert may envision a future state of the board which he would like to achieve and he will explore whether it is achievable. It is rather difficult to specify the rules for this kind of subgoal setting, which rests so heavily in the understanding of the game. Thus whereas earlier studies of thinking and problem solving focused on the general processes, studies of chess expertise have led us to stress the importance of specific knowledge structures, the representation of that knowledge, and knowledge about that knowledge.

Similarly, studies of novices and experts solving physics problems have led to a shift away from explanations of problem solving in terms of processes, or generally applicable procedures, to knowledge-based explanations. The subjects of the study by Chi, Feltovich, and Glaser (1981) were asked to categorise some problems in mechanics. Novices typically saw the problems as being about inclined planes, springs, pulleys and friction, the terms in which the problems were expressed. When they tackled the problems they generated equations that matched the data present in the problem statement. The experts, however, tended to categorise the problems as calling upon principles of mechanics such as the conservation of energy or Newton's force law. Their solutions formed an integrated argument about the problem, whereas many solutions offered by the novices clearly had the style of shuffling equations around to solve for unknowns. The novices' approach is rather as one might write for a simple, data-driven computer program: Match elements of the data presented with algebraic rules held in memory, setting up equations to be solved as though it were simply a mathematical "jigsaw" problem. The method works but the conceptual level implied may not facilitate subsequent learning in physics. Further, following McDermott and Larkin (1978), the representations available to novice and expert differ in line with their different styles of categorisation and solution. The experts can have four stages or levels of representation: (1) the literal elements of the problem; (2) a spatial arrangement of the original objects (e.g., ball on inclined plane); (3) an idealised representation which gives a place to the necessary physical concepts such as centre of gravity or forces; and (4) the mathematical equations that abstract the relations from (3). Novices may lack stages (2) and (3).

The detective as expert is most naively seen as someone who collects evidence for analysis from which logical deductions are made. No doubt there is some truth in this account. A more likely account is that current information about the crime stimulates the imagination of the detective, causing him to seek further evidence, creating further guesses, and so on. At one extreme an unusual factor will create curiosity and the urge to achieve an explanation; at the other, a "hunch" about available data will cause directed evidence-gathering. Just as the chess expert will have much use for well-remembered games and will envision possible positions for testing, so the experienced detective will also have a large number of scripts and plans from previous investigations that can be checked against the possible scenarios for the current crime. In this sense, the skills of chess masters, physicists, and detectives are strongly embedded in their respective knowledge bases. If studies of "mental logic" and "information processing" do not give wholly adequate accounts of how we think and reason about things, how can we combine the "processes" with the "knowledge structures" that are evidently required for expertise?

MENTAL MODELS

In recent years the notions of schemas and mental models have received increasing attention as a mode of explanation of successes and failures in comprehension, thinking, reasoning, and problem solving. The notion of a model, whether explicitly "mental" or otherwise, lies at the core of learning about science and of scientific theorising. The earlier discussion of the differences between experts and novices in physics focused on their differences in levels of conceptualisation of problems. Several studies have provoked a different characterisation of the difference in knowledge structures. Disessa (1983), for example, posed the following problem to novices:

> Think of a vacuum cleaner whose intake nozzle you hold in your hand. If you put your hand over the nozzle, will the pitch of the sound you hear from the motor go up or down?

Some respondents offered the view (View 1) that the speed of the motor, and hence the pitch of its sound, is lowered. They sometimes justified this conclusion by referring to the way in which an electric drill slows when it bites into wood (has to work harder). Others (View 2) concluded that the pitch rises because the motor speeds up, since the motor must work harder to overcome the interference. Which view expresses the correct answer? Strictly, words like "concluded," "because," and "since" in the preceding explanations are used rather loosely. Unless we have a clear memory from direct experience of whether the pitch rises or falls when the nozzle is blocked, we can probably be induced to explain either possibility. Notice how "work harder" has a different consequence in the two explanations. Try the alternative question: Why does the pitch (motor speed) fall when the nozzle is blocked? Many of us will offer a view, rather like View 1 above. In fact, the pitch rises. Disessa suggested that the physics-naive among us operate a "phenomenological primitive" based on an Ohm's law model. Ohm's law connects the measurements of electromotive force (volts), current flow (amps), and electrical resistance (ohms) in electrical circuits. Thus the motor provides an impetus (compare voltage) which meets blockage (resistance) and the flow of air (current) reduces (somehow the motor slows). View 2 given above, although justifying the correct answer, is also seen as being based on the same analogy but with a difference. Instead of the motor slowing as the airflow reduces, the motor, somewhat anthropomorphically, is said to speed up to "compensate" for this reduction.

Similarly, Gentner and Gentner (1983) discuss the way in which novice physicists may use the flow of water from reservoirs and through pipes, or the movement of crowds of people through restricted pathways, as analogues for reasoning about electrical flow in circuits of various designs. These "mental models" may be sufficient for some simpler inferences, but unless the lines of the analogy are very carefully drawn the models break down for more complex problems.

Recall also Johnson-Laird's (1983) account of how we come to assert some logically invalid conclusions and fail to find some valid ones for the Aristotelian syllogisms. To be successful, subjects must gain an integrated mental representation of the premises, and they must be able to explore what alternative models of the premises might exist to determine whether or not some possible conclusion is a necessary conclusion. In general, we can envisage that the act of comprehending problem statements, like the process of comprehending a story, often requires us to acquire some kind of schema. Sometimes the schema is retrieved in a ready-made form for a familiar sort of problem. All we have to do is to slot in the novel parameters, "run" the model fairly effortlessly, and the answer appears. At other times we have to work a little harder and attempt to construct a relatively novel model from the problem statement, hoping that when we "run" it the necessary inferences will follow from the "workings" of the mental model.

The notion of mental model is the topic of much recent research and we are not yet in a position to define it precisely. As indicated in our brief introduction here, a mental model has something in common with the idea of a schema, it is a mental representation, it may have analogical properties, and it can be "run" or operated in some sense to produce inferences.

As we have suggested already, Sherlock Holmes is not merely a clever observer and logician; he builds a scenario within which the critical events might have taken place, and this in turn leads him selectively to seek other clues which by inference ought to exist if the scenario is on the right lines. His knowledge of life and the ways of criminals supply many fragments to the picture he builds up as he surveys the scene. Similarly, some good detective writers seem to know how to cause readers to create and sustain misleading assumptions and to generate wrong inferences. We run the wrong model of events and personalities, forget some bits that do not fit, and sometimes even speculate about the mind of the author who is clearly out to defeat our amateur efforts as detectives. The real detective as an expert of a particular kind has many ready-made frameworks for action and thinking; but the experienced professional also has a store of cautionary tales about cases when standard scenarios have been misleading and when standard practices have failed.

It is variously estimated that it takes about 10 years or 4000 hours to produce an "expert." To account for the thinking and reasoning of experts and to prescribe how more effectively we might gain our chosen expertise continues to be a major challenge for research.

SUMMARY

Many studies of thinking and reasoning have adopted some well-defined forms for deductive inferences developed by logicians, which have often been assumed to provide standards for human inference. By these standards our reasoning is sometimes found to be defective. This is especially the case when the structure of an argument is expressed in abstract terms. If a realistic content and context is given to an argument form, we tend to perform much better; but even here we can be led to make errors. Perceptual and linguistic factors and the limitations of immediate memory may be invoked to account for many of the errors. In this sense, the problems of deductive inference highlight many of the same processes that have been discussed in previous chapters.

The wider range of tasks used in studies of problem solving show that many other skills are required for their successful solution. In novel tasks it may sometimes be necessary to overcome the routine ways of thinking provided by our experience, which may be prompted by the appearances of the task. Some problems require us to trace a path from a current state of knowledge to a "goal state." In well-defined problems we seek a route through a "search space." Our skills lie in the use of heuristic principles which sometimes allow us to avoid exploring every one of a large number of search paths. In less well-defined problems, our skills may reside in the ability to give some preliminary definition to the space that the problem occupies. How we go about solving problems, especially the less well-defined ones, refers to skills—of envisioning or scenario building—beyond those of the routine deductive skills of inference.

In general, the skills of problem solving are an extension of the processes of comprehension rather than, as was once thought, a matter of developing general logical structures in the mind. A current conception of these processes is that we use mental models as representations of the problems. The learner or novice is engaged in building these as acts of comprehension, and sometimes immature mental models will show themselves by being inadequate to the tasks at hand. Experts will have a store of useful mental models from their experience which can often readily take on the special features of the current problem and be "run" to produce answers. These models are, however, not to be taken as equivalent to the general-purpose "logical structures" envisaged by earlier researchers. Rather, attention is currently being given to the role of specialised mental representations for thinking and problem solving in particular domains of knowledge.

To reason and solve problems we have to use a wide range of cognitive processes. Indeed, all the topics covered in earlier chapters in this book have something to contribute to the understanding of how we interact intelligently with the world we live in. Perceptual and linguistic factors may lead us to understand a problem in a particular way, limitations on immediate memory may make it difficult to hold all the relevant information, spatial knowledge may be used when we create a model of a problem, our memory for previous problems or for relevant general knowledge is clearly important, and the whole process can be understood as an extension of comprehension. Finally, when we have solved a problem or made a decision we have to turn our decision into action.

Throughout this book we have broken the cognitive system down in order to try to understand it, but we have continually found that any real-life activity involves many parts of the system and these parts interrelate or overlap. Problem solving is probably the best example of the interrelatedness of the components of the cognitive system in action.

There are many books entitled *Thinking and Problem Solving*, or something similar. *Thinking, Problem Solving and Cognition*, by R. E. Mayer (1983), is an introductory text, and is particularly interesting because it brings together accounts of concept identification, schema, the structure of semantic memory, and cognitive development, along with the usual topics. Further reading on the newer topics raised in this chapter can be found in two books, both with the title *Mental Models*, by P. N. Johnson-Laird (1983) and by D. Gentner and A. L. Stevens (Eds.) (1983). The first focuses on issues in language, logic, and meaning; the second on learning and thinking about the physical world.

References

Alderson, G. J. K., Sully, D. J., & Sully, H. G. (1974) An operational analysis of a one handed catching task using high speed photography. *Journal of Motor Behaviour*, *6*, 217–226.

Allport, D. A. (1980) Attention and performance. In G. Claxton (Ed.), *Cognitive Psychology: New Directions*. London: Routledge & Kegan Paul.

Allport, D. A. (1977) On knowing the meaning of words we are unable to report: the effects of visual masking. In S. Dornic (Ed.), *Attention and Performance, VI*. Hillsdale, N.J.: Lawrence Erlbaum Associates Inc.

Allport, D. A. (1983) Language and cognition. In R. Harris (Ed.), *Approaches to Language*. Oxford: Pergamon.

Allport, D. A., Antonis, B., & Reynolds, P. (1972) On the division of attention: a disproof of the single channel hypothesis. *Quarterly Journal of Experimental Psychology*, *24*, 225–235.

Allport, D. A., & Funnell, E. (1981) Components of the mental lexicon. *Philosophical Transactions of the Royal Society (London)*, *B295*, 397–410.

Anderson, J. R. (1976) *Language, Memory and Thought*. Hillsdale, N.J.: Lawrence Elrbaum Associates Inc.

Anderson, J. R. (1978) Arguments concerning representations for mental imagery. *Psychological Review*, *85*, 249–277.

Anderson, J. R. (1980) *Cognitive Psychology and its Implications*. San Francisco: W. H. Freeman.

Anderson, J. R. (1983) *The Architecture of Cognition*. Cambridge, Mass.: Harvard University Press.

Anderson, J. R. (1984) Spreading activation. In J. R. Anderson & S. M. Kosslyn (Eds.), *Essays in Learning and Memory*. New York: W. H. Freeman & Co.

Anderson, J. R. (1985) *Cognitive Psychology and its Implications* (2nd edn). New York: W. H. Freeman & Co.

Anderson, J. R., & Bower, G. H. (1973) *Human Associative Memory*. Washington DC: Hemisphere Press.

Anderson, J. R., & Kosslyn, S. M. (Eds.) (1984) *Tutorials in Learning and Memory*. San Francisco: W. H. Freeman & Co.

Anderson, R. C., & Pichert, J. W. (1978) Recall of previously unrecallable information following a shift in perspective. *Journal of Verbal Learning and Verbal Behavior*, *17*, 1–12.

Annett, J., Annett, M., Hudson, P. T. W., & Turner, A. (1979) The control of movement in the preferred and non-preferred hands. *Quarterly Journal of Experimental Psychology*, *31*, 641–652.

Appleyard, D. A. (1976) *Planning a Pluralistic City*. Cambridge, Mass.: MIT Press.

Atkinson, R. C., & Shiffrin, R. M. (1968) Human memory: a proposed system and its control processes. In K. W. Spence & J. T. Spence (Eds.), *The Psychology of Learning and Motivation: Advances in Research and Theory*, Vol. 2. New York: Academic Press.

Atkinson, R. C., & Shiffrin, R.M. (1971) The control of short-term memory. *Scientific American*, *225*, 82–90.

Baddeley, A. D. (1976) *The Psychology of Memory*. New York: Basic Books Inc.

Baddeley, A. D. (1978) The trouble with levels: A re-examination of Craik and Lockhart's framework for memory research. *Psychological Review*, *85*, 139–152.

Baddeley, A. D. (1983) Working memory. *Philosophical Transactions of the Royal Society*, Series B, *302*, 311–324.

Baddeley, A. D. (1983) *Your Memory: A User's Guide*. Harmondsworth: Penguin.

Baddeley, A. D., & Hitch, G. J. (1974) Working memory. In G. H. Bower (Ed.), *The Psychology of Learning and Motivation*, Vol. 2. New York: Academic Press.

Baddeley, A. D., & Hitch, G. (1977) Recency re-examined. In S. Dornic (Ed.), *Attention and Performance VI*. London: Academic Press.

Baddeley, A. D. & Lieberman, K. (1980) Spatial working memory. In R. Nickerson (Ed.), *Attention and Performance VIII*. Hillsdale, N.J.: Lawrence Erlbaum Associates Inc.

Baddeley, A. D., Thomson, N., & Buchanan, M. (1975) Word length and the structure of short-term memory. *Journal of Verbal Learning and Verbal Behaviour*, *14*, 575–589.

Bahrick, H. P. (1984) Semantic memory content in permastore: Fifty years of memory for Spanish learned at school. *Journal of Experimental Psychology: General*, *113*, 1–29.

Bahrick, H. P., Bahrick, P. O., & Wittlinger, R. P. (1975) Fifty years of memory for names and faces: A cross-sectional approach. *Journal of Experimental Psychology: General*, *104*, 54–75.

Baker, R. R. (1982) *Human Navigation and the Sixth Sense*. London: Hodder & Stoughton.

Barclay, J. R., Bransford, J. D., Franks, J. J., McCarrell, N. S., & Nitsch, K. (1974) Comprehension and semantic flexibility. *Journal of Verbal Learning and Verbal Behavior*, *13*, 471–481.

Barnes, J. M., & Underwood, B. J. (1959) "Fate" of first-list associations in transfer theory. *Journal of Experimental Psychology*, *58*, 97–105.

Bartlett, F. C. (1932) *Remembering*. Cambridge: Cambridge University Press.

Baum, D. R., & Jonides, J. J. (1979) Cognitive maps: analysis of comparative judgements of distance. *Memory and Cognition*, *7*, 462–468.

Beattie, G. W., & Butterworth, B. (1979) Contextual probability of word frequency as determinants of pauses and errors in spontaneous speech. *Language and Speech*, *22*, 201–211.

Bekerian, D. A., & Baddeley, A. D. (1980) Saturation advertising and the repetition effect. *Journal of Verbal Learning and Verbal Behavior*, *19*, 17–25.

Bekerian, D. A., & Bowers, J. M. (1983) Eyewitness testimony. Were we misled? *Journal of Experimental Psychology: Learning and Cognition*, *9*, 139–145.

Berlin, B. (1978) Ethnobiological classification. In E. Rosch & B. B. Lloyd (Eds.), *Cognition and Categorization*. Hillsdale, N.J.: Lawrence Erlbaum Associates Inc.

Berry, D. C. (1983) Metacognitive experience and transfer of logical reasoning. *Quarterly Journal of Experimental Psychology*, *35A*, 39–49.

Besner, D. (1980) *Visual word recognition: Codes and procedures for accessing the internal lexicon*. Unpublished Ph.D. thesis, University of Reading, England.

Birch, H. G., & Rabinowitz, H. S. (1951) The negative effect of previous experience on productive thinking. *Journal of Experimental Psychology*, *41*, 121–125.

Black, J. B. & Bern, H. (1981) Causal coherence and memory for events in narratives. *Journal of Verbal Learning and Verbal Behavior*, *20*, 267–275.

Book, A., & Garling, T. (1981) Maintenance of orientation during locomotion in unfamiliar environments. *Journal of Experimental Psychology: Human Perception and Performance*, *7*, 995–1006.

Boreas, T. (1930) Experimental studies of memory 2. The rate of forgetting. *Pracktilea Academy, Athens, 5*, 382–396. Quoted by R. S. Woodworth & H. Schlosberg (1954), *Experimental Psychology*. New York: Holt, Rinehart & Winston.

Bouma, H. & Bouwhuis, D. G. (1984) *Attention and Performance X: Control of Language Processes*. London: Lawrence Erlbaum Associates Ltd.

Bousfield, W. A. (1953) The occurrence of clustering in recall of randomly arranged associates. *Journal of General Psychology, 49*, 229–240.

Bower, G. H. (1983) Affect and cognition. *Philosophical Transactions of the Royal Society of London* (Series B), *302* (1110), 387–402.

Bower, G. H., Black, J. B., & Turner, T. J. (1979) Scripts in memory for text. *Cognitive Psychology, 11*, 177–220.

Bower, G. H., Clark, M. C., Lesgold, A. M., & Winzenz, D. (1969) Hierarchical retrieval schemes in recall of categorized word lists. *Journal of Verbal Learning and Verbal Behavior, 8*, 323–343.

Bower, G. H., & Trabasso, T. R. (1964) Concept identification. In R. C. Atkinson (Ed.), *Studies in Mathematical Psychology*. Stanford, Cal.: Stanford University Press.

Bransford, J. D. (1979) *Human Cognition: Learning, Understanding and Remembering*. Belmont, Cal.: Wadworth.

Bransford, J. D., Barclay, J. R., & Franks, J. J. (1972) Sentence memory: A constructive versus interpretive approach. *Cognitive Psychology, 3*, 193–209.

Bransford, J. D. & Franks, J. J. (1971) The abstraction of linguistic ideas. *Cognitive Psychology, 2*, 331–350.

Bransford, J. D., & Johnson, M. K. (1972) Contextual prerequisites for understanding: Some investigations of comprehension and recall. *Journal of Verbal Learning and Verbal Behavior, 11*, 717–726.

Bransford, J. D., & Johnson, M. K. (1973) Considerations of some problems of comprehension. In W. G. Chase (Ed.), *Visual Information Processing*. New York: Academic Press.

Brebner, J. (1977) The search for exceptions to the psychological refractory period. In S. Dornic (Ed.), *Attention and Performance, VI*. Hillsdale, N. J.: Lawrence Erlbaum Associates Inc.

Brewer, W. F., & Lichtenstein, E. H. (1981) Event schemas, story schemas, and story grammars. In J. Long & A. Baddeley (Eds.), *Attention and Performance IX*. Hillsdale, N.J.: Lawrence Erlbaum Associates Inc.

Broadbent, D. E. (1958) *Perception and Communication*. London: Pergamon.

Broadbent, D. E. (1971) *Decision and Stress*. London: Academic Press.

Broadbent, D. E. (1984) The Maltese Cross: A new simplistic model for memory. *Behavioral and Brain Sciences, 7*, 55–94.

Brooks, L. R. (1967) The suppression of visualization by reading. *Quarterly Journal of Experimental Psychology, 19*, 289–299.

Brooks, L. R. (1968) Spatial and verbal components of the act of recall. *Canadian Journal of Psychology, 22*, 349–368.

Brown, J. (1968) Reciprocal facilitation and impairment of face recall. *Psychonomic Science, 10*, 41–42.

Brown, R., & Kulik, J. (1977) Flashbulb memories. *Cognition, 5*, 73–99.

Brown, R., & McNeill, D. (1966) The "tip of the tongue" phenomenon. *Journal of Verbal Learning and Verbal Behavior, 5*, 325–337.

Bruce, V. (1983) Recognizing faces. *Philosophical Transactions of the Royal Society of London*, Series B, *302*, 423–436.

Bruce, V., & Green, P. (1985) *Visual Perception: Psychology, Physiology, Ecology*. London: Lawrence Erlbaum Associates Ltd.

Bruce, V., & Valentine, T. (1986) Semantic priming of familiar faces. *Quarterly Journal of Experimental Psychology, 38A*, 125–150.

Bruner, J. S., Goodnow, J. J., & Austin, G. A. (1956) *A Study of Thinking*. New York: Wiley.

Bryant, P. E., & Trabasso, T. R. (1971) Transitive inference and memory in young children. *Nature, 232*, 456–458.

Bugelski, B. R., & Alampay, D. A. (1962) The role of frequency in developing perceptual sets. *Canadian Journal of Psychology, 15*, 205–211.

Buswell, G. T. (1937) How adults read. *Supplementary Educational Monographs*, No. 45. Chicago: Chicago University Press.

Butterworth, B. (1975) Hesitation and semantic planning in speech. *Journal of Psycholinguistic Research, 4*, 75–87.

Butterworth, B. (1980a) Evidence from pauses. In B. Butterworth (Ed.), *Language Production*, Vol. 1. London: Academic Press.

Butterworth, B. (1980b) *Language Production*, Vol. 1. London: Academic Press.

Butterworth, B. (1983) *Language Production*, Vol. 2. London: Academic Press.

Byrne, R. (1979) Memory for urban geography. *Quarterly Journal of Experimental Psychology, 31*, 147–154.

Campbell, R., & Butterworth, B. (1985) Phonological dyslexia and dysgraphia: A developmental case with associated deficits of phonemic processing and awareness. *Quarterly Journal of Experimental Psychology, 37A*, 435–475.

Caplan, D. (1972) Clause boundaries and recognition latencies for words in sentences. *Perception and Psychophysics, 12*, 73–76.

Caramazza, A., & Zurif, E. B. (1976) Dissociation of algorithmic and heuristic processes in language comprehension: Evidence from aphasia. *Brain and Language, 3*, 572–582.

Carlton, L. G. (1981) Processing visual feedback information for movement control. *Journal of Experimental Psychology: Human Perception and Performance, 7*, 1019–1030.

Chase, W. G., & Simon, H. A. (1973a) Perception in chess. *Cognitive Psychology, 4*, 55–81.

Chase, W. G., & Simon, H. A. (1973b) The mind's eye in chess. In W. G. Chase (Ed.), *Visual Information Processing*. New York: Academic Press.

Cheng, P. W. (1985) Restructuring versus automaticity: alternative accounts of skill acquisition. *Psychological Review, 92*, 414–423.

Chernikoff, R., & Taylor, F. V. (1952) Reaction time to kinaesthetic stimulation resulting from sudden arm displacement. *Journal of Experimental Psychology, 43*, 1–8.

Cherry, E. C. (1953) Some experiments on the recognition of speech with one and two ears. *Journal of the Acoustical Society of America, 25*, 975–979.

Cherry, E. C., & Taylor, W. K. (1954) Some further experiments upon the recognition of speech with one, and with two ears. *Journal of the Acoustical Society of America, 26*, 554–559.

Chi, M. T. H., Feltovich, P. J., & Glaser, R. (1981) Categorisation and representation of physics problems by experts and novices. *Cognitive Science, 5*, 121–152.

Chi, M. T. H., Glaser, R., & Rees, E. (1982) Expertise in problem solving. In R. J. Sternberg (Ed.), *Advances in the Psychology of Human Intelligence*, Vol. 1. Hillsdale, N. J.: Lawrence Erlbaum Associates Inc.

Clark, H. H. (1969) Linguistic processes in deductive reasoning. *Psychological Review, 76*, 387–404.

Clarke, E. F. (1982) Timing in the performance of Erik Satie's "Vexations". *Acta Psychologica, 50*, 1–19.

Claxton, G. (Ed.) (1980) *Cognitive Psychology: New Directions*. London: RKP.

Cofer, C. N. (1951) Verbal behaviour in relation to reasoning and values. In H. Guetzkow (Ed.), *Group Leadership and Men*. Pittsburgh, Pa.: Carnegie Press.

Cohen, G. (1983) *The Psychology of Cognition* (2nd edn). London: Academic Press.

Cohen, G., & Freeman, R. (1978) Individual differences in reading strategies in relation to handedness and cerebral asymmetry. In J. Requin (Ed.), *Attention and Performance VII*. Hillsdale, N.J.: Lawrence Erlbaum Associates Inc.

Cohen, G., & Martin, M. (1975) Hemisphere differences in an auditory Stroop test. *Perception and Psychophysics*, *17*, 79–83.

Colegrove, F. W. (1899) Individual memories. *American Journal of Psychology*, *10*, 228–255.

Collins, A. M., & Loftus, E. F. (1975) A spreading activation theory of semantic processing. *Psychological Review*, *82*, 407–428.

Collins, A. M., & Quillian, M. R. (1969) Retrieval time from semantic memory. *Journal of Verbal Learning and Verbal Behaviour*, *8*, 240–247.

Coltheart, M. (1981) Disorders of reading and their implications for models of normal reading. *Visible Language*, *15*, 245–286.

Combs, B., & Slovic, P. (1979) Causes of death: Biased newspaper coverage and biased judgments. *Journalism Quarterly*, *56*, 837–843. (Cited in Slovic, Fischoff, & Lichtenstein, 1982.)

Conrad, R. (1964) Acoustic confusions in immediate memory. *British Journal of Psychology*, *55*, 75–84.

Conrad, R., & Hull, A. J. (1964) Information, acoustic confusion and memory span. *British Journal of Psychology*, *55*, 429–432.

Coombs, C. H. (1975) Portfolio theory and the measurement of risk. In M. F. Kaplan & S. Schwartz (Eds.), *Human Judgement and Decision Processes*. New York: Academic Press.

Cooper, A. J. R., & Monk, A. (1976) Learning for recall and learning for recognition. In J. Brown (Ed.), *Recall and Recognition*. London: Wiley.

Cotton, J. (1935) Normal "visual hearing". *Science*, *82*, 592–593.

Craik, F. I. M., & Lockhart, R. S. (1972) Levels of processing: a framework for memory research. *Journal of Verbal Learning and Verbal Behavior*, *11*, 671–684.

Craik, F. I. M., & Tulving, E. (1975) Depth of processing and the retention of words in episodic memory. *Journal of Experimental Psychology: General*, *104*, 268–294.

Craik, F. I. M., & Watkins, J. J. (1973) The role of rehearsal in short-term memory. *Journal of Verbal Learning and Verbal Behavior*, *12*, 599–607.

Craik, K. J. W. (1984) Theory of the human operator in control systems. II: Man as an element in a control system. *British Journal of Psychology*, *38*, 142–148.

Crain, S., & Steedman, M. J. (in press) On not being led up the garden path: The use of context by the psychological parser. In A. Zwicky, L. Kartunnen, & D. Dowty (Eds.), *Natural Language Parsing: Psycholinguistic, Theoretical and Computational Perspectives*. Cambridge: Cambridge University Press.

Crossman, E. R. F. W., & Goodeve, P. J. (1963) Feedback control of hand-movement and Fitts' Law. Published in *Quarterly Journal of Experimental Psychology*, 1983, *35A*, 251–278.

Cutler, A. (1982) *Slips of the Tongue*. The Hague: Mouton.

Davidson, D., Suppes, P., & Siegel, S. (1957) *Decision-Making: An Experimental Approach*. Stanford, Cal.: Stanford University Press.

Davies, G., Ellis, H. D., & Shepherd, J. W. (1981) *Perceiving and Remembering Faces*. London: Academic Press.

Davis, R. (1956) The limits of the "psychological refractory period". *Quarterly Journal of Experimental Psychology*, *9*, 119–129.

Deese, J. (1980) *Thought into Speech*. Englewood Cliffs, N.J.: Prentice-Hall.

De Renzi, E., & Nichelli, P. (1975) Verbal and non-verbal short-term memory impairment following hemispheric damage. *Cortex*, *11*, 341–354.

Deutsch, J. A., & Deutsch, D. (1963) Attention: some theoretical considerations. *Psychological Review*, *70*, 80–90.

Devlin, A. S. (1976) The small town cognitive map: adjusting to a new environment. In G. T. Moore & R. G. Golledge (Eds.), *Environmental Knowing*. Strowdsberg, Pa: Dowden, Hutchinson & Ross.

Disessa, A. A. (1983) Phenomenology and the evolution of intuition. In D. Gentner & A. L. Stevens, *Mental Models*. Hillsdale N.J.: Lawrence Erlbaum Associates Inc.

Dodd, B., & Campbell, R. (1986) *Hearing by Eye: The Psychology of Lip Reading*. London: Lawrence Erlbaum Associates Ltd.

Dodge, R. (1900) Visual perception during eye movement. *Psychological Review*, *7*, 454–465.

Donaldson, M. (1978) *Children's Minds*. Glasgow: Fontana.

Duncan, J. (1980) The demonstration of capacity limitation. *Cognitive Psychology*, *12*, 75–96.

Duncker, K. (1945) On problem solving. *Psychological Monographs*, *58*:5, Whole No. 270.

Ebbinghaus, H. (1885) *Uber das Gedachtris*. Leipzig: Dunker. (Trans. H. Ruyer & C. E. Bussenius, *Memory*. New York: Teachers College Press, 1913.)

Eddy, D. M. (1982) Probabilisitic reasoning in clinical medicine: Problems and opportunities. In D. Kahneman, P. Slovic, & A. Tversky (Eds.), *Judgement Under Uncertainty: Heuristics and Biases*. Cambridge: Cambridge University Press.

Edwards, W. (1956) The theory of decision making. *Psychological Bulletin*, *51*, 380–417.

Edwards, W. & Tversky, A. (Eds.) (1967) *Decision Making*. Harmondsworth, Middlesex: Penguin Books Ltd.

Ehrlich, S. F., & Rayner, K. (1981) Contextual effects on word perception and eye movements during reading. *Journal of Verbal Learning and Verbal Behaviour*, *20*, 641–655.

Eich, J. E. (1980) The cue-dependent nature of state-dependent retrieval. *Memory and Cognition*, *8*, 157–173.

Elliott, D., & Allard, F. (1985) The utilization of visual feedback information during rapid pointing movements. *Quarterly Journal of Experimental Psychology*, *37*, 407–425.

Ellis, A. W. (1979) Speech production and short-term memory. In J. Morton & J. C. Marshall (Eds.), *Psycholinguistics Series*, Vol. 2. London: Elek, and Cambridge, Mass.: MIT Press.

Ellis, A. W. (1984) *Reading, Writing and Dyslexia: A Cognitive Analysis*. London: Lawrence Erlbaum Associates Ltd.

Ellis, A. W. (1985a) The cognitive neuropsychology of developmental (and acquired) dyslexia: a critical survey. *Cognitive Neuropsychology*, *2*, 169–205.

Ellis, A. W. (1985b) The production of spoken words: A cognitive neuropsychological perspective. In A. W. Ellis (Ed.), *Progress in the Psychology of Language*, Vol. 2. London: Lawrence Erlbaum Associates Ltd.

Ellis, A. W., & Beattie, G. (1986) *The Psychology of Language and Communication*. London: Weidenfeld & Nicolson; and New York: The Guildford Press.

Ellis, A. W., Miller, D., & Sin, G. (1983) Wernicke's aphasia and normal language processing: A case study in cognitive neuropsychology. *Cognition*, *15*, 111–144.

· Ellis, A. W., & Young, A. W. (in press) *Human Cognitive Neuropsychology*. London: Lawrence Erlbaum Associates Ltd.

Ellis, H. D. (1975) Recognising faces. *British Journal of Psychology*, *66*, 409–426.

Ellis, H. D., Jeeves, M. A., Newcombe, F., & Young, A. W. (1986), *Aspects of face processing*, Dortrecht: Martinus Nijhoff.

Ellis, H. D., Shepherd, J. W., & Davies, G. M. (1979) Identification of familiar and unfamiliar faces from internal and external features: Some implications for theories of face recognition. *Perception*, *8*, 431–439.

Ellis, N. C., & Hennelly, R. A. (1980) A bilingual word-length effect: Implications for intelligence testing and the relative ease of mental calculations in Welsh and English. *British Journal of Psychology*, *71*, 43–52.

Elstein, A. S., Shulman, L. S., & Sprafka, S. A. (1978) *Medical Problem Solving: An Analysis of Clinical Reasoning*. Cambridge, Mass.: Harvard University Press.

Ericsson, K. A., Chase, W. G., & Faloon, S. (1980) Acquisition of a memory skill. *Science*, *208*, 1181–1182.

Ernst, G. W., & Newell, A. (1969) *GPS: A Case Study in Generality and Problem Solving*. New York: Academic Press.

Evans, G. W., Marrero, D. G., & Butler, P. A. (1981) Environmental learning and cognitive mapping. *Environment and Behaviour*, *13*, 83–104.

Evett, L. J., & Humphreys, G. W. (1981) The use of abstract graphemic information in lexical access. *Quarterly Journal of Experimental Psychology*, *33A*, 325–350.

Eysenck, M. W. (1979) Depth, elaboration and distinctiveness. In L. S. Cermack & F. I. M. Craik (Eds.), *Levels of Processing in Human Memory*. Hillsdale, N. J.: Lawrence Erlbaum Associates Inc.

Eysenck, M. W. (1984) *A Handbook of Cognitive Psychology*. London: Lawrence Erlbaum Associates Ltd.

Fildes, B. N., O'Loughlin, B. J., Bradshaw, J. L., & Evans, W. J. (1984) Human orientation with restricted sensory information: No evidence for magnetic sensitivity. *Perception*, **13**, 227–364.

Finke, R. A., & Kosslyn, S. M. (1980) Mental imagery circuitry in the peripheral visual field. *Journal of Experimental Psychology: Human Perception and Performance*, *6*, 126–139.

Fischler, I., & Bloom, P. A. (1979) Automatic and attentional processes in the effects of sentence contexts on word recognition. *Journal of Verbal Learning and Verbal Behavior*, *18*, 1–20.

Fischoff, B., Slovic, P., & Lichtenstein, S. (1978) Fault trees: Sensitivity of estimated failure probabilities to problem representation. *Journal of Experimental Psychology: Human Perception and Performance*, *4*, 330–334.

Fitts, P. M. (1954) The information capacity of the human motor system in controlling the amplitude of movement. *Journal of Experimental Psychology*, *47*, 381–391.

Fodor, J. A. (1983) *The Modularity of Mind*. Cambridge, Mass.: M.I.T. Press.

Folkins, J. W., & Abbs, J. H. (1975) Lip and jaw motor control during speech responses to resistive loading of the jaw. *Journal of Speech and Hearing Research*, *18*, 207–220.

Ford, M., & Holmes, V. (1978) Planning units and syntax in sentence production. *Cognition*, *6*, 35–53.

Forster, K. I. (1981) Priming and effects of sentence and lexical contexts on naming time: Evidence of autonomous lexical processing. *Quarterly Journal of Experimental Psychology*, *33A*, 465–495.

Fredericksen, J. R. (1981) Understanding anaphora: Rules used by readers in assigning pronomial referent. *Discourse Processes*, *4*, 323–347.

Frick, R. W. (1984) Using both an auditory and a visual short term store to increase digit span. *Memory and Cognition*, *12*, 507–514.

Frisby, J. P. (1979) *Seeing: Mind, Brain and Illusion*. London: Oxford University Press.

Fromkin, V. A. (Ed.) (1973) *Speech Errors as Linguistic Evidence*. The Hague: Mouton.

Fromkin, V. A. (Ed.) (1980) *Errors in Linguistic Performance: Slips of the Tongue, Ear, Pen and Hand*. New York: Academic Press.

Funnell, E. (1983) Phonological processes in reading: New evidence from acquired dyslexia. *British Journal of Psychology*, *74*, 159–180.

Garling, T., Book, A., & Lindberg, E. (1984) Cognitive mapping of large scale environments. *Environment and Behaviour*, *16*, 3–34.

Garnham, A. (1985) *Psycholinguistics: Central Topics*. London: Methuen.

Garrett, M. F. (1975) The analysis of sentence production. In G. H. Bower (Ed.), *The Psychology of Learning and Motivation*, Vol. 9. New York: Academic Press.

Garrett, M. F. (1976) Syntactic processes in sentence production. In R. Wales & E. Walker (Eds.), *New Approaches to Language Mechanisms*. Amsterdam: North Holland.

Garrett, M. F. (1980) Levels of processing in sentence production. In B. Butterworth (Ed.), *Language Production*, Vol. 1: *Speech and Talk*. London: Academic Press.

Garrett, M. F. (1982) Production of speech: Observations from normal and pathological language use. In A. W. Ellis (Ed.), *Normality and Pathology in Cognitive Functions*. London: Academic Press.

Garrett, M. F. (1984) The organization of processing structure for language production: Applications to aphasic speech. In D. Caplan, A. R. Lecours, & A. Smith (Eds.), *Biological Perspectives on Language*. Cambridge, Mass.: MIT Press.

Gentner, D. & Gentner, D. R. (1983) Flowing waters or teeming crowds. In D. Gentner & A. L. Stevens (Eds.), *Mental Models*. Hillsdale, N.J.: Lawrence Erlbaum Associates Inc.

Gentner, D., & Stevens, A. L. (Eds.) (1983) *Mental Models*. Hillsdale, N.J.: Lawrence Erlbaum Associates Inc.

Gentner, D. R. (1983) Keystroke timing in transcription typing. In W. E. Cooper (Ed.), *Cognitive Aspects of Skilled Typewriting*. New York: Springer Verlag.

Gentner, D. R., Grudin, J., & Conway, E. (1980) *Finger movements in transcription typing*. (Tech. Rep. 8001) La Jolla Cal. University of California at San Diego, Center for Human Information Processing.

Gibson, J. J. (1966) *The Senses Considered as Perceptual Systems*. Boston, Mass.: Houghton Mifflin.

Gibson, J. J. (1979) *The Ecological Approach to Visual Perception*. Boston, Mass.: Houghton Mifflin.

Gladwin, T. (1970) *East is a Big Bird*. Cambridge, Mass.: Harvard University Press.

Godden, D. R., & Baddeley, A. D. (1975) Context dependent memory in two natural environments: on land and underwater. *British Journal of Psychology*, 66, 325–332.

Goldman-Eisler, F. (1968) *Psycholinguistics: Experiments in Spontaneous Speech*. London: Academic Press.

Gomulicki, B. R. (1956) Recall as an abstractive process. *Acta Psychologica*, 12, 77–94.

Goodman, D., & Kelso, J. A. S. (1980) Are movements prepared in parts? Not under compatible (naturalised) conditions. *Journal of Experimental Psychology*, 109, 475–495.

Gough, P. B., Alford, J. A. Jr., & Holley-Wilcox, P. (1981) Words and contexts. In O. J. L. Tzeng & H. Singer (Eds.), *Perception of a Print: Reading Research in Experimental Psychology*. Hillsdale, N.J.: Lawrence Erlbaum Associates Inc.

Greenspoon, J., & Ranyard, R. (1957) Stimulus conditions and retroactive inhibition. *Journal of Experimental Psychology*, 53, 55–59.

Greenwald, A. G., & Shulman, H. G. (1973) On doing two things at once. II: Elimination of the psychological refractory period. *Journal of Experimental Psychology*, 101, 70–76.

Griggs, R. A., & Cox, J. R. (1982) The elusive thematic materials effect in Wason's selection task. *British Journal of Psychology*, 73, 407–420.

Groff, P. (1975) Shapes as cues to word recognition. *Visible Language*, 9, 67–71.

de Groot, A. D. (1965) *Thought and Choice in Chess*. The Hague: Mouton.

de Groot, A. D. (1966) Perception and memory versus thought: Some old ideas and recent findings. In B. Kleinmuntz (Ed.), *Problem Solving: Research, Method and Theory*. New York: Wiley.

Grudin, J. T. (1983) Error patterns in novice and skilled transcription typing. In W. E. Cooper (Ed.), *Cognitive Aspects of Skilled Typewriting*. New York: Springer Verlag.

Gruneberg, M. M., & Morris, P. E. (1978) *Aspects of Memory*. London: Methuen.

Guenther, R. K., Klatzky, R. L., & Putnam, W. (1980) Commonalities and differences in semantic decisions about pictures and words. *Journal of Verbal Learning and Verbal Behavior*, *19*, 54–74.

Gunkel, M. (1962) Uber relative Koordination bei willkurlichen menschlichen Gliederbewegungen. *Pflugers Archiv fur gesamte Physiologie*, *275*, 472–477.

Haberlandt, K., & Bingham, G. (1978) Verbs contribute to the coherence of brief narrative passages: Reading related and unrelated sentence triplets. *Journal of Verbal Learning and Verbal Behavior*, *17*, 419–425.

Hampton, J. A. (1979) Polymorphous concepts in semantic memory. *Journal of Verbal Learning and Verbal Behavior*, *18*, 441–461.

Haviland, S. E., & Clark, H. H. (1974) What's new? Acquiring new information as a process in comprehension. *Journal of Verbal Learning and Verbal Behavior*, *13*, 512–521.

Hay, D. C., & Young, A. W. (1982) The human face. In A. W. Ellis (Ed.), *Normality and Pathology in Cognitive Functions*. London: Academic Press.

Hayes, J. R. (1973) On the function of visual imagery in elementary mathematics. In W. G. Chase (Ed.), *Visual Information Processing*. New York: Academic Press.

Hayes-Roth, B., & Hayes-Roth, F. (1977) Concept learning and the recognition and classification of exemplars. *Journal of Verbal Learning and Verbal Behavior*, *16*, 321–338.

Hécaen, H. (1981) The neuropsychology of face recognition. In G. Davies, H. Ellis, & J. Shepherd (Eds.), *Perceiving and Remembering Faces*. London: Academic Press.

Heidbreder, E. (1946) The attainment of concepts. 1: Terminology and methodology. *Journal of General Psychology*, *35*, 173–189.

Henderson, L. (1982) *Orthography and Word Recognition in Reading*. London: Academic Press.

Henderson, L. (1985) The psychology of morphemes. In A. W. Ellis (Ed.), *Progress in the Psychology of Language*, Vol. 1. London: Lawrence Erlbaum Associates Ltd.

Henderson, S. E. (1975) Predicting the accuracy of a throw without usual feedback. *Journal of Human Movement Studies*, *1*, 183–189.

Henle, M. (1962) On the relationship between logic and thinking. *Psychological Review*, *69*, 366–378.

Henry, F. M., & Rogers, D. E. (1960) Increased response latency for complicated movements and a "memory drum" theory of neuromotor reaction. *Research Quarterly*, *31*, 448–458.

Hick, W. E. (1948) The discontinuous functioning of the human operator in pursuit tasks. *Quarterly Journal of Experimental Psychology*, *1*, 36–51.

Hinton, G. (1984) Parallel computations for controlling an arm. *Journal of Motor Behaviour*, *16*, 171–194.

Hirst, W., Spelke, E. S., Reaves, C. C., Caharack, G., & Neisser, U. (1980) Dividing attention without alternation or automaticity. *Journal of Experimental Psychology: General*, *109*, 98–117.

Hitch, G. J. (1978) The role of short-term working memory in mental arithmetic. *Cognitive Psychology*, *10*, 302–323.

Hitch, G. (1980) Developing the concept of working memory. In G. Claxton (Ed.), *Cognitive Psychology: New Directions*. London: Routledge & Kegan Paul.

Hoffman, J. E., Nelson, B., & Houek, M. R. (1983) The role of attentional resources in automatic detection. *Cognitive Psychology*, *15*, 379–410.

Holt, E. B. (1903) Eye-movement and central anaesthesia. I. The problem of anaesthesia during eye-movement. *Psychological Review Monographs*, *4*, 3–45.

Howard, I. P., & Templeton, W. B. (1966) *Human Spatial Orientation*. London: Wiley.

Huey, E. B. (1908) *The Psychology and Pedagogy of Reading* (reprinted 1968). Cambridge, Mass.: MIT Press.

Hull, C. L. (1920) Quantitative aspects of the evolution of concepts. *Psychological Monographs*, *28*, No. 123.

Hunter, I. M. L. (1962) An exceptional talent for calculative thinking. *British Journal of Psychology*, *53*, 243–258.

Hunter, I. M. L. (1977) An exceptional memory. *British Journal of Psychology*, *68*, 155–164.

Hunter, I. M. L. (1978) The role of memory in expert mental calculations. In M. M. Gruneberg, P. E. Morris & R. N. Sykes (Eds.), *Practical Aspects of Memory*. London: Academic Press.

Hunter, I. M. L. (1979) Memory in everyday life. In M. M. Gruneberg & P. E. Morris (Eds.), *Applied Problems in Memory*. London: Academic Press.

Hunter, I. M. L. (1985) Lengthy verbatim recall: The role of text. In A. W. Ellis (Ed.), *Progress in the Psychology of Language*, Vol. 1. London: Lawrence Erlbaum Associates Ltd.

Hutchins, E., & Hinton, G E. (1984) Why the islands move. *Perception*, *13*, 629–632.

Ibbotson, N. R., & Morton, J. (1981) Rhythm and dominance. *Cognition*, *9*, 125–138.

Inhoff, A. W., Rosenbaum, D. A., Gordon, A. M., & Campbell, J. A. (1984) Stimulus-response compatibility and motor programming of manual response sequences. *Journal of Experimental Psychology: Human Perception and Performance*, *10*, 724–733.

Jacobs, J. (1887) Experiments on "Prehension". *Mind*, *12*, 75–79.

James, W. (1890) *The Principles of Psychology*. New York: Holt.

Jarvella, R. J. (1970) Effects of syntax on running memory span for connected discourse. *Psychonomic Sequence*, *19*, 235–236.

Jarvella, R. J. (1971) Syntactic processing of connected speech. *Journal of Verbal Learning and Verbal Behavior*, *10*, 409–416.

Jeannerod, M. (1984) The timing of natural prehension movements. *Journal of Motor Behaviour*, *16*, 235–254.

Jeannerod, M., Michel, F., & Prablanc, C. (1984) The control of hand movements in a case of hemianaesthesia following a parietal lesion. *Brain*, *107*, 899–920.

Jenkins, J. J., Wald, J., & Pittenger, J. B. (1978) Apprehending pictorial events: An instance of psychological cohesion. In C. W. Savage (Ed.), *Minnesota Studies in the Philosophy of Science*, Vol. 9. Mineapolis: University of Minnesota Press.

Johnson-Laird, P. N. (1983) *Mental Models*. Cambridge: Cambridge University Press.

Johnson-Laird, P. N., & Bara, B. (1982) The figural effect in syllogistic reasoning. Mimeo cited in Johnson-Laird (1983).

Johnson-Laird, P. N., Gibbs, G., & de Mowbray, J. (1978) Meaning, amount of processing and memory for words. *Memory and Cognition*, *6*, 372–375.

Johnson-Laird, P. N., & Wason, P. C. (Eds.) (1977) *Thinking: Readings in Cognitive Science*. Cambridge: Cambridge University Press.

Jonides, J., Naveh-Benjamin, M., & Palmer, J. (1985) Assessing automaticity. *Acta Psychologica*, *60*, 157–171.

Julesz, B. (1971) *Foundations of Cyclopean Perception*. Chicago: University of Chicago Press.

Kahneman, D. (1973) *Attention and Effort*. Englewood Cliffs. N.J.: Prentice-Hall.

Kahneman, D., & Tversky, A. (1973) On the psychology of prediction. *Psychological Review*, *80*, 237–251.

Kahneman, D., & Tversky, A. (1979) Prospect theory: An analysis of decision under risk. *Econometrica*, *47*, 263–291.

Kahneman, D., & Tversky, A. (1982a) Subjective probability: A judgement of representativeness. In D. Kahneman, P. Slovic, & A. Tversky (Eds.). *Judgement Under Uncertainty: Heuristics and Biases*. Cambridge: Cambridge University Press.

Kahneman, D., & Tversky, A. (1982b) Variants of uncertainty. In D. Kahneman, P. Slovic, & A. Tversky (Eds.), *Judgement Under Uncertainty: Heuristics and Biases*. Cambridge: Cambridge University Press.

Kahneman, D., Slovic, P., & Tversky, A. (Eds.) (1982) *Judgement Under Uncertainty: Heuristics and Biases*. Cambridge: Cambridge University Press.

Keele, S. W. & Posner, M. I. (1968) Processing visual feedback in rapid movements. *Journal of Experimental Psychology*, 77, 155–158.

Keenan, J. M., & Moore, R. E. (1979) Memory for images of concealed objects: a re-examination of Neisser and Kern. *Journal of Experimental Psychology: Human Learning and Memory*, 5, 374–385.

Kelso, J. A. S. (Ed.) (1982) *Human Motor Behavior*. Hillsdale, N.J.: Lawrence Erlbaum Associates Inc.

Kelso, J. A. S., Southard, D. L., & Goodman, D. (1979) On the coordination of two handed movements. *Journal of Experimental Psychology: Human Perception and Performance*, 5, 229–238.

Kintsch, W. (1974) *The Representation of Meaning in Memory*. Hillsdale, N.J.: Lawrence Erlbaum Associates Inc.

Kintsch, W., & Bates, E. (1977) Recognition memory for statements from a classroom lecture. *Journal of Experimental Psychology: Human Learning and Memory*, 3, 150–159.

Kirasic, K. C., Allen, G. L., & Siegel, A. W. (1984) Expression of configurational knowledge of large scale environments. *Environment and Behaviour*, 16, 687–712.

Klapp, S. T. (1979) Doing two things at once: the role of temporal compatibility. *Memory and Cognition*, 5, 375–381.

Klapp, S. T., & Wyatt, E. P. (1976) Motor programming within a sequence of responses. *Journal of Motor Behaviour*, 8, 19–26.

Kosslyn, S. M. (1980) *Image and Mind*. Cambridge, Mass.: Harvard University Press.

Kosslyn, S. M. (1981) The medium and the message in mental imagery: a theory. *Psychological Review*, 88, 46–66.

Kosslyn, S. M., & Pomerantz, J. R. (1979) Imagery, propositions and the form of internal representations. *Cognitive Psychology*, 9, 52–76.

Kosslyn, S. M., & Schwartz, S. P. (1981) Empirical constraints on theories of visual mental imagery. In J. Long & A. Baddeley (Eds.), *Attention and Performance IX*, Hillsdale, N.J.: Lawrence Erlbaum Associates Inc.

Kosslyn, S. M., Pick, H., & Fariello, G. (1974) Cognitive maps in children and men. *Child Development*, 45, 707–716.

Kozlowski, L., & Bryant, K. (1977) Sense of direction, spatial orientation, and cognitive maps. *Journal of Experimental Psychology: Human Perception and Performance*, 3, 590–598.

Kroll, N. E. A., Kellicut, M. H., & Parks, T. E. (1975) Rehearsal of visual and auditory stimuli while shadowing. *Journal of Experimental Psychology: Human Learning and Memory*, 4, 215–222.

Lackner, J. R., & Garrett, M. F. (1972) Resolving ambiguity: Effects of biasing context in the unattended ear. *Cognition*, 1, 359–372.

Lakoff, G., & Johnson, M. (1981) The metaphorical structure. In D. A. Norman (Ed.), *Perspectives on Cognitive Science*. Hillsdale, N.J.: Lawrence Erlbaum Associates Inc.

Larish, D. D., & Frekany, G. A. (1985) Planning and preparing expected and unexpected movements: Re-examining the relationship of arm, direction and extent of movement. *Journal of Motor Behaviour*, 17, 168–189.

Lashley, K. S. (1951) The problem of serial order in behaviour. In L. A. Jeffress (Ed.), *Cerebral Mechanisms in Behaviour*. New York: Wiley.

Latour, P. L. (1962) Visual threshold during eye movements. *Vision Research*, 2, 261–262.

Lee, D. N., Lishman, J. R., & Thomson, J. A. (1982) Regulation of gait in long jumping. *Journal of Experimental Psychology: Human Perception and Performance*, 8, 448–459.

Legge, D., & Barber, P. (1976) *Information and Skill*. London: Methuen.

Leonard, J. A. (1959) Tactual choice reactions. *Quarterly Journal of Experimental Psychology*, 11, 76–83.

Levine, M. (1966) Hypothesis behavior by humans during discrimination learning. *Journal of Experimental Psychology*, 71, 331–338.

Lewis, J. L. (1970) Semantic processing of unattended messages using dichotic listening. *Journal of Experimental Psychology*, 85, 225–228.

Lichtenstein, E. H., & Brewer, W. F. (1980) Memory for goal-directed events. *Cognitive Psychology*, 12, 412–445.

Lichtenstein, S., Slovic, P., & Zink, D. (1969) Effect of instruction in expected value on optimality of gambling decisions. *Journal of Experimental Psychology*, 79, 236–240.

Lieberman, P. (1963) Some effects of semantic and grammatical context on the production and perception of speech. *Language and Speech*, 6, 172–187.

Lindsay, P. H., & Norman, D. A. (1977) *Human Information Processing* (2nd edn). New York: Academic Press.

Linton, M. (1975) Memory for real-world events. In D. A. Norman & D. E. Rumelhart (Eds.), *Explorations in Cognition*. San Francisco: W. H. Freeman & Co.

Linton, M. (1982) Transformations of memory in everyday life. In U. Neisser (Ed.), *Memory Observed*. San Francisco: W. H. Freeman & Co.

Loftus, E. F. (1979) *Eyewitness Testimony*. Cambridge, Mass.: Harvard University Press.

Loftus, E. F. (1981) Mentalmorphosis: Alterations in memory produced by the mental bonding of new information to old. In J. Long & A. Baddeley (Eds.), *Attention and Performance IX*. Hillsdale, N.J.: Lawrence Erlbaum Associates Inc.

Loftus, E. F. (1983) Misfortunes of memory. *Philosophical Transactions of the Royal Society of London* (Series B), 302, 413–421.

Loftus, E. F., & Loftus, G. R. (1980) On the permanence of stored information in the human brain. *American Psychologist*, 35, 409–420.

Loftus, E. F., Manber, M., & Keating, J. P. (1983) Recollection of naturalistic events: Context enhancement versus negative cueing. *Human Learning*, 2, 83–92.

Loftus, E. F., Miller, D. G., & Burns, H. J. (1978) Semantic integration of verbal information into a visual memory. *Journal of Experimental Psychology: Human Learning and Memory*, 4, 19–31.

Loftus, E. F., & Palmer, J. C. (1974) Reconstruction of automobile destruction: An example of the interaction between language and memory. *Journal of Verbal Learning and Verbal Behavior*, 13, 585–589.

McClelland, J. L. (1976) Preliminary letter identification in the perception of words and nonwords. *Journal of Experimental Psychology: Human Perception and Performance*, 2, 80–91.

McClelland, J. L., & Rumelhart, D. E. (1981) An interactive activation model of context effects in letter perception. Part 1. An account of basic findings. *Psychological Review*, 88, 375–407.

McConkie, G. W. (1983) Eye movements and perception during reading. In K. Rayner (Ed.), *Eye Movements in Reading: Perceptual and Language Processes*. New York: Academic Press.

McConkie, G. W., & Zola, D. (1979) Is visual information integrated across successive fixations in reading? *Perception and Psychophysics*, 25, 221–224.

McDermott, J., & Larkin, J. H. (1978) Re-representing textbook physics problems. *Proceedings of the 2nd National Conference, Canadian Society for Computational Studies of Intelligence*. Toronto: University of Toronto Press. Cited in Chi, Glaser and Rees (1982).

McGeoch, J. A., & MacDonald, W. T. (1931) Meaningful relation and retroactive inhibition. *American Journal of Psychology*, *43*, 579–588.

McGurk, H., & MacDonald, J. (1976) Hearing lips and seeing voices. *Nature*, *264*, 746–748.

McLeod, P. D. (1977) A dual-task response modality effect: support for multiprocessor models of attention. *Quarterly Journal of Experimental Psychology*, *29*, 651–667.

McLeod, P. (1978) Does probe RT measure control processing demand? *Quarterly Journal of Experimental Psychology*, *30*, 83–89.

McLeod, P., & Posner, M. I. (1984) Privileged loops from percept to act. In H. Bouma & D. G. Bouwhuis (Eds.), *Attention and Performance X*. Hillsdale, N.J.: Lawrence Erlbaum Associates Inc.

MacKay, D. G. (1973) Aspects of the theory of comprehension, memory and attention. *Quarterly Journal of Experimental Psychology*, *25*, 22–40.

MacNeilage, P.F. (1970) Motor control of serial ordering of speech. *Psychological Review*, *77*, 182–196.

MacNeilage, P. F. (1980) Speech production. *Language and Speech*, *23*, 3–23.

Maier, N. R. F. (1930) Reasoning in humans. I: On direction. *Journal of Comparative Psychology*, *10*, 115–143.

Maier, N. R. F. (1931) Reasoning in humans. II: The solution of a problem and its appearance in consciousness. *Journal of Comparative Psychology*, *12*, 181–194.

Maier, N. R. F. (1945) Reasoning in humans. III: The mechanisms of equivalent stimuli and of reasoning. *Journal of Experimental Psychology*, *35*, 349–360.

Malpass, R. S. & Devine, P. G. (1981) Guided memory in eyewitness identification. *Journal of Applied Psychology*, *66*, 343–350.

Marcel, A. F. (1983a) Conscious and unconscious perception: Experiments on visual masking and word recognition. *Cognitive Psychology*, *15*, 197–237.

Marcel, A. J. (1983b) Conscious and unconscious perception: An approach to the relations between phenomenal experience and perceptual processes. *Cognitive Psychology*, *15*, 238–300.

Margrain, S. A. (1967) Short-term memory as a function of input modality. *Quarterly Journal of Experimental Psychology*, *25*, 368–377.

Marslen-Wilson, W. D. (1980) Speech understanding as a psychological process. In J. C. Simon (Ed.), *Spoken Language Generation and Understanding*. Dortrecht: D. Reidel.

Marslen-Wilson, W. D. (1984) Function and process in spoken word recognition—A tutorial review. In H. Bouma & D. G. Bouwhuis (Eds.), *Attention and Performance X*. London: Lawrence Erlbaum Associates Ltd.

Marslen-Wilson, W. D. & Tyler, L. K. (1980) The temporal structure of spoken language understanding. *Cognition*, *8*, 1–71.

Marslen-Wilson, W. D. & Welsh, A. (1978) Processing interactions and lexical access during word recognition in continuous speech. *Cognitive Psychology*, *10*, 29–63.

Mayer, R. E. (1983) *Thinking, Problem Solving and Cognition*. New York: W. H. Freeman & Co.

Medin, D. L. & Smith, E. E. (1982) Concepts and concept formation. *Annual Review of Psychology*, *16*, 125–167.

Melton, A. W. & Irwin, J. M. (1940) The influence of degree of interpolated learning on retroactive inhibition and the overt transfer of specific responses. *American Journal of Psychology*, *53*, 173–203.

Mervis, C. B. & Crisafi, M. A. (1982) Order of acquisition of subordinate-, basic- and superordinate-level categories. *Child Development*, *53*, 258–266.

Metzler, J. & Shepard, R. N. (1974) Transformational studies of the internal representation of three dimensional objects. In R. L. Solso (Ed.) *Theories of Cognitive Psychology: The Loyola Symposium*. Hillsdale, N.J.: Lawrence Erlbaum Associates Inc.

Meyer, D. E. & Schvaneveldt, R. W. (1971) Facilitation in recognizing pairs of words: Evidence of a dependence between retrieval operations. *Journal of Experimental Psychology*, *90*, 227–234.

Meyer, D. E., Smith, J. E. K., & Wright, C. E. (1982) Models for the speed and accuracy of aimed limb movements. *Psychological Review*, *89*, 449–482.

Miller, G. A. (1956) The magic number seven, plus or minus two: Some limits on our capacity for processing information. *Psychological Review*, *63*, 81–97.

Miller, G. A., Galanter, E., & Pribram, K. H. (1960) *Plans and the Structure of Behavior*. New York: Holt, Rinehart & Winston.

Miller, G. A., Heise, G. A., & Lichten, W. (1951) The intelligibility of speech as a function of the context of the test materials. *Journal of Experimental Psychology*, *41*, 329–335.

Milner, B. (1970) Memory and the medial temporal regions of the brain. In K. H. Pribram & D. E. Broadbent (Eds.), *Biology of Memory*. New York: Academic Press.

Minsky, M. (1975) A framework for representing knowledge. In P. H. Winston (Ed.), *The Psychology of Computer Vision*. New York: McGraw-Hill.

Mitchell, D. C. (1982) *The Process of Reading*. Chichester, Sussex: J. Wiley.

Moar, I. (1979) *The internal geometry of cognitive maps*. Unpublished doctoral dissertation. Cambridge University.

Moar, I. & Carleton, L. R. (1982) Memory for routes. *Quarterly Journal of Experimental Psychology*, *34*, 381–394.

Monsell, S. (1984) Components of working memory underlying verbal skills: A "distributed capacities" view. In H. Bouma & D. G. Bouwhuis (Eds.), *Attention and Performance X*. London: Lawrence Erlbaum Associates Ltd.

Morris, P. E. (1979) Strategies for learning and recall. In M. M. Gruneberg and P. E. Morris (Eds.), *Applied Problems in Memory*. London: Academic Press.

Morris, P. E. (in press) Memory images. In D. G. Russell & D. F. Marks (Eds.), *Proceedings of the Second International Imagery Conference*.

Morris, P. E., Gruneberg, M. M., Sykes, R. N., & Merrick, A. (1981) Football knowledge and the acquisition of new results. *British Journal of Psychology*, *72*, 479–483.

Morris, P. E. & Hampson, P. J. (1983) *Imagery and Consciousness*. London: Academic Press.

Morris, P. E., Tweedy, M., & Gruneberg, M. M. (1985) Interest, knowledge and the memorizing of soccer scores. *British Journal of Psychology*, *76*, 417–425.

Morris, V., & Morris, P. E. (1985) The influence of question order on eyewitness accuracy. *British Journal of Psychology*, *76*, 365–371.

Morton, J. (1964) The effect of context on the visual duration threshold for words. *British Journal of Psychology*, *55*, 165–180.

Morton, J. (1967) A singular lack of incidental learning. *Nature*, *215*, 203–204.

Morton, J. (1969) Interaction of information in word recognition. *Psychological Review*, *76*, 165–178.

Morton, J. (1970) A functional model for memory. In D. A. Norman (Ed.), *Models of Human Memory*. New York: Academic Press.

Morton, J. (1979) Word recognition. In J. Morton & J. C. Marshall (Eds.), *Psycholinguistics Series*, Vol. 2. London: Elek Science, and Cambridge, Mass.: MIT Press.

Murdock, B. B. Jr. (1962) The serial position effect in free recall. *Journal of Experimental Psychology*, *64*, 482–488.

Murdock, B. B. Jr., & Walker, K. D. (1969) Modality effects in free recall. *Journal of Verbal Learning and Verbal Behavior*, *8*, 665–676.

Navon, D. (1978) The importance of being conservative: Some reflections on human Bayesian behaviour. *British Journal of Mathematical and Statistical Psychology*, *31*, 33–48.

Navon, D. (1984) Resources—A theoretical soup stone? *Psychological Review*, *91*, 216–234.

Neisser, U. (1976) *Cognition and Reality*. San Francisco: W. H. Freeman & Co.

Neisser, U. (1982) *Memory Observed*. San Francisco: W. H. Freeman & Co.

Nelson, T. O. (1977) Repetition and depth of processing. *Journal of Verbal Learning and Verbal Behavior*, *16*, 151–171.

Neumann, P. G. (1977) Visual prototype formation with discontinuous representation of dimensions of variability. *Memory and Cognition*, *5*, 187–197.

Newell, A., & Simon, H. A. (1972) *Human Problem Solving*. Englewood Cliffs, N.J.: Prentice-Hall.

Newport, E. L., & Bellugi, U. (1978) Linguistic expression of category levels in a visual-gestural language: A flower is a flower is a flower. In E. Rosch & B. B. Lloyd (Eds.), *Cognition and Categorization*. Hillsdale, N.J.: Lawrence Erlbaum Associates Inc.

Nickerson, R. S., & Adams, M. J. (1979) Long-term memory for a common object. *Cognitive Psychology*, *11*, 287–307.

Norman, D. A. (1981) Categorisation of action slips. *Psychological Review*, *88*, 1–15.

Norman, D. A., & Rumelhart, D. E. (1975) *Explorations in Cognition*. New York: W. H. Freeman & Co.

Norman, D. A., & Rumelhart, D. E. (1983) Studies of typing from the LNR research group. In W. E. Cooper (Ed.), *Cognitive Aspects of Skilled Typewriting*. New York: Springer-Verlag.

Oldfield, R. C., & Wingfield, A. (1965) Response latencies in naming objects. *Quarterly Journal of Experimental Psychology*, *17*, 273–281.

O'Regan, K. (1980) The control of saccadic size and fixation duration in reading: The limits of linguistic control. *Perception and Psychophysics*, *28*, 112–117.

Palmer, S. E. (1975) The effects of contextual scenes on the identification of objects. *Memory and Cognition*, *3*, 519–526.

Patterson, K. E. (1982) The relation between reading and phonological coding: Further neuropsychological observations. In A. W. Ellis (Ed.), *Normality and Pathology in Cognitive Functions*. London: Academic Press.

Patterson, K. E., Marshall, J. C., & Coltheart, M. (Eds.) (1985) *Surface Dyslexia: Neuropsychological and Cognitive Analyses of Phonological Reading*. London: Lawrence Erlbaum Associates Ltd.

Perrett, D. I., Smith, P. A. J., Potter, D. D., Mistlin, A. J., Head, A. S., Milner, A. D., & Jeeves, M. A. (1984) Neurones responsive to faces in the temporal cortex: Studies in functional organization, sensitivity to identity and relation to perception. *Human Neurobiology*, *3*, 197–208.

Peters, R. (1973) Cognitive maps in wolves and men. In W. P. Preiser (Ed.), *Environmental Design Research*, Vol. 2. Stroudsburg, Pa.: Dowden, Hutchinson & Ross.

Peterson, L. (1969) Concurrent verbal activity. *Psychological Review*, *76*, 376–386.

Pew, R. W. (1974) Human perceptual-motor performance. In B. H. Kantowitz (Ed.), *Human Information Processing: Tutorials in Performance and Cognition*. Hillsdale, N.J.: Lawrence Erlbaum Associates Inc.

Phillips, L., & Edwards, W. (1966) Conservatism in a simple probability task. *Journal of Experimental Psychology*, *72*, 346–354.

Phillips, W. A. (1983) Short term visual memory *Philosophical Transactions of the Royal Society*, series B, *302*, 295–309.

Phillips, W. A., & Baddeley, A. D. (1971) Reaction time and short-term visual memory. *Psychonomic Science*, *22*, 73–74.

Phillips, W. A., & Christie, D. F. M. (1977) Components of visual memory. *Quarterly Journal of Experimental Psychology*, *29*, 117–133.

Piaget, J. (1953) *Logic and Psychology*. Manchester: Manchester University Press.

Piaget, J. (1972) Intellectual evolution from adolescence to adulthood. *Human Development*, *15*, 1–12.

Pick, H. L., & Acredolo, L. P. (Eds.) (1983) *Spatial Orientation; Theory, Research and Application*. New York: Plenum Press.

Pick, H. L., & Lockman, J. J. (1981) From frames of reference to spatial representations. In L. S. Liben, A. H. Patterson, & N. Newcombe (Eds.), *Spatial Representation and Behavior across the Life Span*. New York: Academic Press.

Pillsbury, W. B. (1897) A study in apperception. *American Journal of Psychology*, *8*, 315–393.

Pollatsek, A., Bolozky, S., Well, A. D., & Rayner, K. (1981) Asymmetries in the perceptual span for Israeli readers. *Brain and Language*, *14*, 174–180.

Posner, M. I. (1973) *Cognition: An Introduction*. Glenview Ill.: Scott Foresman. .

Posner, M. I., & Boies, S. J. (1971) Components of attention. *Psychological Review*, *78*, 391–408.

Posner, M. I., & Marin, O. S. M. (Eds.) (1985) *Attention and Performance XI*. Hillsdale, N.J.: Lawrence Erlbaum Associates Inc.

Potter, J. M. (1980) What was the matter with Dr. Spooner? In V. A. Fromkin (Ed.), *Errors in Linguistic Performance: Slips of the tongue, ear, pen and hand*. New York: Academic Press.

Potter, M. C., & Faulconer, B. A. (1975) Time to understand pictures and words. *Nature (London)*, *253*, 437–438.

Pullman, S. G. (1987) Computational models of parsing. In A. W. Ellis (Ed.), *Progress in the Psychology of Language*, Vol. 3. London: Lawrence Erlbaum Associates Ltd.

Pylyshyn, Z. W. (1973) What the mind's eye tells the mind's brain: A critique of mental imagery. *Psychological Bulletin*, *80*, 1–24.

Pylyshyn, Z. (1981) The imagery debate: analogue media versus tacit knowledge. *Psychological Review*, *86*, 16–45.

Rayner, K. (1978) Eye movements in reading and information processing. *Psychological Bulletin*, *85*, 618–660.

Rayner, K., & Posnansky, C. (1978) Stages of processing in word identification. *Journal of Experimental Psychology: General*, *107*, 64–80.

Rayner, K., Well, A. D., & Pollatsek, A. (1980) Asymmetry of the effective visual field in reading. *Perception and Psychophysics*, *27*, 537–544.

Read, J. D., & Bruce, D. (1982) Longitudinal tracking of difficult memory retrievals. *Cognitive Psychology*, *14*, 280–300.

Reason, J. T. (1979) Actions not as planned. In G. Underwood, & R. Stevens (Eds.), *Aspects of Consciousness*. London: Academic Press.

Reason, J. T., & Lucas, D. (1984) Using cognitive diaries to investigate naturally occurring memory blocks. In J. E. Harris & P. E. Morris (Eds.), *Everyday Memory, Actions and Absentmindedness*. London: Academic Press.

Reason, J. T., & Mycielska, K. (1982) *Absent Minded? The Psychology of Mental Lapses and Everyday Errors*, Englewood Cliffs, N. J.: Prentice-Hall.

Reber, A. S., & Allen, R. (1978) Analogy and abstraction strategies in synthetic grammar learning: A function interpretation. *Cognition*, *6*, 189–221.

Reber, A. S., Kassin, S. M., Lewis, S., & Cantor, G. (1980) On the relationship between implicit and explicit modes in the learning of a complex rule structure. *Journal of Experimental Psychology: Human Learning and Memory*, *6*, 492–502.

Reed, S. K. (1972) Pattern recognition and categorization. *Cognitive Psychology*, *3*, 382–407.

Reed, S. K., & Friedman, M. P. (1973) Perceptual vs. conceptual categorization. *Memory and Cognition, 1*, 157–163.

Reicher, G. M. (1969) Perceptual recognition as a function of meaningfulness of stimulus material. *Journal of Experimental Psychology, 81*, 274–280.

Restle, F. (1962) The selection of strategies in cue learning. *Psychological Review, 69*, 329–343.

Rips, L. J. (1983) Cognitive processes in propositional reasoning. *Psychological Review, 90*, 38–71.

Rosch, E. (1978) Principles of categorization. In E. Rosch & B. B. Lloyd (Eds.), *Cognition and Categorization*. Hillsdale, N.J.: Lawrence Erlbaum Associates Inc.

Rosch, E., & Lloyd, B. B. (Eds.) (1978) *Cognition and Categorization*. Hillsdale, N.J.: Lawrence Erlbaum Associates Inc.

Rosch, E., & Mervis, C. B. (1975) Family resemblances: Studies in the internal structure of categories. *Cognitive Psychology, 7*, 573–605.

Rosch, E., Mervis, C. B., Gray, W., Johnson, D., & Boyes-Braem, P. (1976) Basic objects in natural categories. *Cognitive Psychology, 8*, 382–439.

Rosenbaum, D. A. (1980) Human movement imitation: Specification of arm, direction and extent. *Journal of Experimental Psychology: General, 109*, 444–474.

Rosenbaum, D. A., Kenny, S. B., & Derr, M. A. (1983) Hierarchical control of rapid movement sequences. *Journal of Experimental Psychology: Human Perception and Performance, 9*, 86–102.

Rumelhart, D. E. (1975) Notes on a schema for stories. In D. G. Bobrow and A. M. Collins (Eds.), *Representation and Understanding*. New York: Academic Press.

Rumelhart, D. E., & McClelland, J. L. (1982) An interactive activation model of context effects in letter perception. Part 2: The contextual enhancement effect and some tests and extensions of the model. *Psychological Review, 89*, 60–94.

Rumelhart, D. E., & Norman, D. A. (1982) Simulating a skilled typist: A study of skilled perceptual motor performance. *Cognitive Science, 6*, 1–36.

Rundus, D. (1973) Negative effects of using list items as recall cues. *Journal of Verbal Learning and Verbal Behavior, 12*, 43–50.

Sachs, J. S. (1967) Recognition memory for syntactic and semantic aspects of connected discourse. *Perception and Psychophysics, 2*, 437–442.

Saffran, E. M. (1982) Neuropsychological approaches to the study of language. *British Journal of Psychology, 73*, 317–337.

Saffran, E. M., Schwartz, M. F., & Marin, O. S. M. (1980) The word order problem in agrammatism. II. Production. *Brain and Language, 10*, 249–262.

Salame, P., & Baddeley, A. D. (1982) Disruption of short-term memory by unattended speech: Implications for the structure of working memory. *Journal of Verbal Learning and Verbal Behavior, 21*, 150–164.

Schank, R. C. (1975) *Conceptual Information Processing*. Amsterdam: North-Holland.

Schank, R. C. (1982) *Dynamic Memory*. Cambridge: Cambridge University Press.

Schank, R. C., & Abelson, R. (1977) *Scripts, Plans, Goals and Understanding*. Hillsdale, N.J.: Lawrence Erlbaum Associates Inc.

Schmidt, R. A. (1975) A schema theory of discrete motor skill learning. *Psychological Review, 82*, 225–260.

Schmidt, R. A., Zelaznik, H. N., Hawkins, B., Frank, J. S., & Quinn, J. T. Jr. (1979) Motor-output variability: A theory for the accuracy of rapid motor acts. *Psychological Review, 86*, 415–451.

Schneider, W., & Fisk, A. D. (1982) Concurrent automatic and controlled visual research: can processing occur without resource cost? *Journal of Experimental Psychology: Learning, Memory and Cognition, 8*, 261–279.

Schneider, W., & Shiffrin, R. M. (1977) Controlled and automatic information processing. I. Detection, search and attention. *Psychological Review*, *84*, 1–66.

Sergent, J. (1984) An investigation into component and configural processes underlying face perception. *British Journal of Psychology*, *75*, 221–242.

Seymour, P. H. K. (1973) A model for reading, naming and comparison. *British Journal of Psychology*, *64*, 35–49.

Shaffer, L. H. (1973) Latency mechanisms in transcription. In S. Kornblum (Ed.), *Attention and Performance IV*. New York: Academic Press.

Shaffer, L. H. (1975) Multiple attention in continuous verbal tasks. In P. M. A. Rabbitt & S. Dornic (Eds.), *Attention and Performance V*. New York: Academic Press.

Shaffer, L. H. (1978) Timing in the motor programming of typing. *Quarterly Journal of Experimental Psychology*, *30*, 333–345.

Shaffer, L. H. (1981) Performances of Chopin, Bach and Bartok: Studies in motor programming. *Cognitive Psychology*, *13*, 327–376.

Shaffer, L. H. (1982) Rhythm and timing in skill. *Psychological Review*, *89*, 109–122.

Shallice, T., & Warrington, E. K. (1970) Independent functioning of verbal memory stores: a neuropsychological study. *Quarterly Journal of Experimental Psychology*, *22*, 261–273.

Shallice, T., & Warrington, E. K. (1974) The dissociation between short-term retention of meaningful sounds and verbal material. *Neuropsychologia*, *12*, 553–555.

Shallice, T., McLeod, P., & Lewis, K. (1985) Isolating cognitive modules with the dual task paradigm: are speech perception and production separate processes? *Quarterly Journal of Experimental Psychology*, *37A*, 507–532.

Shepherd, J., Davies, G., & Ellis, H. D. (1981) Studies of cue saliency. In G. Davies, H. Ellis, & J. Shepherd (Eds.), *Perceiving and Remembering Faces*. London: Academic Press.

Sherrington, C. S. (1906) *Integrative Action of the Nervous System*. New Haven, Conn.: Yale University Press (reset edition, 1947).

Shiffrin, R. M., & Schneider, W. (1977) Controlled and automatic human information processing. II. Perceptual learning, automatic attending, and a general theory. *Psychological Review*, *84*, 127–190.

Shiffrin, R. M., Dumais, S. T., & Schneider, W. (1981) Characteristics of automatism. In J. Long, & A. Baddeley (Eds.), *Attention and Performance IX*. Hillsdale, N.J.: Lawrence Erlbaum Associates Inc.

Siegel, A. W., & White, S. H. (1975) The development of spatial representations of large scale environments. In H. W. Reese (Ed.), *Advances in Child Development and Behavior*, Vol. 10. New York: Academic Press.

Simon, H. A. (1979) *Models of Thought*. New Haven: Yale University Press.

Simon, H. A., & Gilmartin, K. (1973) Simulation of memory for chess positions. *Cognitive Psychology*, *5*, 29–46.

Sloboda, J. A. (1983) The communication of musical metre in piano performance. *Quarterly Journal of Experimental Psychology*, *35*, 377–396.

Slovic, P., Fischoff, B., & Lichtenstein, S. (1980) Facts vs. fears: Understanding perceived risk. In R. Schwing, & W. A. Albers, Jr. (Eds.), *Societal Risk Assessment: How Safe is Safe Enough?* New York: Plenum.

Smith, E. E., & Collins, A. M. (1981) Use of goal-plan knowledge in understanding stories. *Proceedings of the Third Annual Conference of the Cognitive Science Society*. Berkeley, Cal., 115–116.

Smith, E. E., Shoben, E. J., & Rips, L. J. (1974) Structure and process in semantic memory: A feature model of semantic decisions. *Psychological Review*, *81*, 214–241.

Smith, S. M. (1979) Remembering in and out of context. *Journal of Experimental Psychology: Human Learning and Memory*, *5*, 466–471.

Smith, W. F. (1933) Direction orientation in children. *Journal of Genetic Psychology*, *42*, 154–166.

Smyth, M. M., & Kennedy, J. E. (1982) Orientation and spatial representation within multiple frames of reference. *British Journal of Psychology*, *73*, 527–535.

Smyth, M. M., & Wing, A. M. (Eds.) (1984) *The Psychology of Human Movement*. Orlando, Fla.: Academic Press.

Solomons, L., & Stein, G. (1896) Normal motor automatism. *Psychological Review*, *3*, 492–512.

Spelke, E., Hirst, W., & Neisser, U. (1976) Skills of divided attention. *Cognition*, *4*, 215–230.

Sperber, R. D., McCauley, C., Ragain, R., & Weil, C. M. (1979) Semantic priming effects on picture and word processing. *Memory and Cognition*, *7*, 339–345.

Spilich, G. J., Vesonder, G. T., Chiesi, H. L., & Voss, J. F. (1979) Text processing of domain-related information for individuals with high and low domain knowledge. *Journal of Verbal Learning and Verbal Behavior*, *18*, 275–290.

Squire, L. R., & Slater, P. C. (1975) Forgetting in very long term memory as assessed by an improved questionnaire technique. *Journal of Experimental Psychology: Human Learning and Memory*, *104*, 50–54.

Stanovich, K. E. (1980) Toward an interactive-compensatory model of individual differences in the development of reading fluency. *Reading Research Quarterly*, *16*, 32–71.

Stanovich, K. E., & West, R. F. (1979) Mechanisms of sentence context effects in reading: Automatic activation and conscious attention. *Memory and Cognition*, *7*, 77–85.

Stanovich, K. E., West, R. F., & Freeman, D. J. (1981) A longitudinal study of sentence context effects in second-grade children: Tests of an interactive-compensatory model. *Journal of Experimental Child Psychology*, *32*, 185–199.

Sternberg, S. (1966) High-speed scanning in human memory. *Science*, *153*, 652–654.

Sternberg, S. (1969) Memory-scanning: Mental processes revealed by reaction-time experiments. *American Scientist*, *57*, 421–457.

Stevens, A., & Coupe, P. (1978) Distortions in judged spatial relations. *Cognitive Psychology*, *10*, 422–437.

Stroop, J. R. (1935) Studies of interference in spatial verbal reactions. *Journal of Experimental Psychology*, *18*, 643–662.

Teasdale, J. D. (1983) Affect and accessibility. *Philosophical Transactions of the Royal Society of London* (Series B), *302*, 403–412.

Thagard, P., & Nisbett, R. E. (1982) Variability and confirmation. *Philosophical Studies*, *42*, 379–394.

Thorndyke, P. W. (1977) Cognitive structures in comprehension and memory of narrative discourse. *Cognitive Psychology*, *9*, 77–110.

Thorndyke, P. W. (1981) Distance estimation from cognitive maps. *Cognitive Psychology*, *13*, 526–550.

Thorndyke, P. W. (1984) Applications of schema theory in cognitive research. In J. R. Anderson, & S. M. Kosslyn (Eds.), *Tutorials in Learning and Memory*. New York: W. H. Freeman & Co.

Thorndyke, P. W., & Hayes-Roth, B. (1982) Differences in spatial knowledge acquired from maps and navigation. *Cognitive Psychology*, *14*, 560–589.

Tolman, E. C. (1948) Cognitive maps in rats and men. *Psychological Review*, *55*, 189–208.

Trabasso, T. R. (1963) Stimulus emphasis and all-or-none learning in concept identification. *Journal of Experimental Psychology*, *65*, 398–406.

Treisman, A. M., & Geffen, G. (1967) Selective attention: perception or response? *Quarterly Journal of Experimental Psychology*, *19*, 1–17.

Treisman, A. M., & Gelade, G. (1980) Feature-integration theory of attention. *Cognitive Psychology*, *12*, 97–136.

Treisman, A. M., Squire, R., & Green, J. (1974) Semantic processing in dichotic listening? A replication. *Memory and Cognition*, *2*, 641–646.

Tulving, E. (1972) Episodic and semantic memory. In E. Tulving and W. Donaldson (Eds.), *Organisation of Memory*. London: Academic Press.

Tulving, E. (1983) *Elements of Episodic Memory*. Oxford: Oxford University Press.

Tulving, E., & Gold, C. (1963) Stimulus information and contextual information as determinants of tachistoscopic recognition of words. *Journal of Experimental Psychology*, *66*, 319–327.

Tulving, E., & Thomson, D. M. (1973) Encoding specificity and retrieval processes in episodic memory. *Psychological Review*, *80*, 352–373.

Tulving, E., Mandler, G., & Baumal, R. (1964) Interaction of two sources of information in tachistoscopic word recognition. *Canadian Journal of Psychology*, *18*, 62–71.

Turvey, M. T. (1977) Preliminaries to a theory of action with reference to vision. In R. Shaw, & J. Bransford (Eds.), *Perceiving, Acting and Knowing: Toward an Ecological Psychology*. Hillsdale, N.J.: Lawrence Erlbaum Associates Inc.

Tversky, A. (1967) Additivity, utility and subjective probability. *Journal of Mathematical Psychology*, *4*, 175–202.

Tversky, B. (1981) Distortions in memory for maps. *Cognitive Psychology*, *13*, 407–433.

Underwood, B. J. (1957) Interference and forgetting. *Psychological Review*, *64*, 49–60.

Underwood, B. J., & Richardson, J. (1956) Some verbal materials for the study of concept formation. *Psychological Bulletin*, *53*, 84–95.

Vince, M. A., & Welford, A. T. (1967) Time taken to change the speed of a response. *Nature*, *213*, 532–533.

Vredenbregt, J., & Koster, W. G. (1971) Analysis and synthesis of handwriting. *Philips Technical Review*, *32*, 73–78.

Vygotsky, L. S. (1962) *Thought and Language* (Translated and edited by E. Hanfmann, & G. Vakar from the 1934 original publication). Cambridge, Mass.: MIT Press.

Wagstaff, G. F., & Sykes, C. T. (1984) Hypnosis and the recall of emotionally-toned material. *IRCS Medical Science*, *12*, 137–138.

Wallace, S. A., & Newell, K. M. (1983) Visual control of discrete aiming movements. *Quarterly Journal of Experimental Psychology*, *35*, 311–321.

Wanner, H. E. (1968) *On remembering, forgetting and understanding sentences. A study of the deep structure hypothesis*. Unpublished doctoral dissertation. Harvard University. Cited in J. R. Anderson (1985), *Cognitive Psychology and its Implications*. New York: W. H. Freeman.

Warren, C., & Morton, J. (1982) The effects of priming on picture recognition. *British Journal of Psychology*, *73*, 117–130.

Wason, P. C. (1966) Reasoning. In B. Foss (Ed.), *New Horizons in Psychology*: 1. Harmondsworth, Middlesex: Penguin.

Waugh, N. C., & Norman, D. A. (1965) Primary memory. *Psychological Review*, *72*, 89–104.

Webb, L. W. (1917) Transfer of training and retroaction: A comparative study. *Psychological Monographs*, *24*; whole no. 104.

Welford, A. T. (1968) *Fundamentals of Skill*. London: Methuen.

Wertheimer, M. (1959) *Productive Thinking*. New York: Harper & Row.

Wheeler, D. D. (1970) Processes in word recognition. *Cognitive Psychology*, *1*, 59–85.

Whipple, G. M. (1912) Psychology of testimony and report. *Psychological Bulletin*, *9*, 264–269.

Wing, A. M. (1980) The height of handwriting. *Acta Psychologica*, *46*, 141–151.

Wingfield, A. (1968) Effects of frequency on identification and naming of objects. *American Journal of Psychology*, *81*, 226–234.

Winograd, T. (1972) *Understanding Natural Language*. New York: Academic Press.

Wittgenstein, I. (1958) *Philosophical Investigations* (2nd edn translated by G. E. M. Anscombe). Oxford: Blackwell.

Woodworth, R. S. (1899) The accuracy of voluntary movement. *Psychological Review*, *Monograph Supplement*, *3*, No. 3.

Woodworth, R. S. (1938) *Experimental Psychology*. New York: Holt, Rinehart & Winston.

Woodworth, R. S., & Sells, S. B. (1935) An atmosphere effect in formal syllogistic reasoning. *Journal of Experimental Psychology*, *18*, 451–460.

Wright, G. (1984) *Behavioural Decision Theory: An Introduction*. Harmondsworth, Middlesex: Penguin Books Ltd.

Wundt, W. (1905) *Grundriss der Psychologie*. Leipzig: Engelmann.

Young, A. W., Hay, D. C., & Ellis, A. W. (1985) The faces that launched a thousand slips: Everyday difficulties and errors in recognising people. *British Journal of Psychology*, *76*, 495–523.

Young, A. W., McWeeny, K. H., Ellis, A. W., & Hay, D. C. (1986) Naming and categorizing faces and written names. *Quarterly Journal of Experimental Psychology*, *38A*, 297–318.

Zangwill, O. L. (1946) Some qualitative observations on verbal memory in cases of cerebral lesion. *British Journal of Psychology*, *37*, 8–19.

Author Index

Subject Index